INUYASHA™

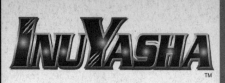

VOL. 21
Action Edition

Story and Art by
RUMIKO TAKAHASHI

English Adaptation by Gerard Jones

Translation/Mari Morimoto
Touch-Up Art & Lettering/Bill Schuch
Graphic Design/Yuki Ameda
Editor/Avery Gotoh
Supervising Editor/Michelle Pangilinan

Managing Editor/Annette Roman
Director ofProduction/Noboru Watanabe
VP of Publishing/Alvin Lu
Sr. Director of Acquisitions/Rika Inouye
VP of Sales & Marketing/Liza Coppola
Publisher/Hyoe Narita

Printed in Canada.

Published by VIZ Media, LLC
P.O. Box 77010
San Francisco, CA 94107

Action Edition
10 9 8 7 6 5 4 3 2
First printing, March 2005
Second printing, June 2005

RATED T+ FOR OLDER TEEN

PARENTAL ADVISORY
INUYASHA is rated T+ for Older Teen. This book contains violence. It is recommended for ages 16 and up.

INU YASHA

™

VOL. 21   Action Edition

STORY AND ART BY
RUMIKO TAKAHASHI

CONTENTS

THE STORY THUS FAR

Long ago, in the "Warring States" era of Japan's Muromachi period (*Sengoku-jidai*, approximately 1467-1568 CE), a legendary dog-like half-demon called "Inu-Yasha" attempted to steal the Shikon Jewel—or "Jewel of Four Souls"—from a village, but was stopped by the enchanted arrow of the village priestess, Kikyo. Inu-Yasha fell into a deep sleep, pinned to a tree by Kikyo's arrow, while the mortally wounded Kikyo took the Shikon Jewel with her into the fires of her funeral pyre. Years passed.

Fast-forward to the present day. Kagome, a Japanese high-school girl, is pulled into a well one day by a mysterious centipede monster, and finds herself transported into the past—only to come face to face with the trapped Inu-Yasha. She frees him, and Inu-Yasha easily defeats the centipede monster.

The residents of the village, now 50 years older, readily accept Kagome as the reincarnation of their deceased priestess Kikyo, a claim supported by the fact that the Shikon Jewel emerges from a cut on Kagome's body. Unfortunately, the jewel's rediscovery means that the village is soon under attack by a variety of demons in search of this treasure. Then, the jewel is accidentally shattered into many shards, each of which may have the fearsome power of the entire jewel.

Although Inu-Yasha says he hates Kagome because of her resemblance to Kikyo, the woman who "killed" him, he is forced to team up with her when Kaede, the village leader, binds him to Kagome with a powerful spell. Now the two grudging companions must fight to reclaim and reassemble the shattered shards of the Shikon Jewel before they fall into the wrong hands....

THIS VOLUME Locked in battle with Ryōkotsusei—the same demon responsible for his father's death—Inu-Yasha may have a chance at victory…but not if he can't master the "Backlash Wave" (Bakuryū-ha). Meanwhile, when Kagome is bitten by Tsubaki's familiar, the Shikon Jewel shards themselves are affected. What can it mean for the shards to turn black…?

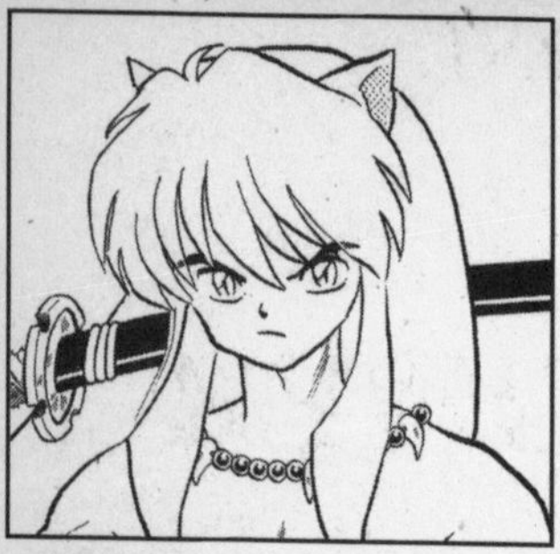

INU-YASHA
Half-demon hybrid, son of a human mother and demon father. His necklace is enchanted, allowing Kagome to control him with a word.

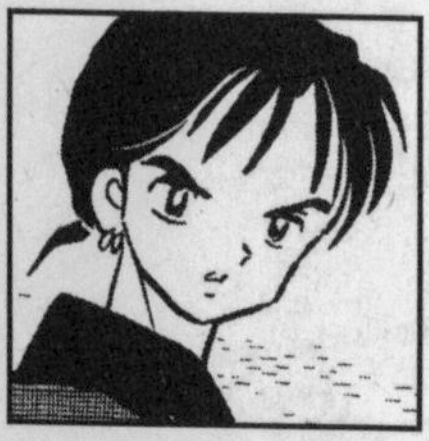

MIROKU
Lecherous Buddhist priest cursed with a mystical "hellhole" in his hand that's slowly killing him.

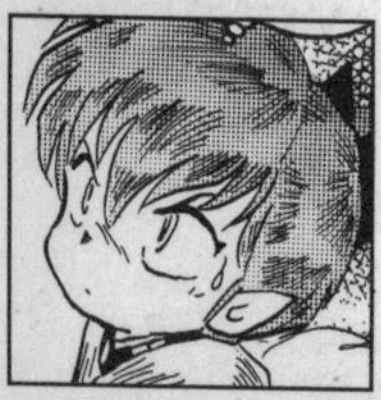

SHIPPO
Orphaned young fox-demon who likes to play shape-changing tricks.

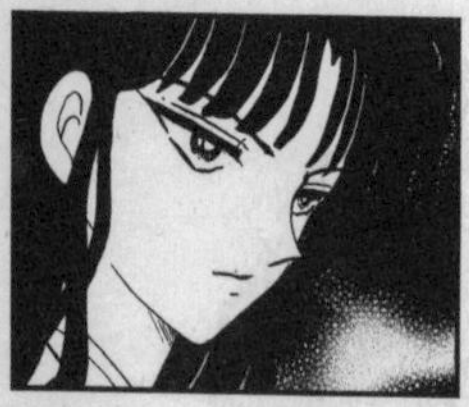

NARAKU
Enigmatic demon-mastermind behind the miseries of nearly everyone in the story.

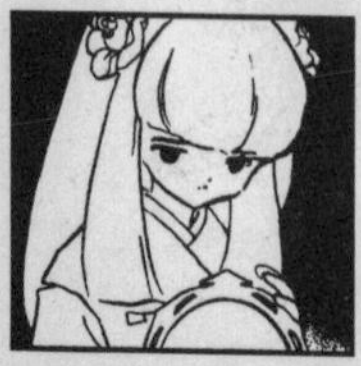

KANNA
Another one of Naraku's splinter-selves, Kanna carries a mirror, which she uses to steal human souls. Unlike her sister, Kagura, Kanna is resigned to her fate as Naraku's puppet.

KAGOME
Modern-day Japanese schoolgirl who can travel back and forth between the past and present through an enchanted well.

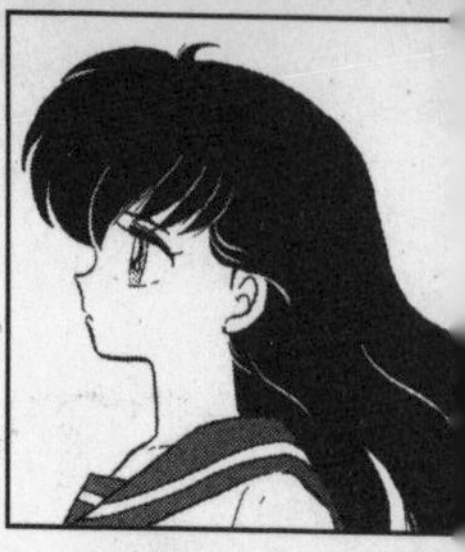

SANGO
"Demon Exterminator" or slayer from the village where the Shikon Jewel was first born.

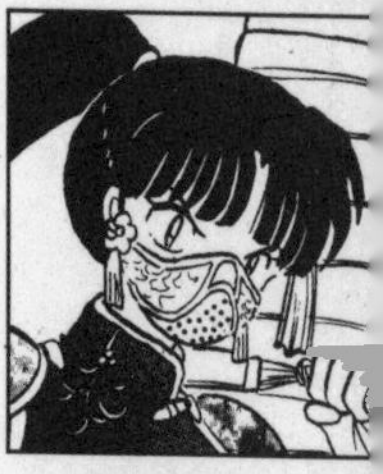

KOGA
Leader of the Wolf Clan, Koga is himself a Wolf Demon and, because of several Shikon shards in his legs, possesses super speed. Enamored of Kagome, he quarrels with Inu-Yasha frequently.

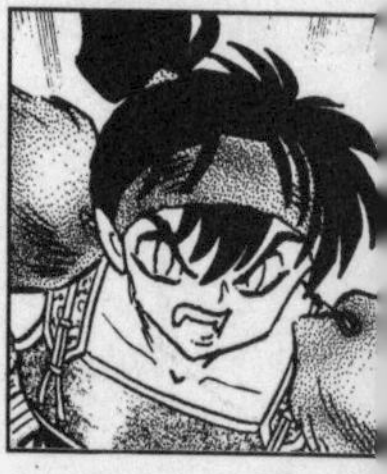

KAGURA
A demon created by Naraku from parts of his own body, Kagura the Wind Demon is Naraku's second incarnation. Unlike others, however, Kagura resents Naraku's control over her and aids him only for her own survival.

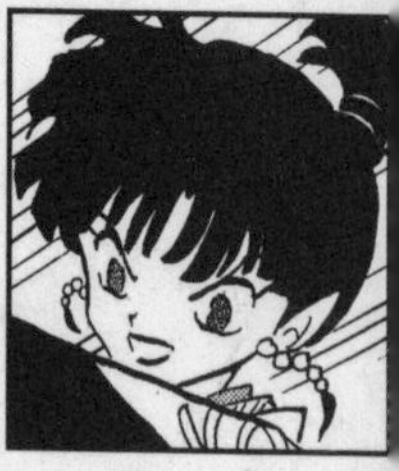

SESSHÔMARU
Inu-Yasha's half-brother and full-demon son of their mutual father. His (literally) toadish lackey is Jaken.

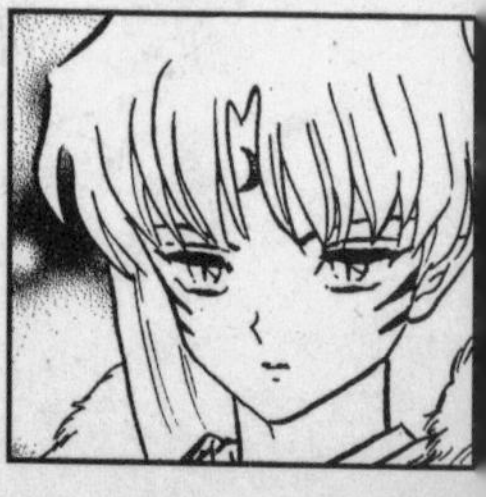

SCROLL ONE

THE
STONE FLOWER

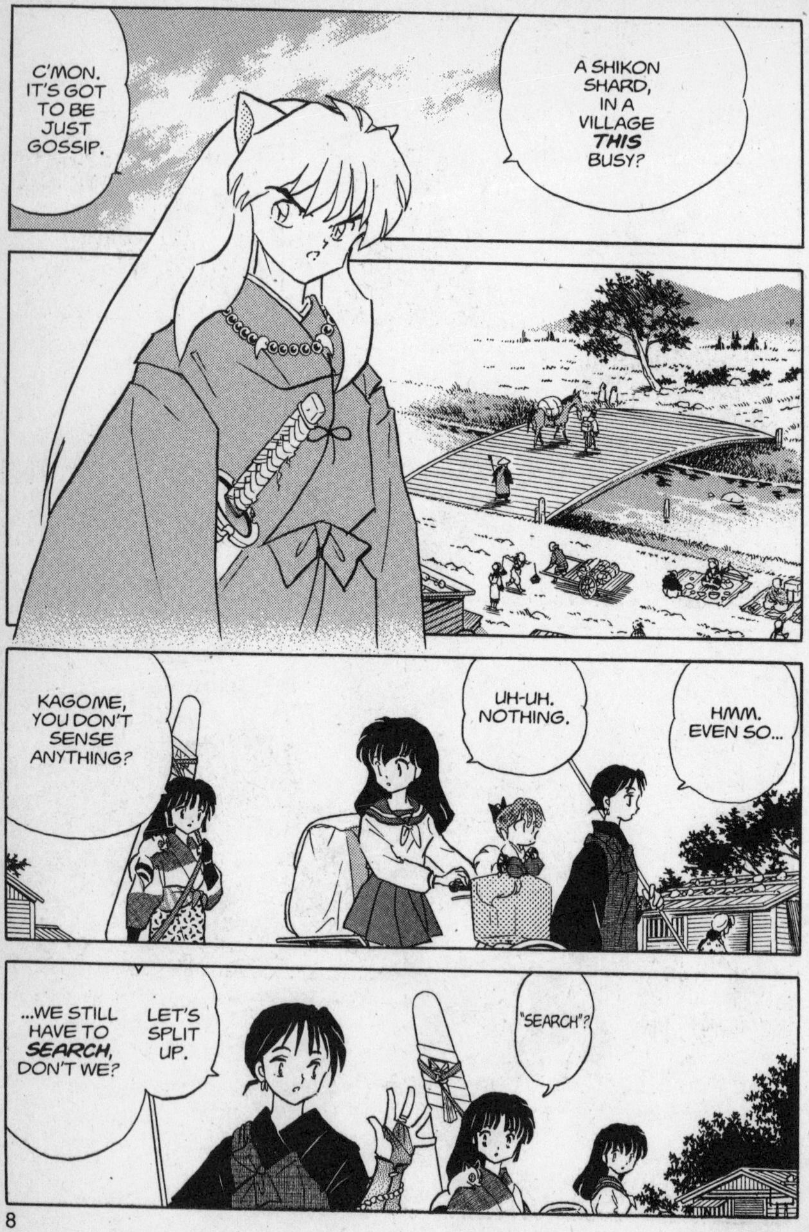
C'MON. IT'S GOT TO BE JUST GOSSIP.
A SHIKON SHARD, IN A VILLAGE **THIS** BUSY?
KAGOME, YOU DON'T SENSE ANYTHING?
UH-UH. NOTHING.
HMM. EVEN SO...
...WE STILL HAVE TO ***SEARCH***, DON'T WE?
LET'S SPLIT UP.
"SEARCH"?

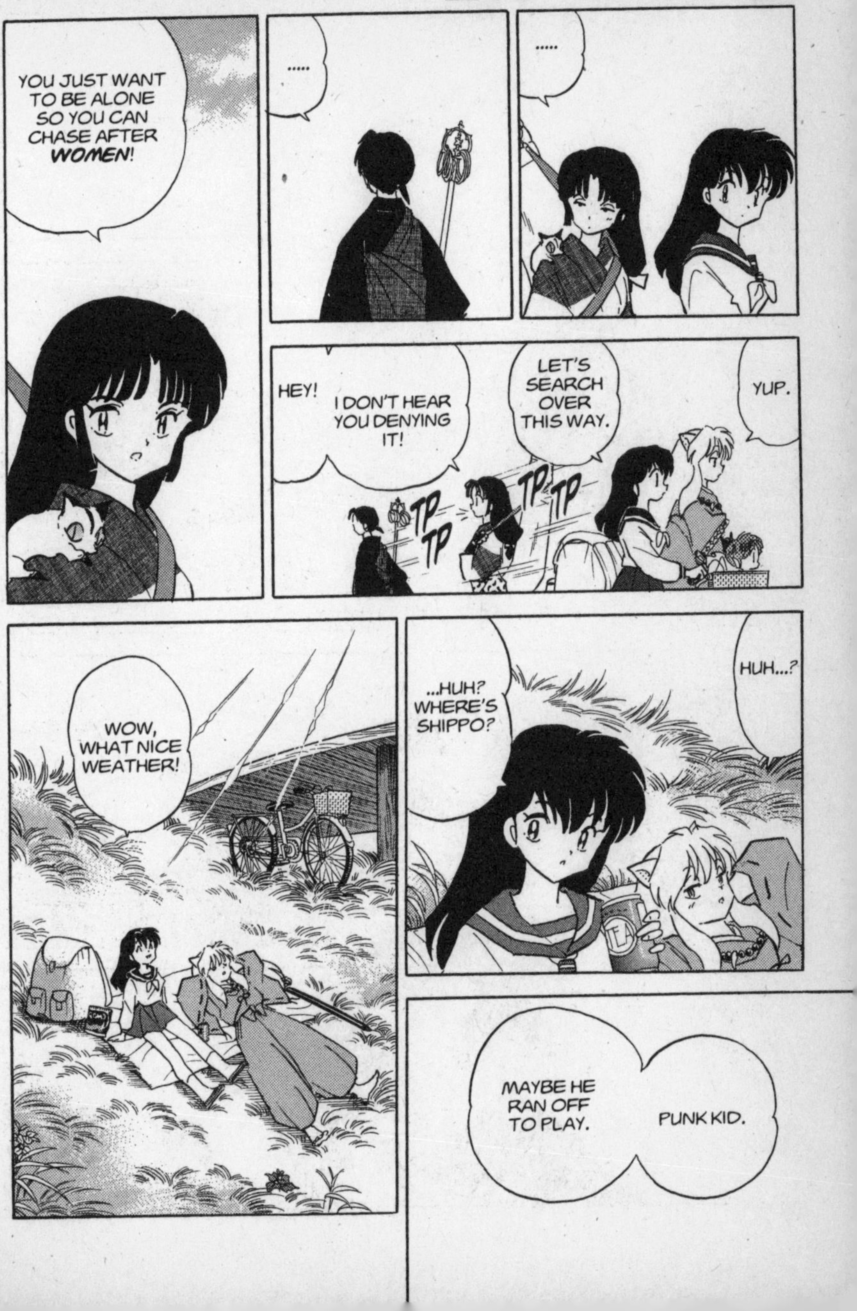
YOU JUST WANT TO BE ALONE SO YOU CAN CHASE AFTER **WOMEN**!
.....
.....
HEY!
I DON'T HEAR YOU DENYING IT!
LET'S SEARCH OVER THIS WAY.
YUP.
TP TP
TP TP
WOW, WHAT NICE WEATHER!
...HUH? WHERE'S SHIPPO?
HUH...?
MAYBE HE RAN OFF TO PLAY.
PUNK KID.

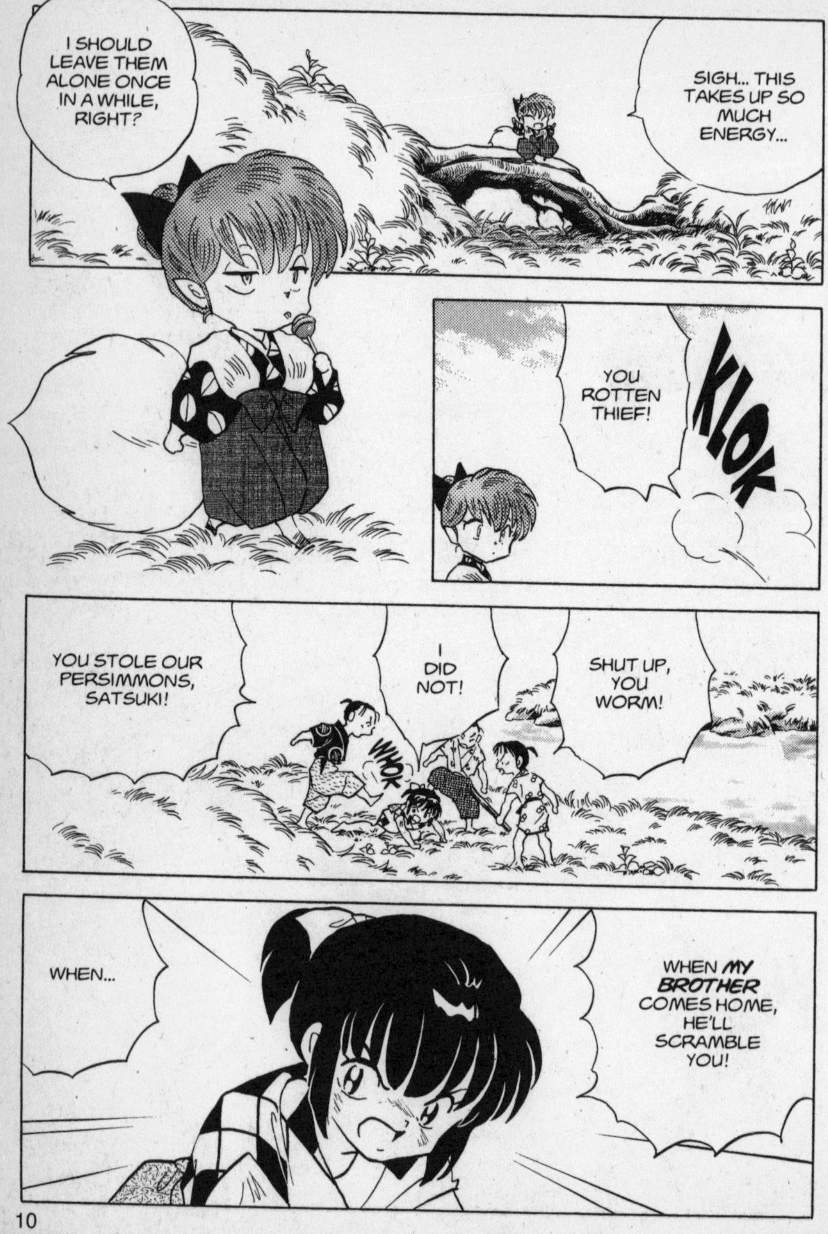
I SHOULD LEAVE THEM ALONE ONCE IN A WHILE, RIGHT?
SIGH... THIS TAKES UP SO MUCH ENERGY...
YOU ROTTEN THIEF!
KLOK
YOU STOLE OUR PERSIMMONS, SATSUKI!
WHOK
I DID NOT!
SHUT UP, YOU WORM!
WHEN...
WHEN MY BROTHER COMES HOME, HE'LL SCRAMBLE YOU!

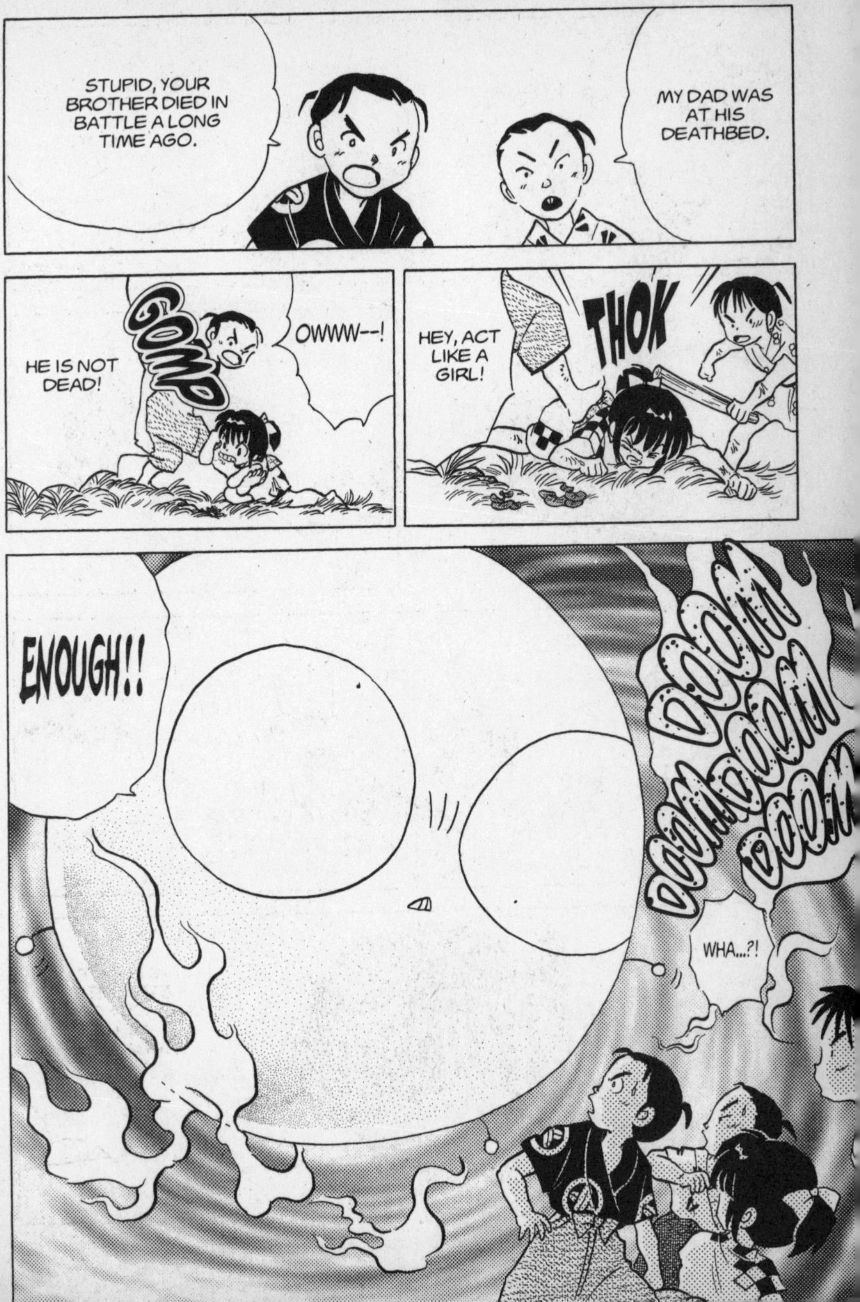
STUPID, YOUR BROTHER DIED IN BATTLE A LONG TIME AGO.
MY DAD WAS AT HIS DEATHBED.
HE IS NOT DEAD!
GOMP
OWWW--!
HEY, ACT LIKE A GIRL!
THOK
ENOUGH!!
DOOM DOOM DOOM DOOM DOOM
WHA...?!

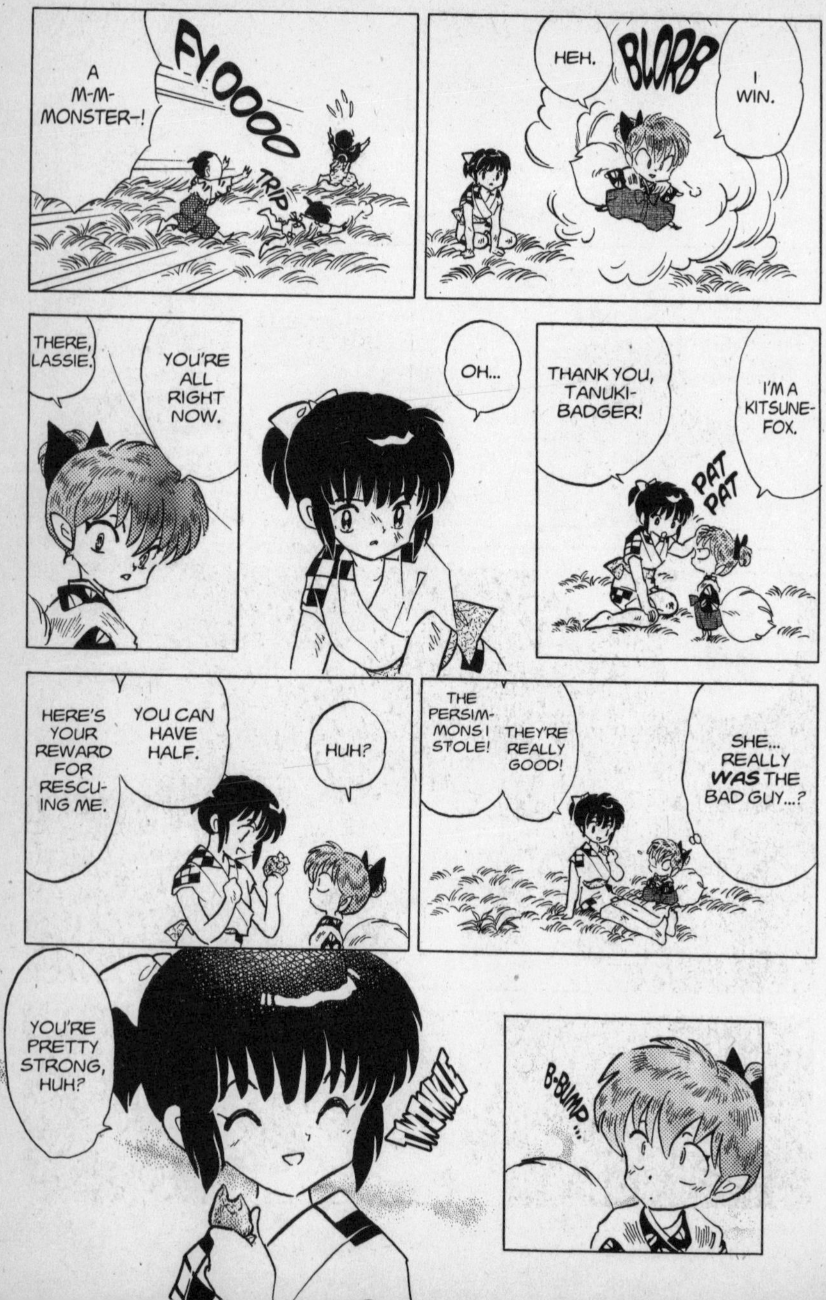
A M-M-MONSTER-!
FYOOOOO
TRIP
HEH.
BLORB
I WIN.
THERE, LASSIE.
YOU'RE ALL RIGHT NOW.
OH...
THANK YOU, TANUKI-BADGER!
I'M A KITSUNE-FOX.
PAT PAT
HERE'S YOUR REWARD FOR RESCUING ME.
YOU CAN HAVE HALF.
HUH?
THE PERSIMMONS I STOLE!
THEY'RE REALLY GOOD!
SHE... REALLY WAS THE BAD GUY...?
YOU'RE PRETTY STRONG, HUH?
TWINKLE
B-BUMP...

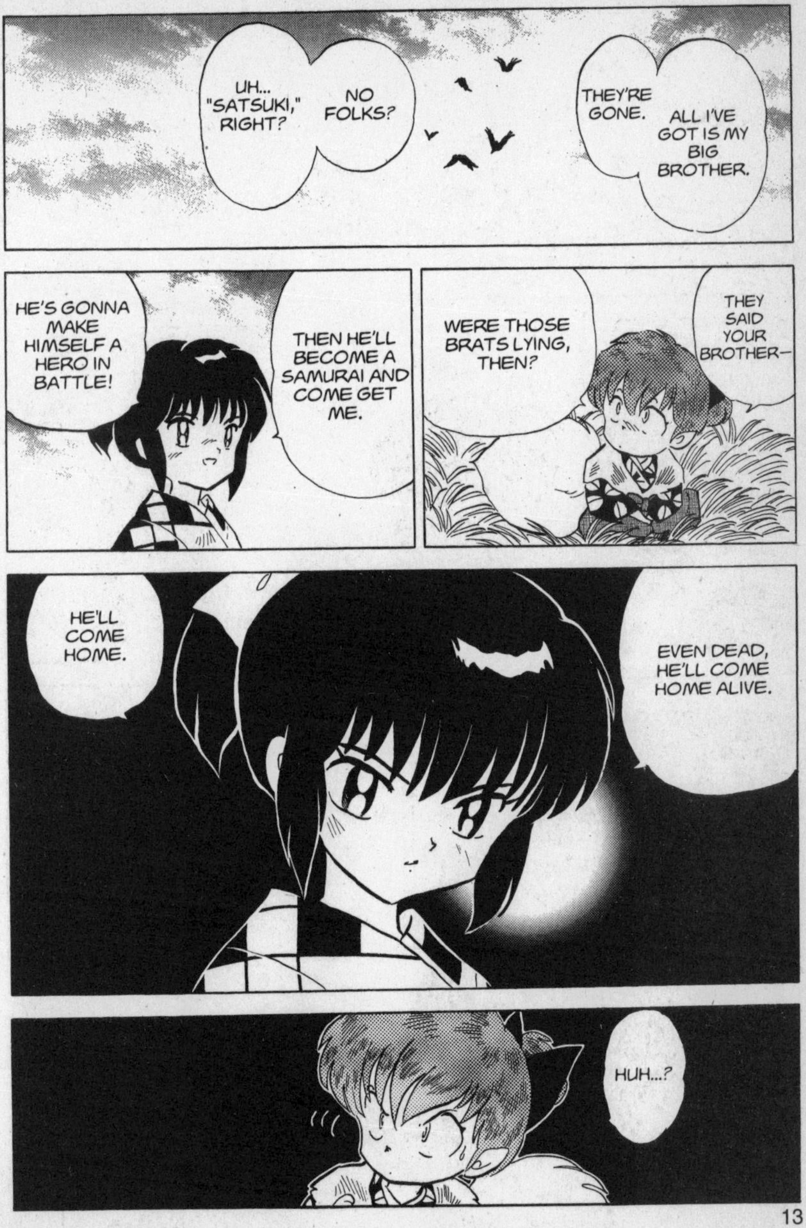
UH... "SATSUKI," RIGHT?
NO FOLKS?
THEY'RE GONE.
ALL I'VE GOT IS MY BIG BROTHER.
HE'S GONNA MAKE HIMSELF A HERO IN BATTLE!
THEN HE'LL BECOME A SAMURAI AND COME GET ME.
WERE THOSE BRATS LYING, THEN?
THEY SAID YOUR BROTHER—
HE'LL COME HOME.
EVEN DEAD, HE'LL COME HOME ALIVE.
HUH...?

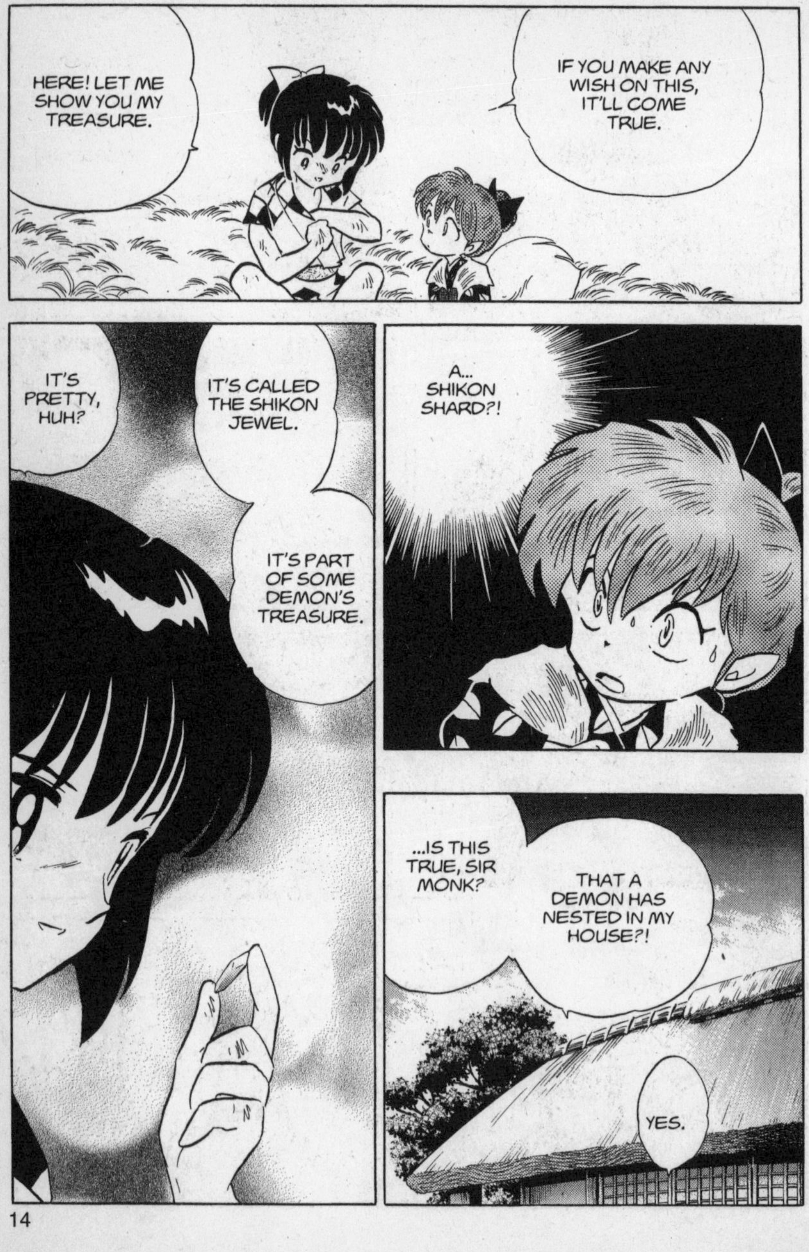
HERE! LET ME SHOW YOU MY TREASURE.
IF YOU MAKE ANY WISH ON THIS, IT'LL COME TRUE.
IT'S PRETTY, HUH?
IT'S CALLED THE SHIKON JEWEL.
IT'S PART OF SOME DEMON'S TREASURE.
A... SHIKON SHARD?!
...IS THIS TRUE, SIR MONK?
THAT A DEMON HAS NESTED IN MY HOUSE?!
YES.

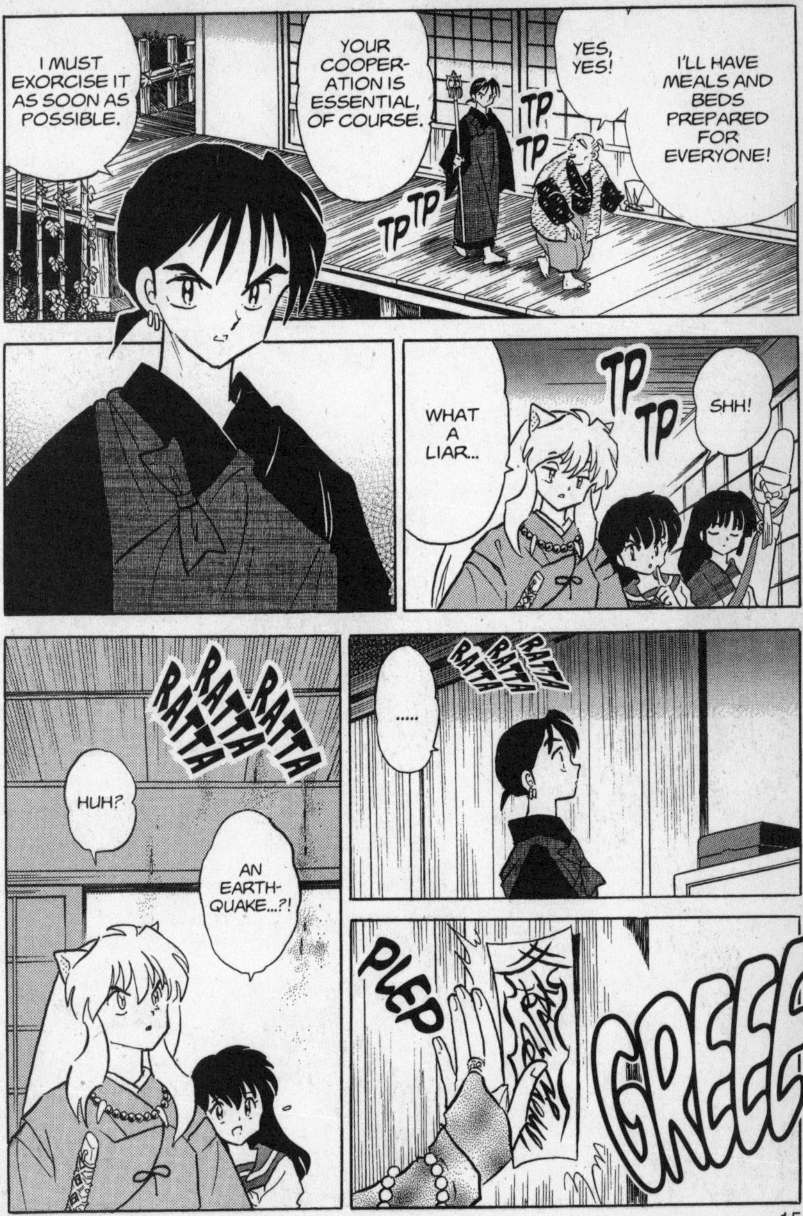
I MUST EXORCISE IT AS SOON AS POSSIBLE.
YOUR COOPER-ATION IS ESSENTIAL, OF COURSE.
TP TP
TP TP
YES, YES!
I'LL HAVE MEALS AND BEDS PREPARED FOR EVERYONE!
WHAT A LIAR...
TP TP
SHH!
RATTA RATTA RATTA
HUH?
AN EARTH-QUAKE...?!
.....
RATTA RATTA RATTA
PLEP
GREEE

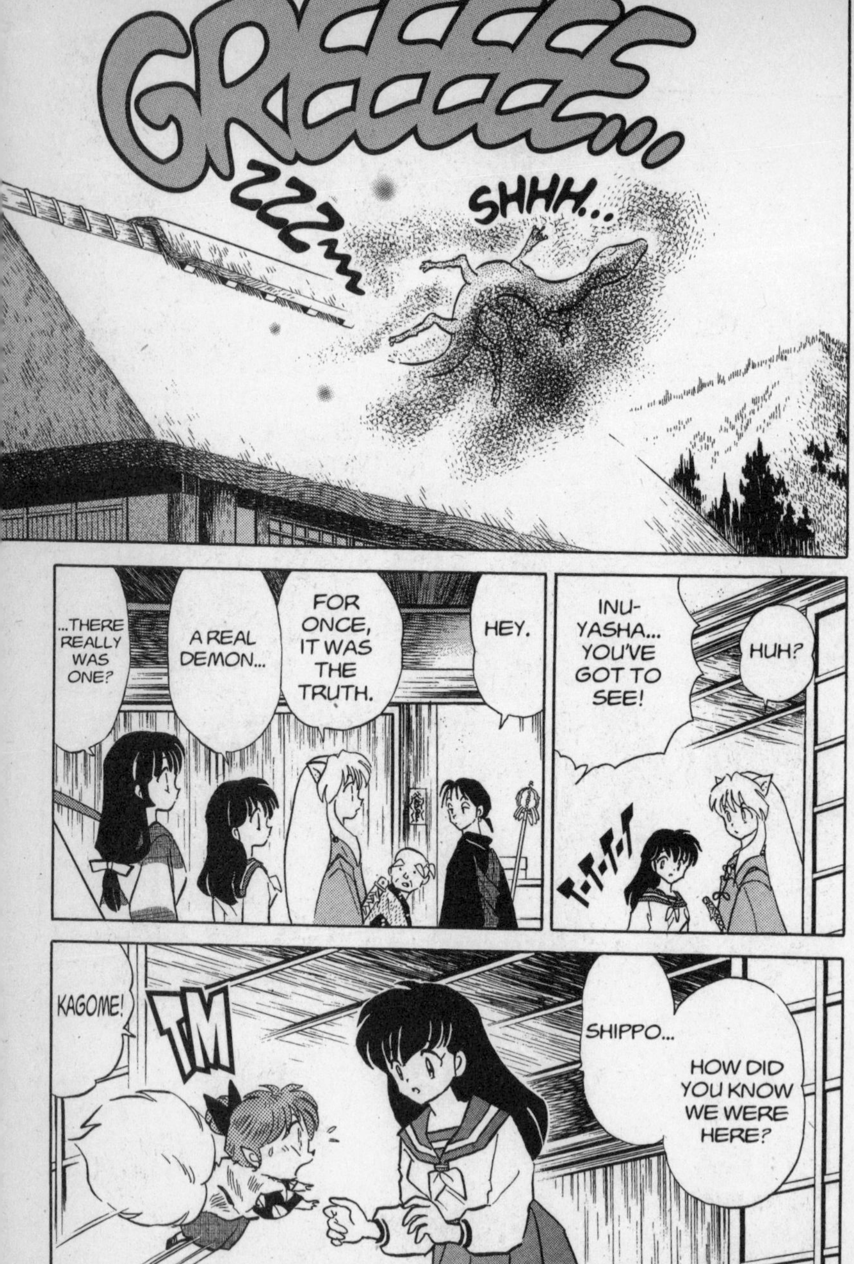
GREEEEE...
ZZZ
SHHH...
...THERE REALLY WAS ONE?
A REAL DEMON...
FOR ONCE, IT WAS THE TRUTH.
HEY.
INU-YASHA... YOU'VE GOT TO SEE!
HUH?
T-T-T-T
KAGOME!
TM
SHIPPO...
HOW DID YOU KNOW WE WERE HERE?

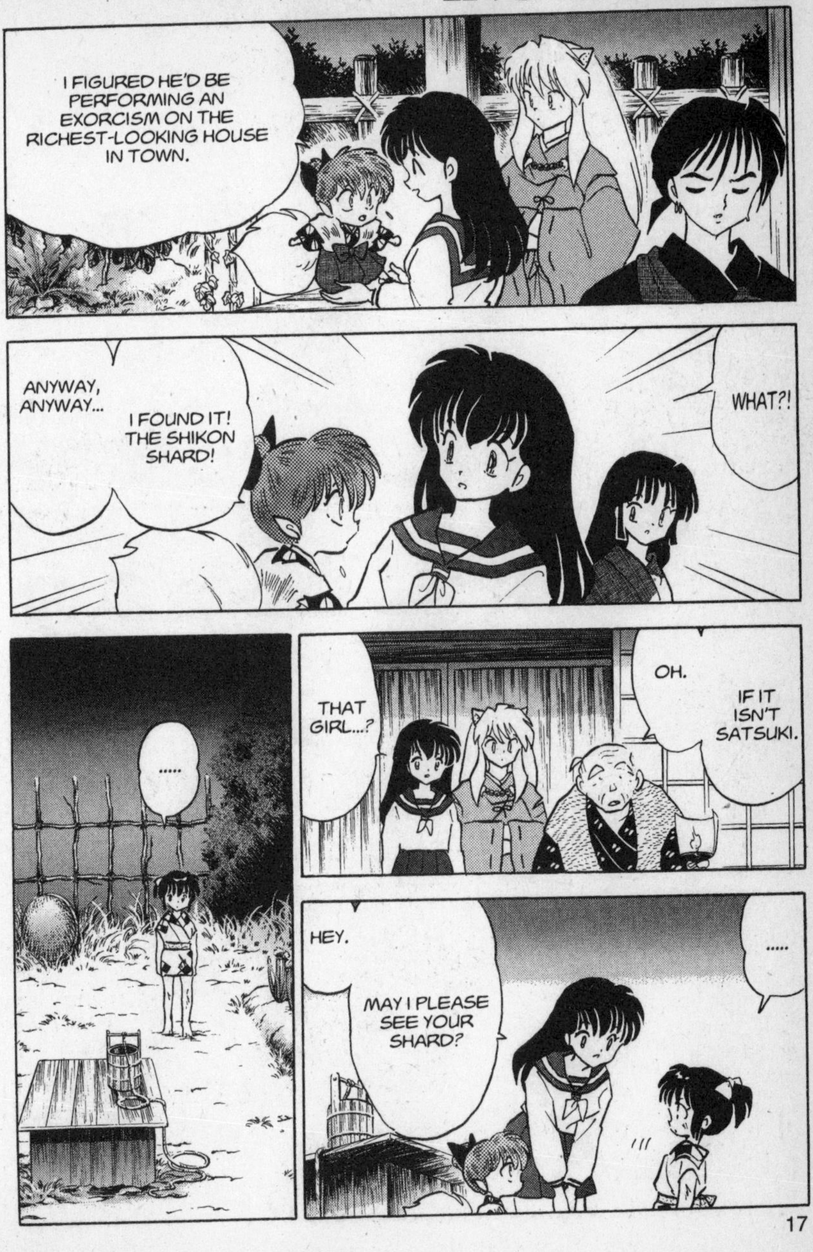
I FIGURED HE'D BE PERFORMING AN EXORCISM ON THE RICHEST-LOOKING HOUSE IN TOWN.
ANYWAY, ANYWAY...
I FOUND IT! THE SHIKON SHARD!
WHAT?!
.....
THAT GIRL...?
OH.
IF IT ISN'T SATSUKI.
HEY.
MAY I PLEASE SEE YOUR SHARD?
.....

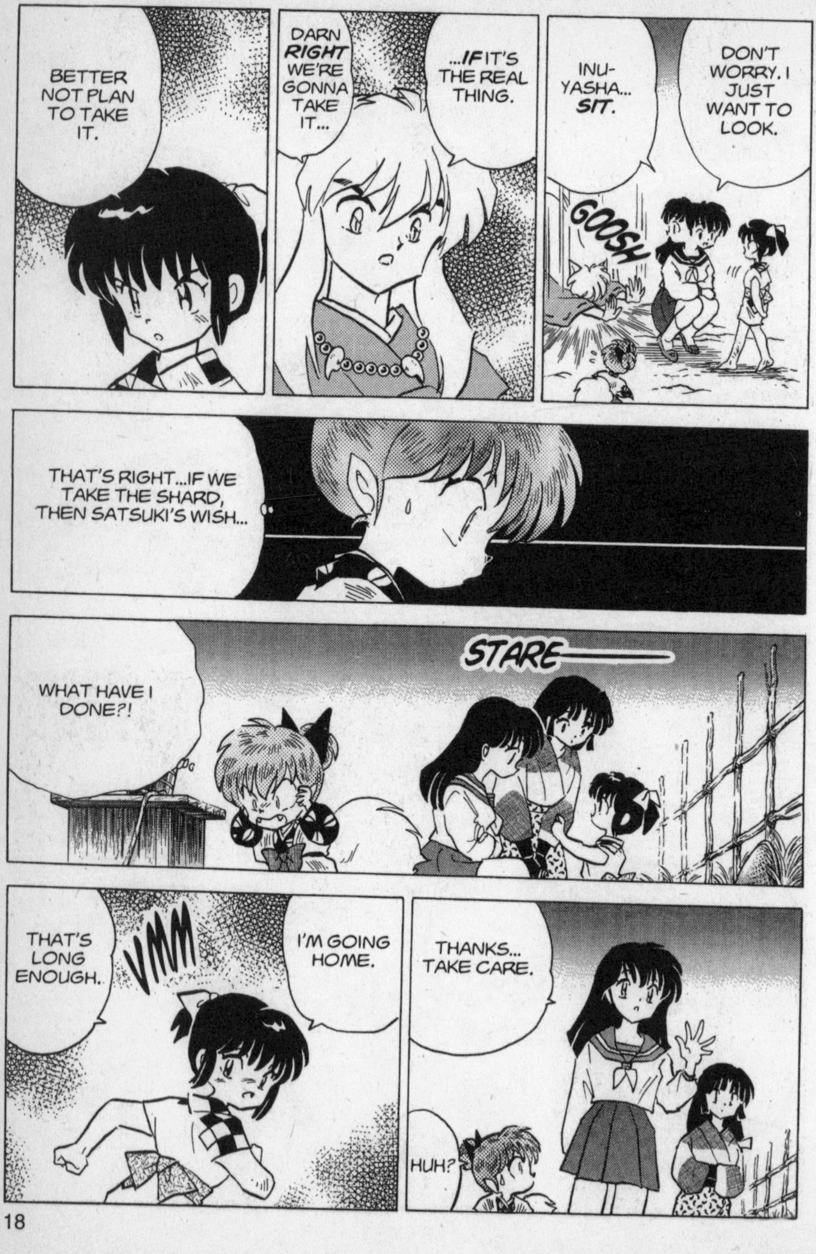
BETTER NOT PLAN TO TAKE IT.
DARN RIGHT WE'RE GONNA TAKE IT...
...IF IT'S THE REAL THING.
INU-YASHA... SIT.
DON'T WORRY. I JUST WANT TO LOOK.
GOOSH
THAT'S RIGHT...IF WE TAKE THE SHARD, THEN SATSUKI'S WISH...
WHAT HAVE I DONE?!
STARE
THAT'S LONG ENOUGH..
VMM
I'M GOING HOME.
THANKS... TAKE CARE.
HUH?

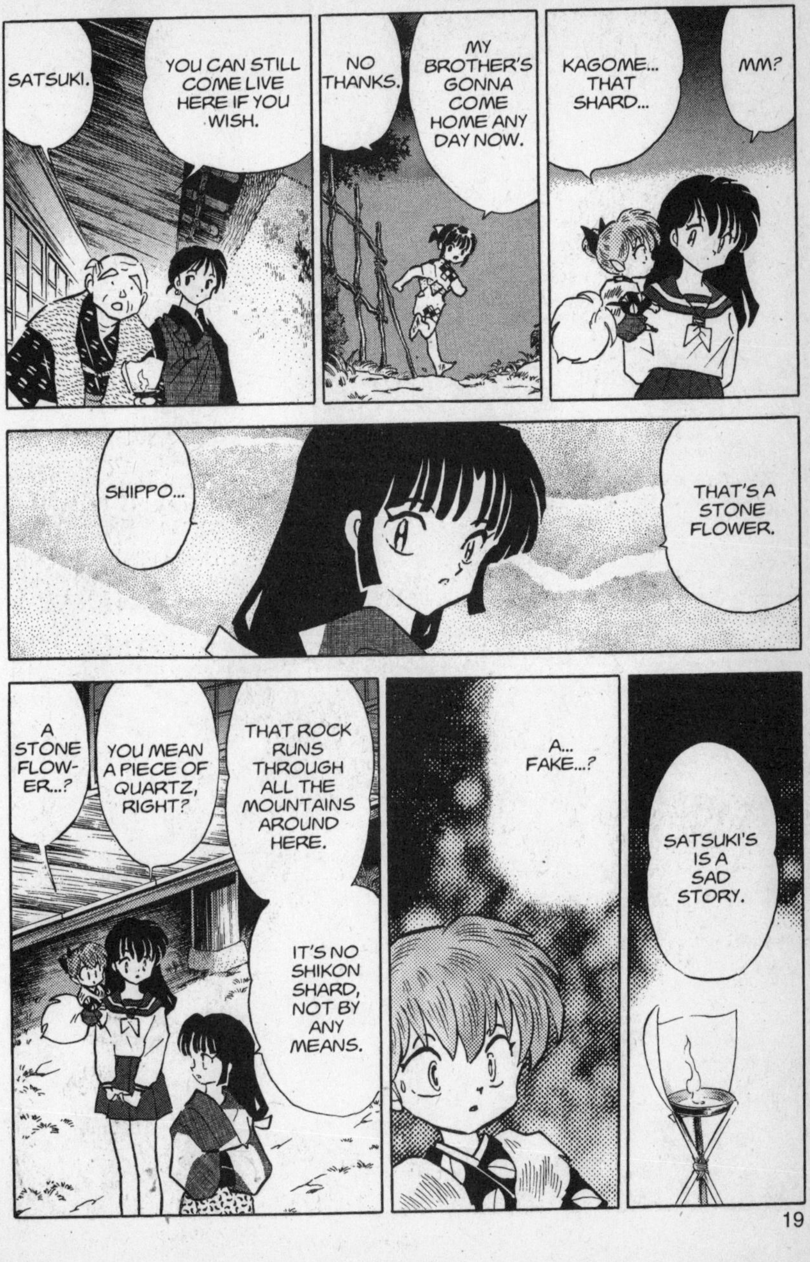
SATSUKI.
YOU CAN STILL COME LIVE HERE IF YOU WISH.
NO THANKS.
MY BROTHER'S GONNA COME HOME ANY DAY NOW.
KAGOME... THAT SHARD...
MM?
SHIPPO...
THAT'S A STONE FLOWER.
A STONE FLOW-ER...?
YOU MEAN A PIECE OF QUARTZ, RIGHT?
THAT ROCK RUNS THROUGH ALL THE MOUNTAINS AROUND HERE.
IT'S NO SHIKON SHARD, NOT BY ANY MEANS.
A... FAKE...?
SATSUKI'S IS A SAD STORY.

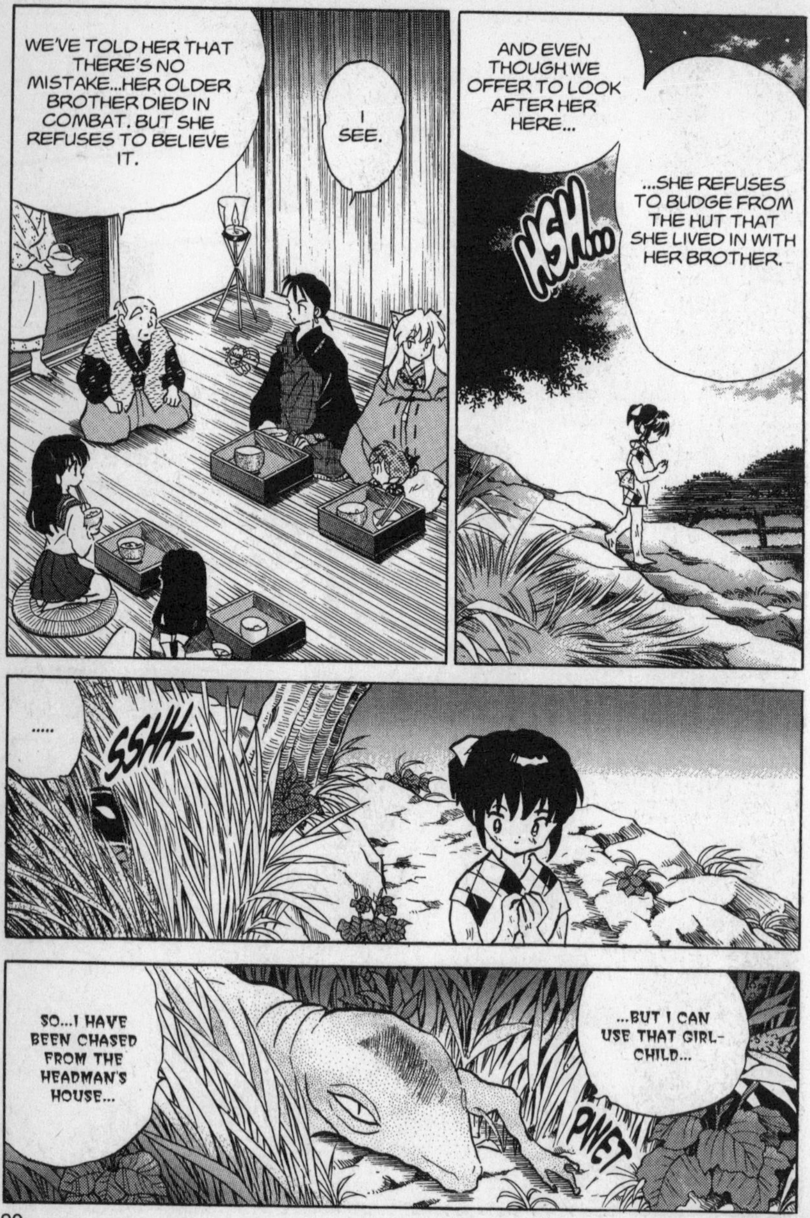
WE'VE TOLD HER THAT THERE'S NO MISTAKE...HER OLDER BROTHER DIED IN COMBAT. BUT SHE REFUSES TO BELIEVE IT.
I SEE.
AND EVEN THOUGH WE OFFER TO LOOK AFTER HER HERE...
HSH...
...SHE REFUSES TO BUDGE FROM THE HUT THAT SHE LIVED IN WITH HER BROTHER.
.....
SSHH
SO...I HAVE BEEN CHASED FROM THE HEADMAN'S HOUSE...
...BUT I CAN USE THAT GIRL-CHILD...
PWET

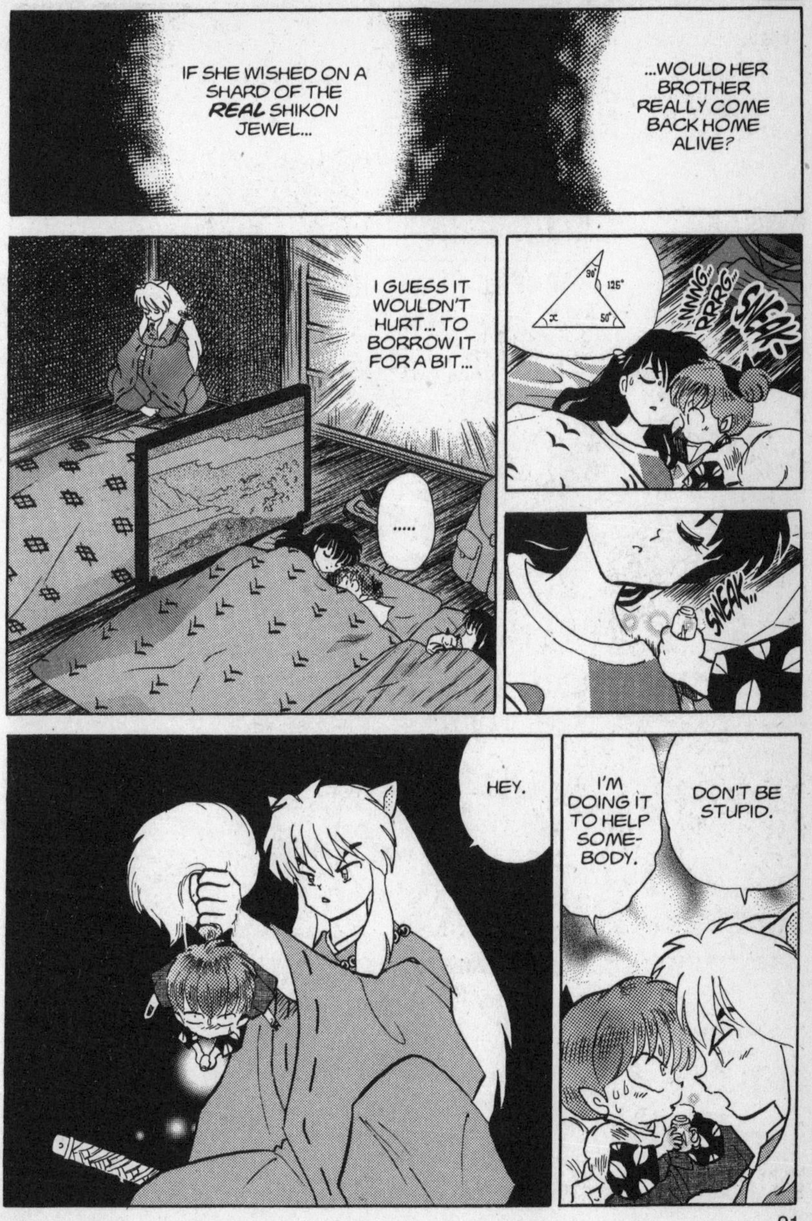
IF SHE WISHED ON A SHARD OF THE REAL SHIKON JEWEL...
...WOULD HER BROTHER REALLY COME BACK HOME ALIVE?
I GUESS IT WOULDN'T HURT... TO BORROW IT FOR A BIT...
.....
90°
125°
x
50°
NNNG... RRRG...
SNEAK-
SNEAK...
HEY.
I'M DOING IT TO HELP SOME-BODY.
DON'T BE STUPID.

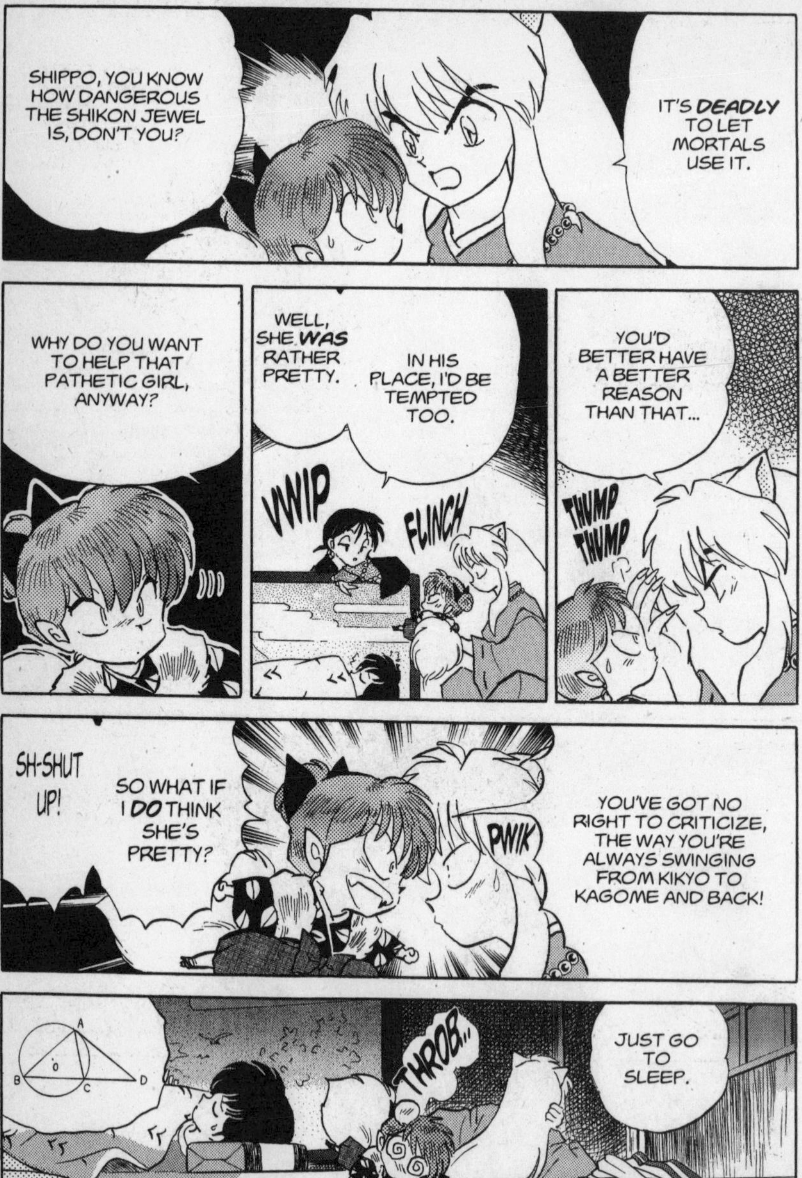
SHIPPO, YOU KNOW HOW DANGEROUS THE SHIKON JEWEL IS, DON'T YOU?
IT'S DEADLY TO LET MORTALS USE IT.
WHY DO YOU WANT TO HELP THAT PATHETIC GIRL, ANYWAY?
WELL, SHE WAS RATHER PRETTY.
IN HIS PLACE, I'D BE TEMPTED TOO.
VWIP
FLINCH
YOU'D BETTER HAVE A BETTER REASON THAN THAT...
THUMP THUMP
SH-SHUT UP!
SO WHAT IF I DO THINK SHE'S PRETTY?
PWIK
YOU'VE GOT NO RIGHT TO CRITICIZE, THE WAY YOU'RE ALWAYS SWINGING FROM KIKYO TO KAGOME AND BACK!
A
O
B
C
D
THROB...
JUST GO TO SLEEP.

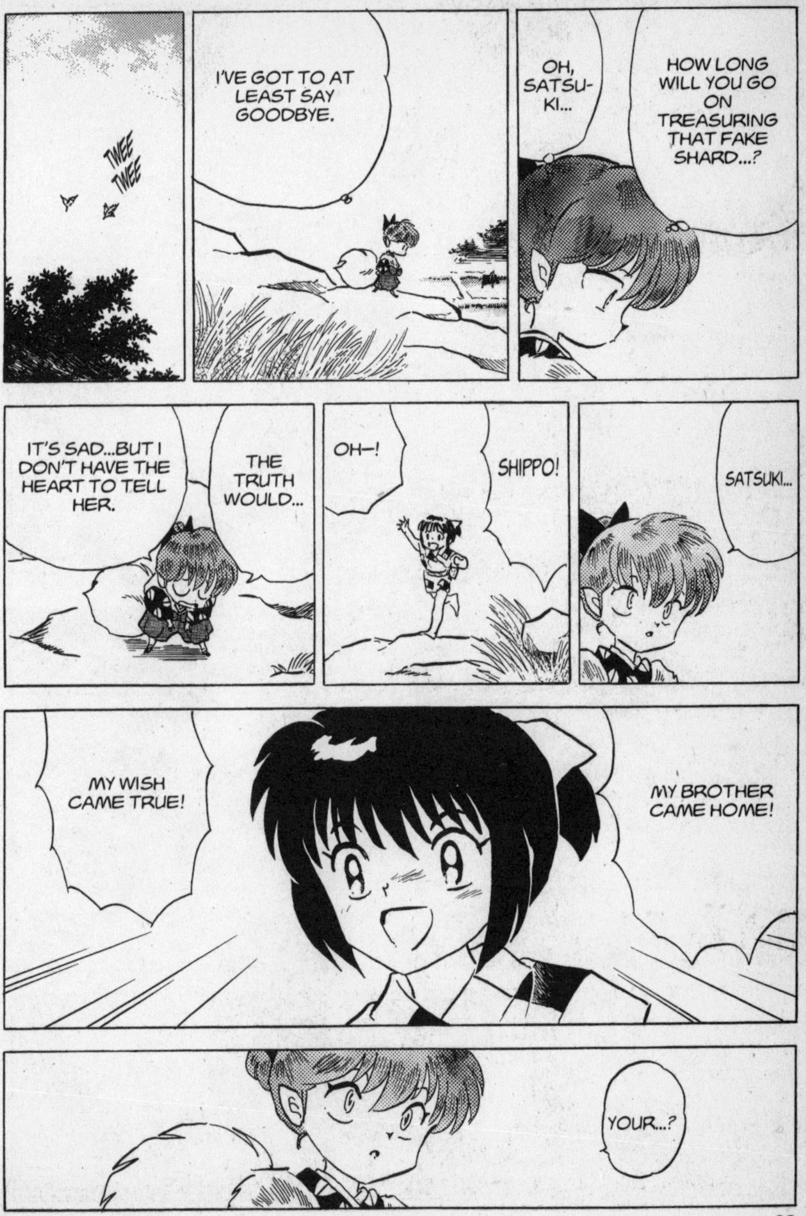
TWEE TWEE
I'VE GOT TO AT LEAST SAY GOODBYE.
OH, SATSU-KI...
HOW LONG WILL YOU GO ON TREASURING THAT FAKE SHARD...?
IT'S SAD...BUT I DON'T HAVE THE HEART TO TELL HER.
THE TRUTH WOULD...
OH—!
SHIPPO!
SATSUKI...
MY WISH CAME TRUE!
MY BROTHER CAME HOME!
YOUR...?

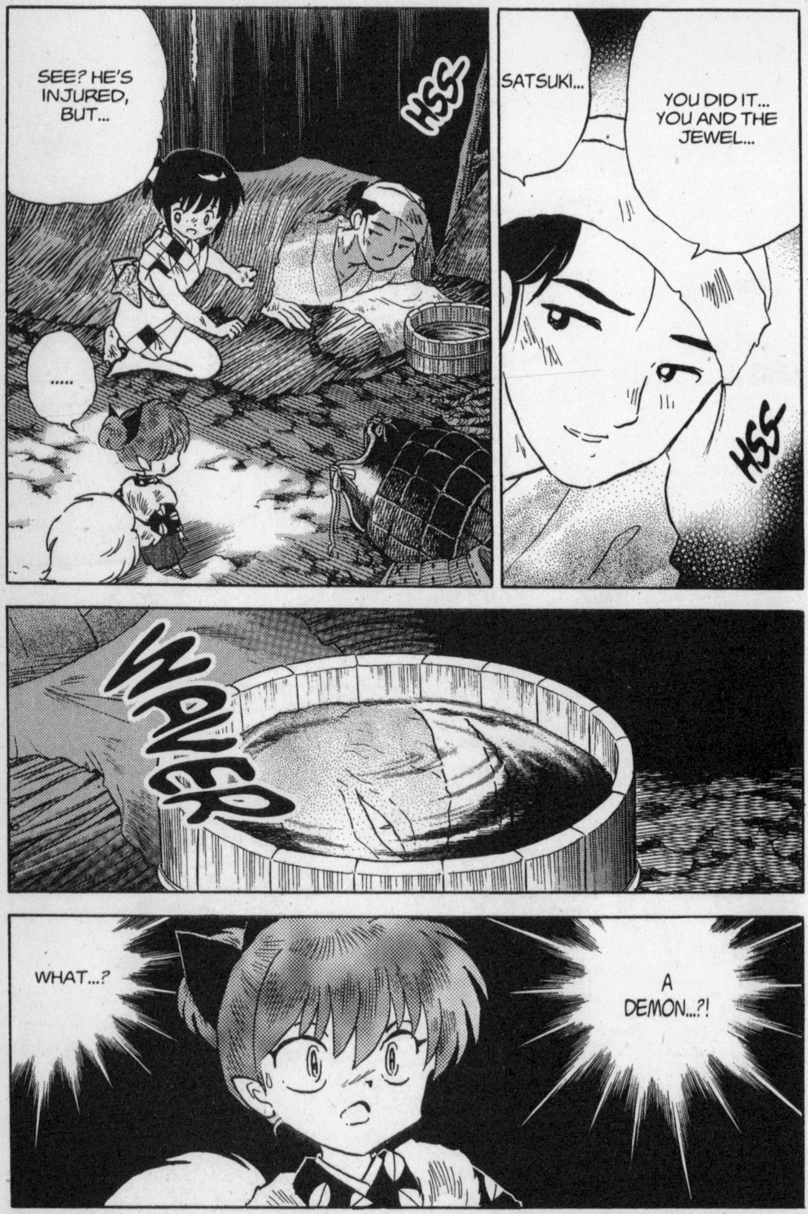
SEE? HE'S INJURED, BUT...
HSS
......
SATSUKI...
YOU DID IT... YOU AND THE JEWEL...
HSS
WAVER
WHAT...?
A DEMON...?!

SCROLL TWO

SHATTERED DREAM

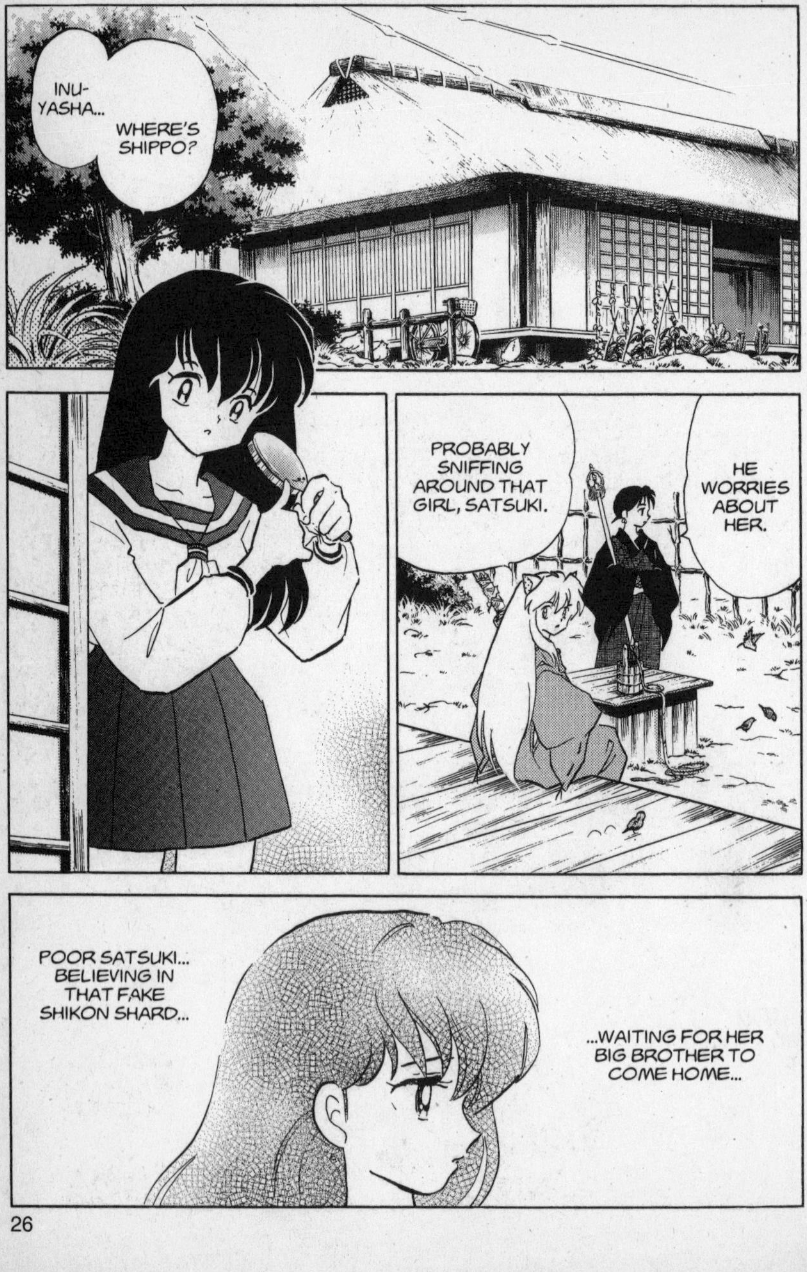
INU-YASHA...
WHERE'S SHIPPO?
PROBABLY SNIFFING AROUND THAT GIRL, SATSUKI.
HE WORRIES ABOUT HER.
POOR SATSUKI... BELIEVING IN THAT FAKE SHIKON SHARD...
...WAITING FOR HER BIG BROTHER TO COME HOME...

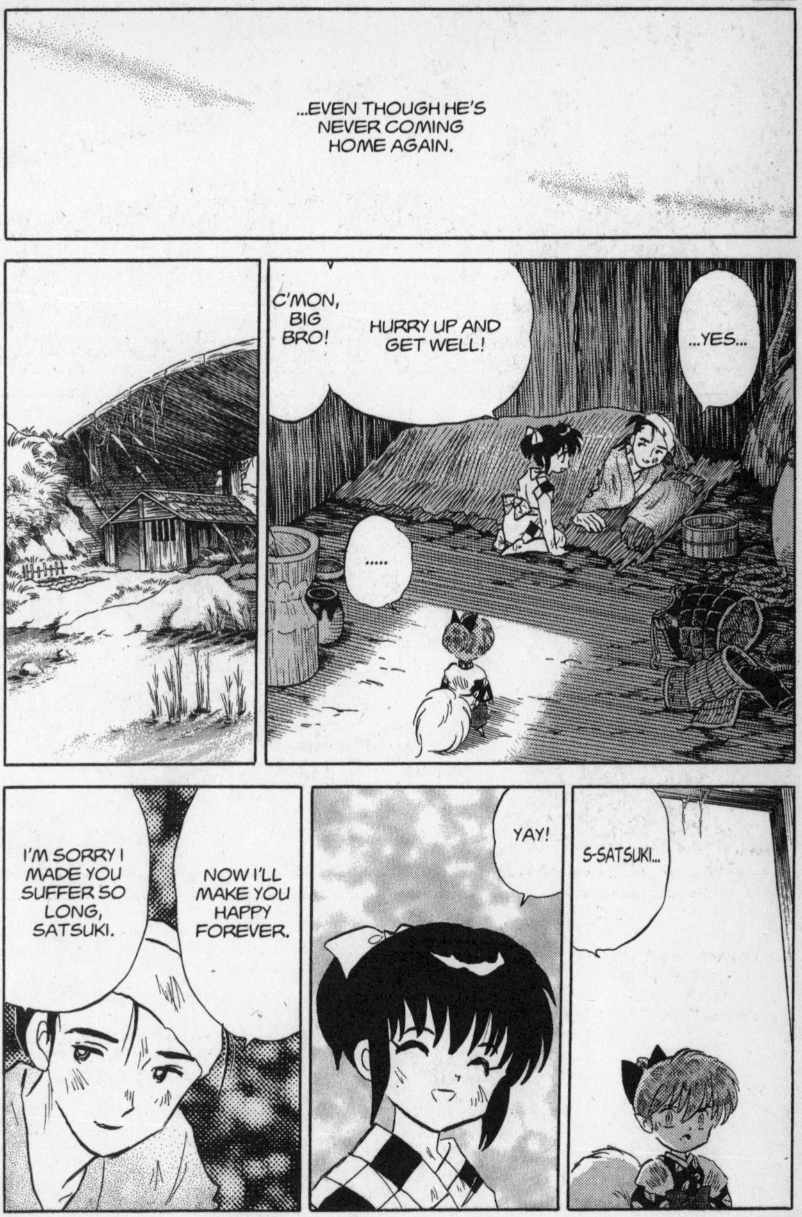
...EVEN THOUGH HE'S NEVER COMING HOME AGAIN.
C'MON, BIG BRO!
HURRY UP AND GET WELL!
.....
...YES...
I'M SORRY I MADE YOU SUFFER SO LONG, SATSUKI.
NOW I'LL MAKE YOU HAPPY FOREVER.
YAY!
S-SATSUKI...

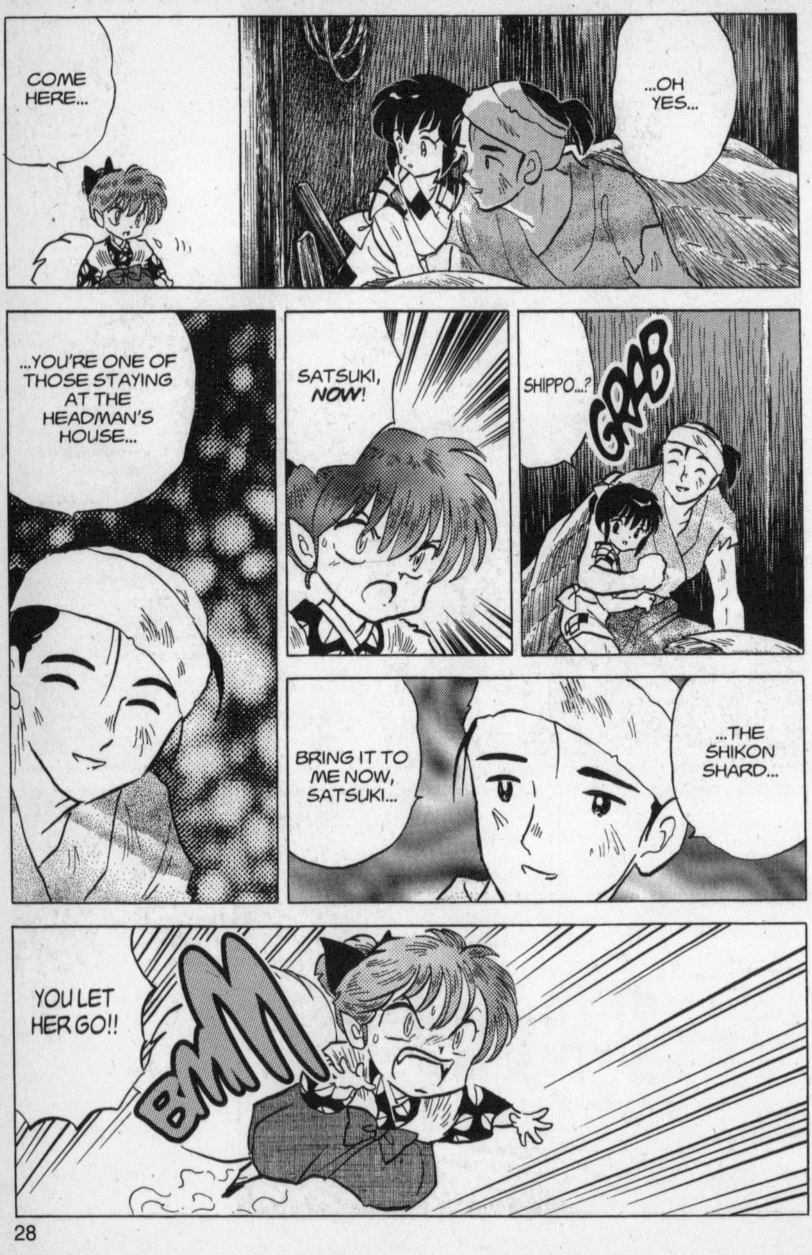
COME HERE...
...OH YES...
...YOU'RE ONE OF THOSE STAYING AT THE HEADMAN'S HOUSE...
SATSUKI, *NOW*!
SHIPPO...?
GRAB
BRING IT TO ME NOW, SATSUKI...
...THE SHIKON SHARD...
YOU LET HER GO!!
BAM

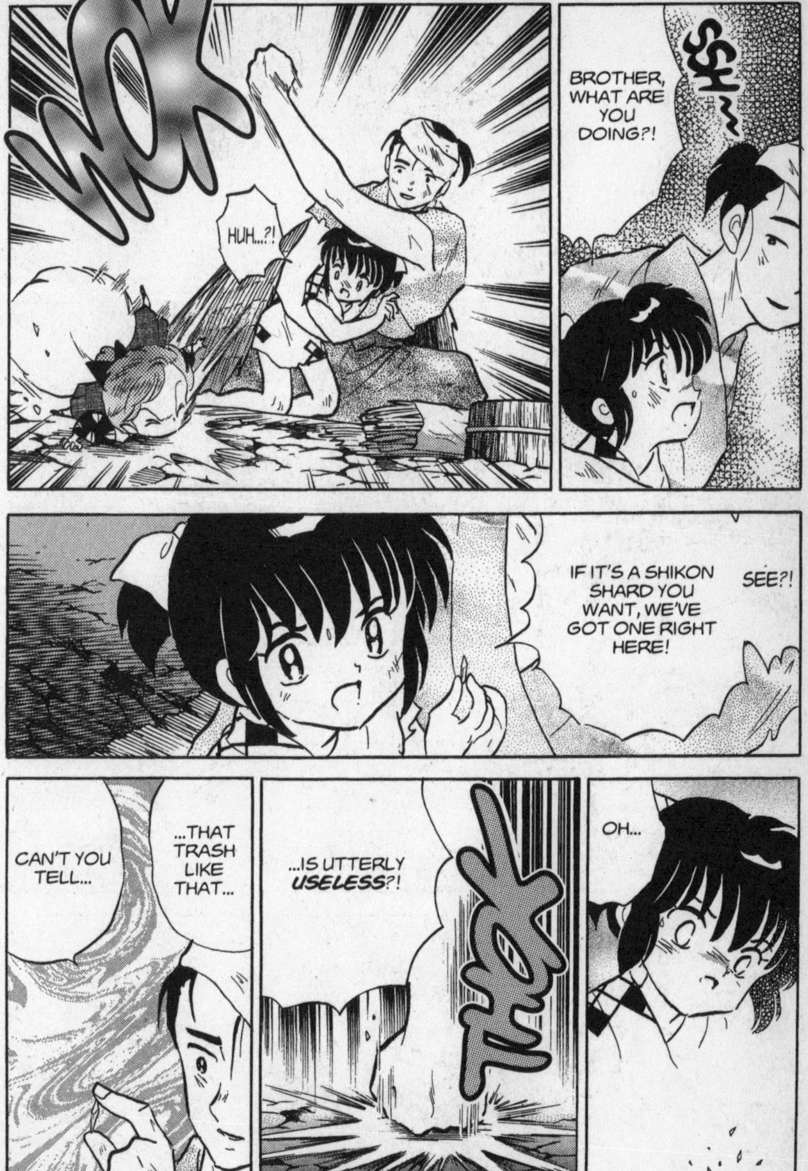
WOK
HUH...?!
SSH~
BROTHER, WHAT ARE YOU DOING?!
IF IT'S A SHIKON SHARD YOU WANT, WE'VE GOT ONE RIGHT HERE!
SEE?!
CAN'T YOU TELL...
...THAT TRASH LIKE THAT...
...IS UTTERLY *USELESS*?!
THOK
OH...

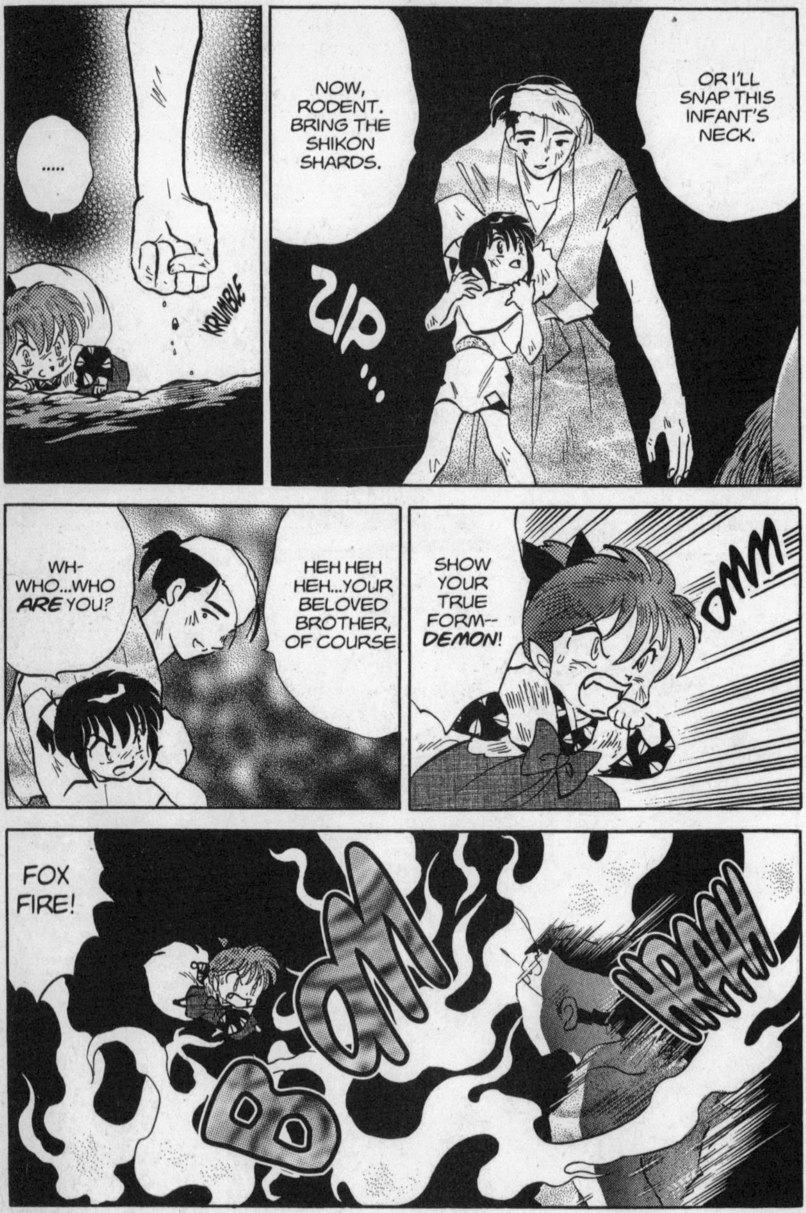
.....
KRUMBLE
NOW, RODENT. BRING THE SHIKON SHARDS.
ZIP...
OR I'LL SNAP THIS INFANT'S NECK.
WH- WHO...WHO ARE YOU?
HEH HEH HEH...YOUR BELOVED BROTHER, OF COURSE
SHOW YOUR TRUE FORM-- DEMON!
FOX FIRE!

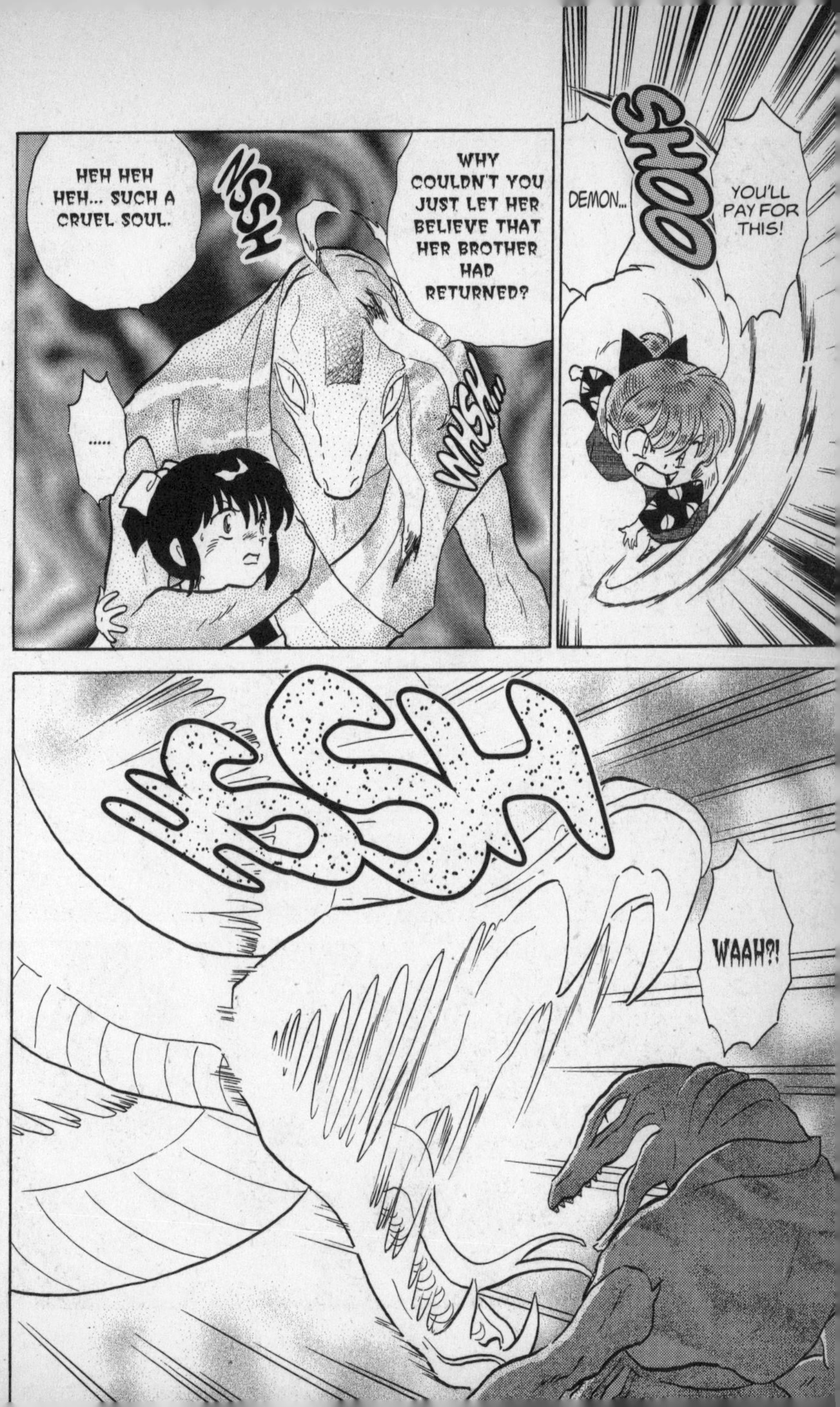
HEH HEH HEH... SUCH A CRUEL SOUL.
NSSH
WHY COULDN'T YOU JUST LET HER BELIEVE THAT HER BROTHER HAD RETURNED?
.....
WHSH
SHOO
DEMON...
YOU'LL PAY FOR THIS!
WAAH?!

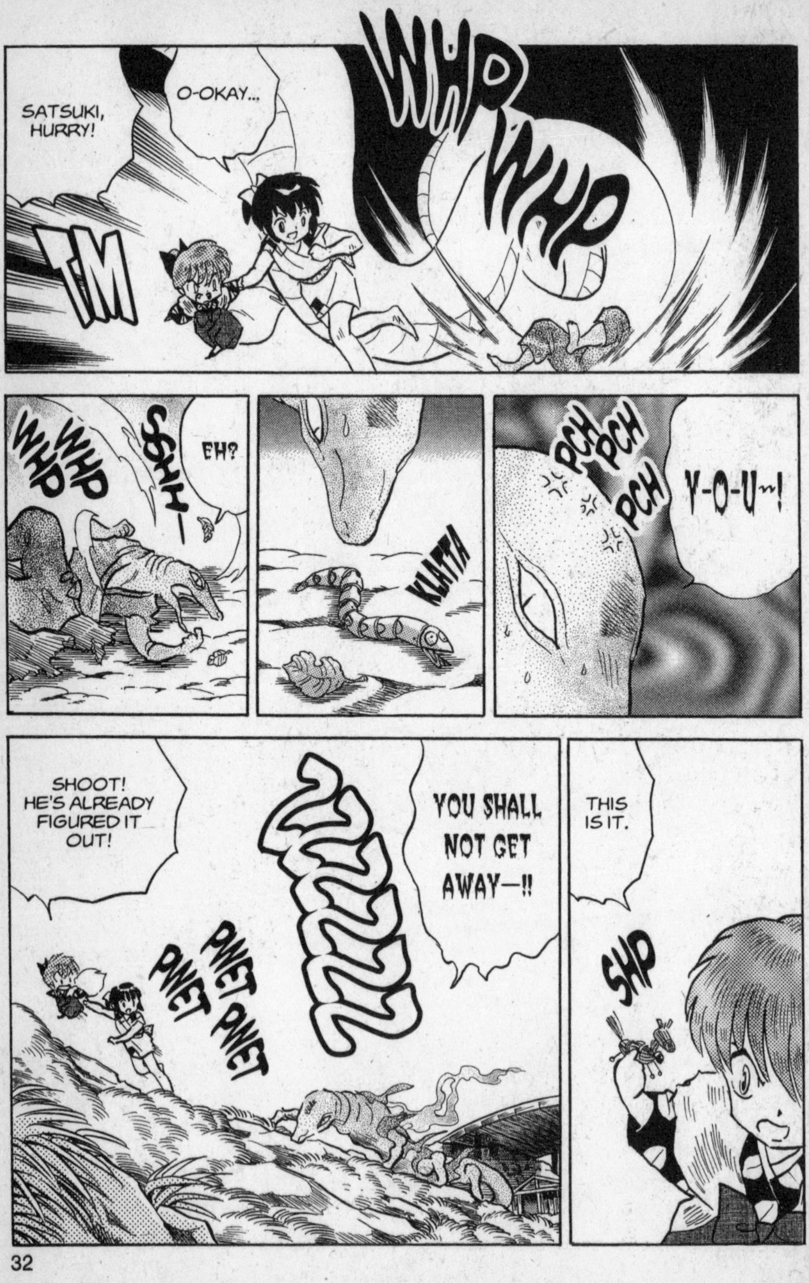
SATSUKI, HURRY!
O-OKAY...
WHP WHP
TM
WHP WHP
SGHH—
EH?
KLATTA
PCH PCH PCH PCH
Y-O-U~!
SHOOT! HE'S ALREADY FIGURED IT OUT!
YOU SHALL NOT GET AWAY—!!
PWET PWET PWET PWET
THIS IS IT.
SHP

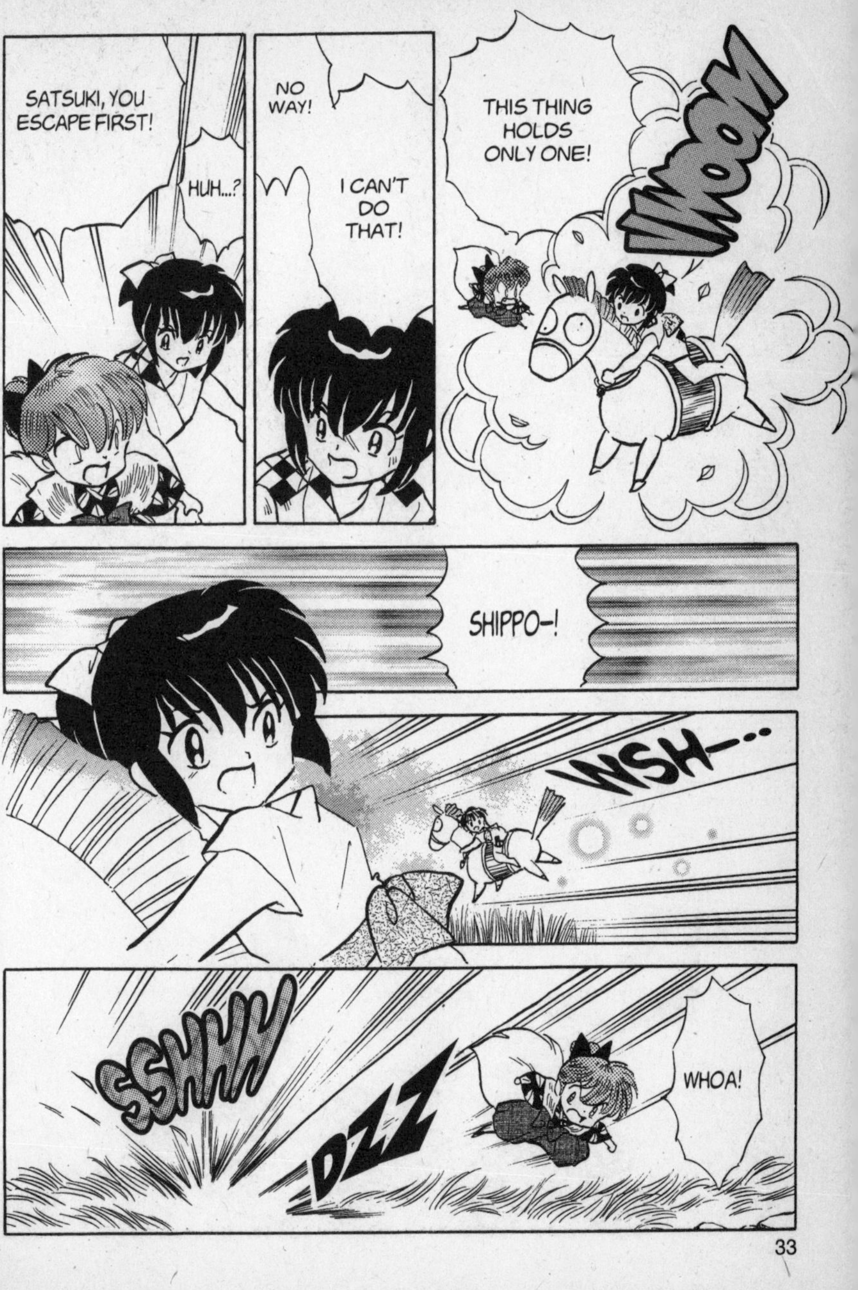
SATSUKI, YOU ESCAPE FIRST!
HUH...?
NO WAY!
I CAN'T DO THAT!
THIS THING HOLDS ONLY ONE!
WOOM
SHIPPO-!
WSH---
SSHHH
DZZ
WHOA!

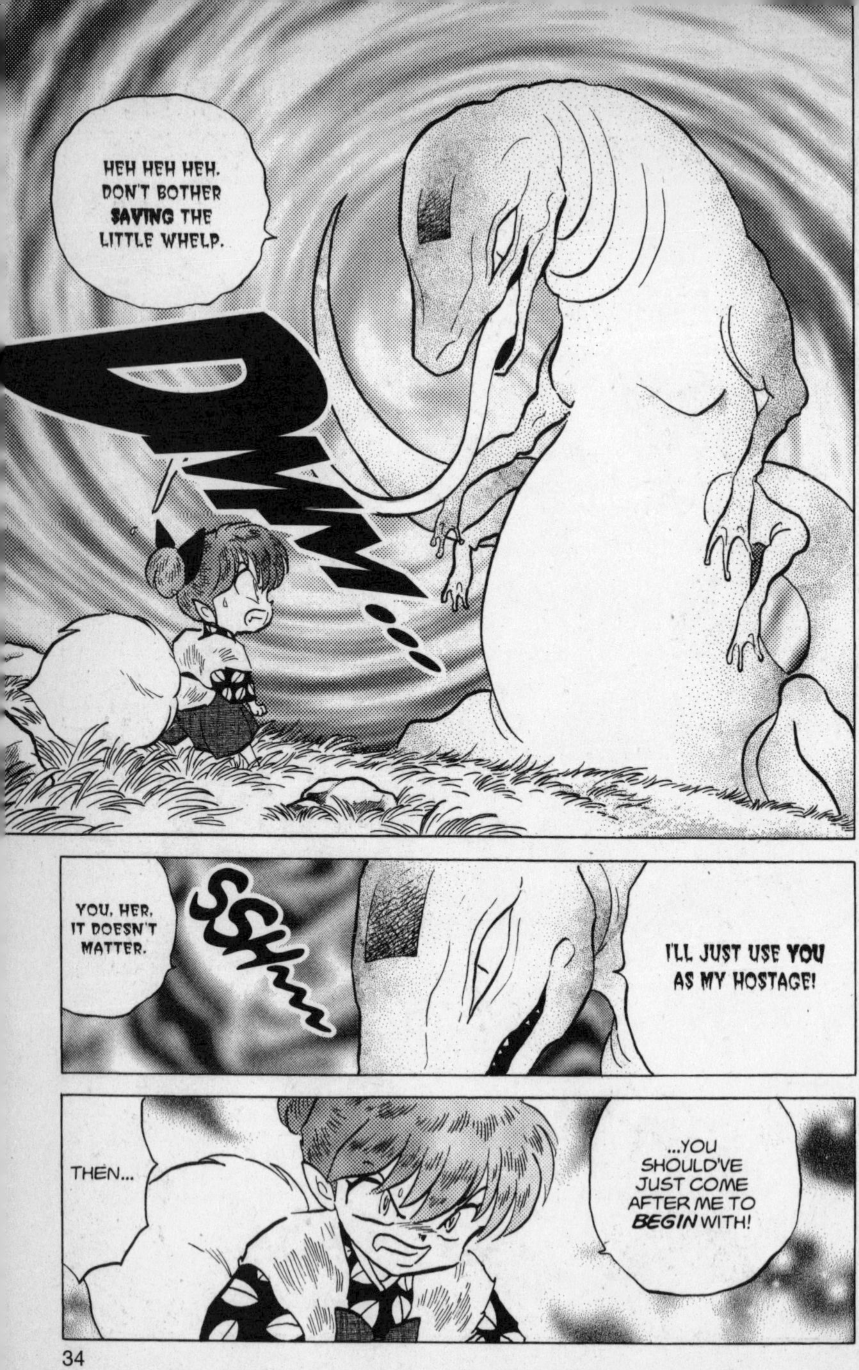
HEH HEH HEH. DON'T BOTHER SAVING THE LITTLE WHELP.
YOU, HER, IT DOESN'T MATTER.
I'LL JUST USE YOU AS MY HOSTAGE!
THEN...
...YOU SHOULD'VE JUST COME AFTER ME TO BEGIN WITH!

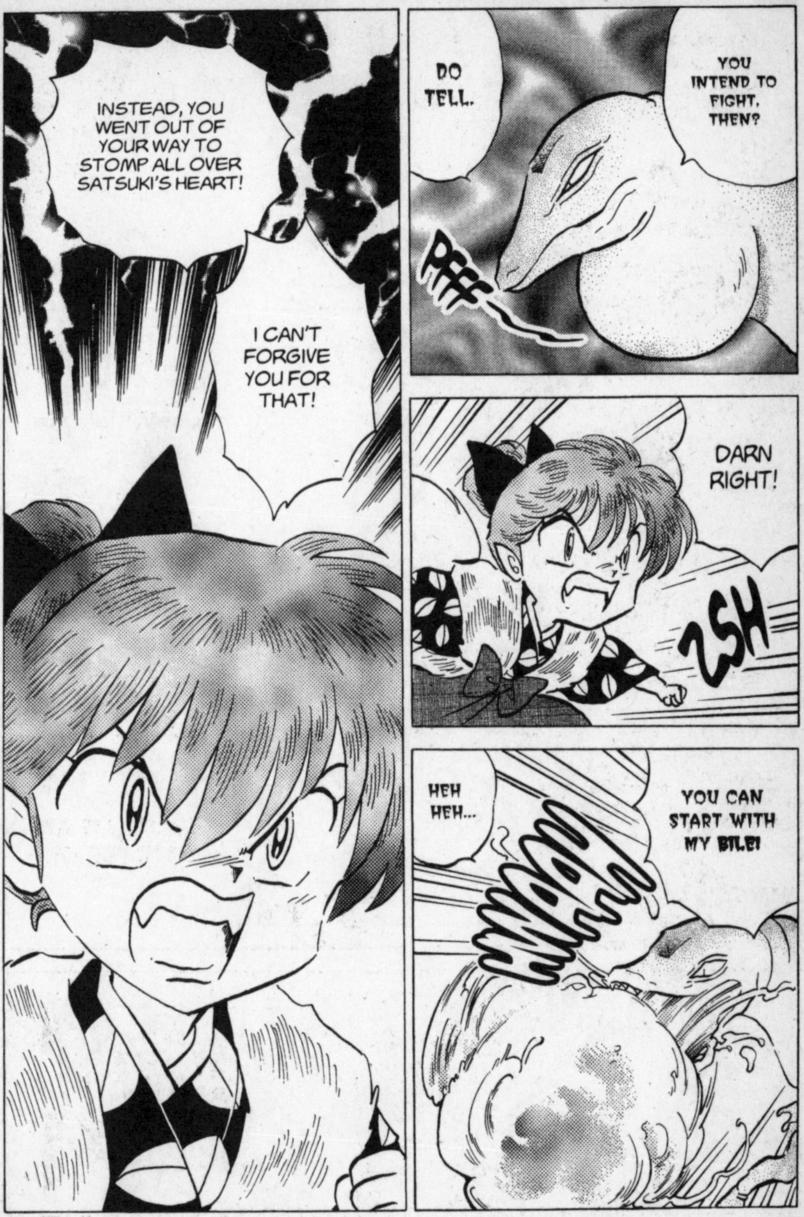
INSTEAD, YOU WENT OUT OF YOUR WAY TO STOMP ALL OVER SATSUKI'S HEART!
I CAN'T FORGIVE YOU FOR THAT!
DO TELL.
YOU INTEND TO FIGHT, THEN?
PFFF
DARN RIGHT!
ZSH
HEH HEH...
YOU CAN START WITH MY BILE!

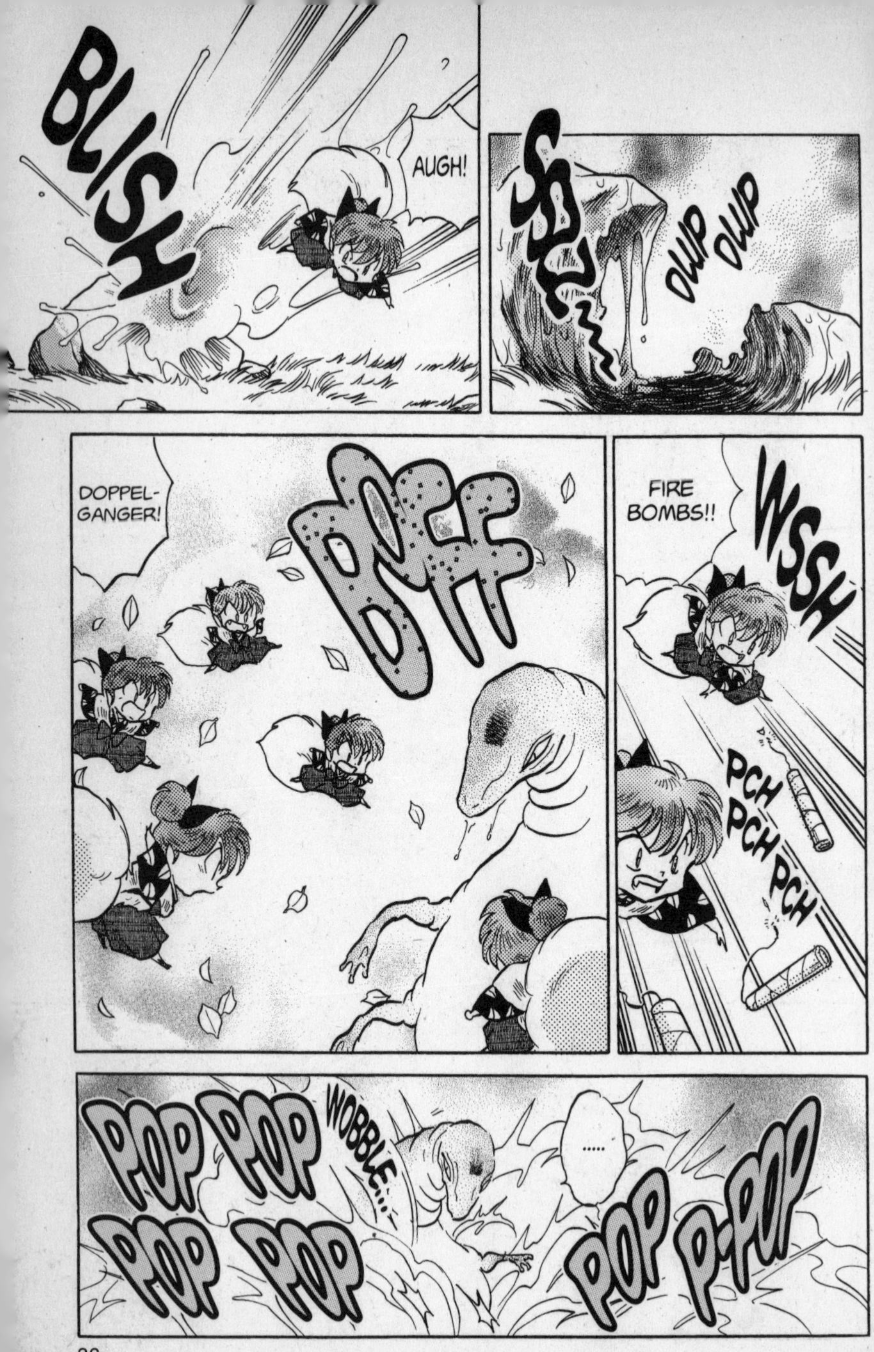
BLISH
AUGH!
SPLOOSH
DWP DWP
DOPPEL-
GANGER!
BOFF
FIRE
BOMBS!!
WSSH
PCH
PCH
PCH
PCH
POP POP
POP POP
WOBBLE...
......
POP P-POP

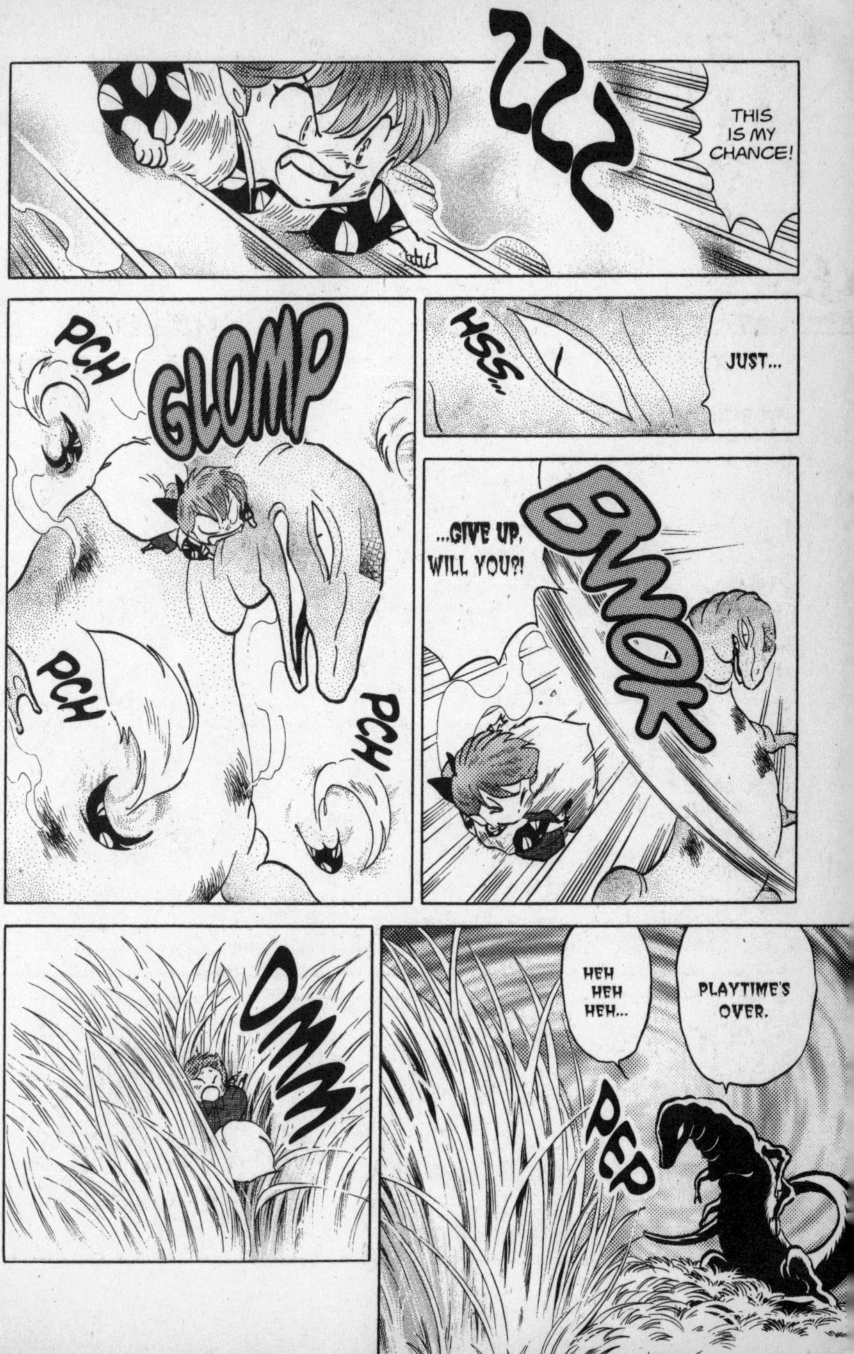
ZZZ
THIS IS MY CHANCE!
PCH
GLOMP
PCH
PCH
HSS...
JUST...
...GIVE UP, WILL YOU?!
BWOK
DMM
HEH HEH HEH...
PLAYTIME'S OVER.
PEP

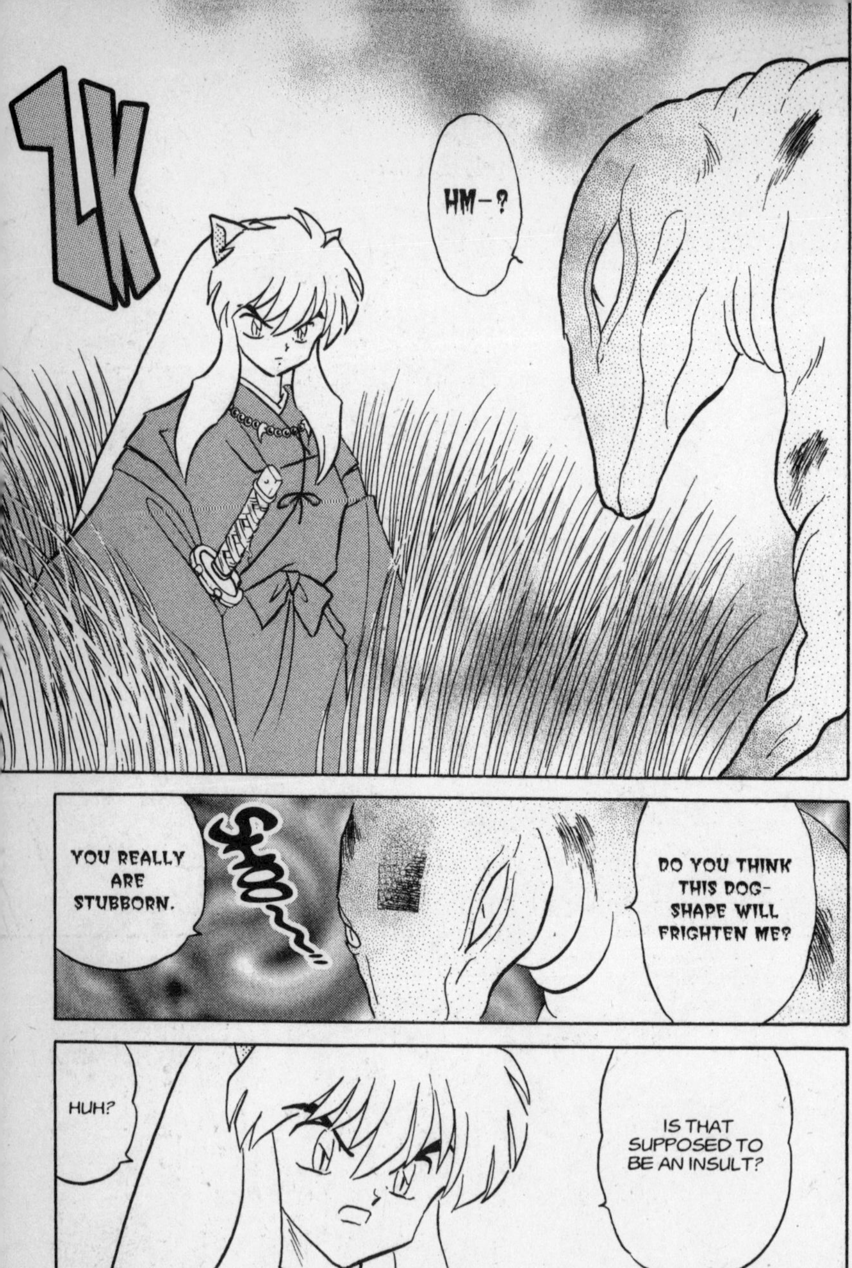
ZK
HM-?
YOU REALLY ARE STUBBORN.
SHOO~~!!
DO YOU THINK THIS DOG-SHAPE WILL FRIGHTEN ME?
HUH?
IS THAT SUPPOSED TO BE AN INSULT?

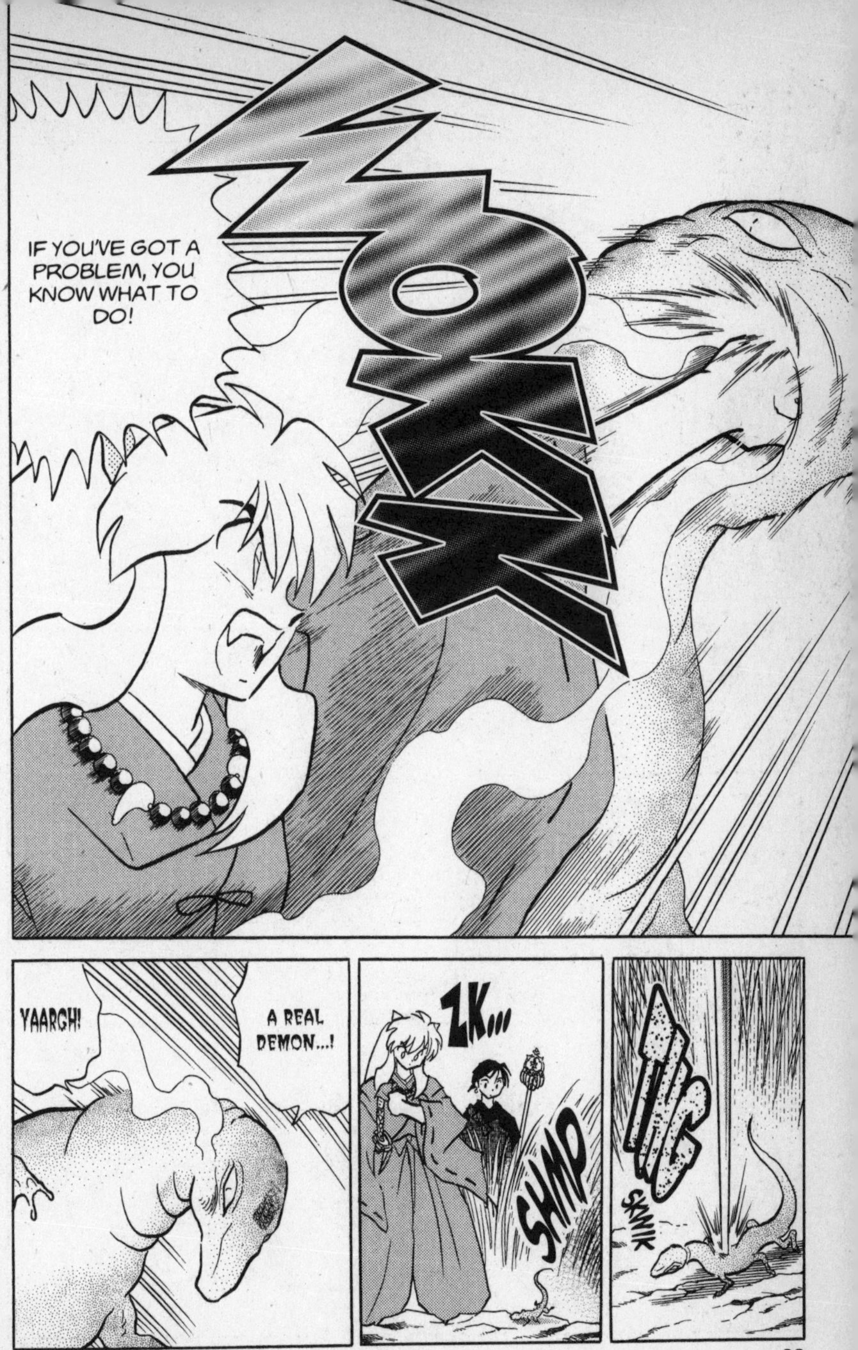
IF YOU'VE GOT A PROBLEM, YOU KNOW WHAT TO DO!
YAARGH!
A REAL DEMON...!
ZK...
SHMP
SKWIK

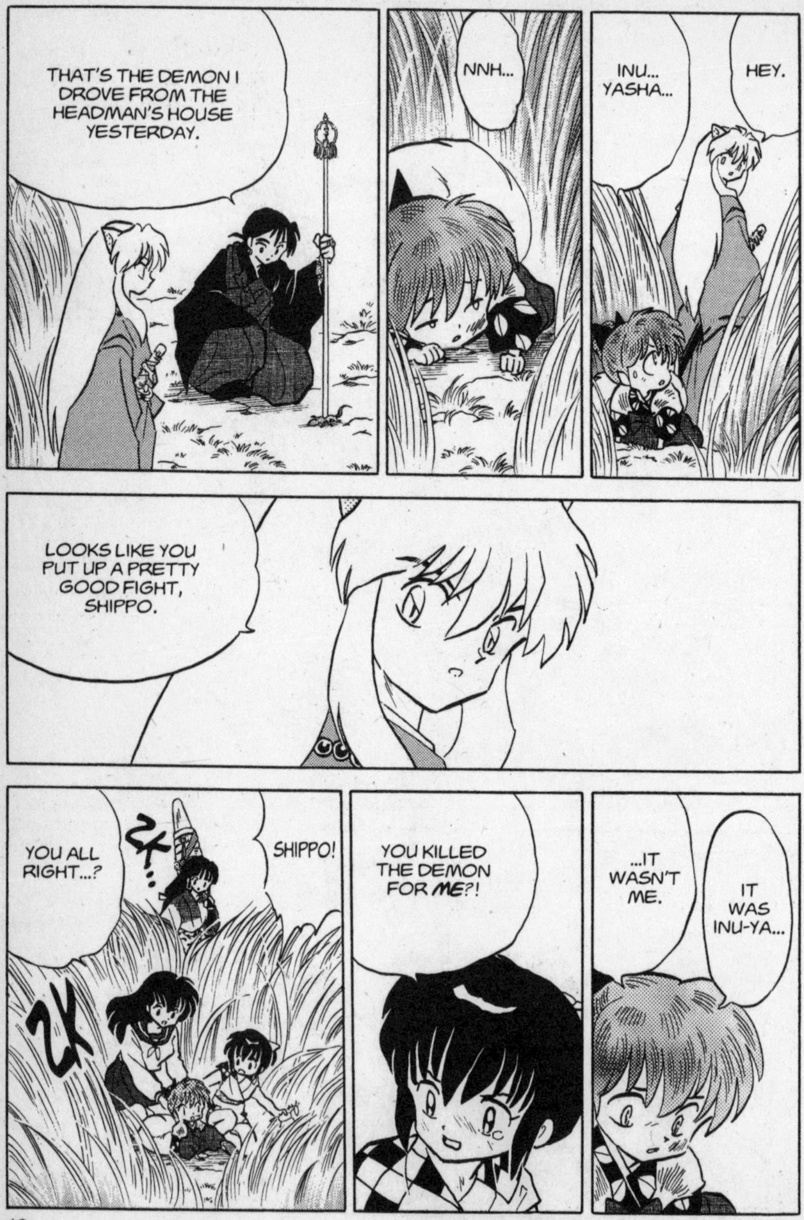
THAT'S THE DEMON I DROVE FROM THE HEADMAN'S HOUSE YESTERDAY.
NNH...
INU... YASHA...
HEY.
LOOKS LIKE YOU PUT UP A PRETTY GOOD FIGHT, SHIPPO.
YOU ALL RIGHT...?
ZK...
SHIPPO!
ZK
YOU KILLED THE DEMON FOR ME?!
...IT WASN'T ME.
IT WAS INU-YA...

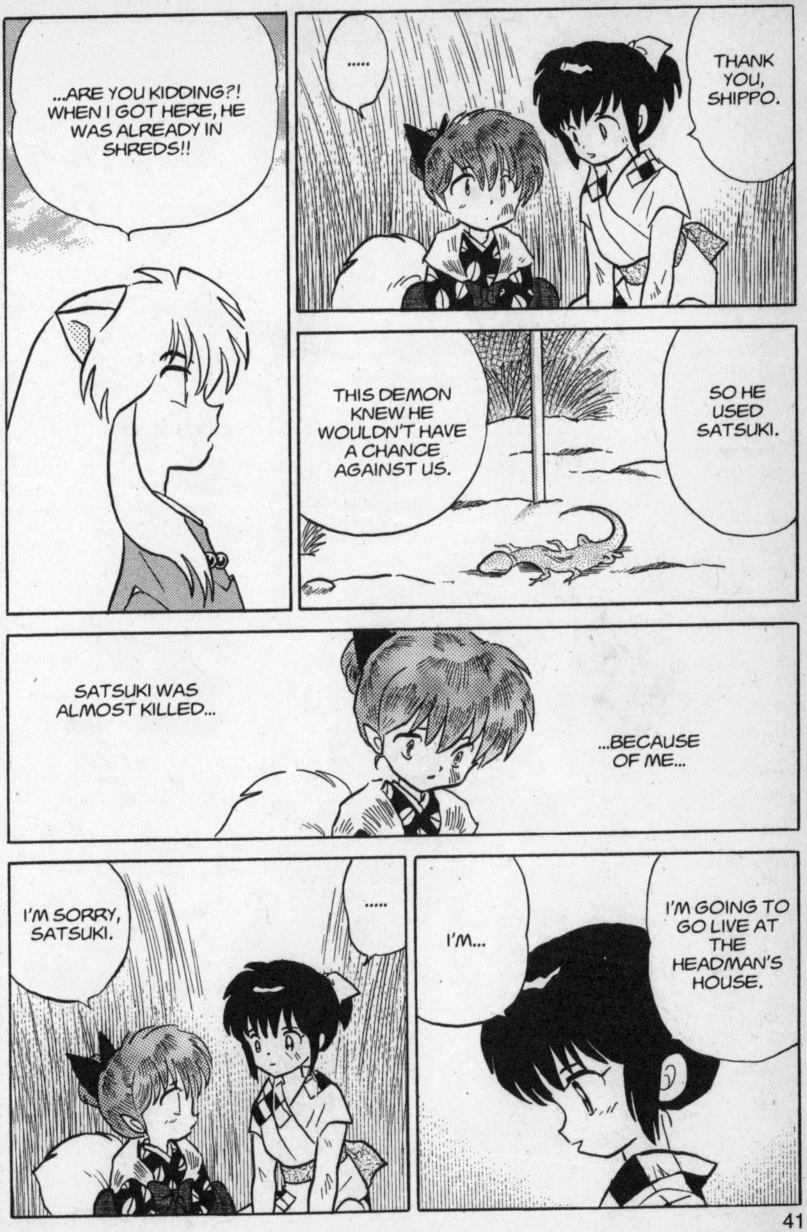
...ARE YOU KIDDING?! WHEN I GOT HERE, HE WAS ALREADY IN SHREDS!!
.....
THANK YOU, SHIPPO.
THIS DEMON KNEW HE WOULDN'T HAVE A CHANCE AGAINST US.
SO HE USED SATSUKI.
SATSUKI WAS ALMOST KILLED...
...BECAUSE OF ME...
I'M SORRY, SATSUKI.
.....
I'M...
I'M GOING TO GO LIVE AT THE HEADMAN'S HOUSE.

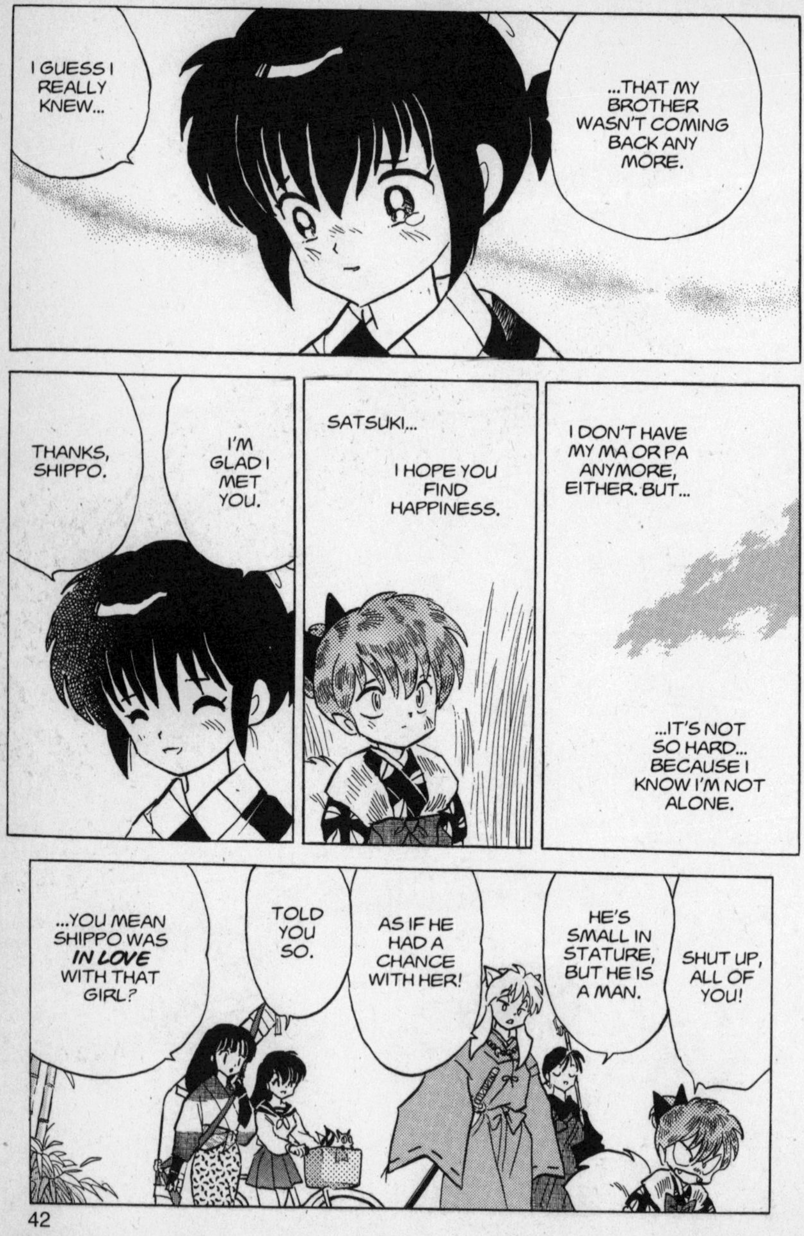
I GUESS I REALLY KNEW...
...THAT MY BROTHER WASN'T COMING BACK ANY MORE.
THANKS, SHIPPO.
I'M GLAD I MET YOU.
SATSUKI,...
I HOPE YOU FIND HAPPINESS.
I DON'T HAVE MY MA OR PA ANYMORE, EITHER. BUT...
...IT'S NOT SO HARD... BECAUSE I KNOW I'M NOT ALONE.
...YOU MEAN SHIPPO WAS ***IN LOVE*** WITH THAT GIRL?
TOLD YOU SO.
AS IF HE HAD A CHANCE WITH HER!
HE'S SMALL IN STATURE, BUT HE IS A MAN.
SHUT UP, ALL OF YOU!

SCROLL THREE

NARAKU'S SCENT

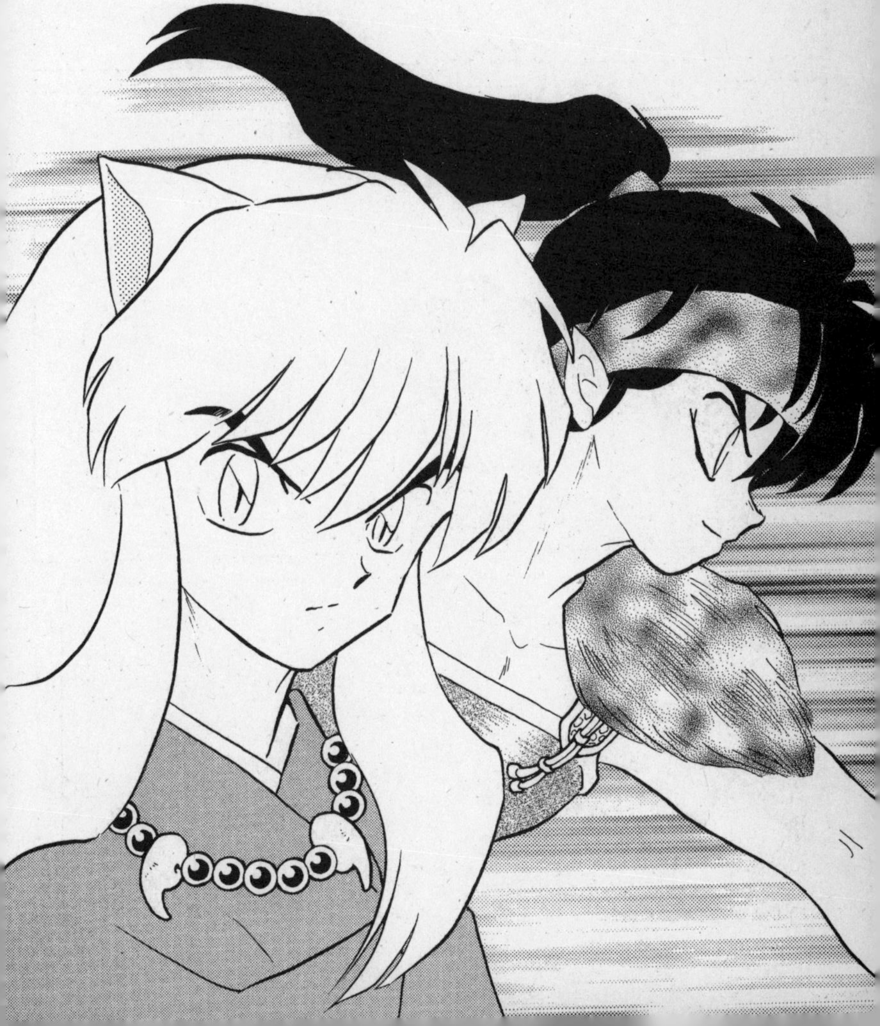

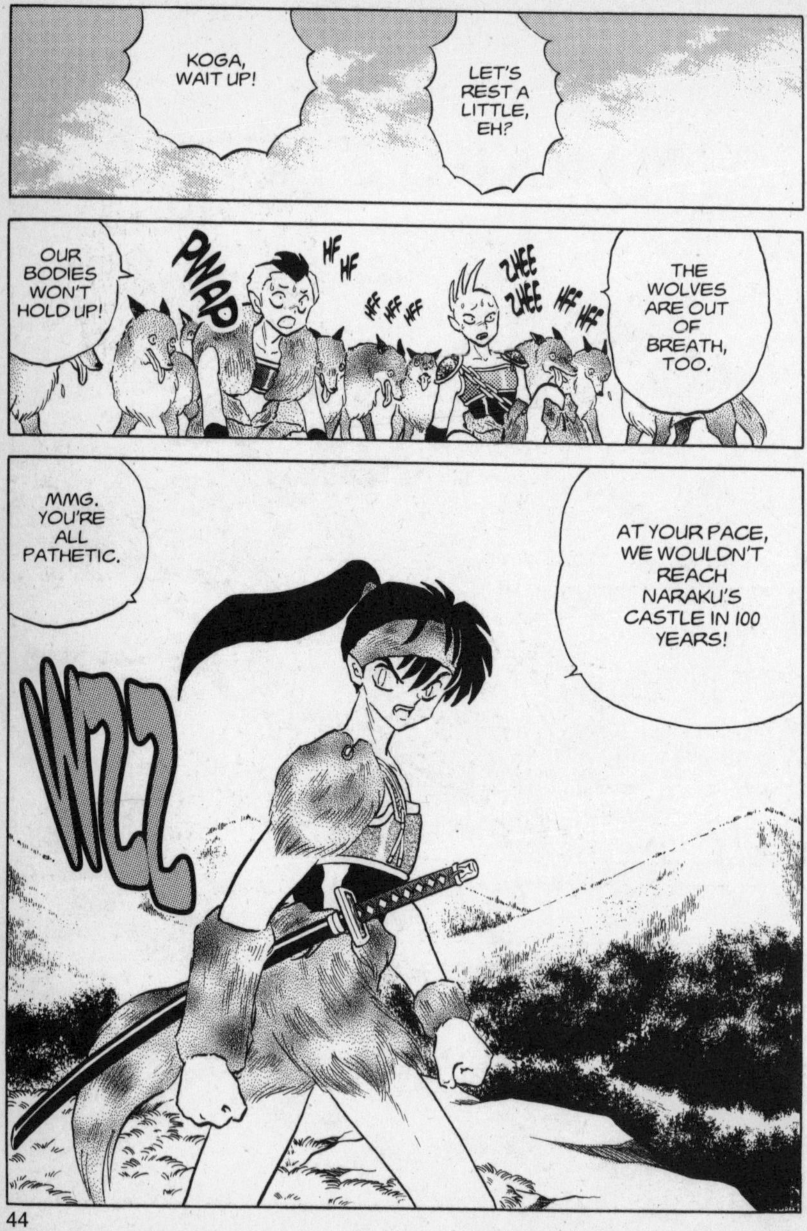
KOGA, WAIT UP!
LET'S REST A LITTLE, EH?
OUR BODIES WON'T HOLD UP!
PWAP
HF HF
HFF HFF HFF
ZHEE ZHEE
HFF HFF
THE WOLVES ARE OUT OF BREATH, TOO.
MMG. YOU'RE ALL PATHETIC.
AT YOUR PACE, WE WOULDN'T REACH NARAKU'S CASTLE IN 100 YEARS!
WZZ

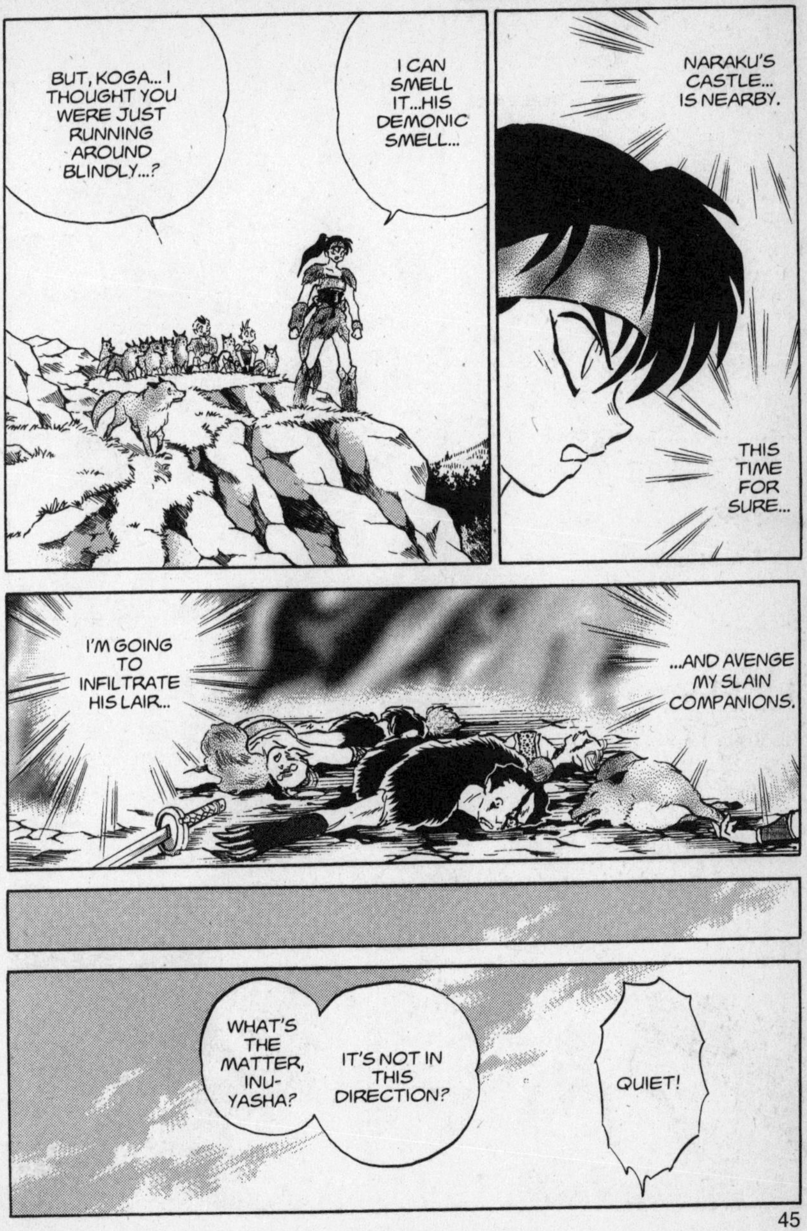
BUT, KOGA... I THOUGHT YOU WERE JUST RUNNING AROUND BLINDLY...?
I CAN SMELL IT...HIS DEMONIC SMELL...
NARAKU'S CASTLE... IS NEARBY.
THIS TIME FOR SURE...
I'M GOING TO INFILTRATE HIS LAIR..
...AND AVENGE MY SLAIN COMPANIONS.
WHAT'S THE MATTER, INU-YASHA?
IT'S NOT IN THIS DIRECTION?
QUIET!

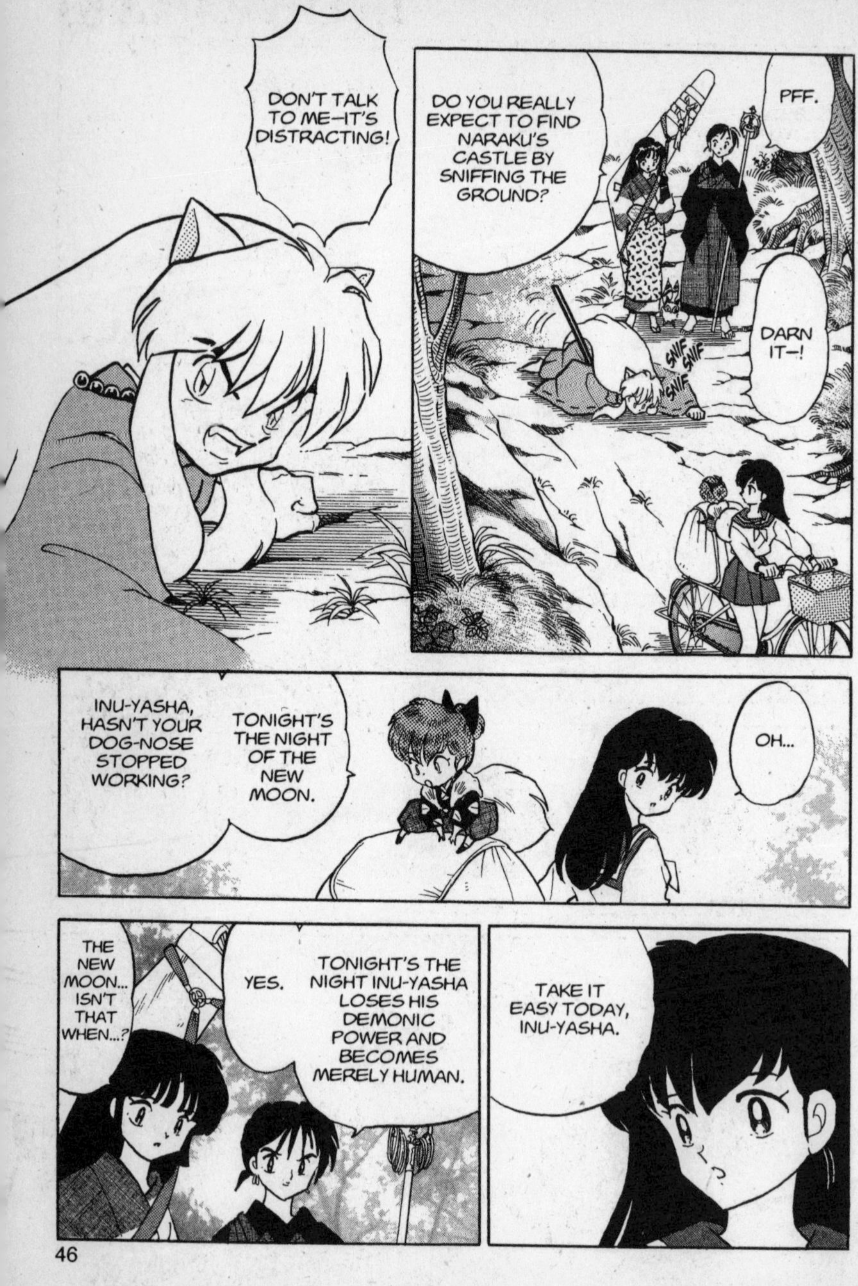
DON'T TALK TO ME—IT'S DISTRACTING!
DO YOU REALLY EXPECT TO FIND NARAKU'S CASTLE BY SNIFFING THE GROUND?
PFF.
SNIF SNIF SNIF
DARN IT—!
INU-YASHA, HASN'T YOUR DOG-NOSE STOPPED WORKING?
TONIGHT'S THE NIGHT OF THE NEW MOON.
OH...
THE NEW MOON... ISN'T THAT WHEN...?
YES.
TONIGHT'S THE NIGHT INU-YASHA LOSES HIS DEMONIC POWER AND BECOMES MERELY HUMAN.
TAKE IT EASY TODAY, INU-YASHA.

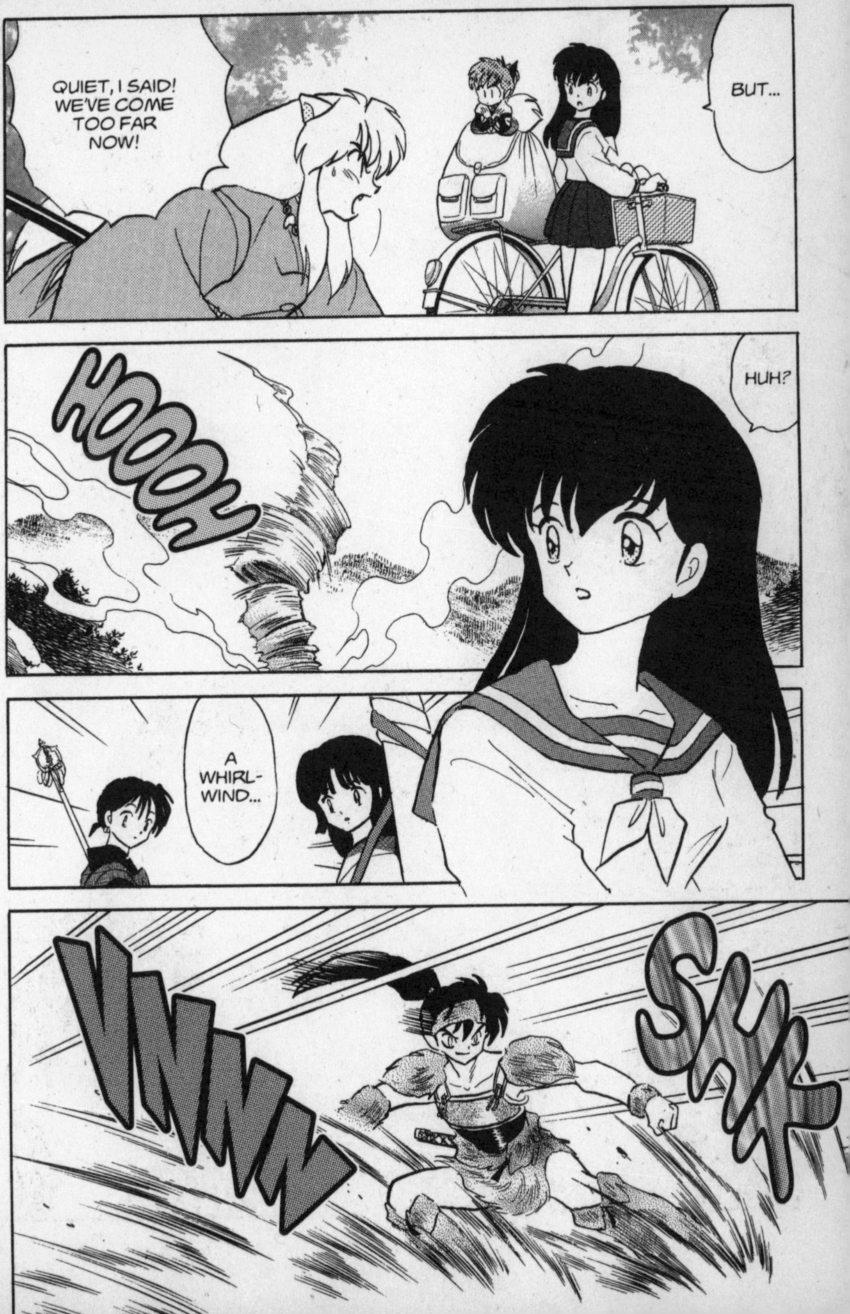
QUIET, I SAID! WE'VE COME TOO FAR NOW!
BUT...
HOOOH
HUH?
A WHIRL-WIND...
VNNNN
SHK

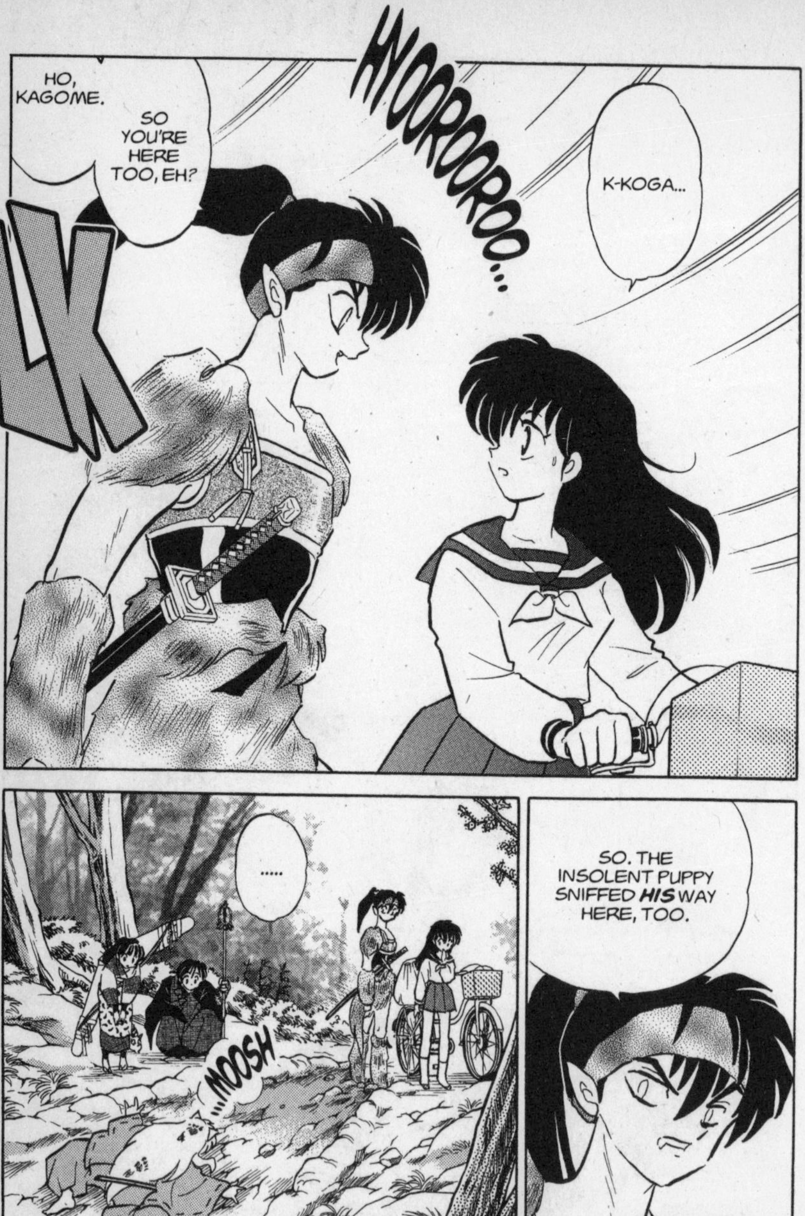
HO, KAGOME.
SO YOU'RE HERE TOO, EH?
ZK
HYOOROOROO...
K-KOGA...
.....
...MOOSH
SO. THE INSOLENT PUPPY SNIFFED **HIS** WAY HERE, TOO.

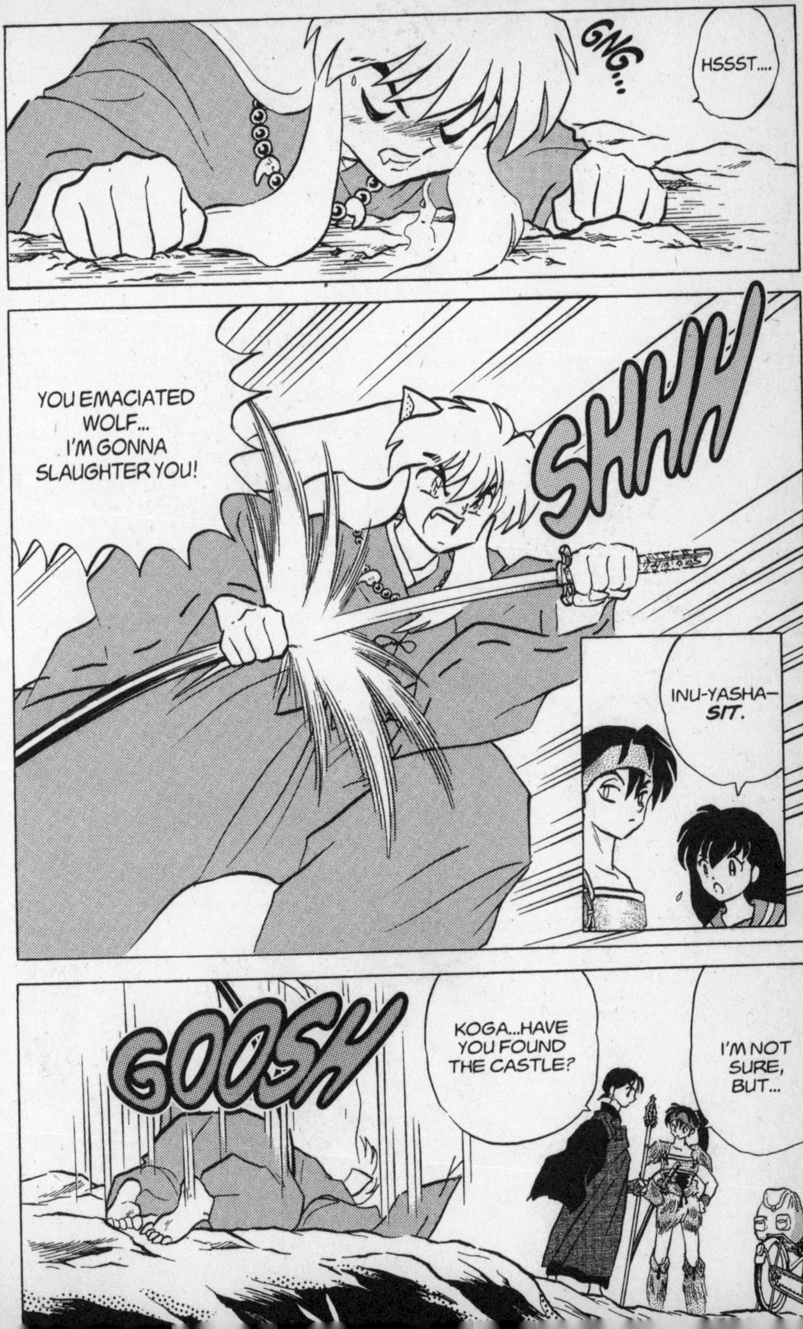
GNG...
HSSST....
YOU EMACIATED WOLF... I'M GONNA SLAUGHTER YOU!
SHHH
INU-YASHA— *SIT*.
GOOSH
KOGA...HAVE YOU FOUND THE CASTLE?
I'M NOT SURE, BUT...

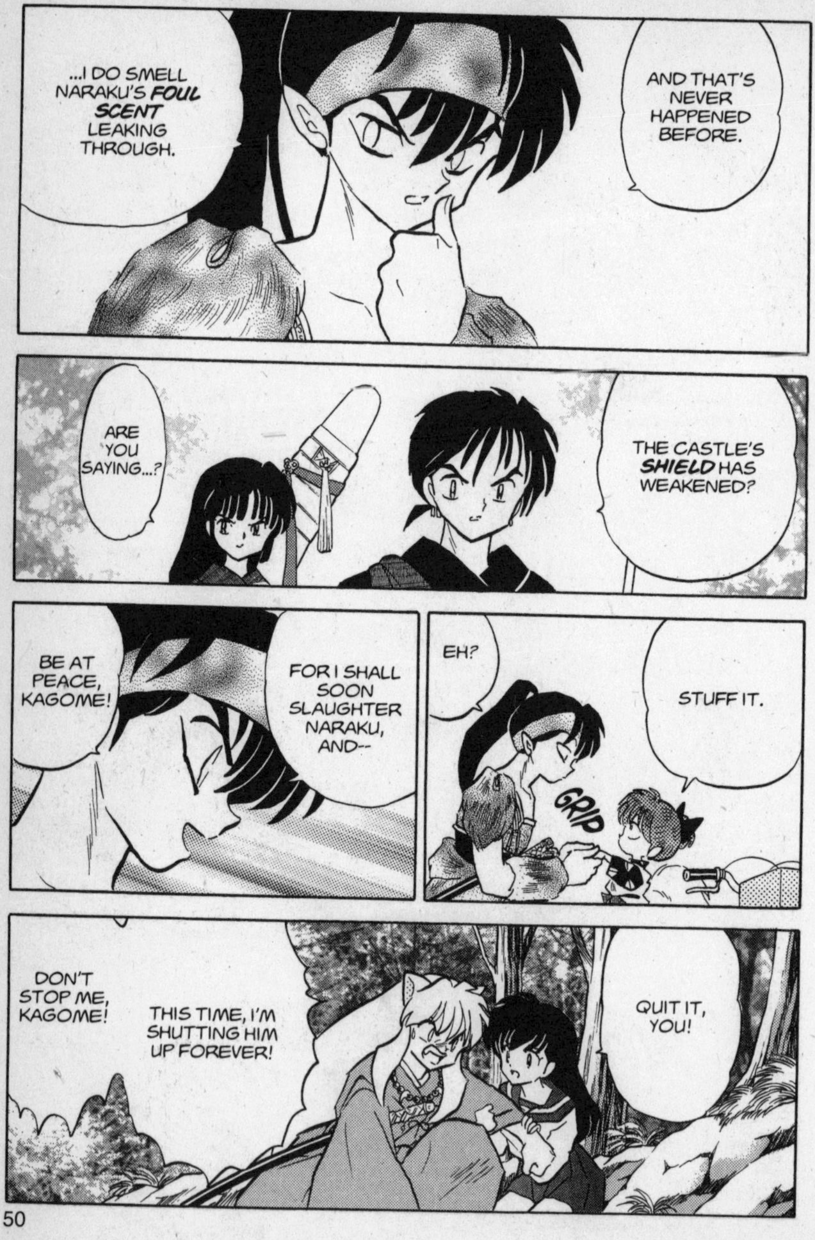

...I DO SMELL NARAKU'S **FOUL SCENT** LEAKING THROUGH.
AND THAT'S NEVER HAPPENED BEFORE.
ARE YOU SAYING...?
THE CASTLE'S **SHIELD** HAS WEAKENED?
BE AT PEACE, KAGOME!
FOR I SHALL SOON SLAUGHTER NARAKU, AND--
EH?
STUFF IT.
GRIP
DON'T STOP ME, KAGOME!
THIS TIME, I'M SHUTTING HIM UP FOREVER!
QUIT IT, YOU!

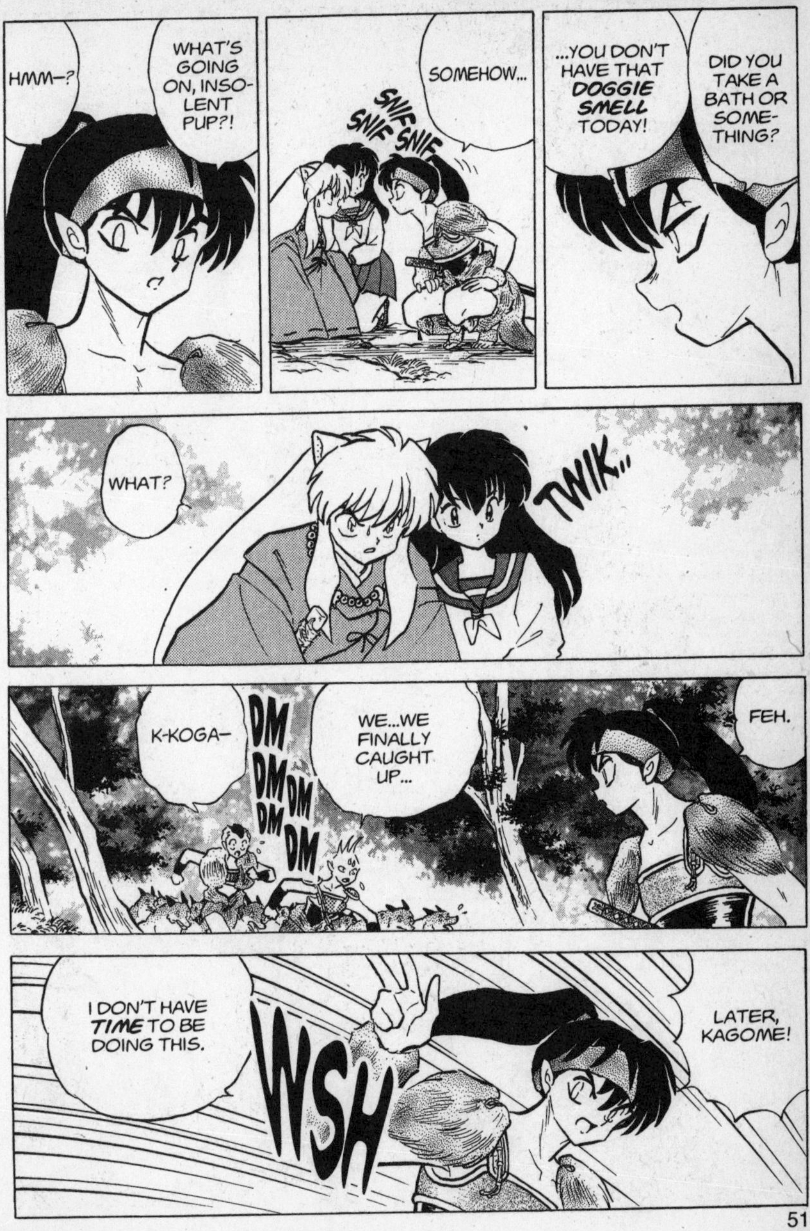
HMM–?
WHAT'S GOING ON, INSO-LENT PUP?!
SNIF SNIF SNIF
SOMEHOW...
...YOU DON'T HAVE THAT **DOGGIE SMELL** TODAY!
DID YOU TAKE A BATH OR SOME-THING?
WHAT?
TWIK...
K-KOGA–
DM DM DM DM DM DM
WE...WE FINALLY CAUGHT UP...
FEH.
I DON'T HAVE ***TIME*** TO BE DOING THIS.
WSH
LATER, KAGOME!

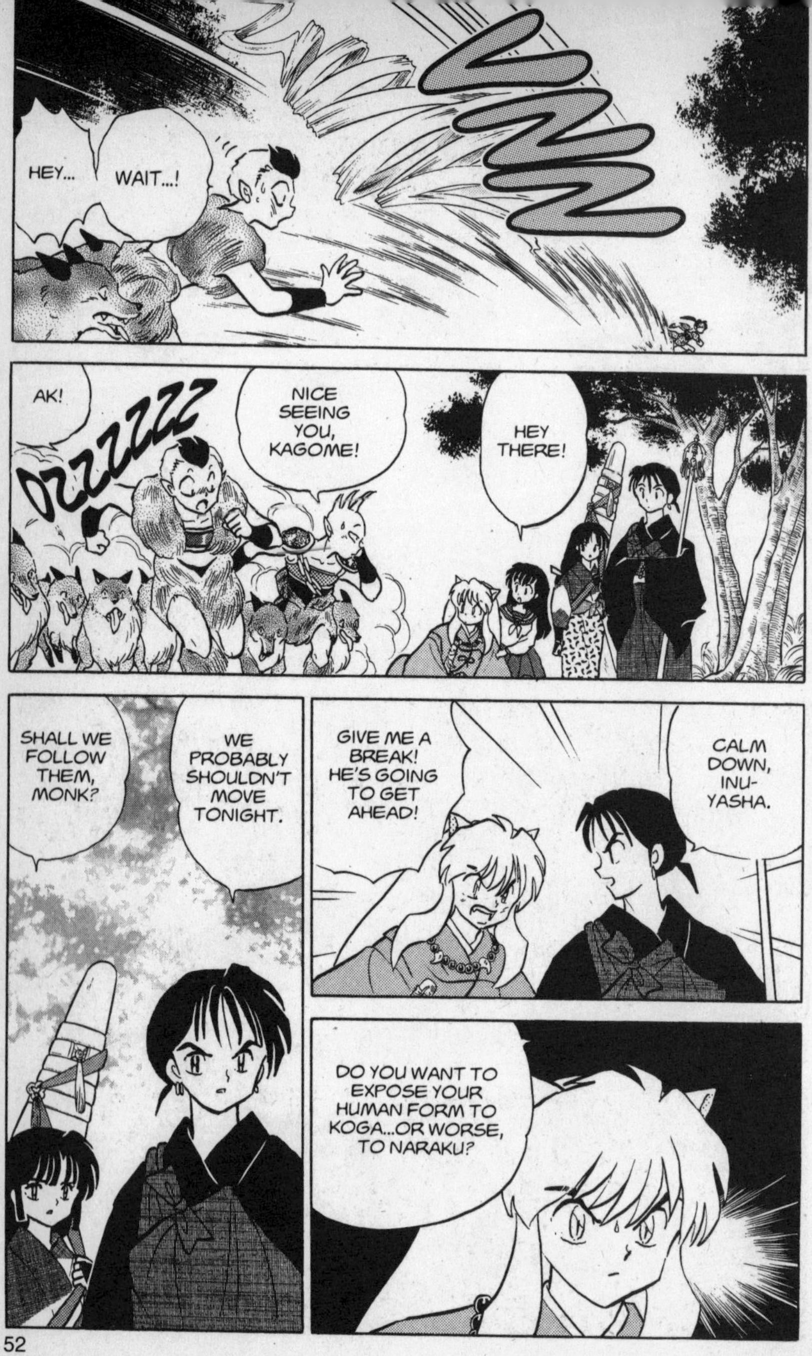
HEY...
WAIT...!
AK!
DZZZZZZ
NICE SEEING YOU, KAGOME!
HEY THERE!
SHALL WE FOLLOW THEM, MONK?
WE PROBABLY SHOULDN'T MOVE TONIGHT.
GIVE ME A BREAK! HE'S GOING TO GET AHEAD!
CALM DOWN, INU-YASHA.
DO YOU WANT TO EXPOSE YOUR HUMAN FORM TO KOGA...OR WORSE, TO NARAKU?

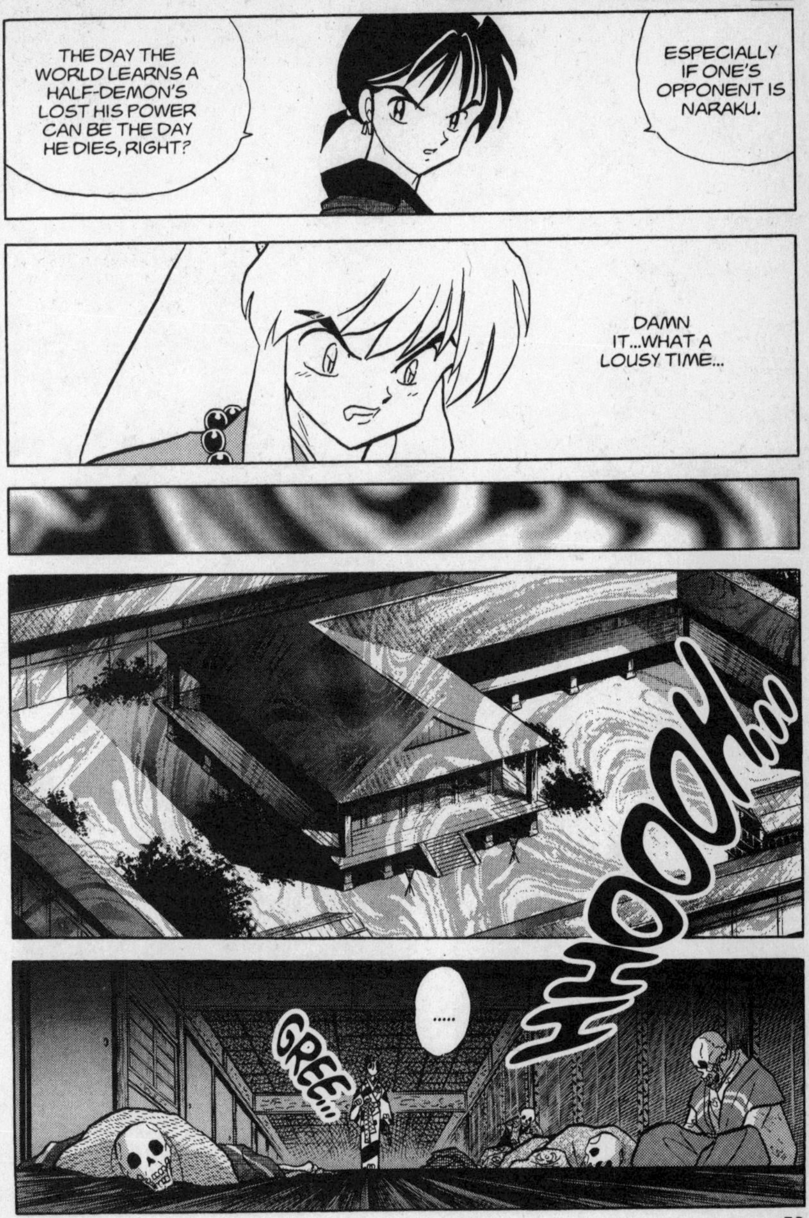
THE DAY THE WORLD LEARNS A HALF-DEMON'S LOST HIS POWER CAN BE THE DAY HE DIES, RIGHT?
ESPECIALLY IF ONE'S OPPONENT IS NARAKU.
DAMN IT...WHAT A LOUSY TIME...
GREE...
......
WHOOOhooo

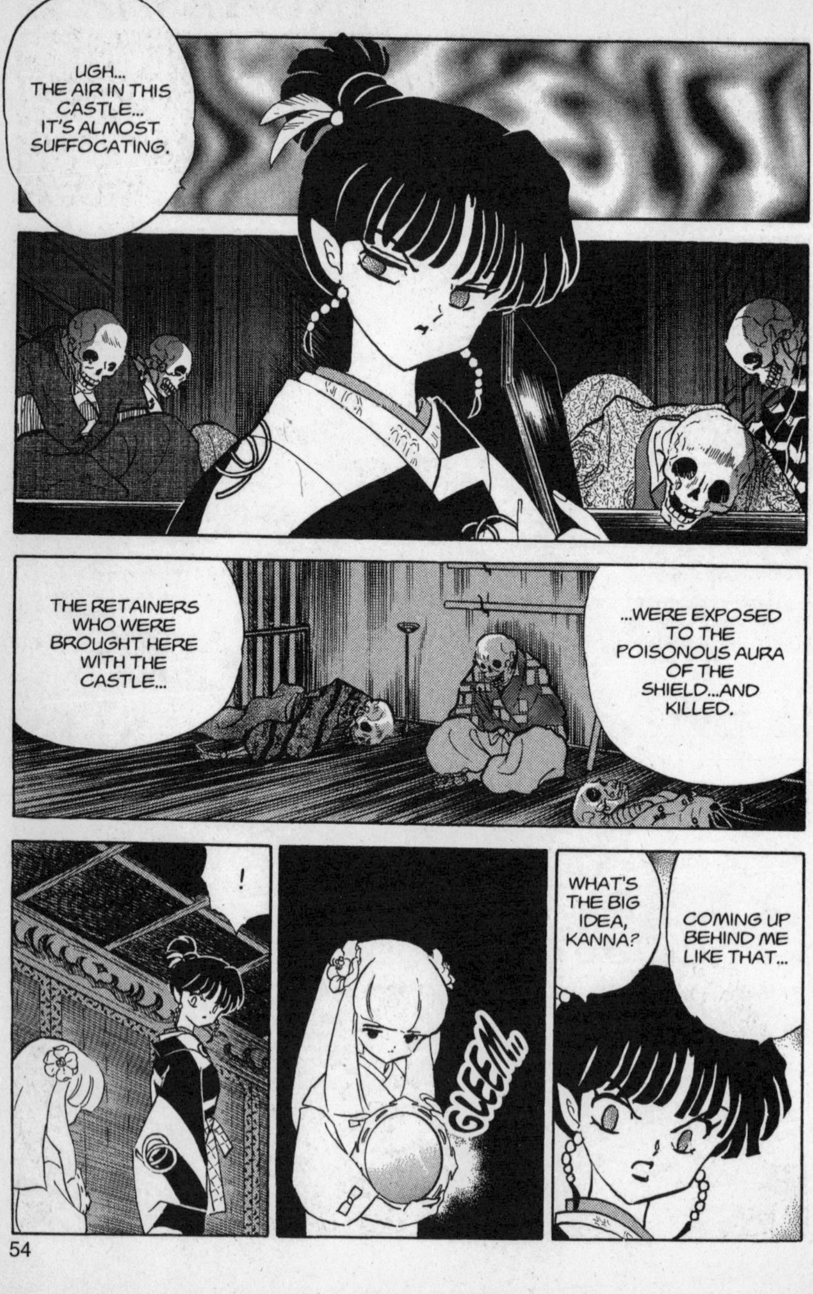
UGH... THE AIR IN THIS CASTLE... IT'S ALMOST SUFFOCATING.
THE RETAINERS WHO WERE BROUGHT HERE WITH THE CASTLE...
...WERE EXPOSED TO THE POISONOUS AURA OF THE SHIELD...AND KILLED.
!
GLEEM...
WHAT'S THE BIG IDEA, KANNA?
COMING UP BEHIND ME LIKE THAT...

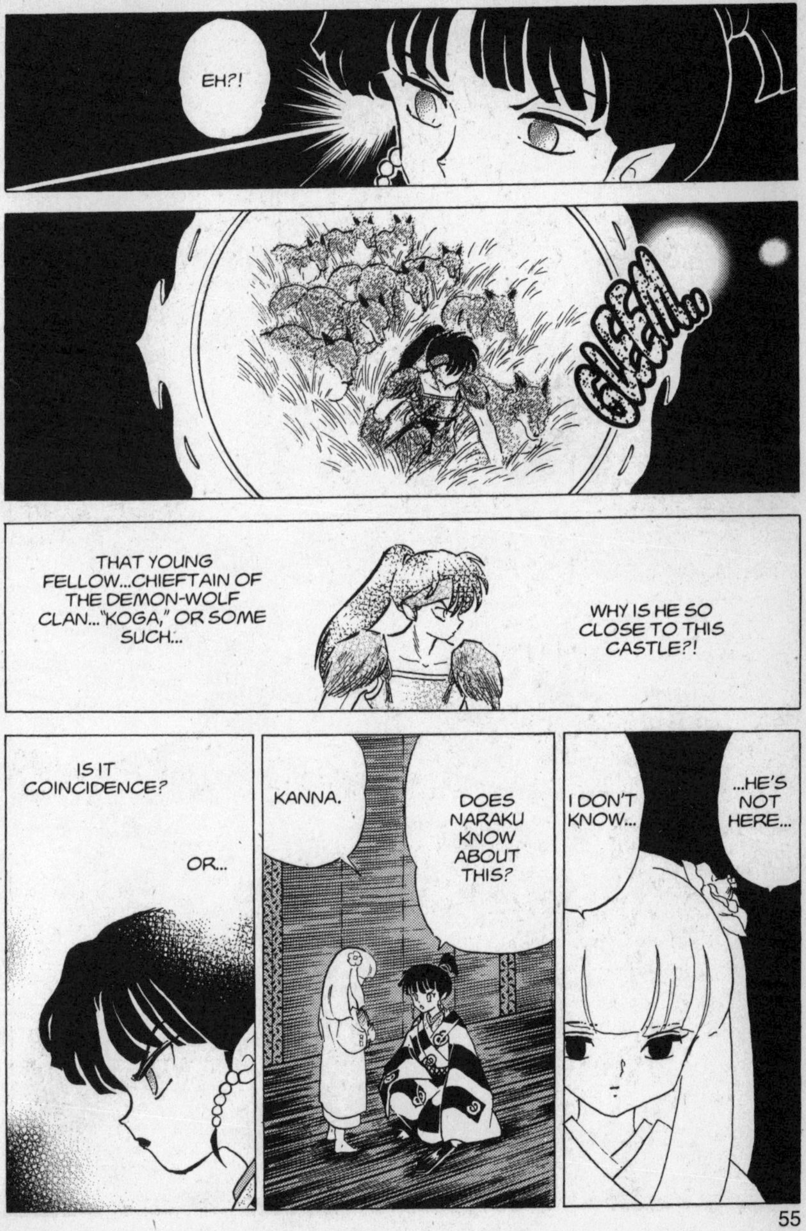
EH?!
THAT YOUNG FELLOW...CHIEFTAIN OF THE DEMON-WOLF CLAN..."KOGA," OR SOME SUCH...
WHY IS HE SO CLOSE TO THIS CASTLE?!
IS IT COINCIDENCE?
OR...
KANNA.
DOES NARAKU KNOW ABOUT THIS?
I DON'T KNOW...
...HE'S NOT HERE...

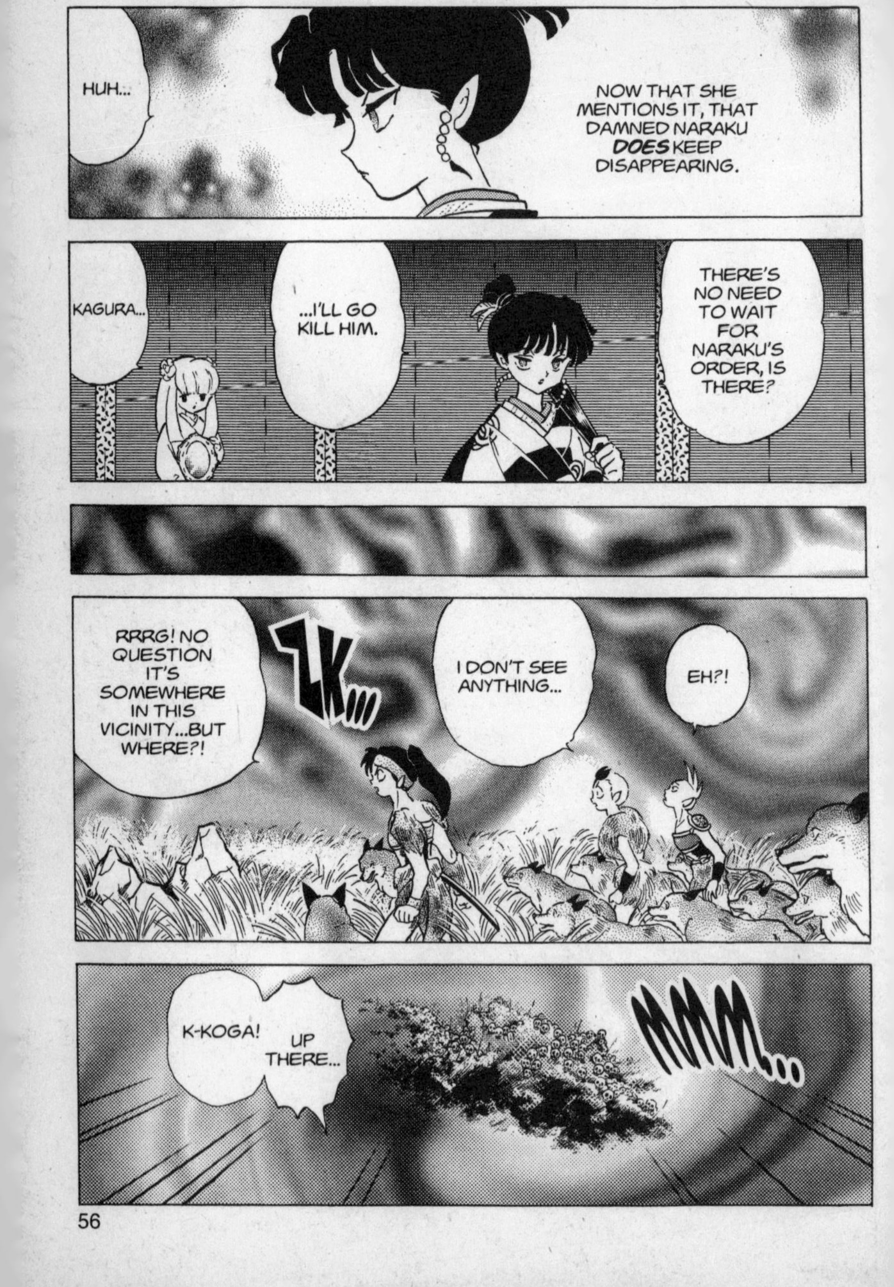
HUH...
NOW THAT SHE MENTIONS IT, THAT DAMNED NARAKU **DOES** KEEP DISAPPEARING.
KAGURA...
...I'LL GO KILL HIM.
THERE'S NO NEED TO WAIT FOR NARAKU'S ORDER, IS THERE?
RRRG! NO QUESTION IT'S SOMEWHERE IN THIS VICINITY...BUT WHERE?!
LK...
I DON'T SEE ANYTHING...
EH?!
K-KOGA!
UP THERE...
MMM...

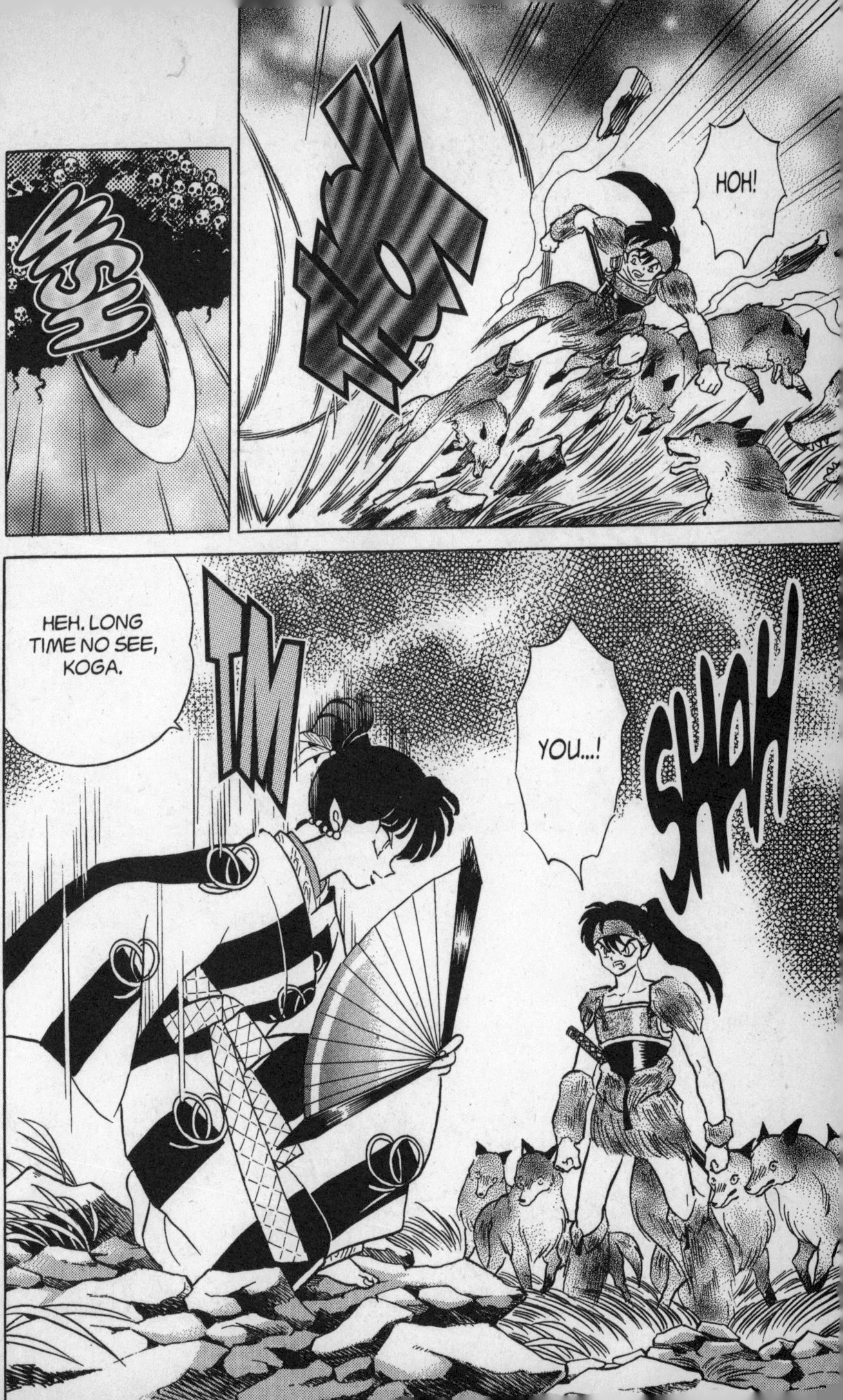
WSH
HOH!
HEH. LONG TIME NO SEE, KOGA.
YOU...!

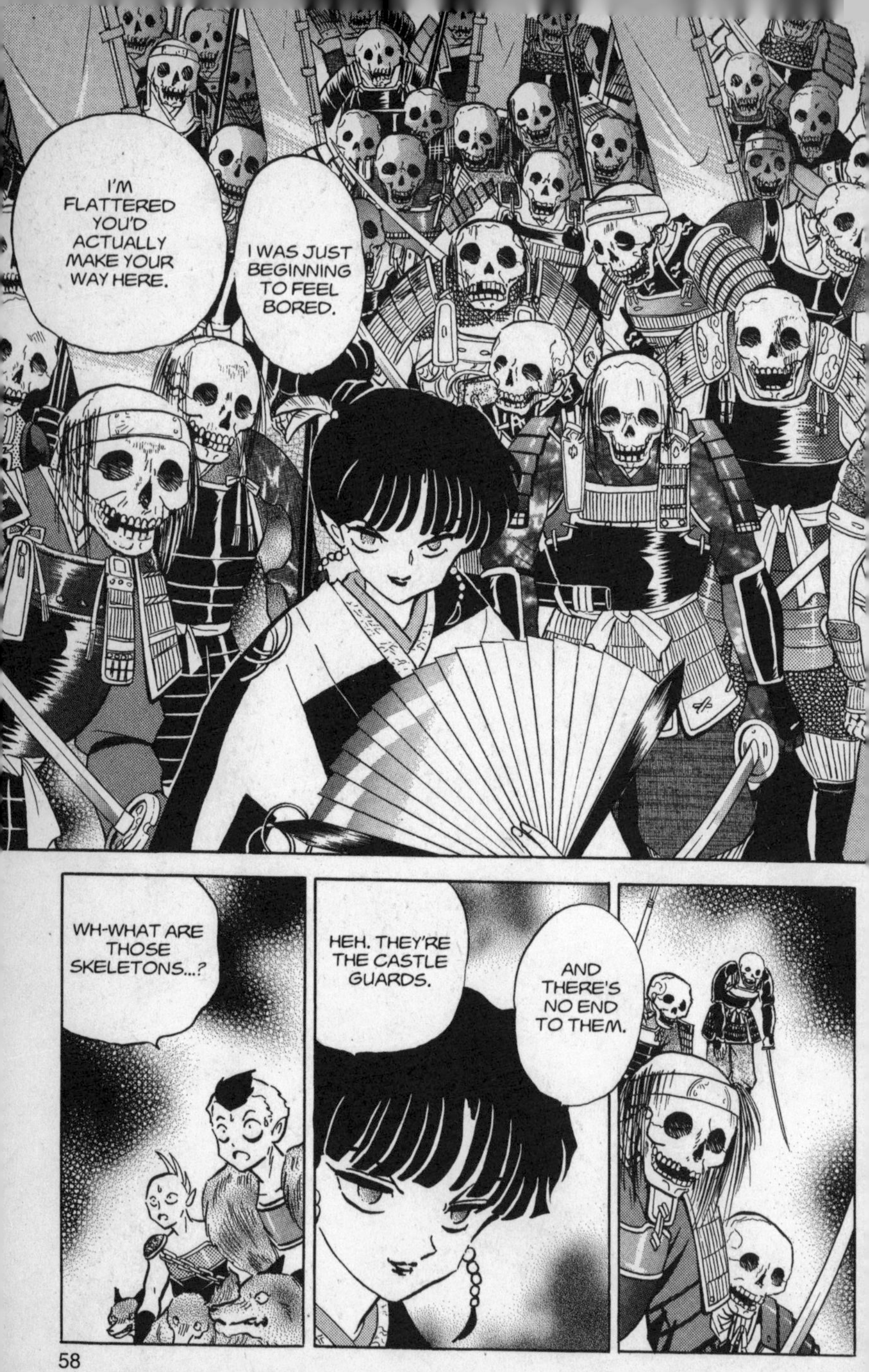
I'M FLATTERED YOU'D ACTUALLY MAKE YOUR WAY HERE.
I WAS JUST BEGINNING TO FEEL BORED.
WH-WHAT ARE THOSE SKELETONS...?
HEH. THEY'RE THE CASTLE GUARDS.
AND THERE'S NO END TO THEM.

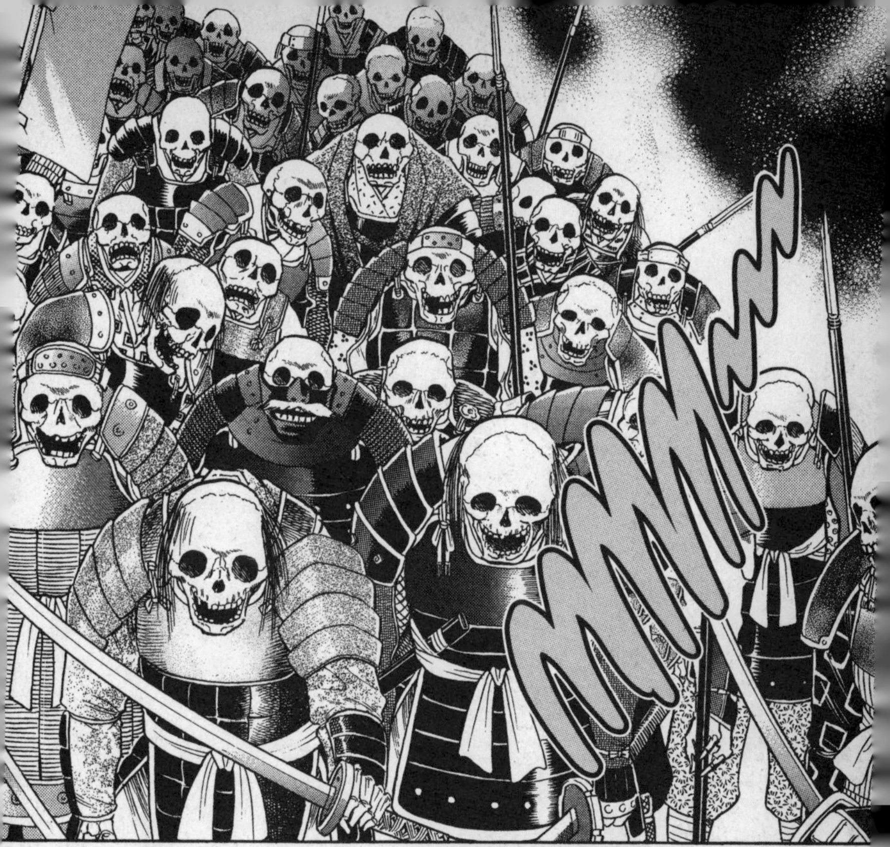

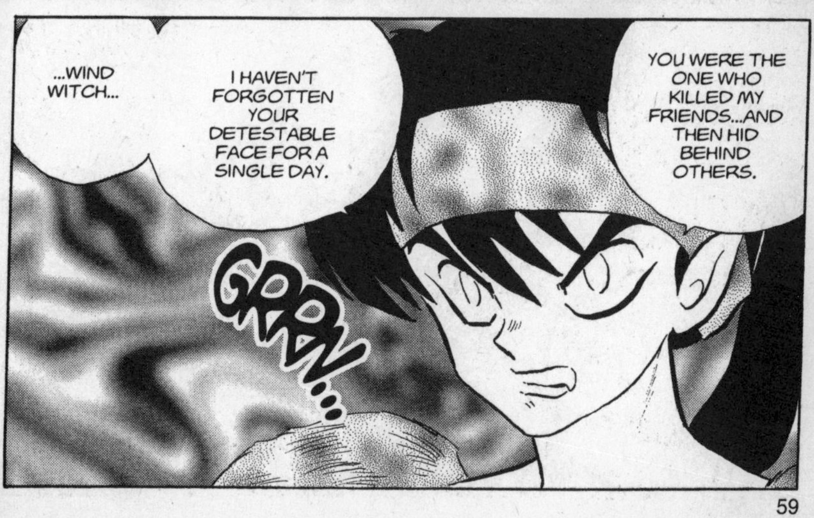
...WIND WITCH...
I HAVEN'T FORGOTTEN YOUR DETESTABLE FACE FOR A SINGLE DAY.
YOU WERE THE ONE WHO KILLED MY FRIENDS...AND THEN HID BEHIND OTHERS.
GRRN...

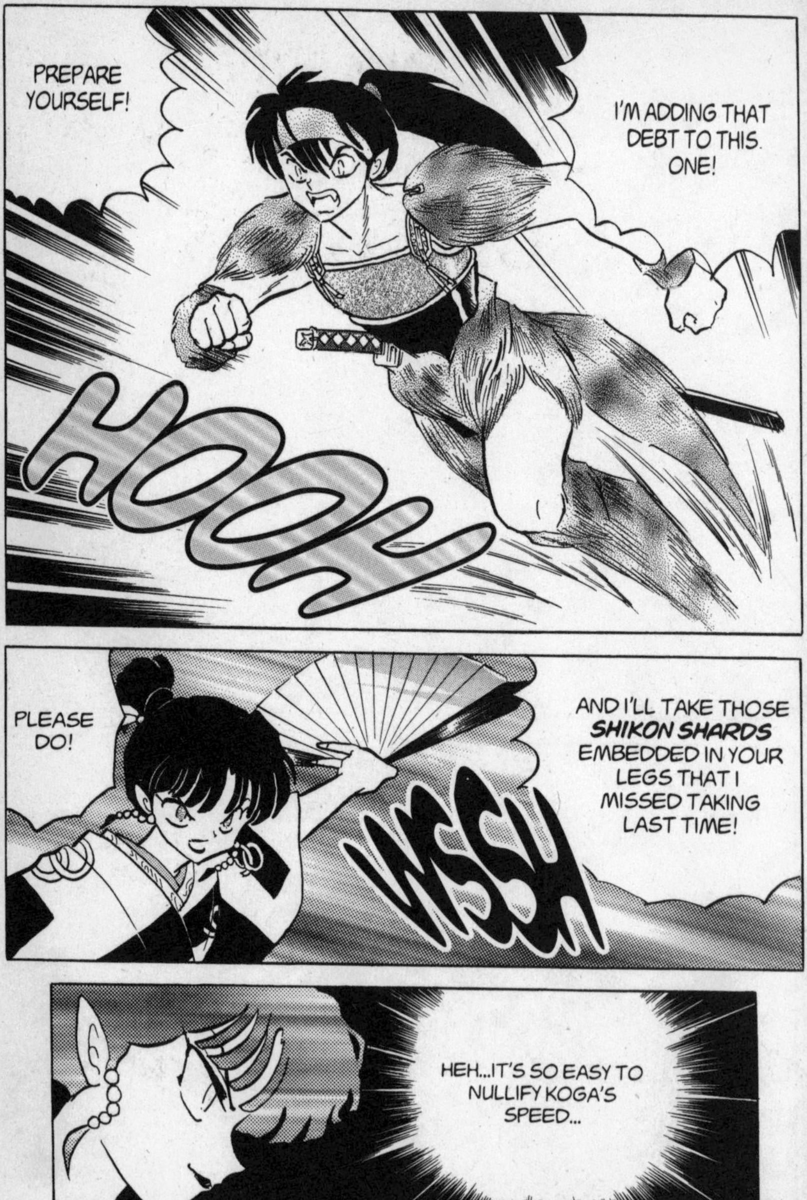
PREPARE YOURSELF!
I'M ADDING THAT DEBT TO THIS ONE!
HOOOH
PLEASE DO!
AND I'LL TAKE THOSE ***SHIKON SHARDS*** EMBEDDED IN YOUR LEGS THAT I MISSED TAKING LAST TIME!
WSSH
HEH...IT'S SO EASY TO NULLIFY KOGA'S SPEED...

SCROLL FOUR

THE VORTEX OF BONES

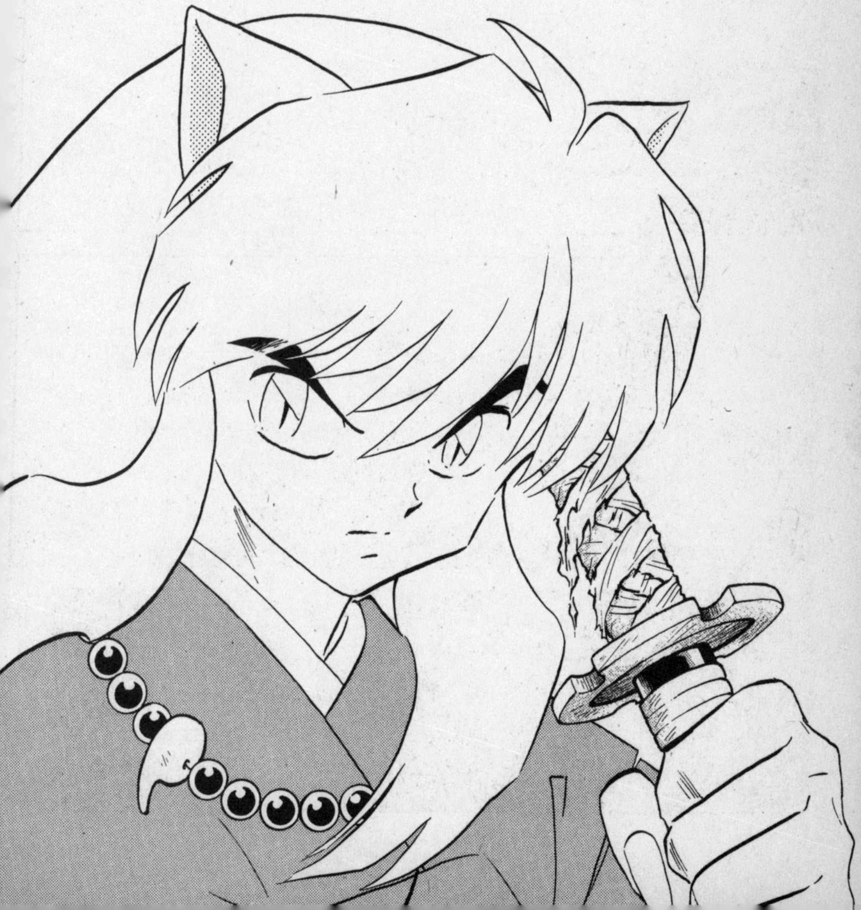

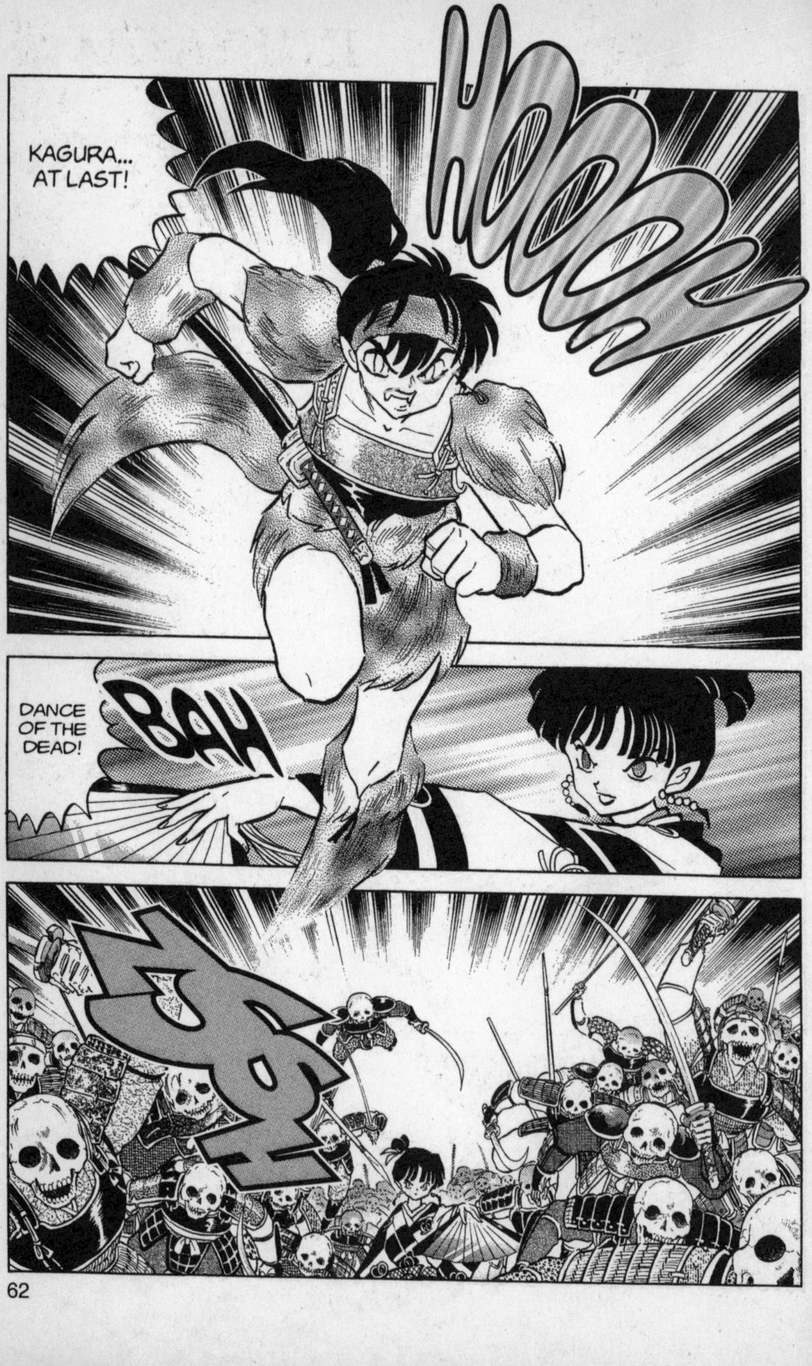

KAGURA... AT LAST!
DANCE OF THE DEAD!
BAH

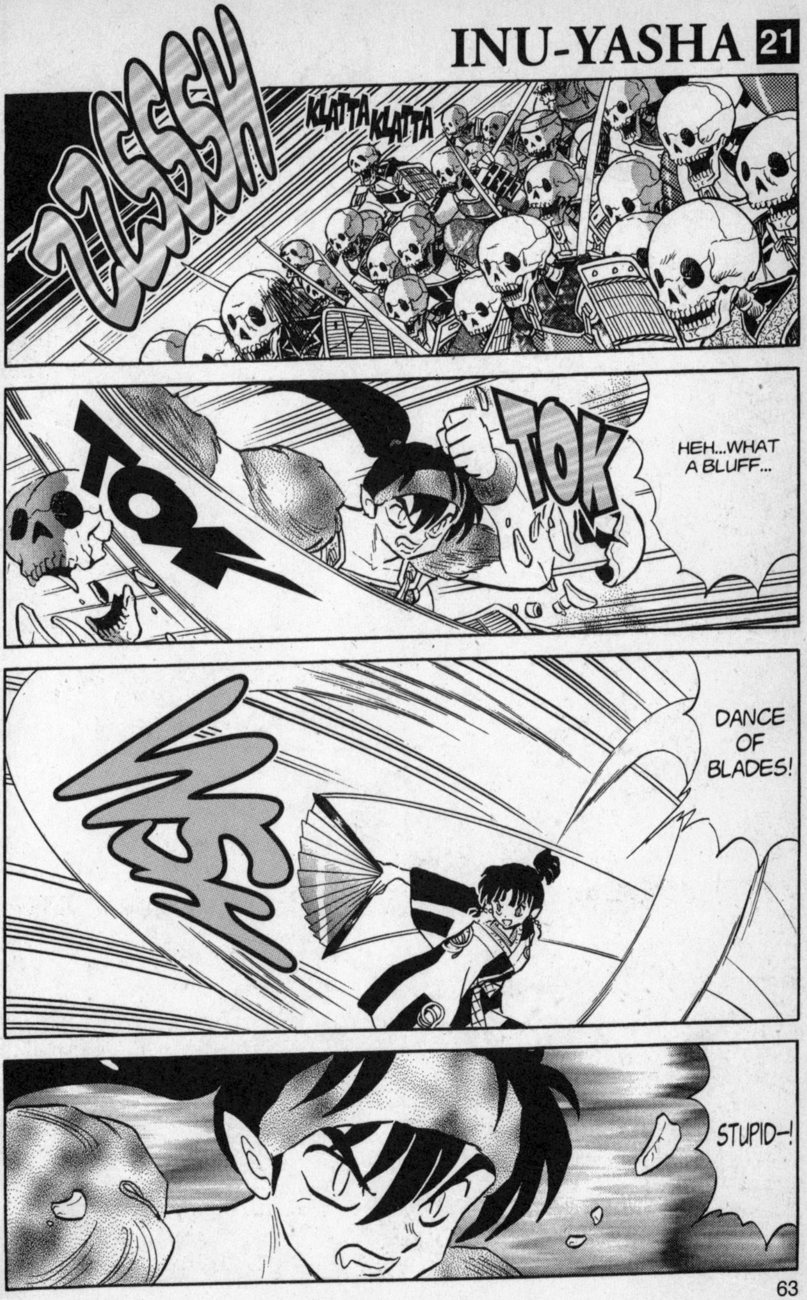
ZZESSH
KLATTA KLATTA
TOK
TOK
HEH...WHAT A BLUFF...
DANCE OF BLADES!
STUPID—!

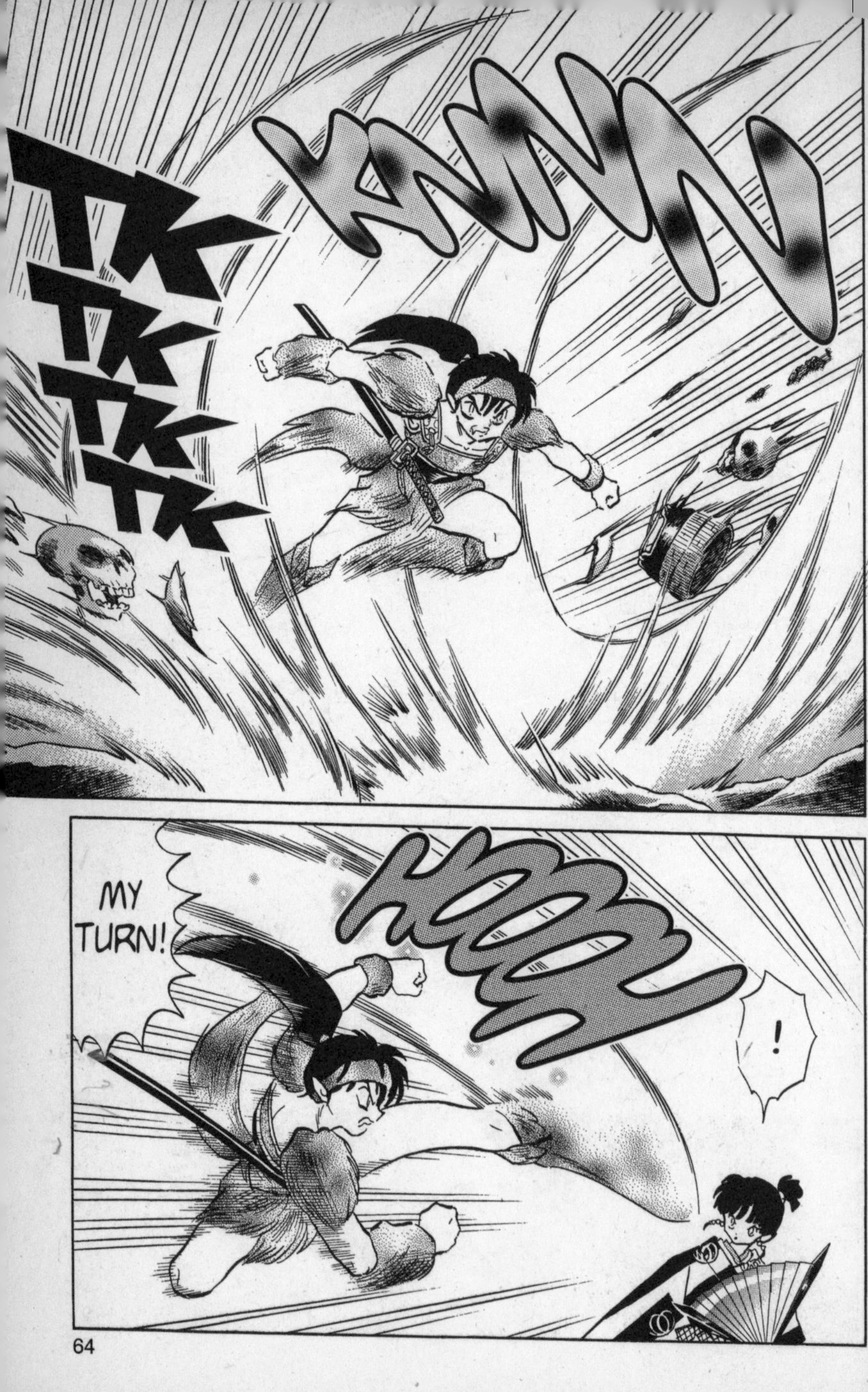
TK TK TK TK
MY TURN!
!

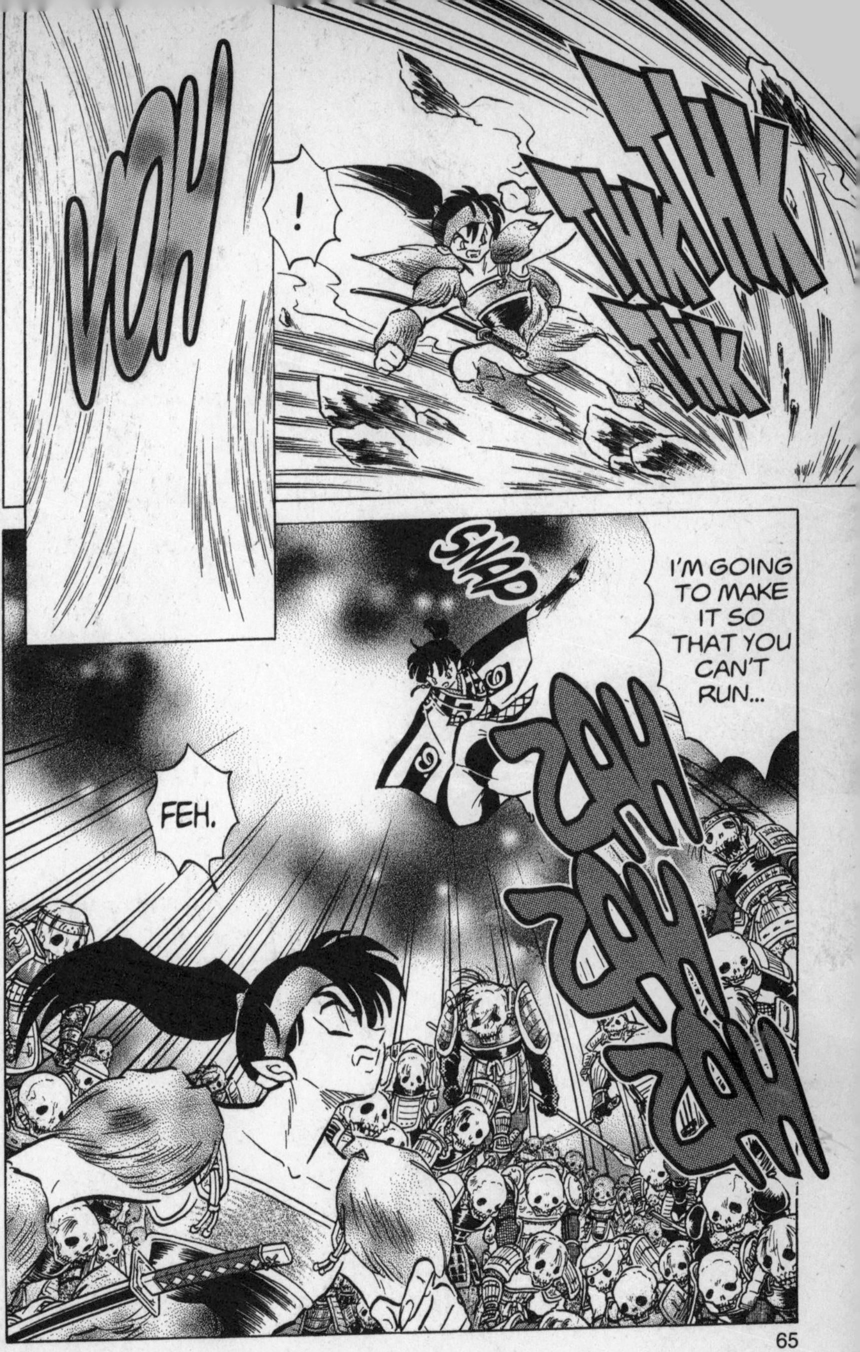
VOOH
!
THUNK
THUNK
THUNK
SNAP
I'M GOING TO MAKE IT SO THAT YOU CAN'T RUN...
FEH.
ZAH
ZAH
ZAH
ZAH

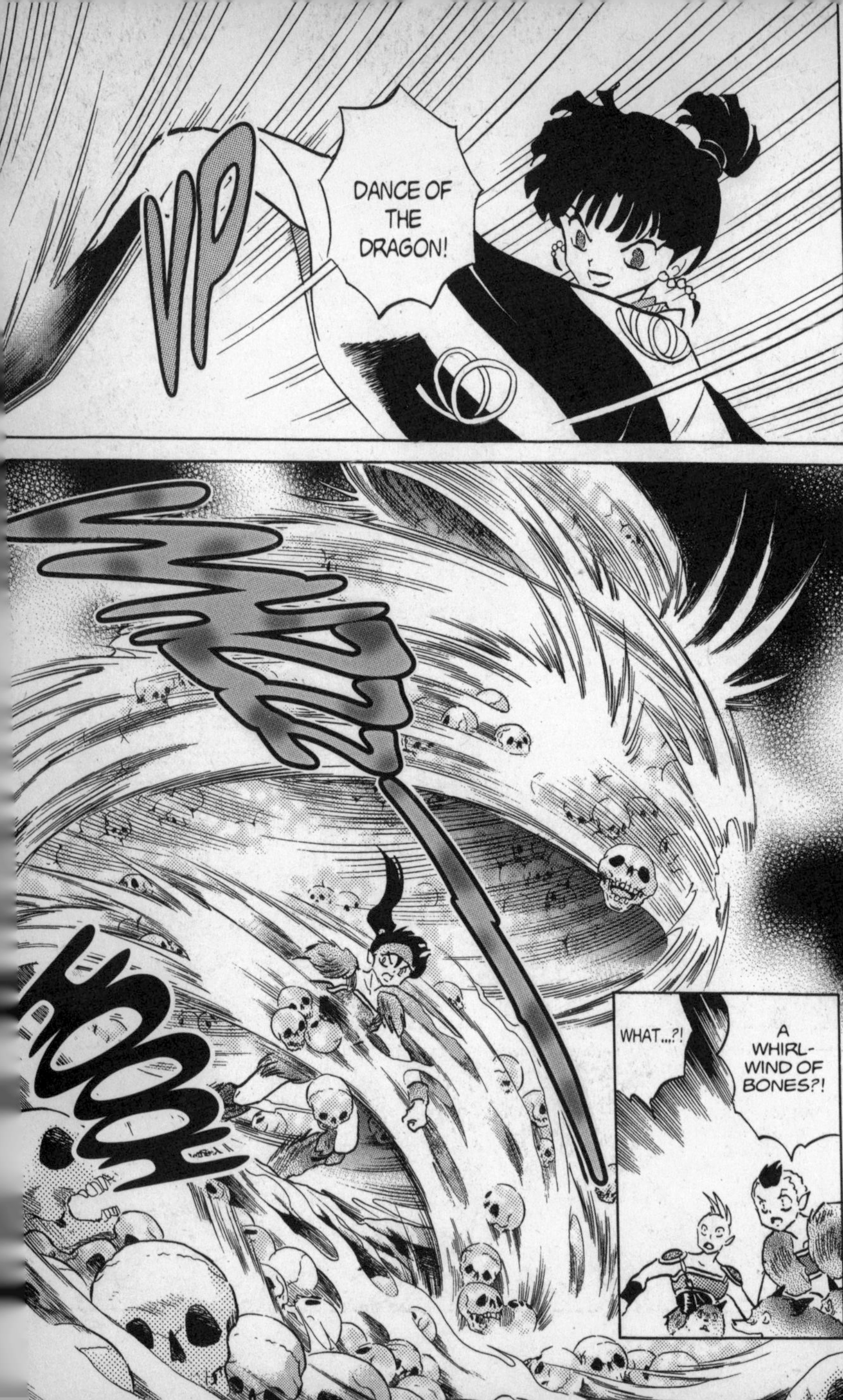
DANCE OF THE DRAGON!
WHAT...?!
A WHIRL-WIND OF BONES?!

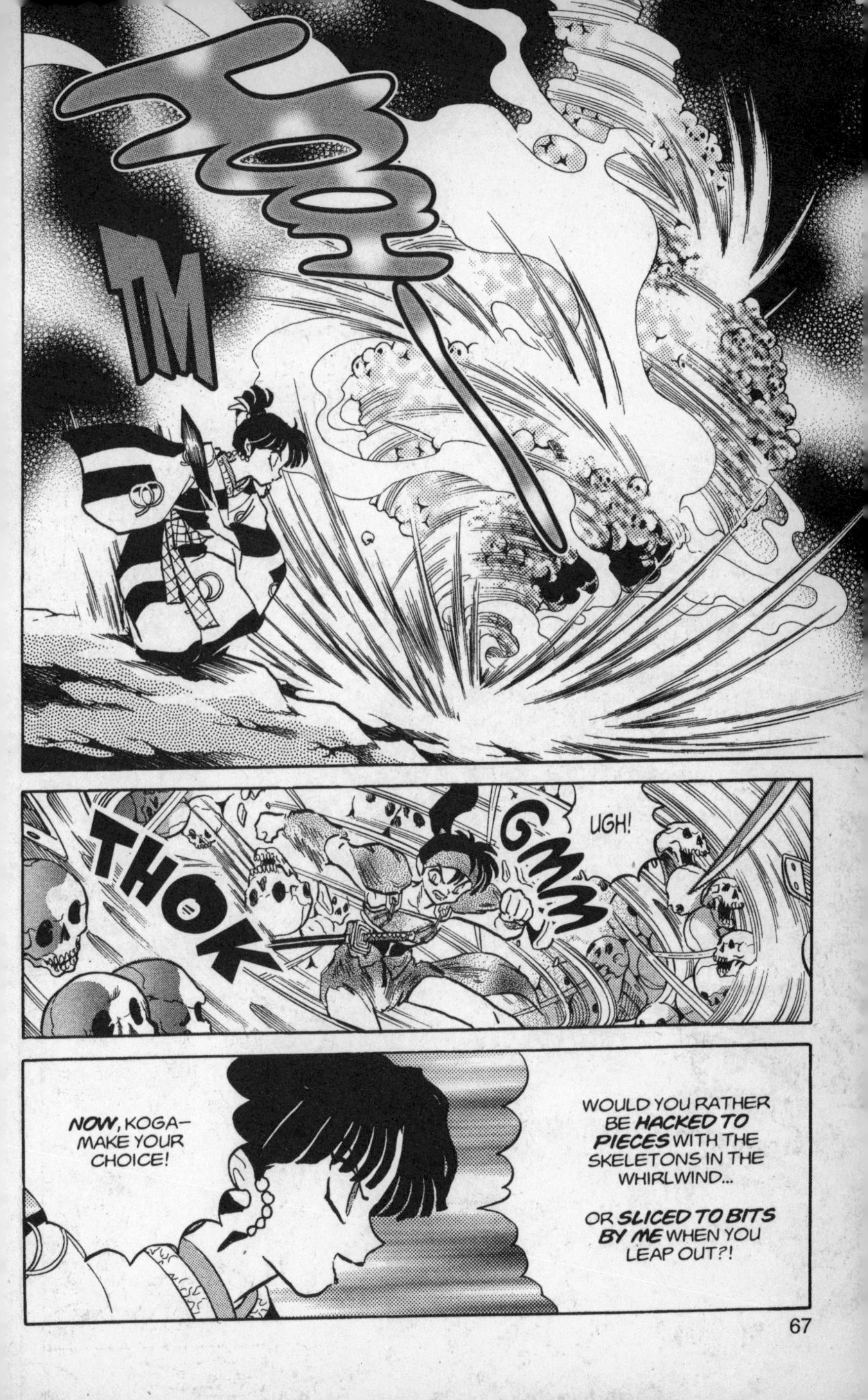
TM
THOK
GMM
UGH!
NOW, KOGA—MAKE YOUR CHOICE!
WOULD YOU RATHER BE HACKED TO PIECES WITH THE SKELETONS IN THE WHIRLWIND...
OR SLICED TO BITS BY ME WHEN YOU LEAP OUT?!

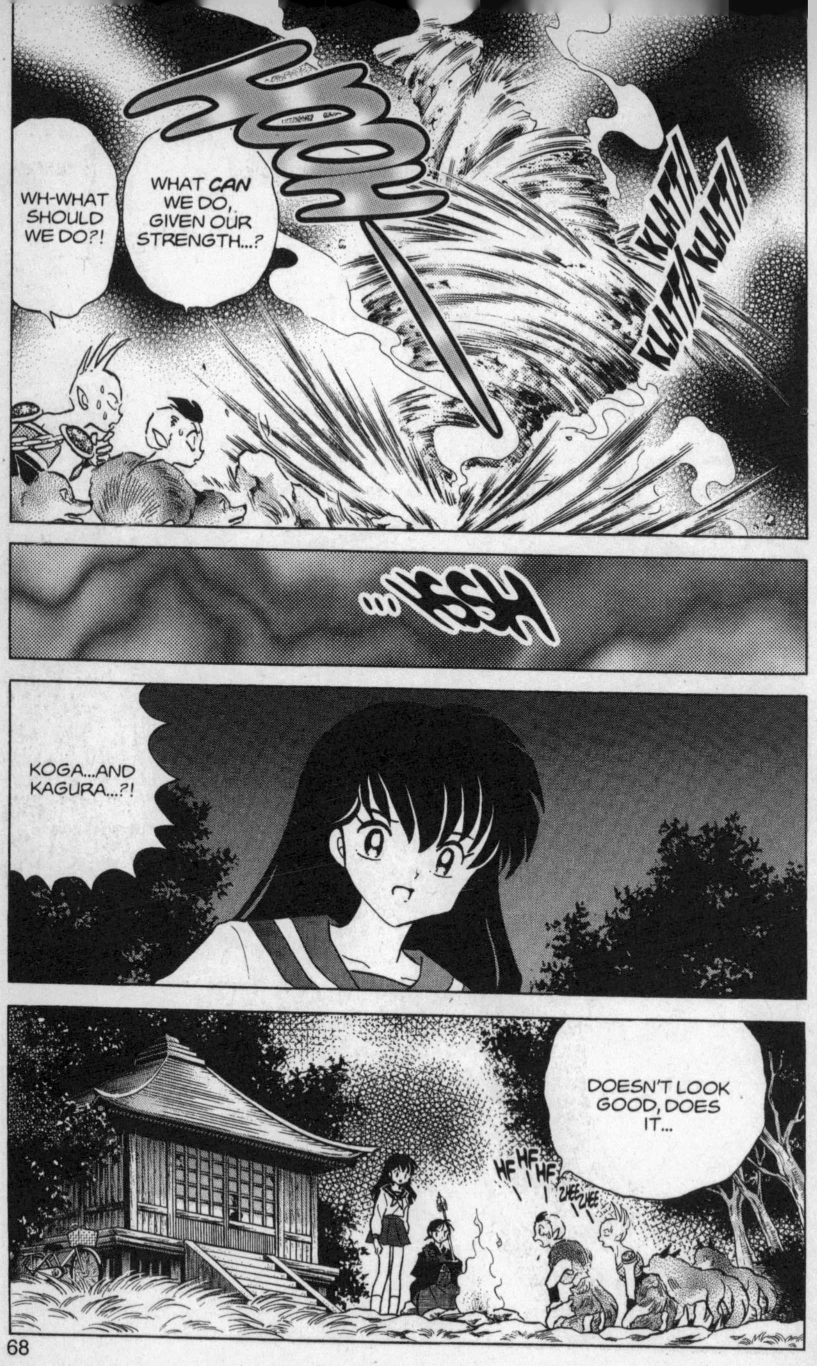
WH-WHAT SHOULD WE DO?!
WHAT *CAN* WE DO, GIVEN OUR STRENGTH...?
KLATTA KLATTA KLATTA
KOGA...AND KAGURA...?!
DOESN'T LOOK GOOD, DOES IT...
HF HF HF
ZHEE ZHEE

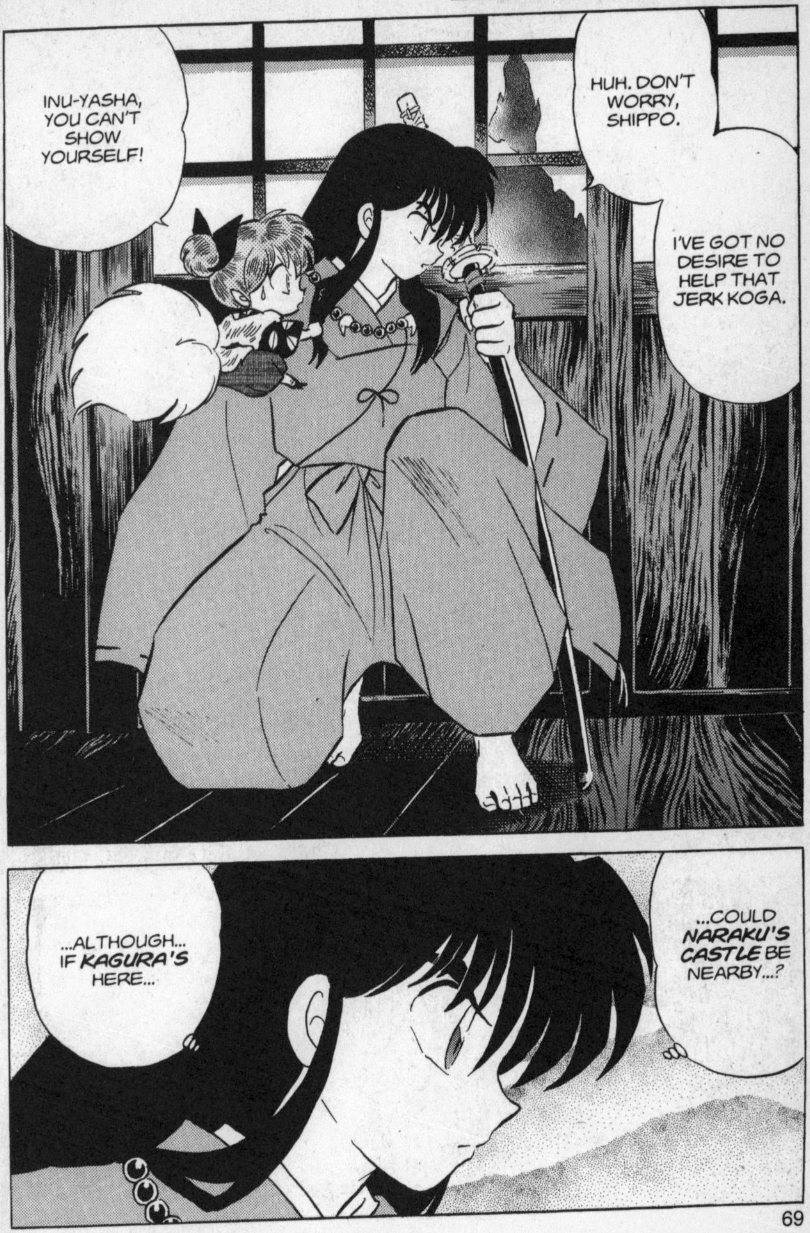
INU-YASHA, YOU CAN'T SHOW YOURSELF!
HUH. DON'T WORRY, SHIPPO.
I'VE GOT NO DESIRE TO HELP THAT JERK KOGA.
...ALTHOUGH... IF *KAGURA'S* HERE...
...COULD *NARAKU'S CASTLE* BE NEARBY...?

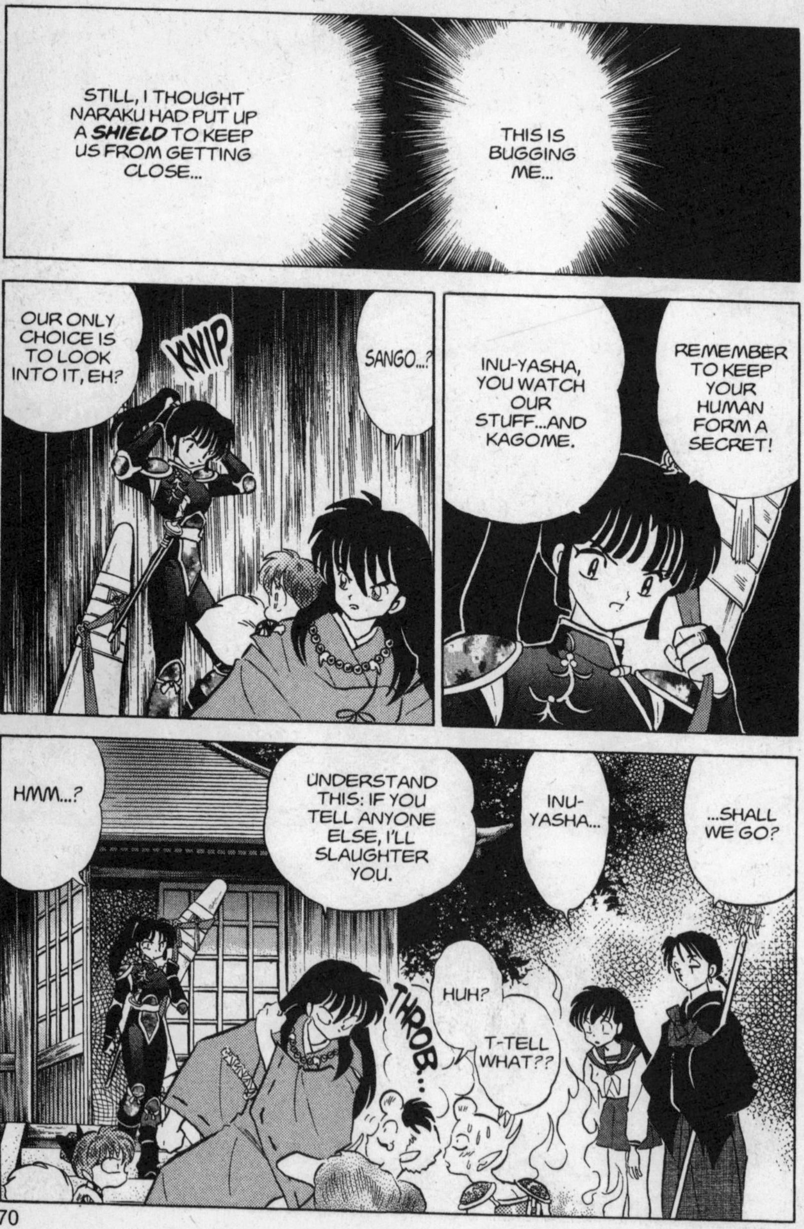
STILL, I THOUGHT NARAKU HAD PUT UP A SHIELD TO KEEP US FROM GETTING CLOSE...
THIS IS BUGGING ME...
OUR ONLY CHOICE IS TO LOOK INTO IT, EH?
KWIP
SANGO...?
INU-YASHA, YOU WATCH OUR STUFF...AND KAGOME.
REMEMBER TO KEEP YOUR HUMAN FORM A SECRET!
HMM...?
UNDERSTAND THIS: IF YOU TELL ANYONE ELSE, I'LL SLAUGHTER YOU.
INU-YASHA...
...SHALL WE GO?
THROB...
HUH?
T-TELL WHAT??

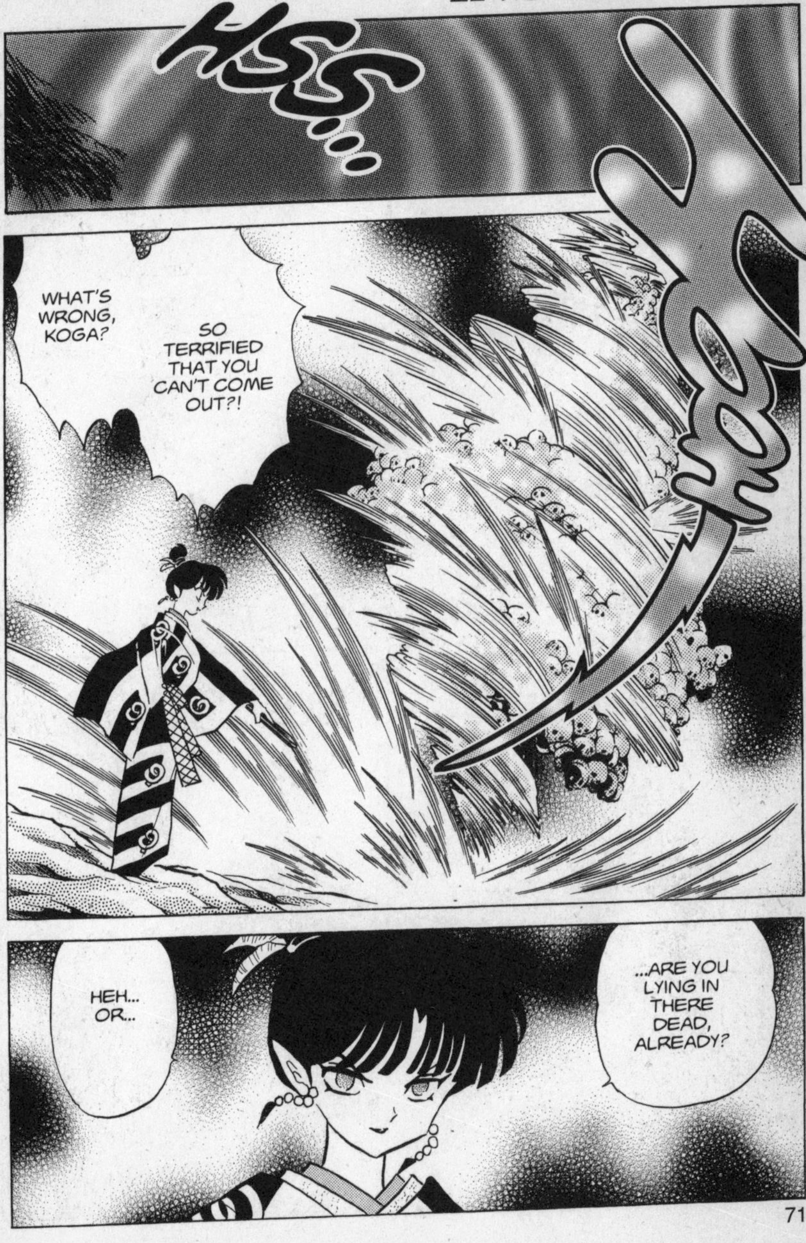
HSS...
WHAT'S WRONG, KOGA?
SO TERRIFIED THAT YOU CAN'T COME OUT?!
HEH... OR...
...ARE YOU LYING IN THERE DEAD, ALREADY?

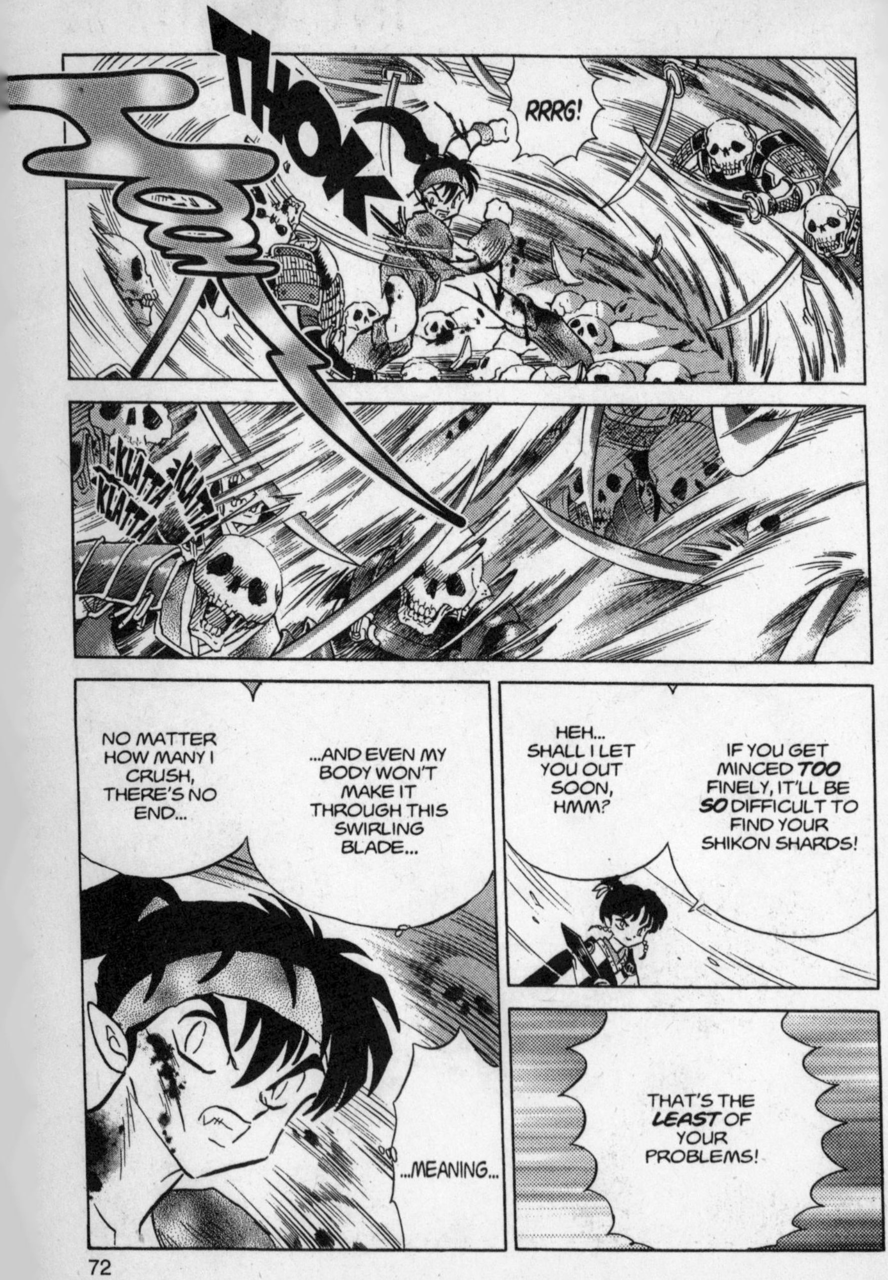
THOK
RRRG!
KLATTA KLATTA
KLATTA KLATTA
NO MATTER HOW MANY I CRUSH, THERE'S NO END...
...AND EVEN MY BODY WON'T MAKE IT THROUGH THIS SWIRLING BLADE...
...MEANING...
HEH... SHALL I LET YOU OUT SOON, HMM?
IF YOU GET MINCED TOO FINELY, IT'LL BE SO DIFFICULT TO FIND YOUR SHIKON SHARDS!
THAT'S THE LEAST OF YOUR PROBLEMS!

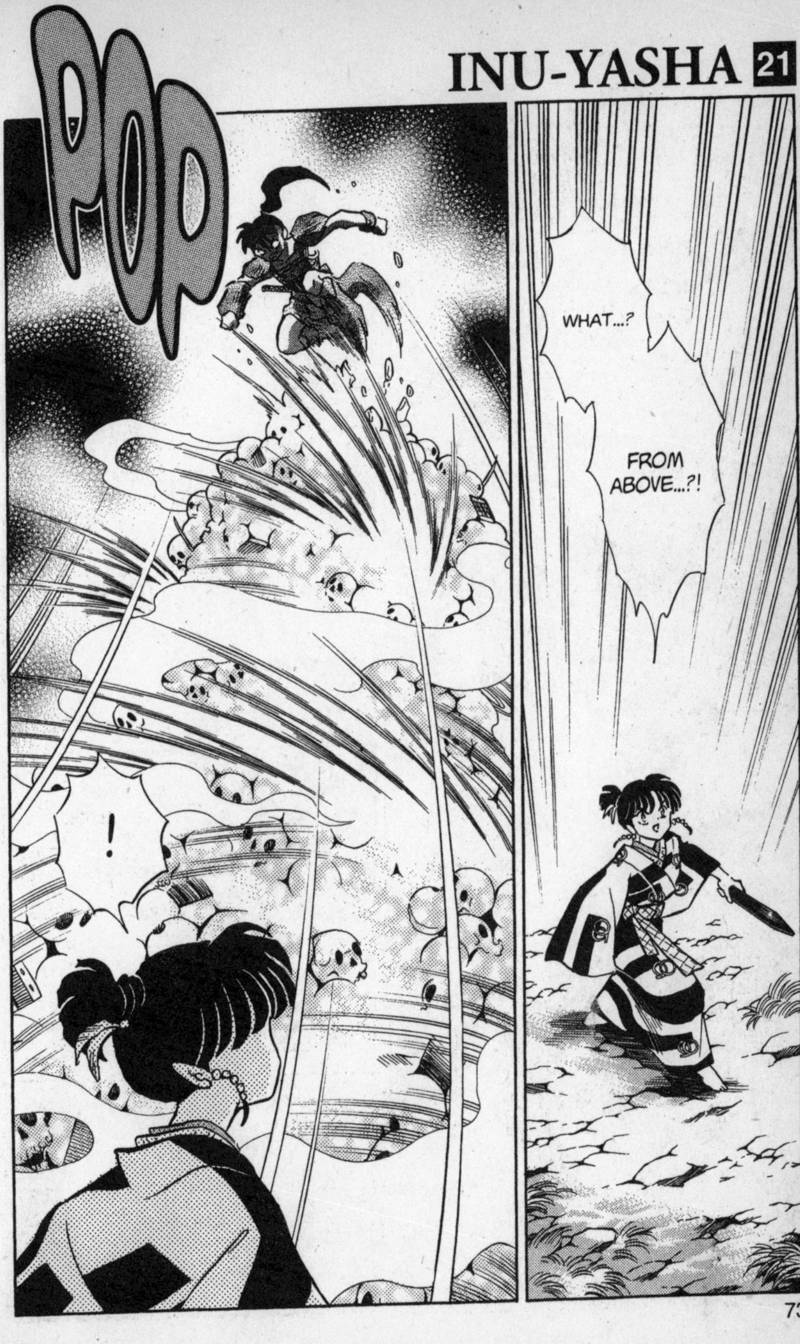
POP
!
WHAT...?
FROM ABOVE...?!

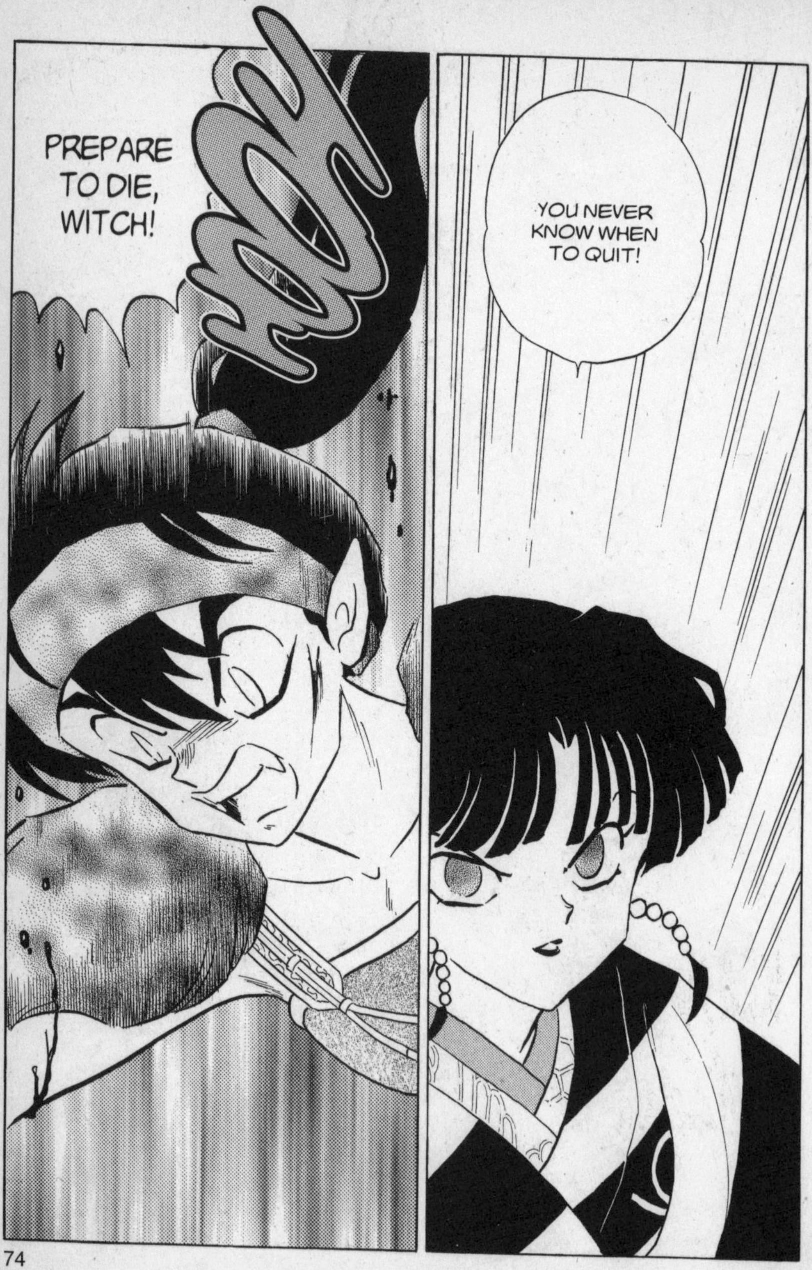
PREPARE TO DIE, WITCH!
YOU NEVER KNOW WHEN TO QUIT!

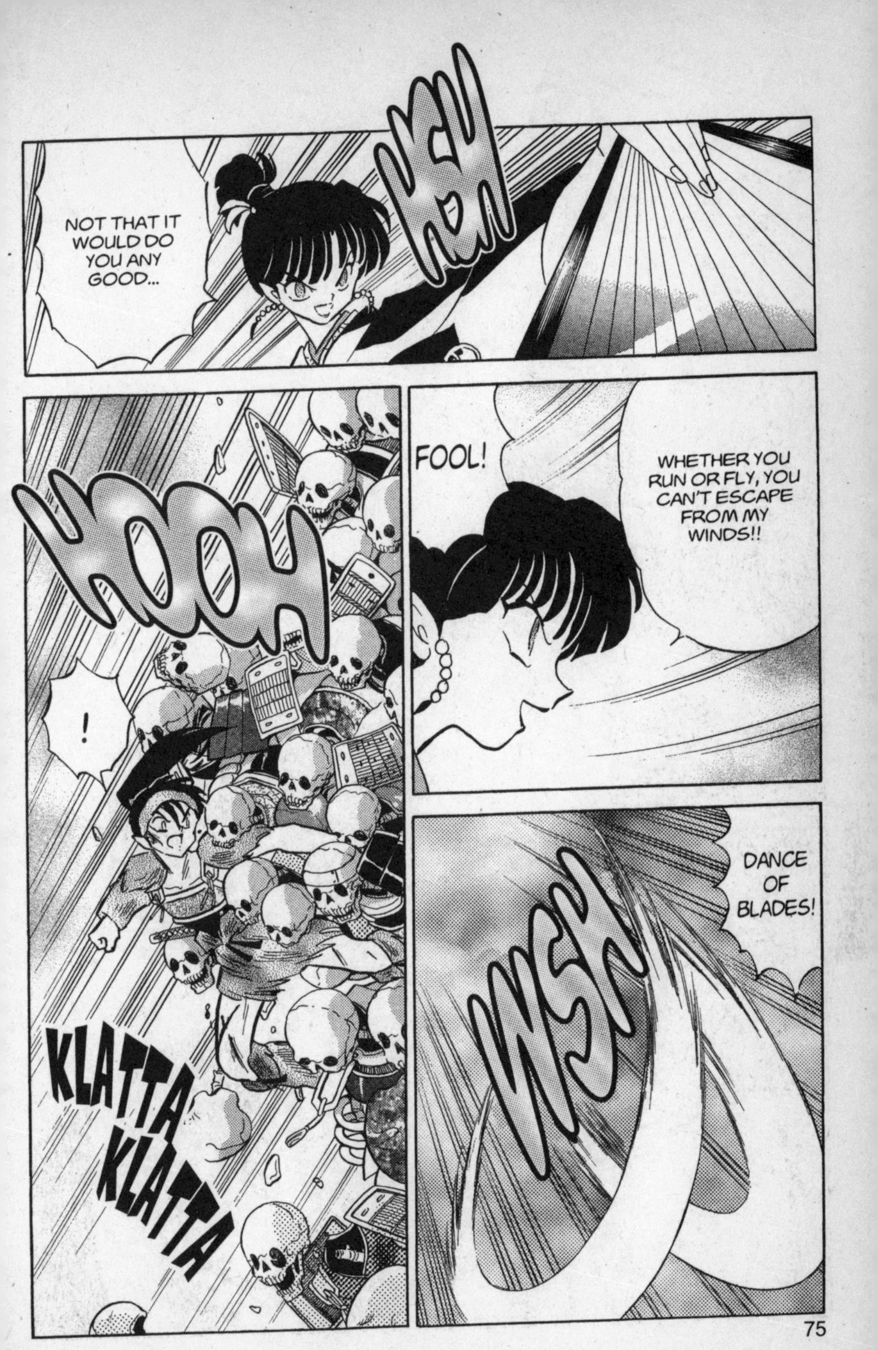
NOT THAT IT WOULD DO YOU ANY GOOD...
!
KLATTA KLATTA
FOOL!
WHETHER YOU RUN OR FLY, YOU CAN'T ESCAPE FROM MY WINDS!!
DANCE OF BLADES!

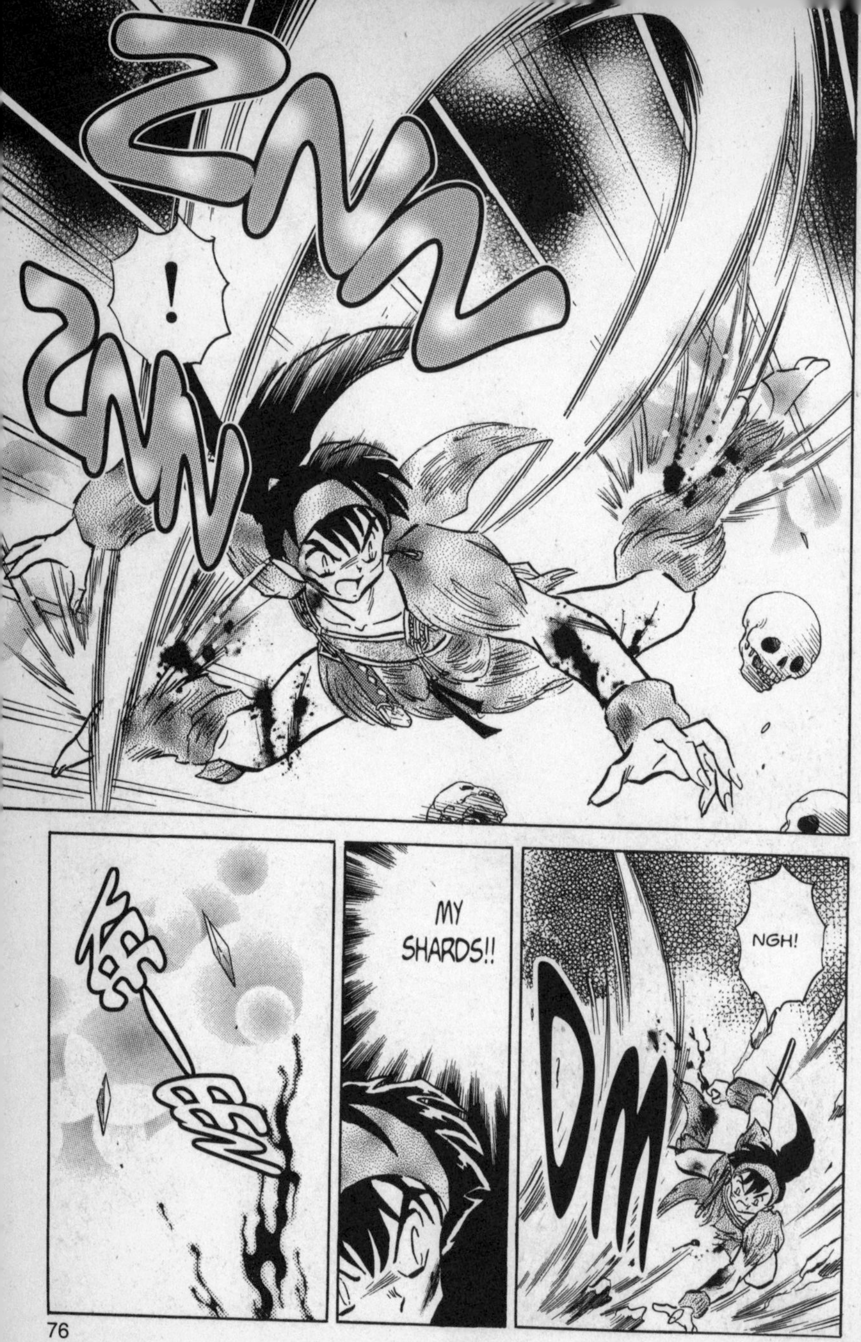
!
MY SHARDS!!
NGH!

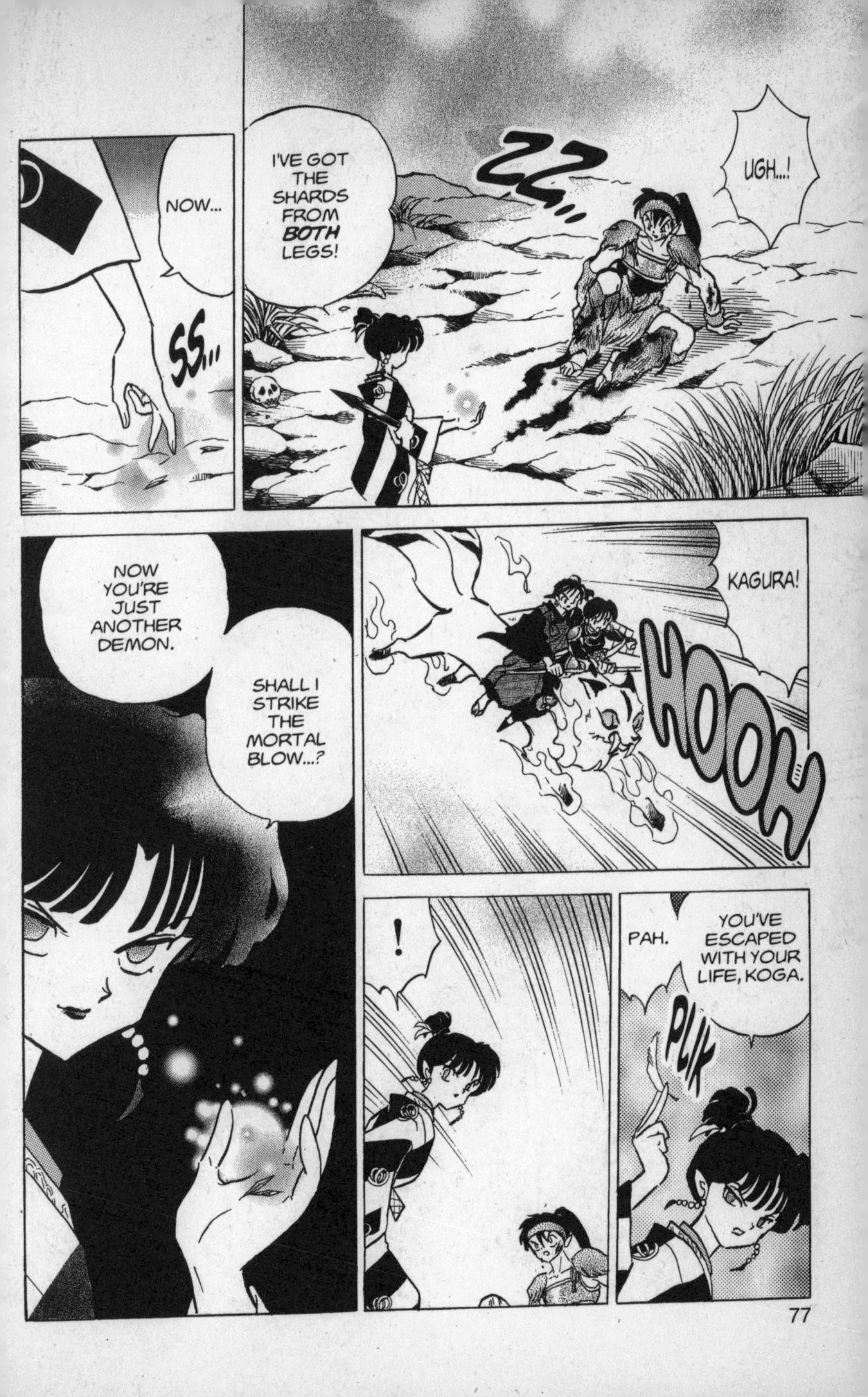
NOW...
SS...
I'VE GOT THE SHARDS FROM **BOTH** LEGS!
ZZ
UGH...!
NOW YOU'RE JUST ANOTHER DEMON.
SHALL I STRIKE THE MORTAL BLOW...?
KAGURA!
HOOOH
!
PAH.
YOU'VE ESCAPED WITH YOUR LIFE, KOGA.
PLIK

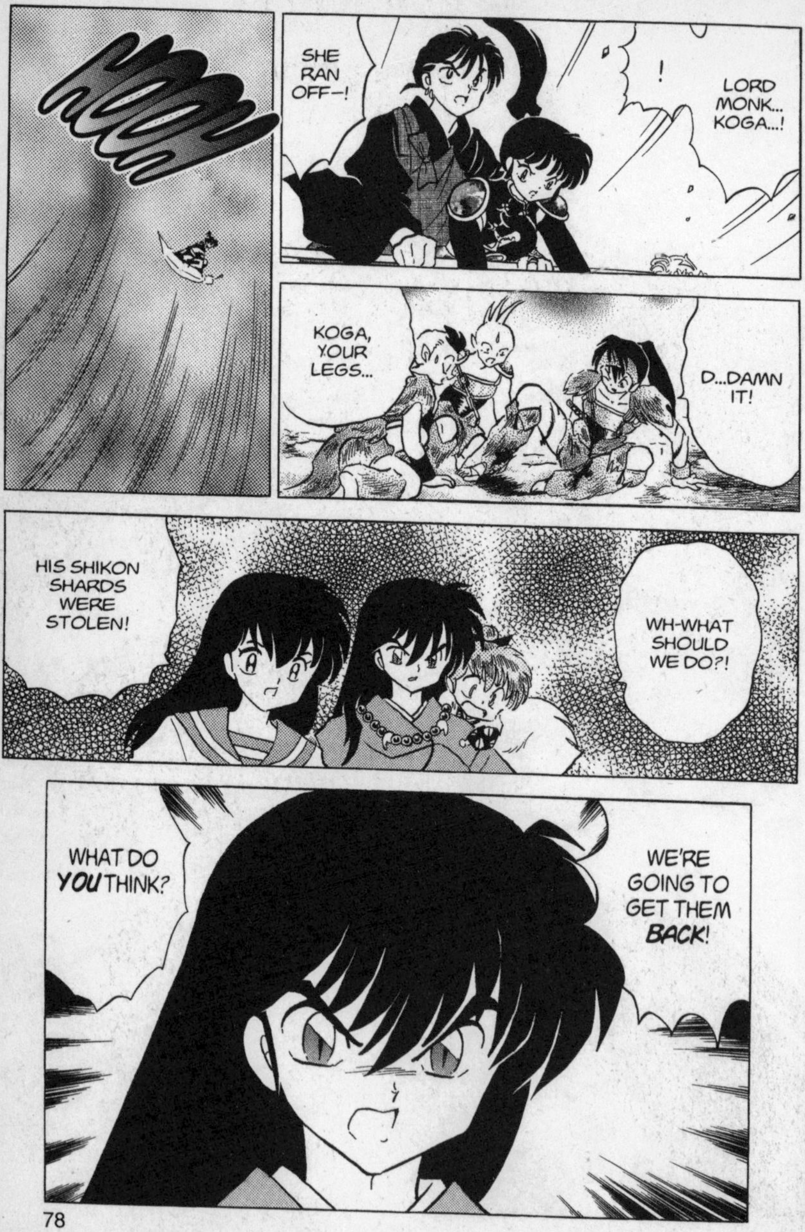
SHE RAN OFF—!
!
LORD MONK... KOGA...!
KOGA, YOUR LEGS...
D...DAMN IT!
HIS SHIKON SHARDS WERE STOLEN!
WH-WHAT SHOULD WE DO?!
WHAT DO ***YOU*** THINK?
WE'RE GOING TO GET THEM ***BACK***!

SCROLL FIVE

DESERTION

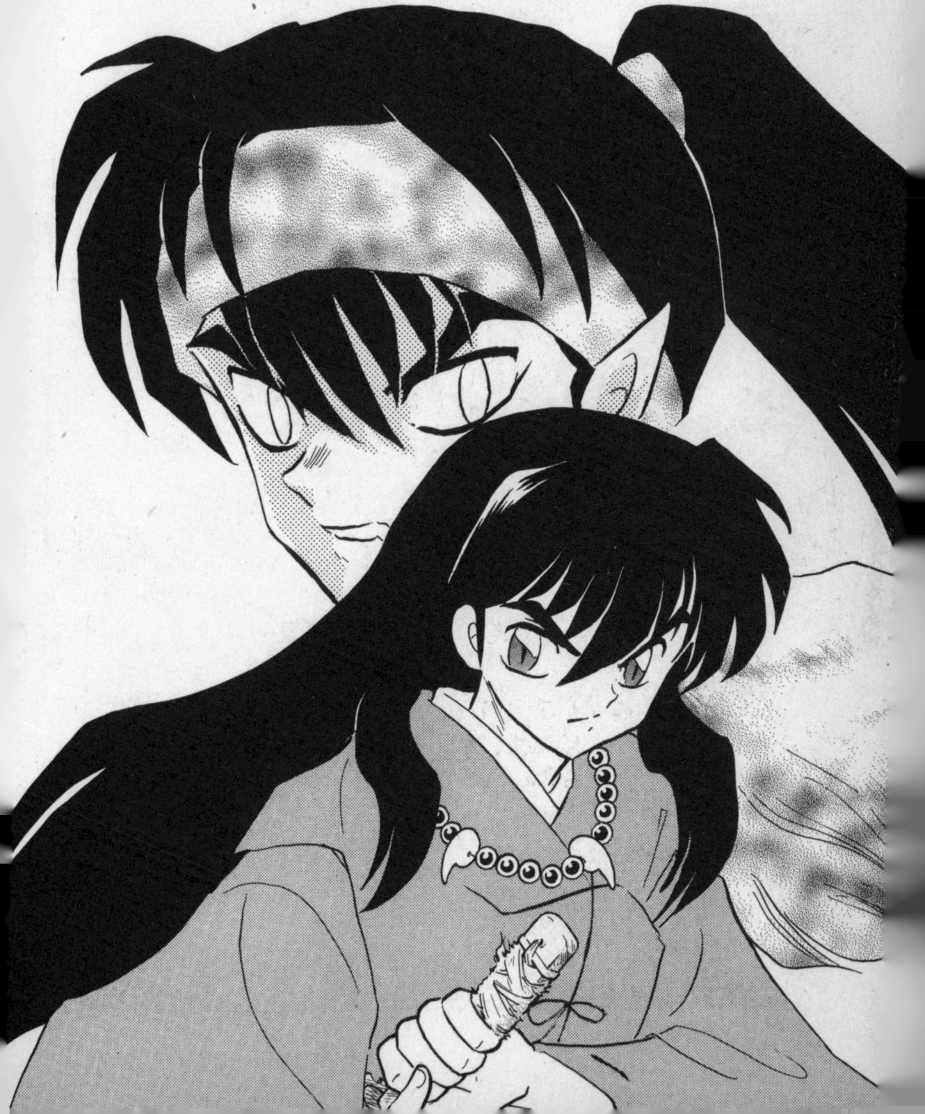

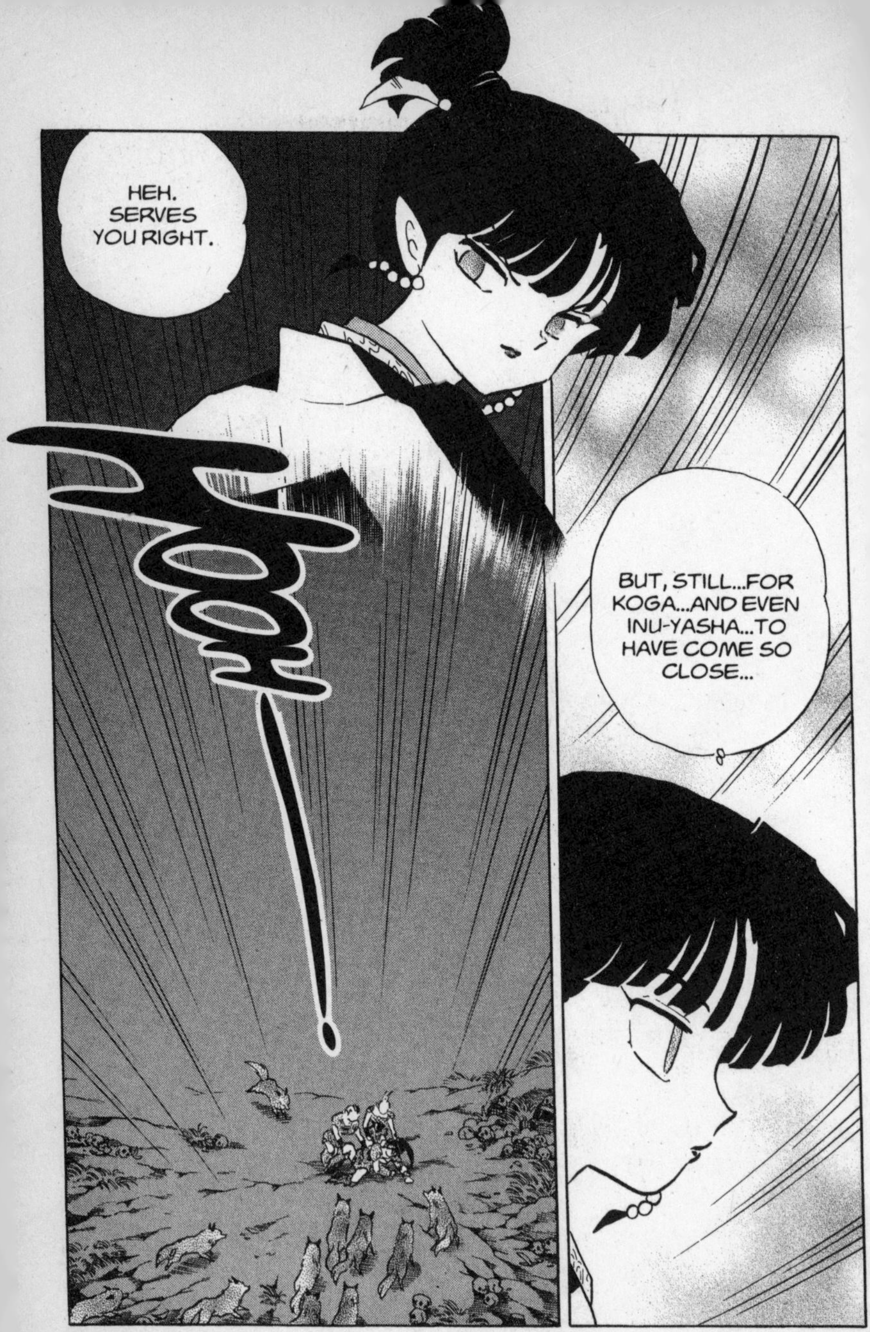
HEH. SERVES YOU RIGHT.
BUT, STILL...FOR KOGA...AND EVEN INU-YASHA...TO HAVE COME SO CLOSE...

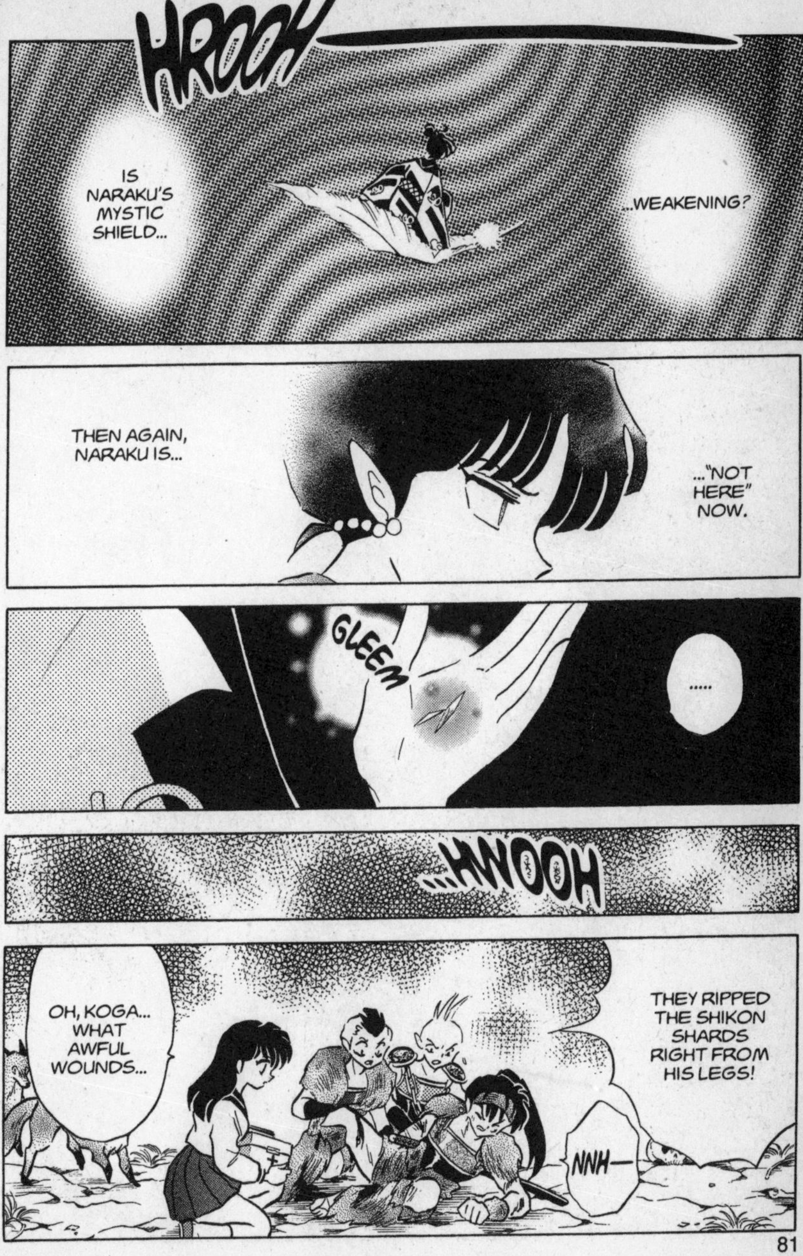
HROOH
IS NARAKU'S MYSTIC SHIELD...
...WEAKENING?
THEN AGAIN, NARAKU IS...
..."NOT HERE" NOW.
GLEEM
.....
OH, KOGA... WHAT AWFUL WOUNDS...
THEY RIPPED THE SHIKON SHARDS RIGHT FROM HIS LEGS!
NNH—

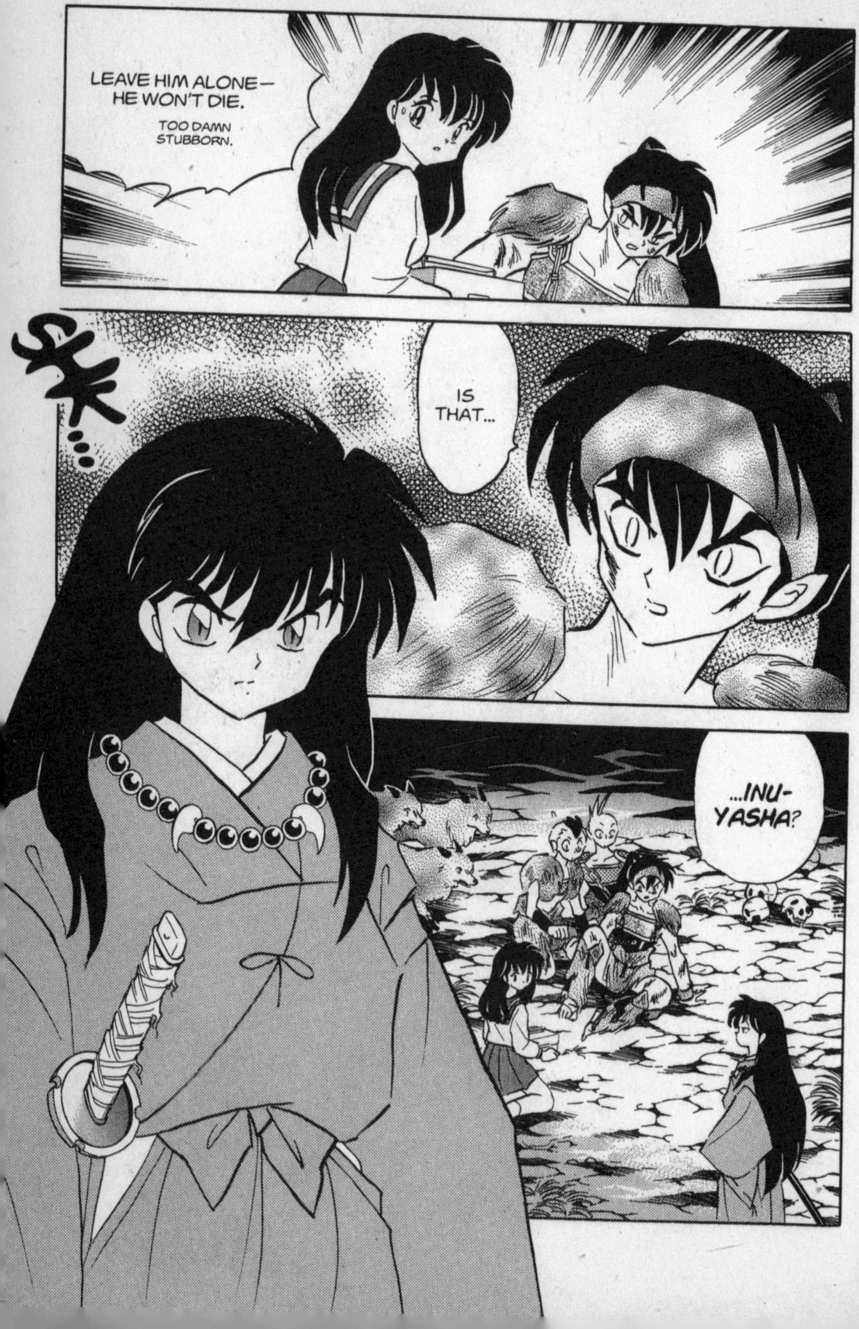
LEAVE HIM ALONE— HE WON'T DIE.
TOO DAMN STUBBORN.
SHK...
IS THAT...
...INU-YASHA?

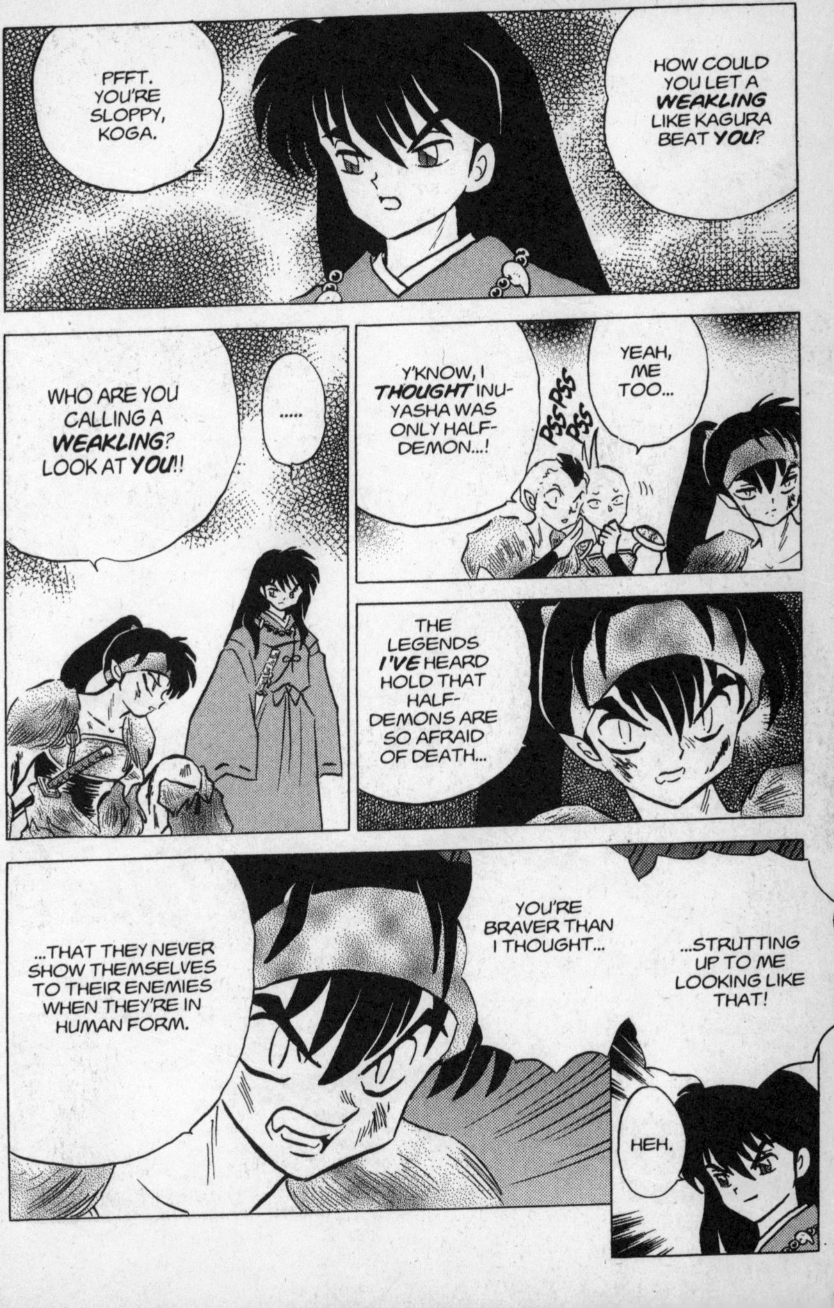
PFFT. YOU'RE SLOPPY, KOGA.
HOW COULD YOU LET A WEAKLING LIKE KAGURA BEAT YOU?
WHO ARE YOU CALLING A WEAKLING? LOOK AT YOU!!
.....
Y'KNOW, I THOUGHT INU-YASHA WAS ONLY HALF-DEMON...!
PSS PSS PSS
YEAH, ME TOO...
THE LEGENDS I'VE HEARD HOLD THAT HALF-DEMONS ARE SO AFRAID OF DEATH...
...THAT THEY NEVER SHOW THEMSELVES TO THEIR ENEMIES WHEN THEY'RE IN HUMAN FORM.
YOU'RE BRAVER THAN I THOUGHT...
...STRUTTING UP TO ME LOOKING LIKE THAT!
HEH.

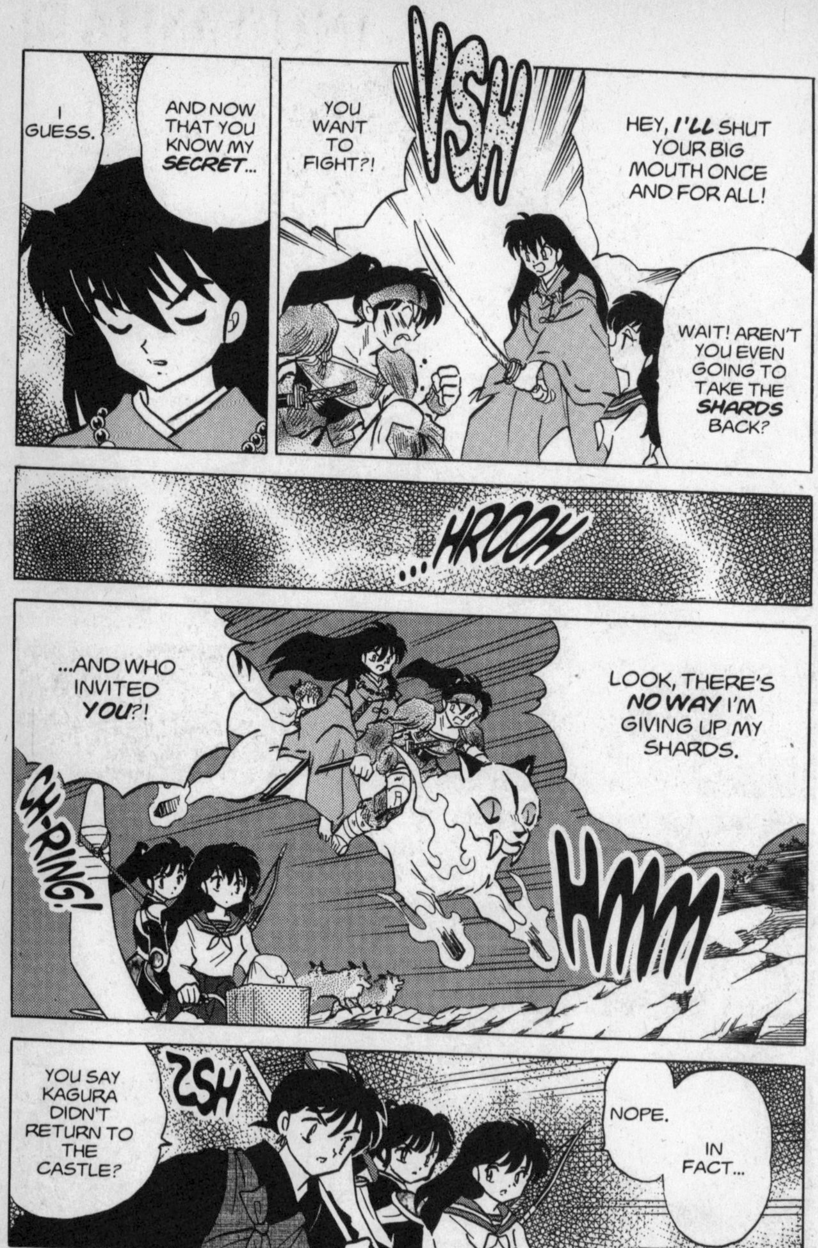
I GUESS.
AND NOW THAT YOU KNOW MY SECRET...
YOU WANT TO FIGHT?!
VSH
HEY, I'LL SHUT YOUR BIG MOUTH ONCE AND FOR ALL!
WAIT! AREN'T YOU EVEN GOING TO TAKE THE SHARDS BACK?
...HROOH
...AND WHO INVITED YOU?!
LOOK, THERE'S NO WAY I'M GIVING UP MY SHARDS.
CH-RING!
HWM
YOU SAY KAGURA DIDN'T RETURN TO THE CASTLE?
ZSH
NOPE.
IN FACT...

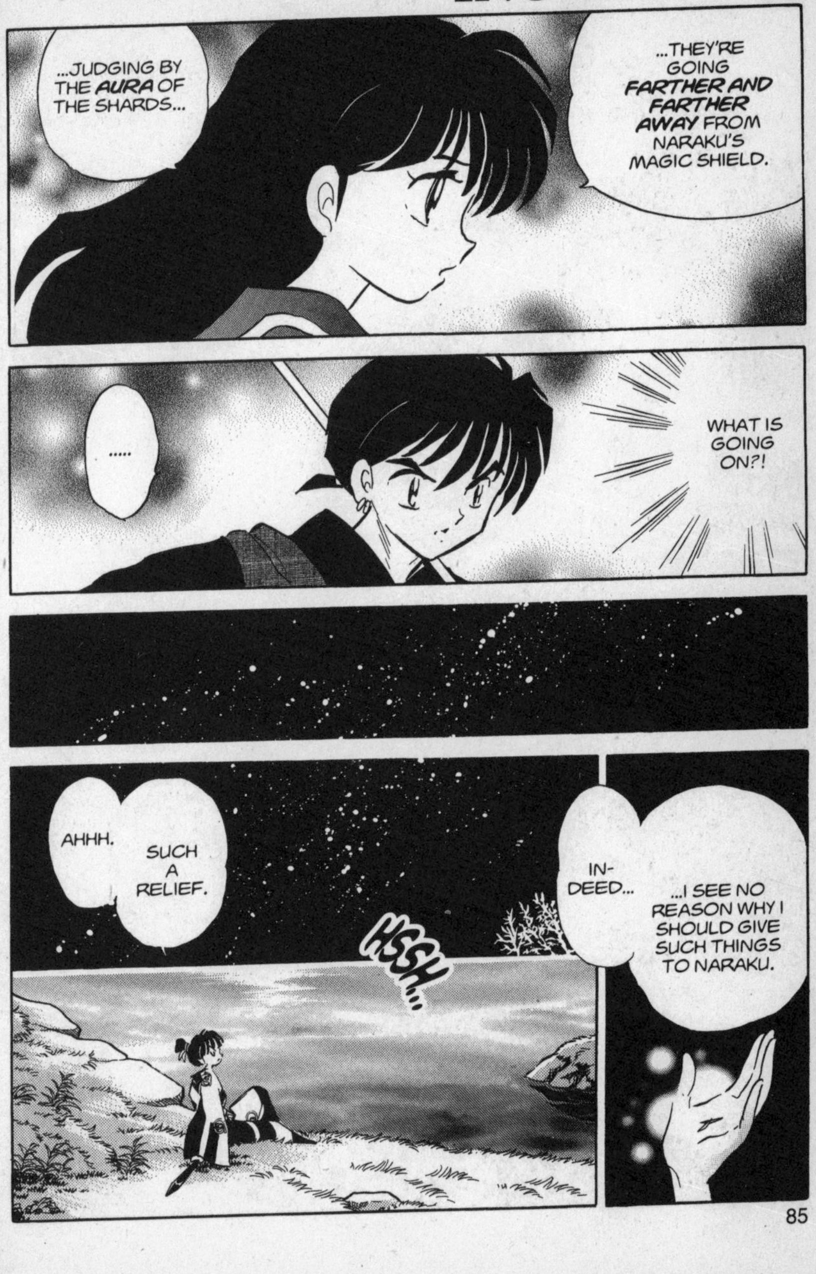
...JUDGING BY THE *AURA* OF THE SHARDS...
...THEY'RE GOING *FARTHER AND FARTHER AWAY* FROM NARAKU'S MAGIC SHIELD.
.....
WHAT IS GOING ON?!
AHHH.
SUCH A RELIEF.
HSSH...
IN-DEED...
...I SEE NO REASON WHY I SHOULD GIVE SUCH THINGS TO NARAKU.

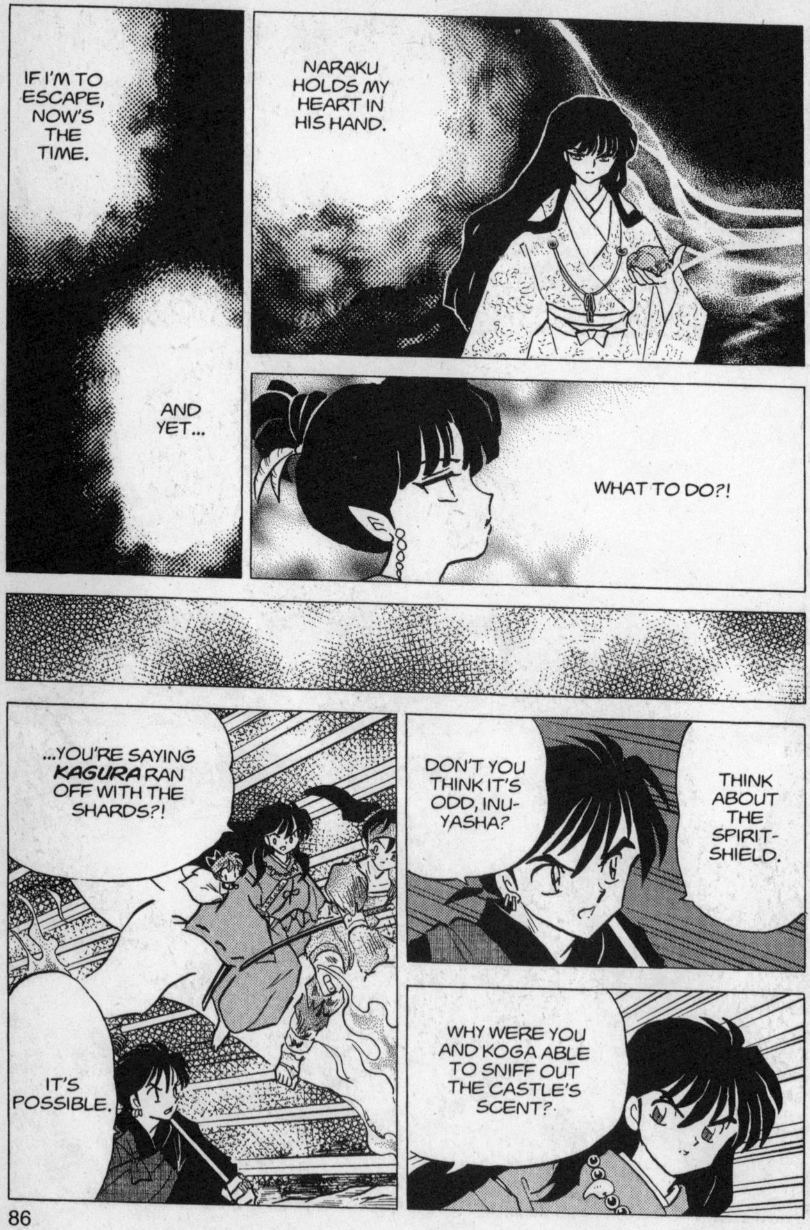
IF I'M TO ESCAPE, NOW'S THE TIME.
NARAKU HOLDS MY HEART IN HIS HAND.
AND YET...
WHAT TO DO?!
...YOU'RE SAYING KAGURA RAN OFF WITH THE SHARDS?!
IT'S POSSIBLE.
DON'T YOU THINK IT'S ODD, INU-YASHA?
THINK ABOUT THE SPIRIT-SHIELD.
WHY WERE YOU AND KOGA ABLE TO SNIFF OUT THE CASTLE'S SCENT?

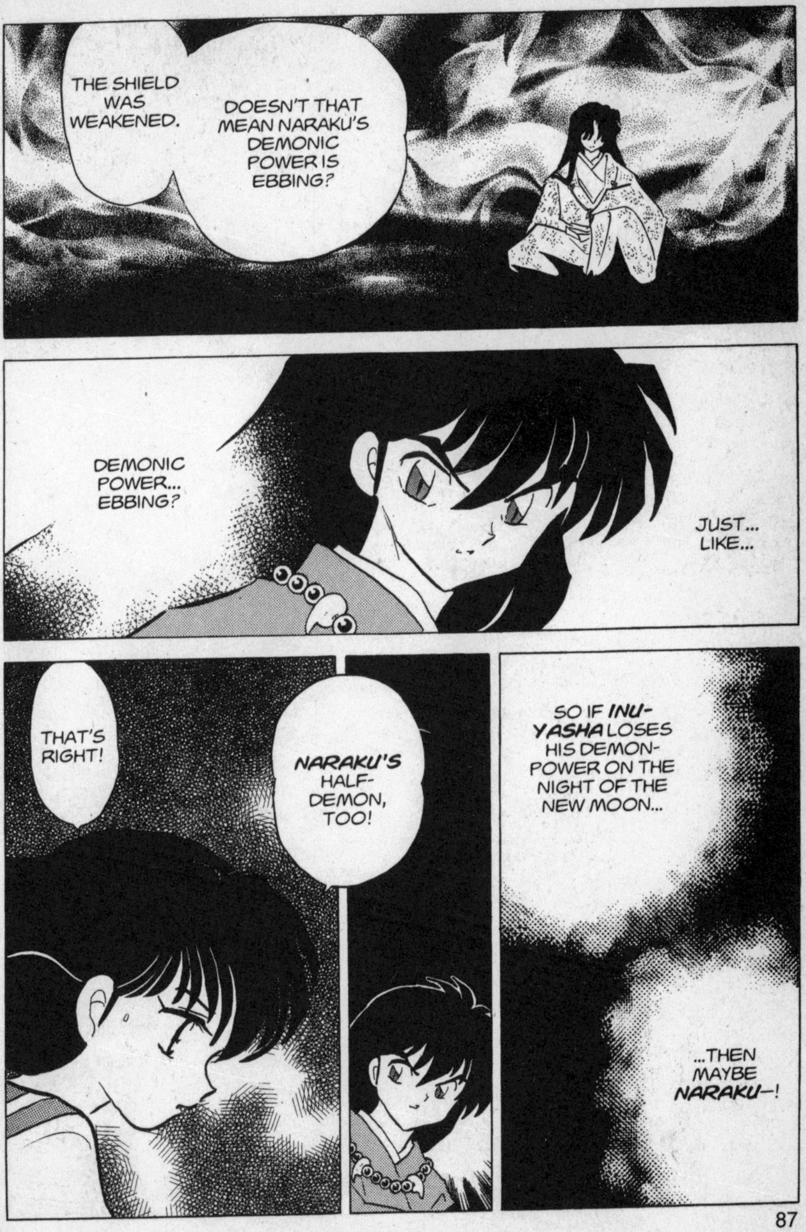
THE SHIELD WAS WEAKENED.
DOESN'T THAT MEAN NARAKU'S DEMONIC POWER IS EBBING?
DEMONIC POWER... EBBING?
JUST... LIKE...
THAT'S RIGHT!
NARAKU'S HALF-DEMON, TOO!
SO IF INU-YASHA LOSES HIS DEMON-POWER ON THE NIGHT OF THE NEW MOON...
...THEN MAYBE NARAKU–!

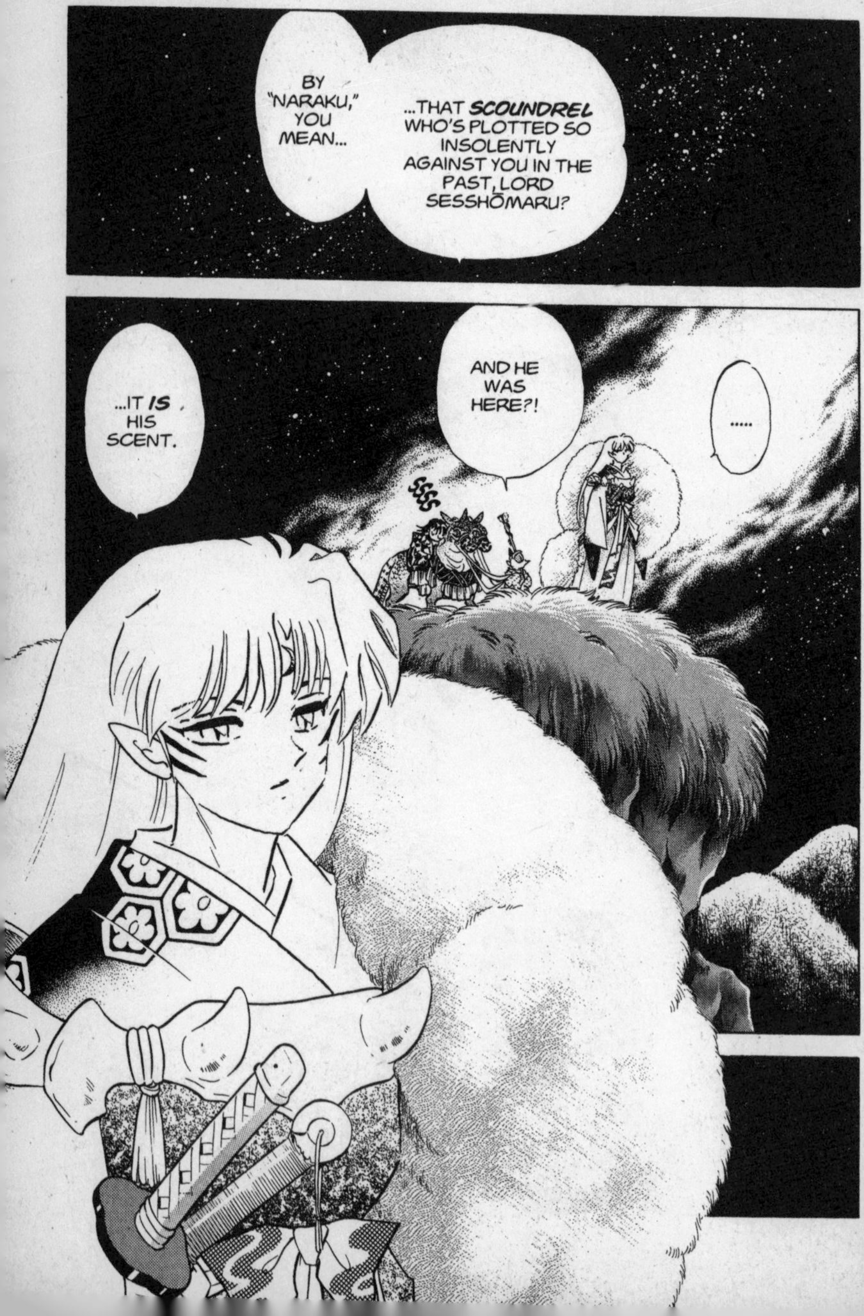
BY "NARAKU," YOU MEAN...
...THAT SCOUNDREL WHO'S PLOTTED SO INSOLENTLY AGAINST YOU IN THE PAST, LORD SESSHŌMARU?
...IT IS HIS SCENT.
AND HE WAS HERE?!
.....
SSSS

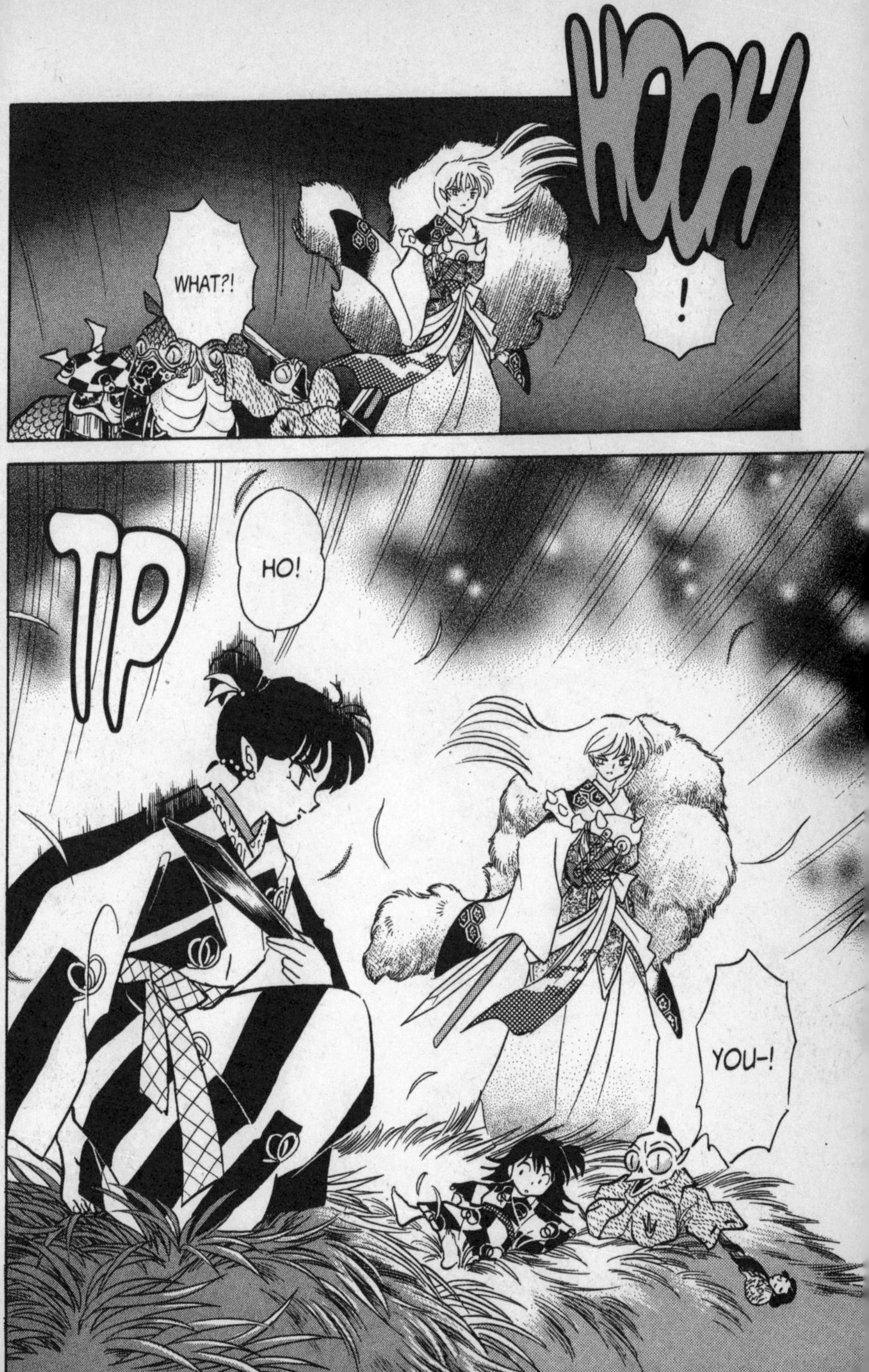

WHOOH
WHAT?!
!
TIP
HO!
YOU-!

SO, SESSHŌMARU. HAVE YOU COME SNIFFING NARAKU'S SCENT, TOO?

L-LORD SESSHŌMARU... THIS WOMAN...SHE WAS BIRTHED BY *HIM*...

.....

"KAGURA THE WIND WITCH"... ISN'T IT?

SHP...

MM. I'M FLATTERED.

YOU REMEMBER ME.

NOW, TAKE YOUR HAND FROM YOUR SWORD.

I DIDN'T COME HERE TO BATTLE YOU.

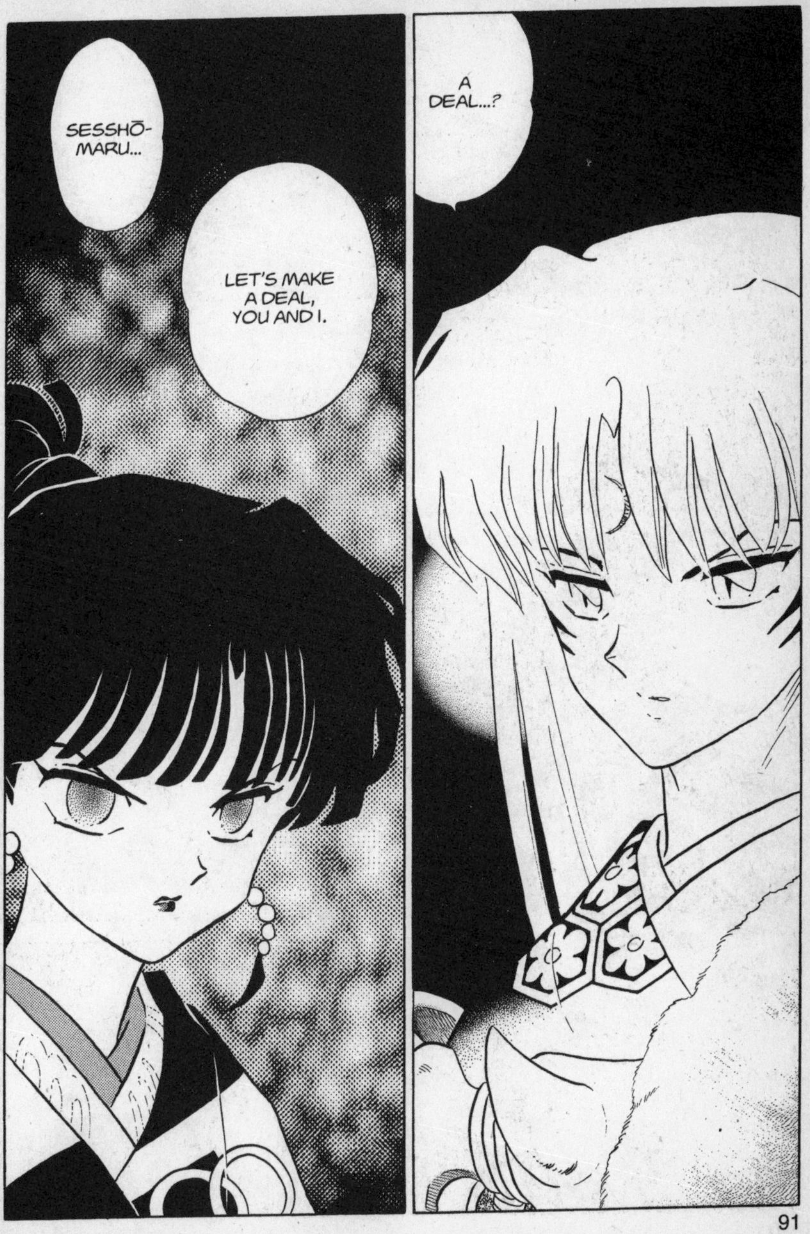
SESSHŌ-MARU...
LET'S MAKE A DEAL, YOU AND I.
A DEAL...?

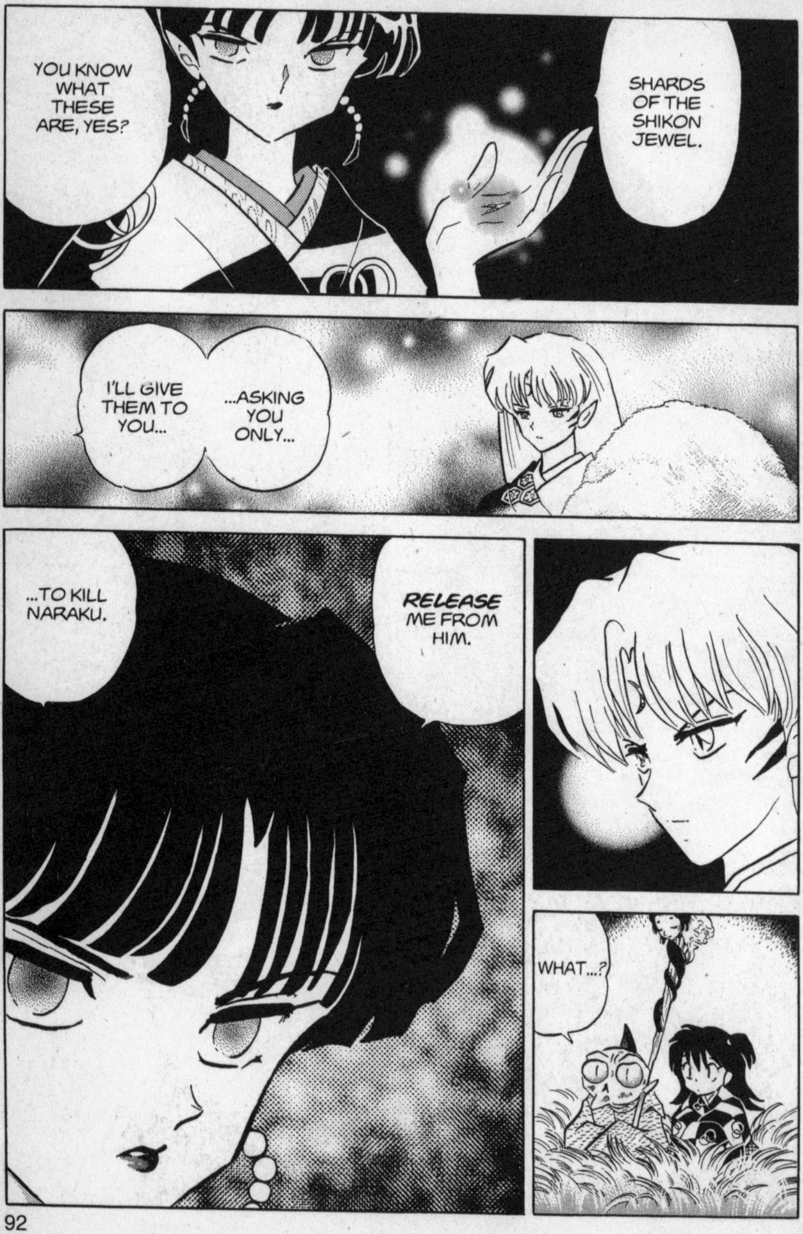
YOU KNOW WHAT THESE ARE, YES?
SHARDS OF THE SHIKON JEWEL.
I'LL GIVE THEM TO YOU...
...ASKING YOU ONLY...
...TO KILL NARAKU.
RELEASE ME FROM HIM.
WHAT...?

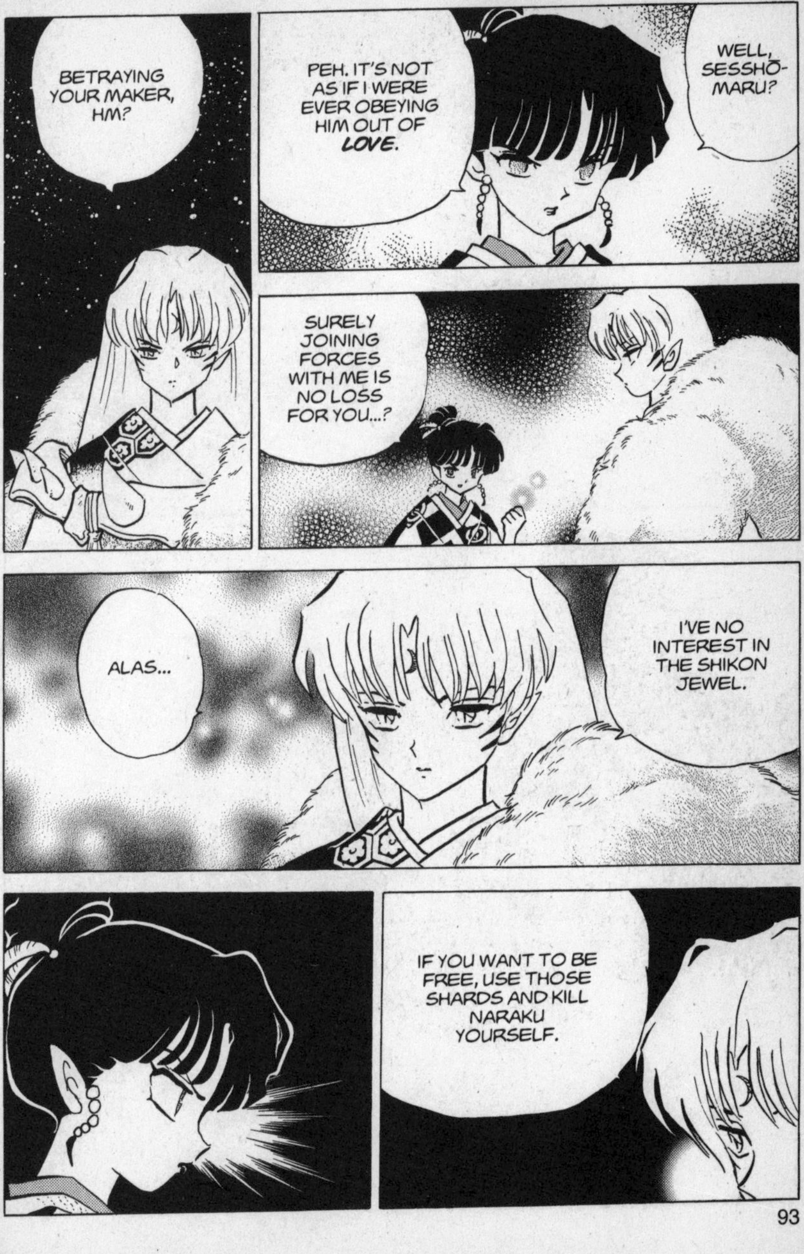
BETRAYING YOUR MAKER, HM?
PEH. IT'S NOT AS IF I WERE EVER OBEYING HIM OUT OF **LOVE**.
WELL, SESSHŌ-MARU?
SURELY JOINING FORCES WITH ME IS NO LOSS FOR YOU...?
ALAS...
I'VE NO INTEREST IN THE SHIKON JEWEL.
IF YOU WANT TO BE FREE, USE THOSE SHARDS AND KILL NARAKU YOURSELF.

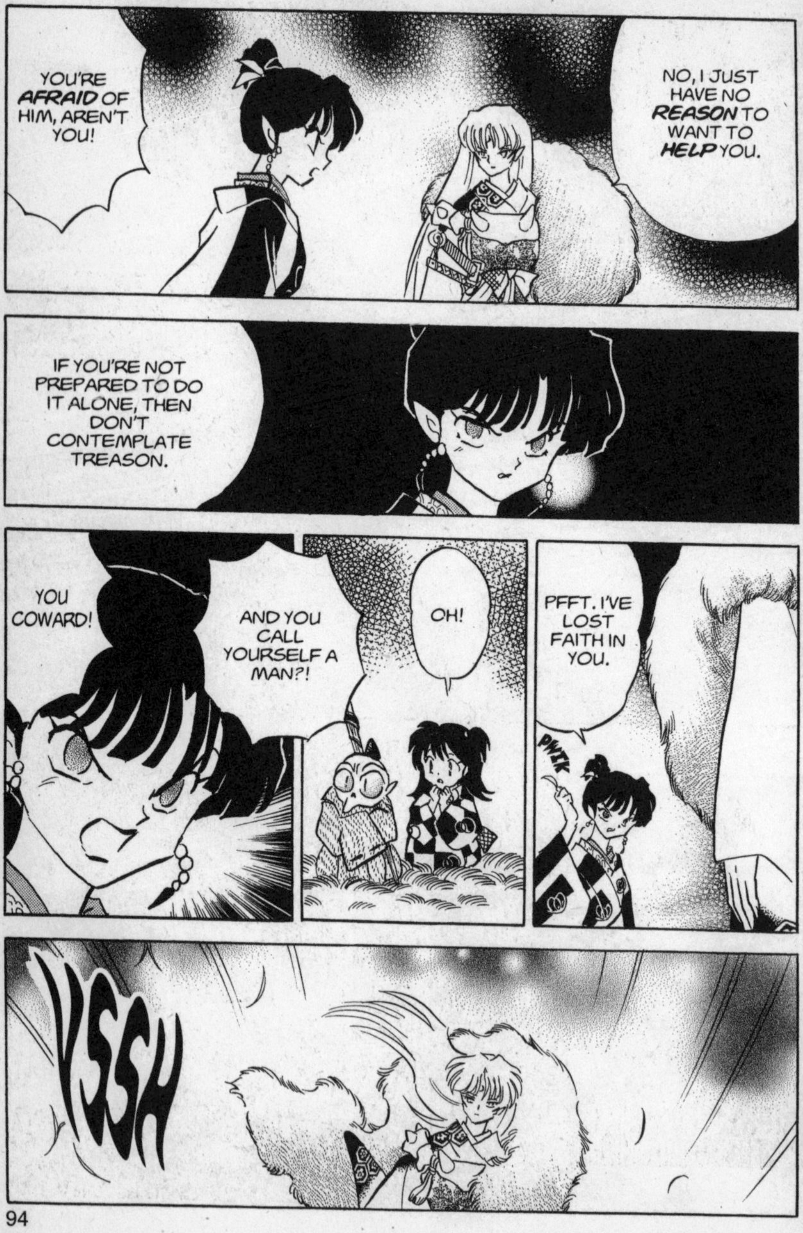
YOU'RE **AFRAID** OF HIM, AREN'T YOU!
NO, I JUST HAVE NO **REASON** TO WANT TO **HELP** YOU.
IF YOU'RE NOT PREPARED TO DO IT ALONE, THEN DON'T CONTEMPLATE TREASON.
YOU COWARD!
AND YOU CALL YOURSELF A MAN?!
OH!
PFFT. I'VE LOST FAITH IN YOU.
PWIK
VSSH

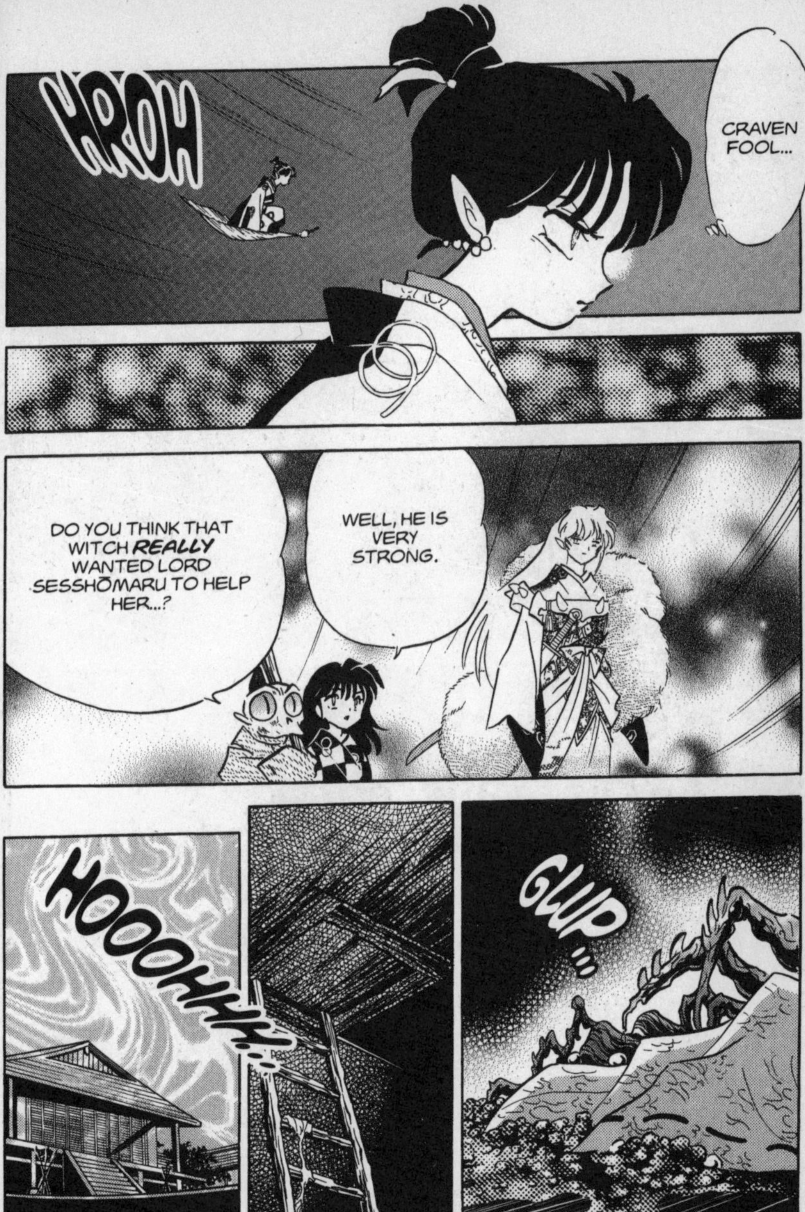
HROOH
CRAVEN FOOL...
DO YOU THINK THAT WITCH REALLY WANTED LORD SESSHŌMARU TO HELP HER...?
WELL, HE IS VERY STRONG.
HOOOHHH!!
GLIP...

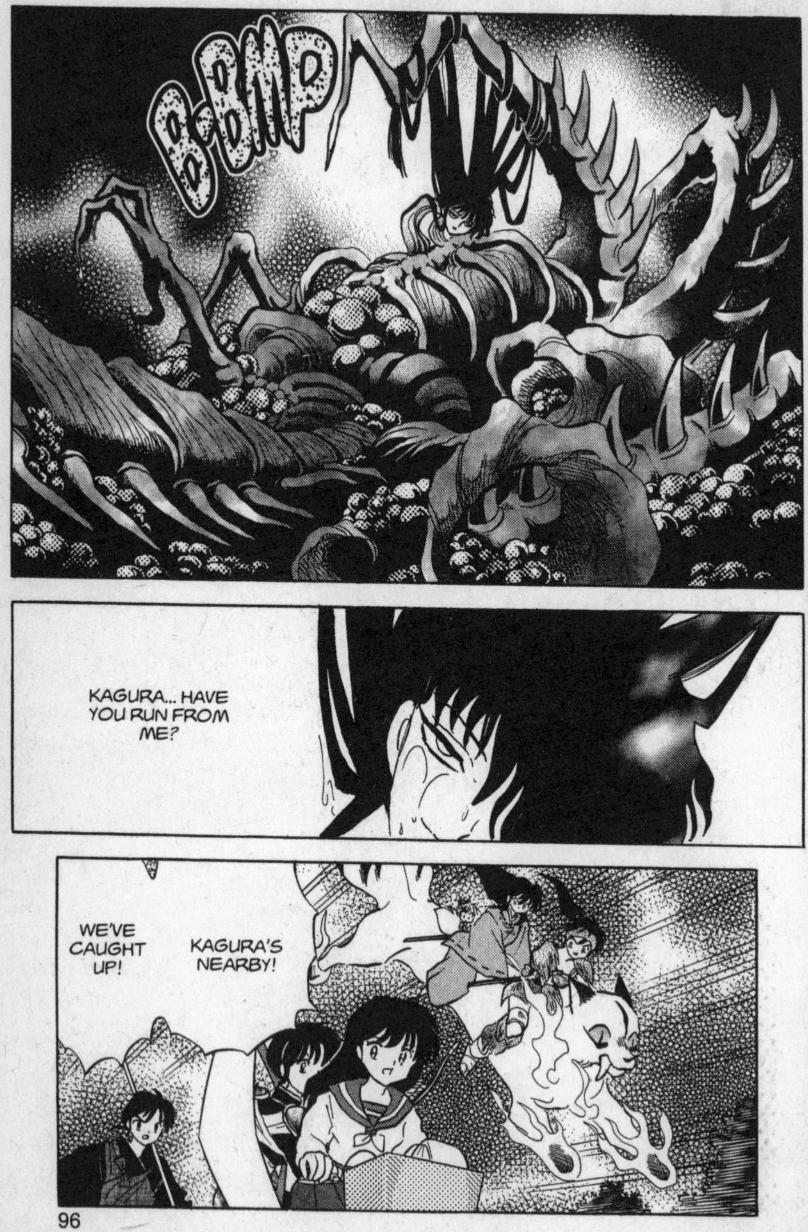
B-BMP
KAGURA... HAVE YOU RUN FROM ME?
WE'VE CAUGHT UP!
KAGURA'S NEARBY!

SCROLL SIX

SUNRISE

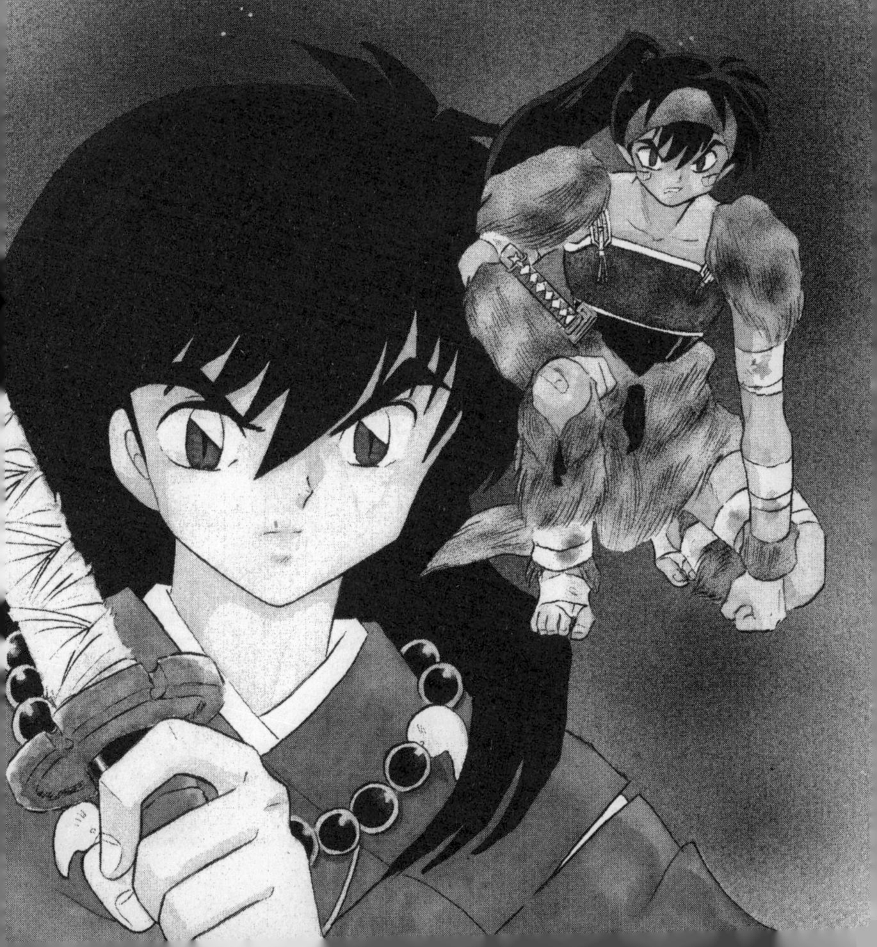

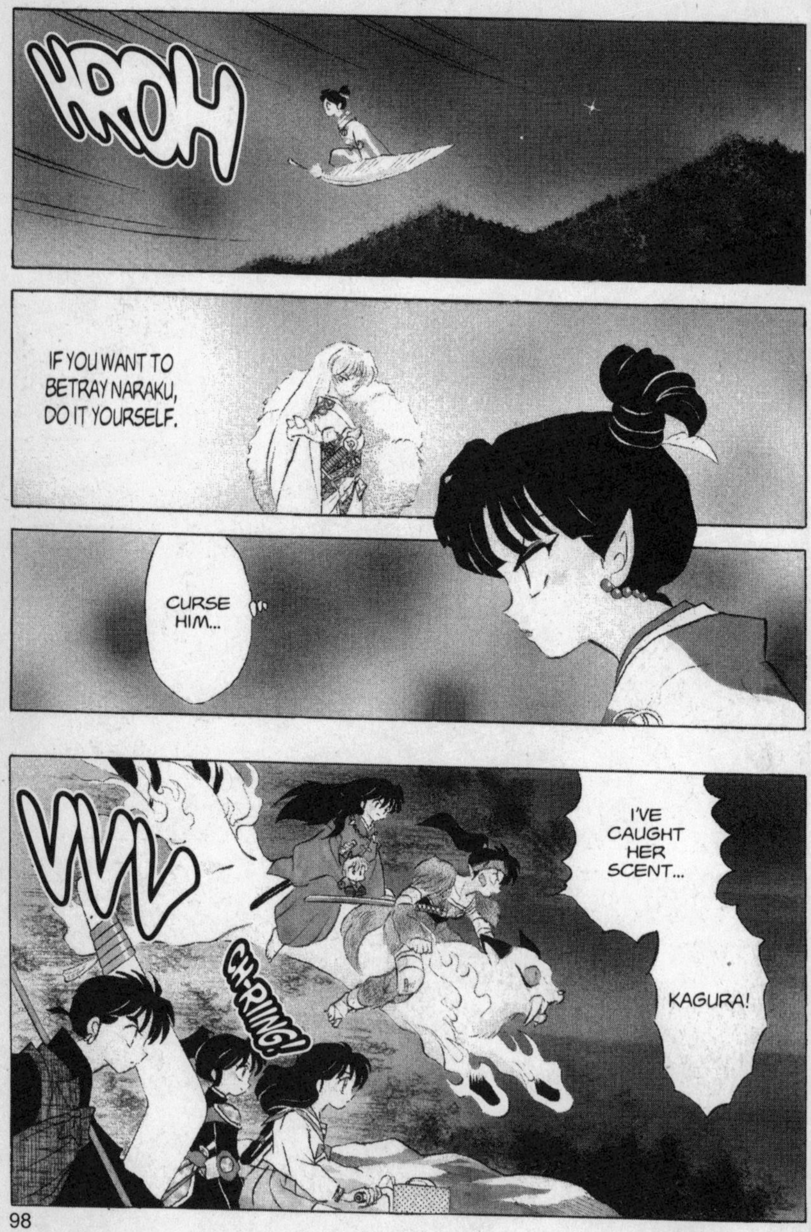
HROH
IF YOU WANT TO BETRAY NARAKU, DO IT YOURSELF.
CURSE HIM...
VVVV
CH-RING!
I'VE CAUGHT HER SCENT...
KAGURA!

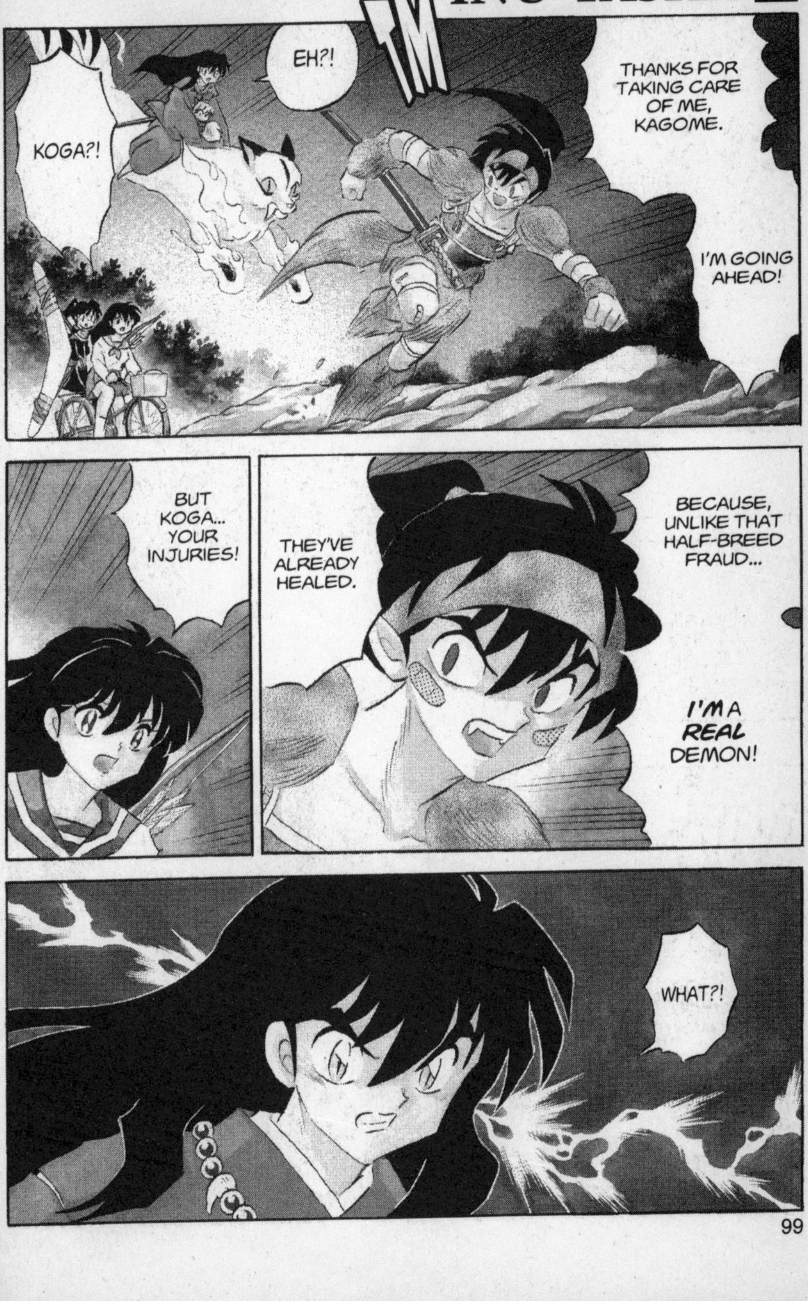
KOGA?!
EH?!
TM
THANKS FOR TAKING CARE OF ME, KAGOME.
I'M GOING AHEAD!
BUT KOGA... YOUR INJURIES!
THEY'VE ALREADY HEALED.
BECAUSE, UNLIKE THAT HALF-BREED FRAUD...
I'M A REAL DEMON!
WHAT?!

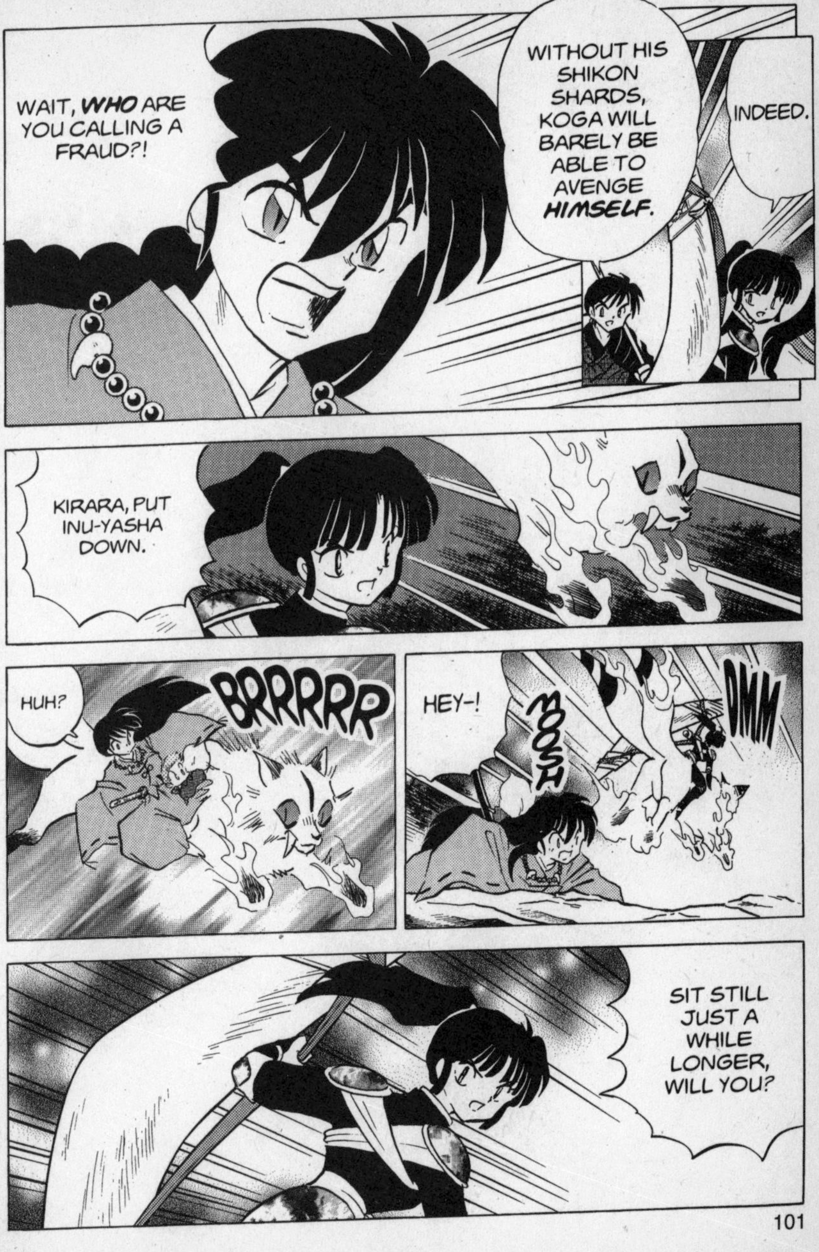
WAIT, ***WHO*** ARE YOU CALLING A FRAUD?!
WITHOUT HIS SHIKON SHARDS, KOGA WILL BARELY BE ABLE TO AVENGE ***HIMSELF***.
INDEED.
KIRARA, PUT INU-YASHA DOWN.
HUH?
BRRRRR
HEY-!
WOOSH
DMM
SIT STILL JUST A WHILE LONGER, WILL YOU?

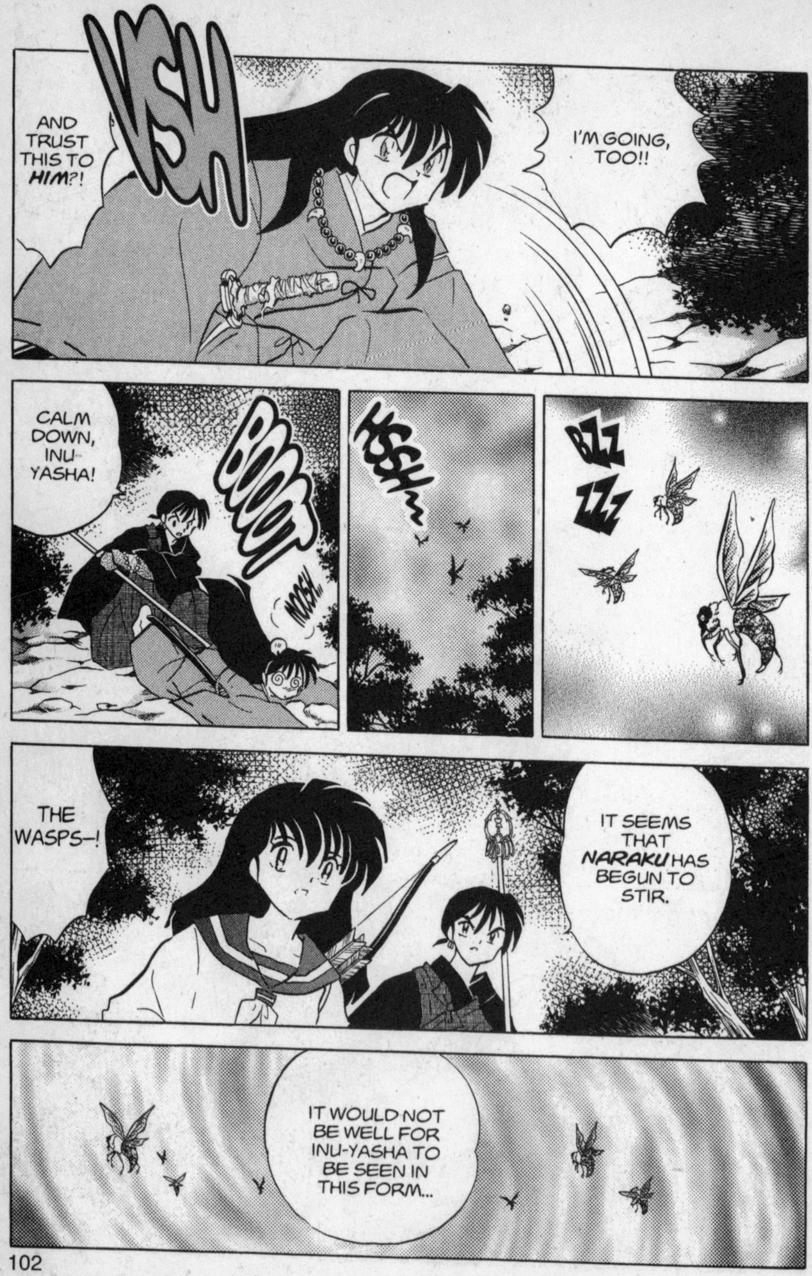
VSH
AND TRUST THIS TO HIM?!
I'M GOING, TOO!!
CALM DOWN, INU-YASHA!
BOOOT
MOOSH...
HSSH
BZZ ZZZ
THE WASPS—!
IT SEEMS THAT NARAKU HAS BEGUN TO STIR.
IT WOULD NOT BE WELL FOR INU-YASHA TO BE SEEN IN THIS FORM...

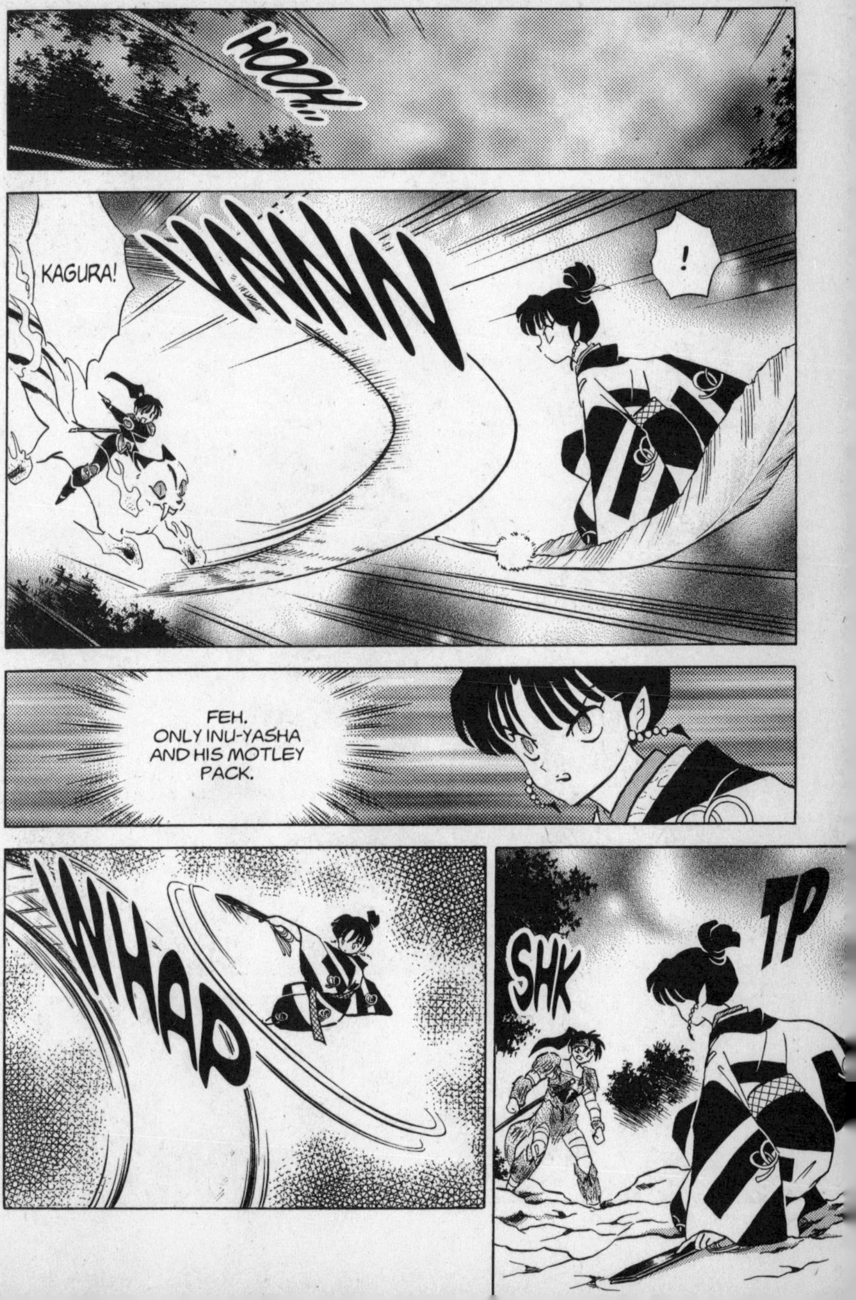
HOOH...
!
KAGURA!
FEH.
ONLY INU-YASHA
AND HIS MOTLEY
PACK.
TP
SHK
WHAP

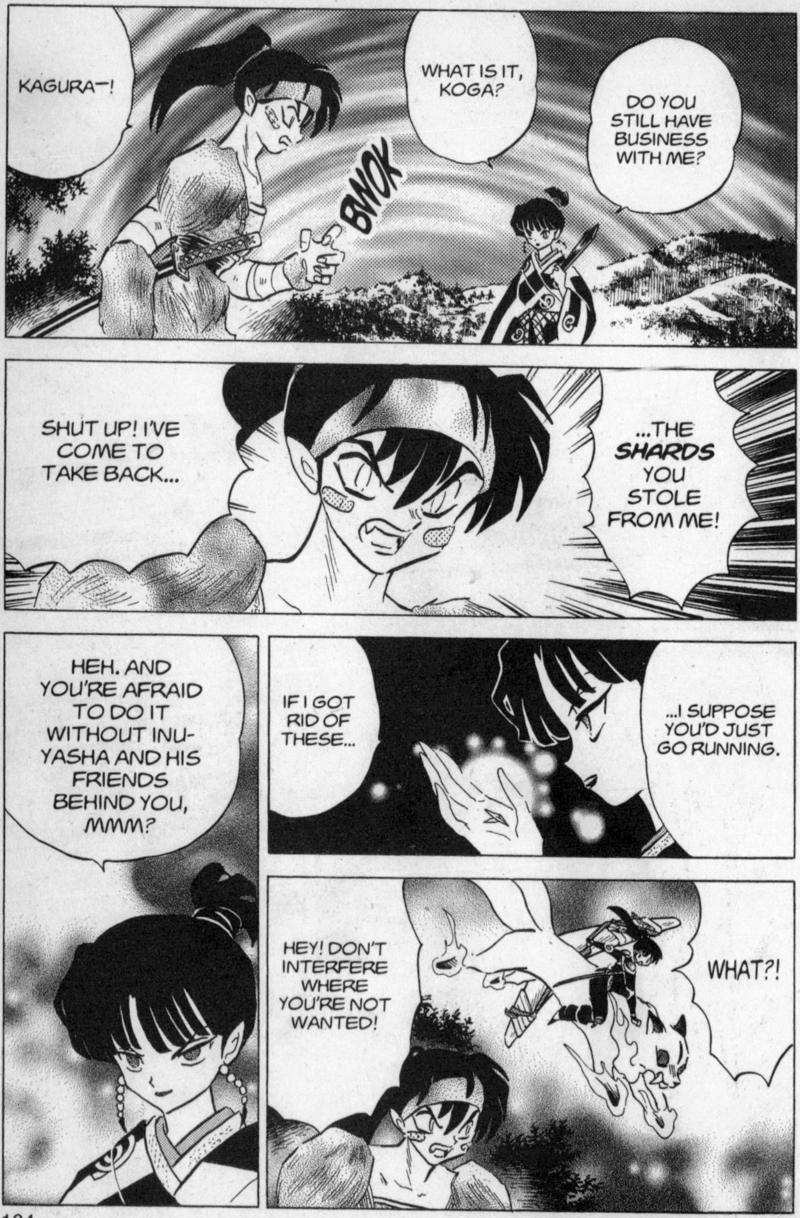
KAGURA—!
WHAT IS IT, KOGA?
DO YOU STILL HAVE BUSINESS WITH ME?
BWOK
SHUT UP! I'VE COME TO TAKE BACK...
...THE SHARDS YOU STOLE FROM ME!
HEH. AND YOU'RE AFRAID TO DO IT WITHOUT INU-YASHA AND HIS FRIENDS BEHIND YOU, MMM?
IF I GOT RID OF THESE...
...I SUPPOSE YOU'D JUST GO RUNNING.
HEY! DON'T INTERFERE WHERE YOU'RE NOT WANTED!
WHAT?!

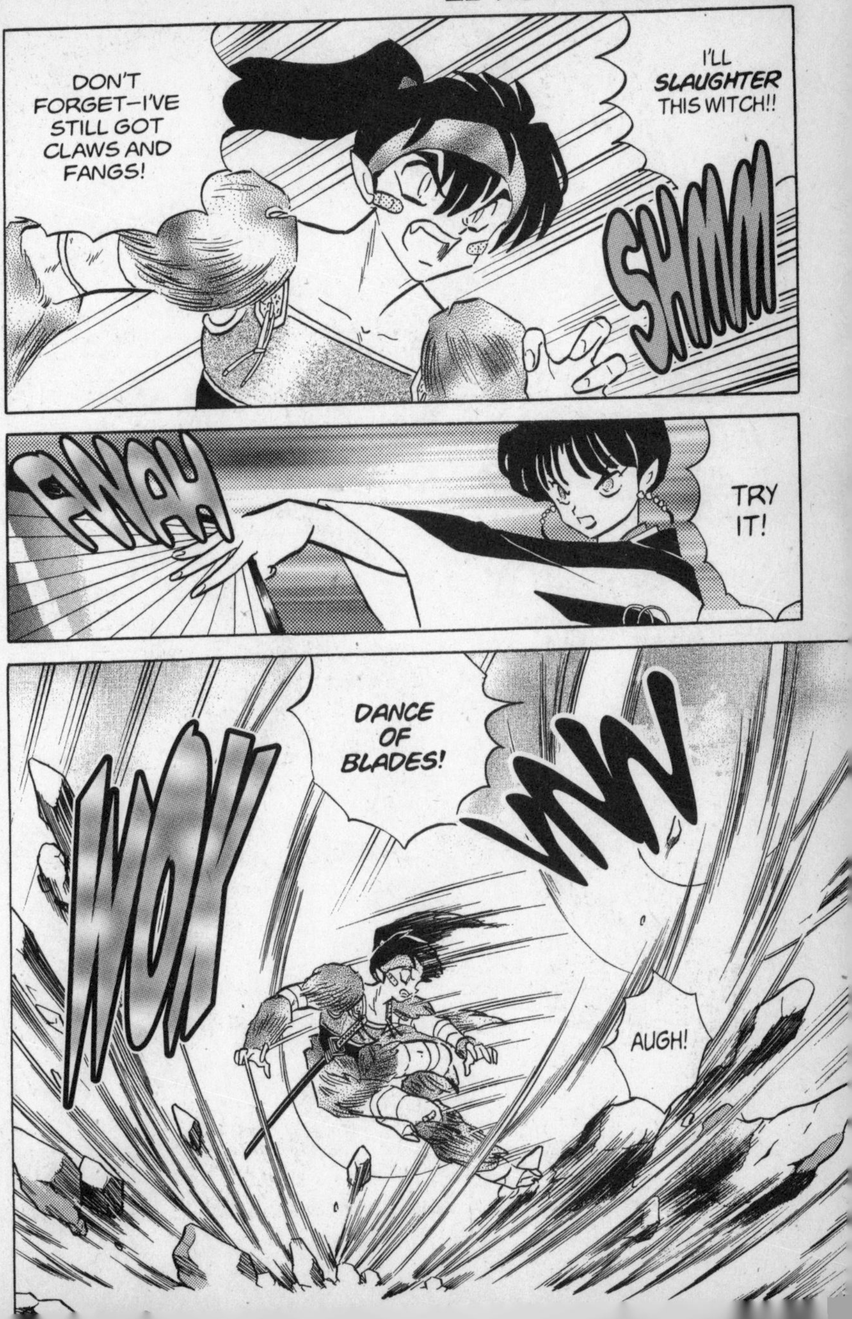
DON'T FORGET—I'VE STILL GOT CLAWS AND FANGS!
I'LL SLAUGHTER THIS WITCH!!
TRY IT!
DANCE OF BLADES!
AUGH!

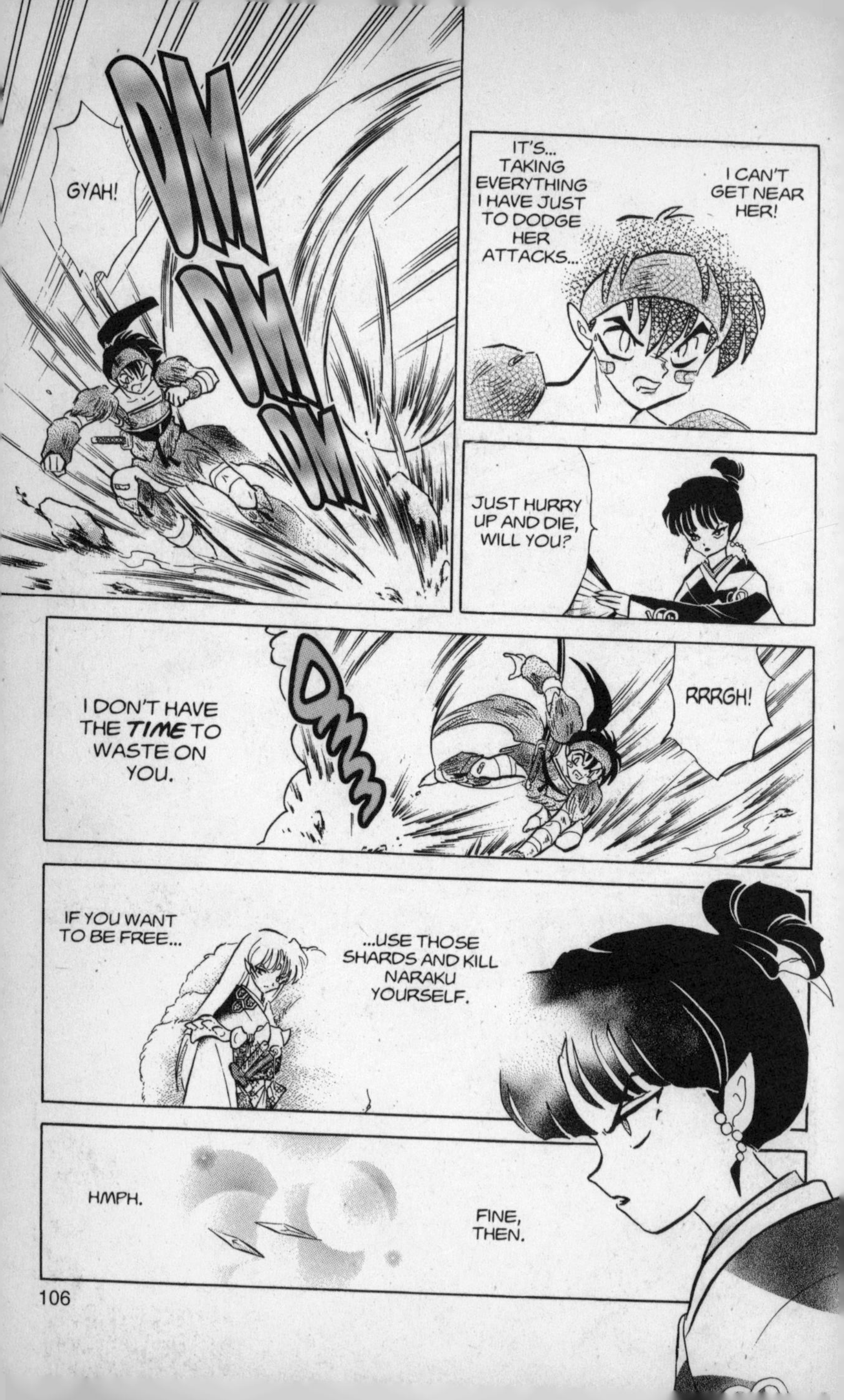

GYAH!
DIM DIM DIM DIM
IT'S... TAKING EVERYTHING I HAVE JUST TO DODGE HER ATTACKS...
I CAN'T GET NEAR HER!
JUST HURRY UP AND DIE, WILL YOU?
I DON'T HAVE THE *TIME* TO WASTE ON YOU.
DMM
RRRGH!
IF YOU WANT TO BE FREE...
...USE THOSE SHARDS AND KILL NARAKU YOURSELF.
HMPH.
FINE, THEN.

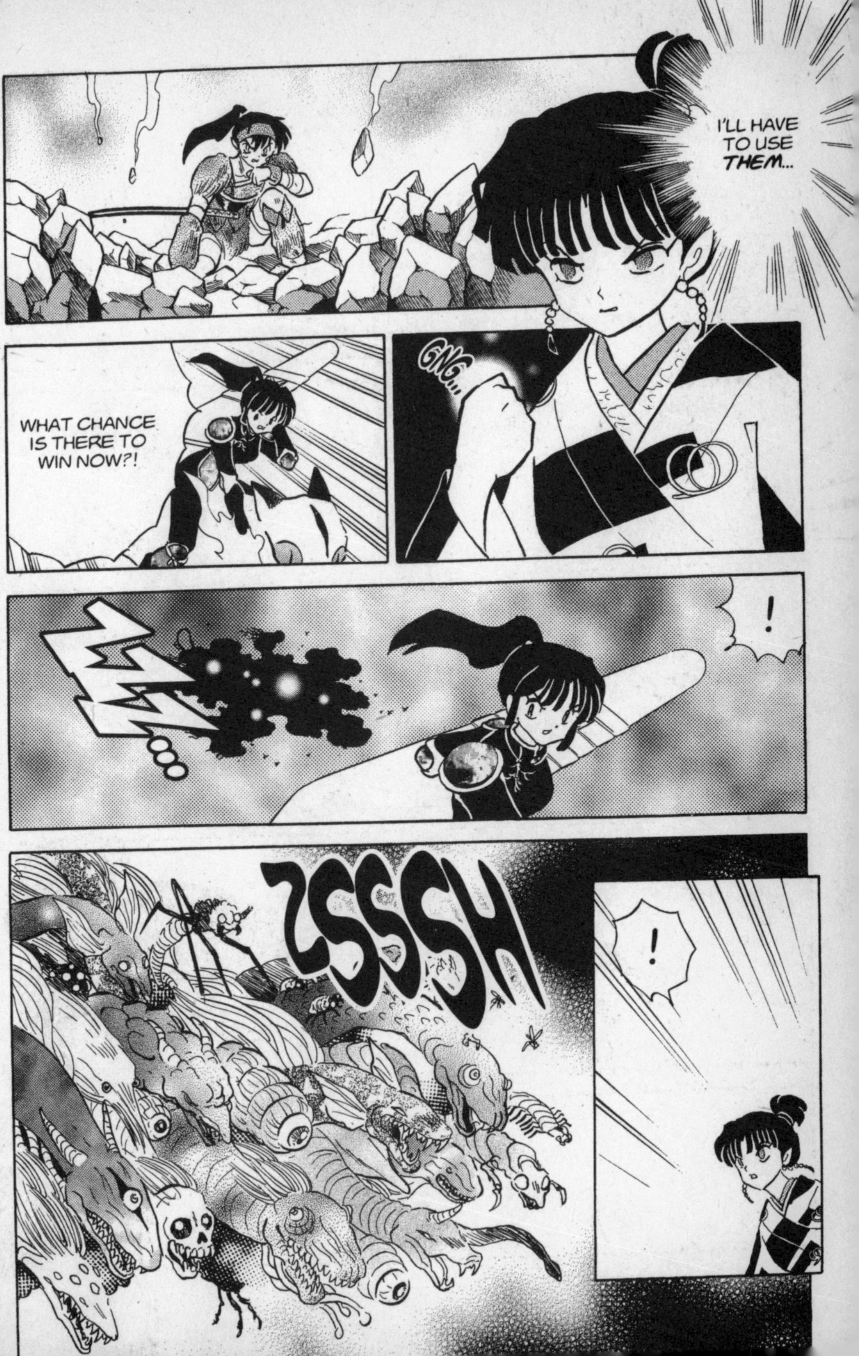
I'LL HAVE TO USE THEM...
WHAT CHANCE IS THERE TO WIN NOW?!
GNG...
!
!
ZSSSH

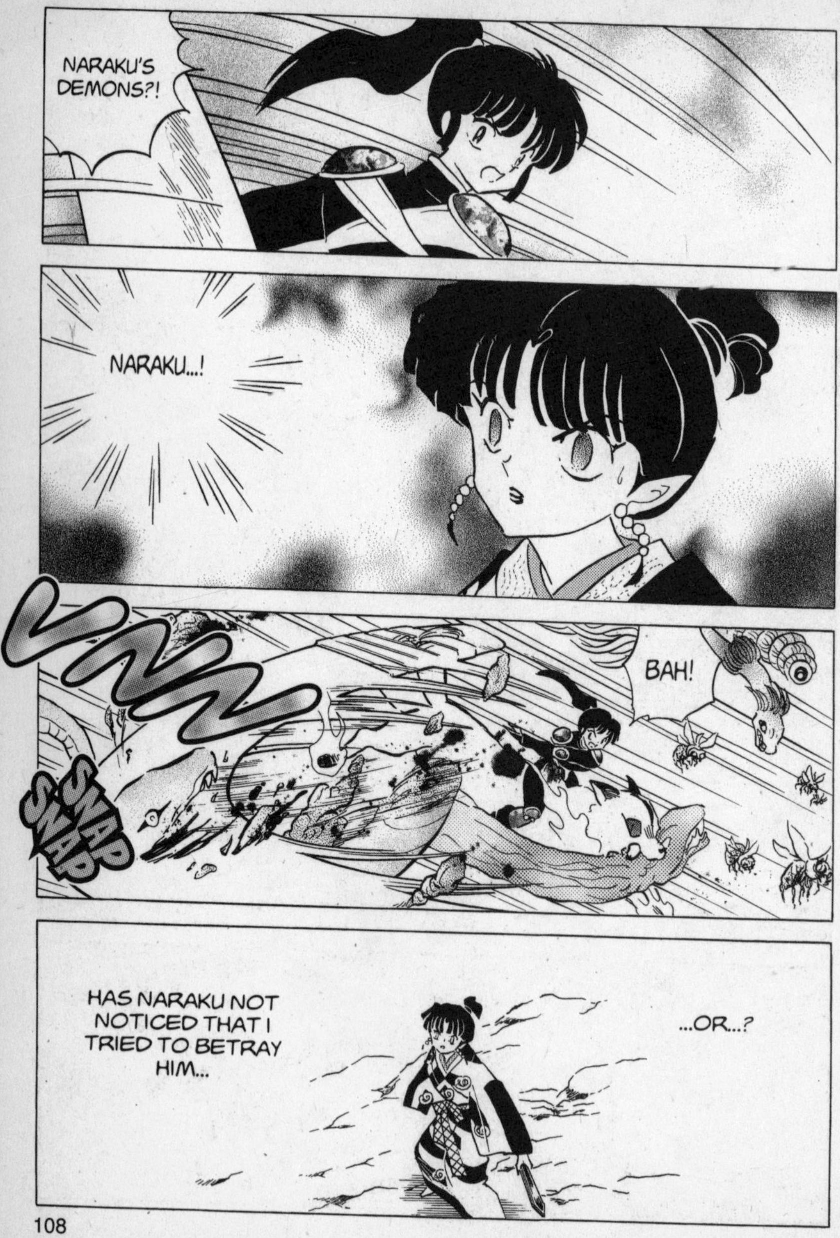
NARAKU'S DEMONS?!
NARAKU...!
BAH!
VNNN
SNAP SNAP
HAS NARAKU NOT NOTICED THAT I TRIED TO BETRAY HIM...
...OR...?

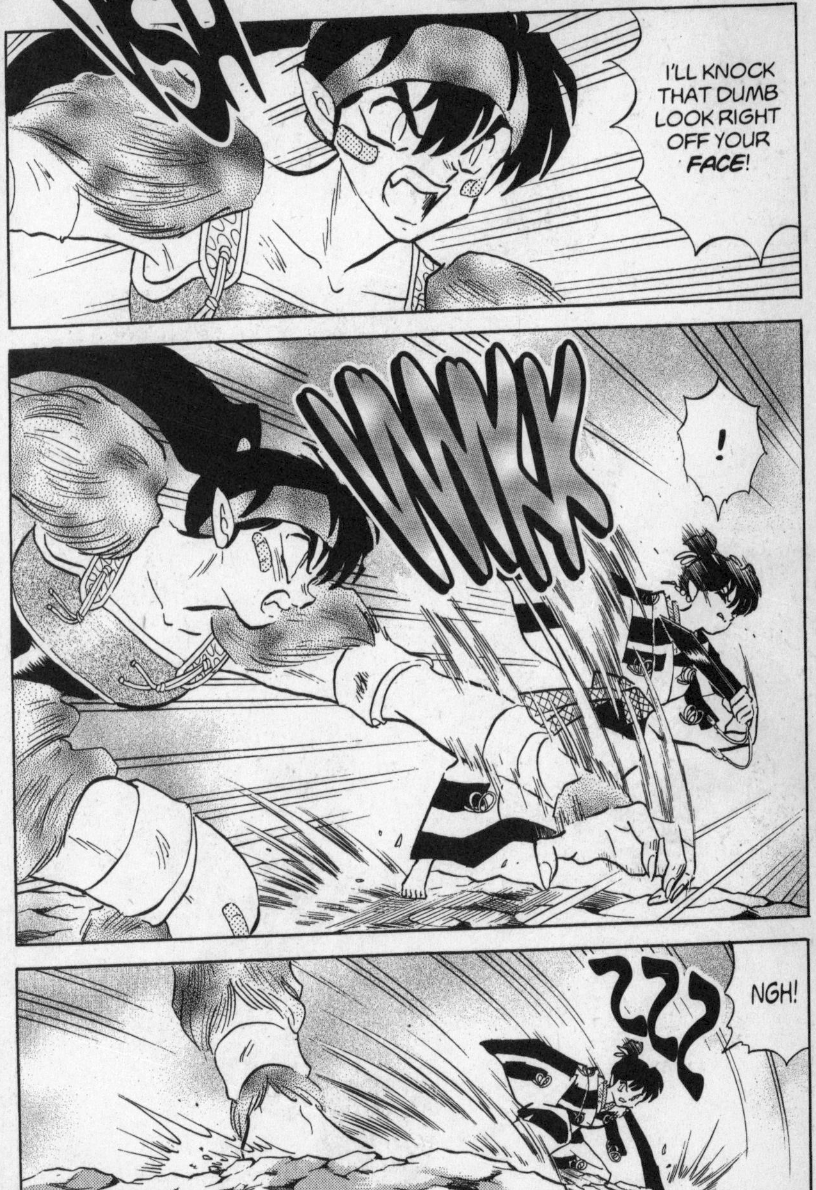
VSSH
I'LL KNOCK THAT DUMB LOOK RIGHT OFF YOUR *FACE*!
!
NGH!

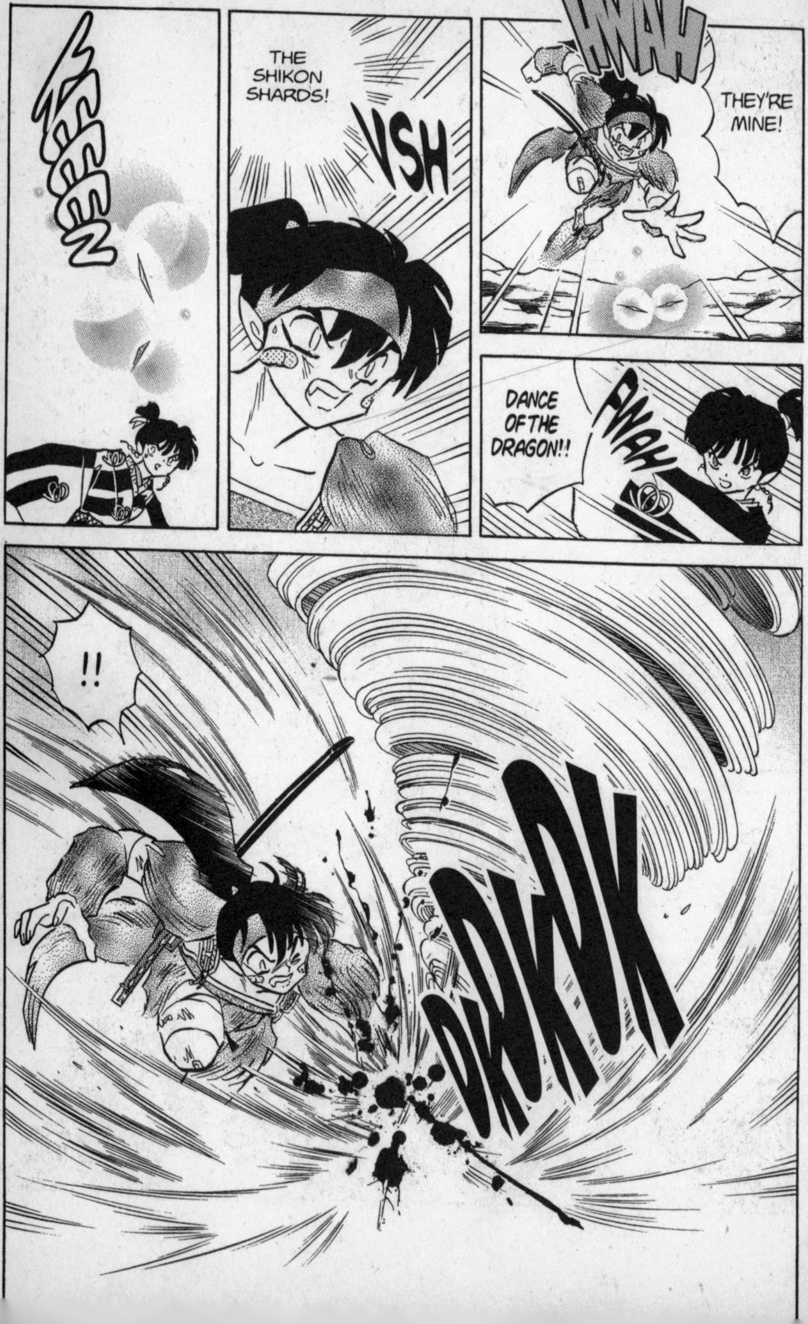
KEEEEN
THE SHIKON SHARDS!
VSH
HWAH
THEY'RE MINE!
DANCE OF THE DRAGON!!
AWAH
!!
DKRRK

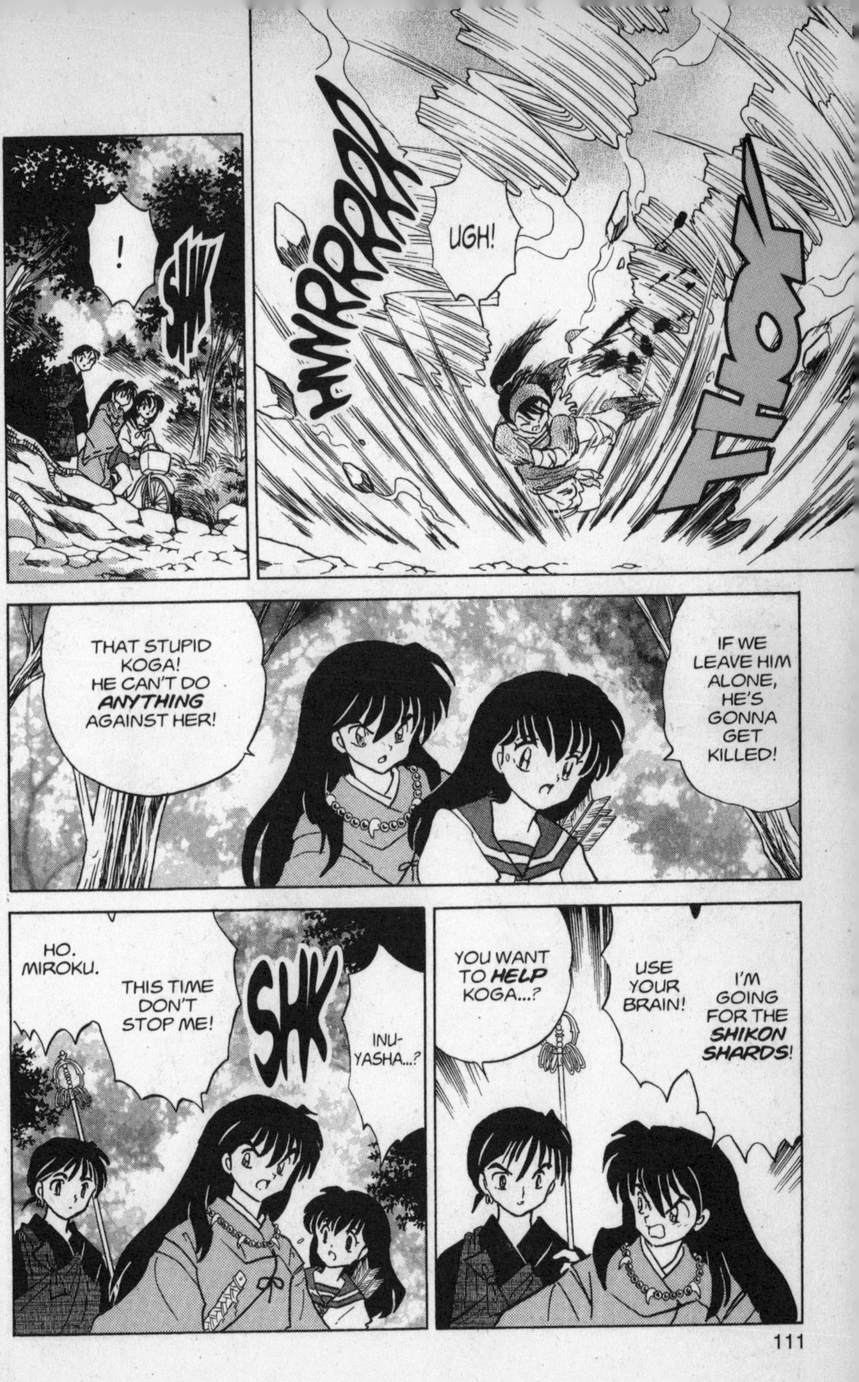
!
SHK
HWRRRPP
UGH!
THOK
THAT STUPID KOGA! HE CAN'T DO ***ANYTHING*** AGAINST HER!
IF WE LEAVE HIM ALONE, HE'S GONNA GET KILLED!
HO. MIROKU.
THIS TIME DON'T STOP ME!
SHK
INU-YASHA...?
YOU WANT TO ***HELP*** KOGA...?
USE YOUR BRAIN!
I'M GOING FOR THE ***SHIKON SHARDS***!

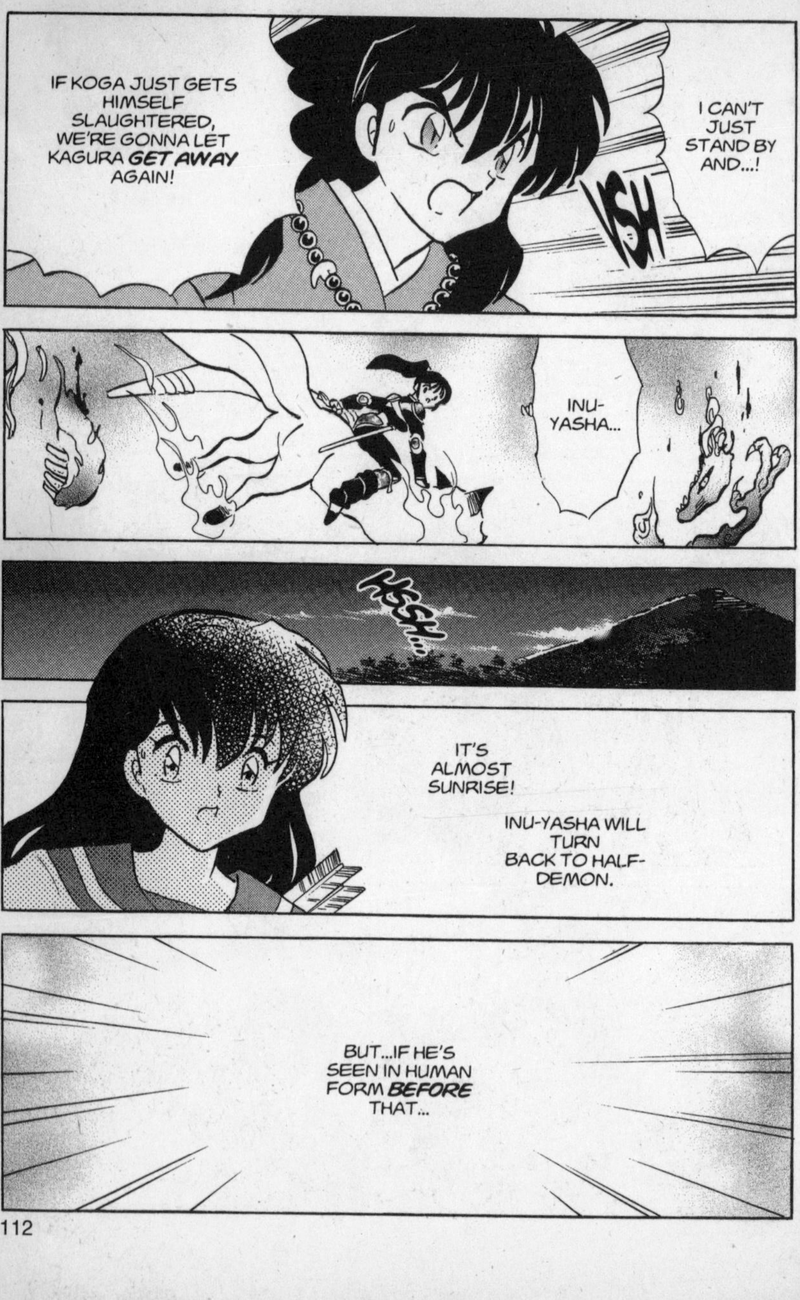
IF KOGA JUST GETS HIMSELF SLAUGHTERED, WE'RE GONNA LET KAGURA GET AWAY AGAIN!
I CAN'T JUST STAND BY AND...!
VSH
INU-YASHA...
VSSH...
IT'S ALMOST SUNRISE!
INU-YASHA WILL TURN BACK TO HALF-DEMON.
BUT...IF HE'S SEEN IN HUMAN FORM BEFORE THAT...

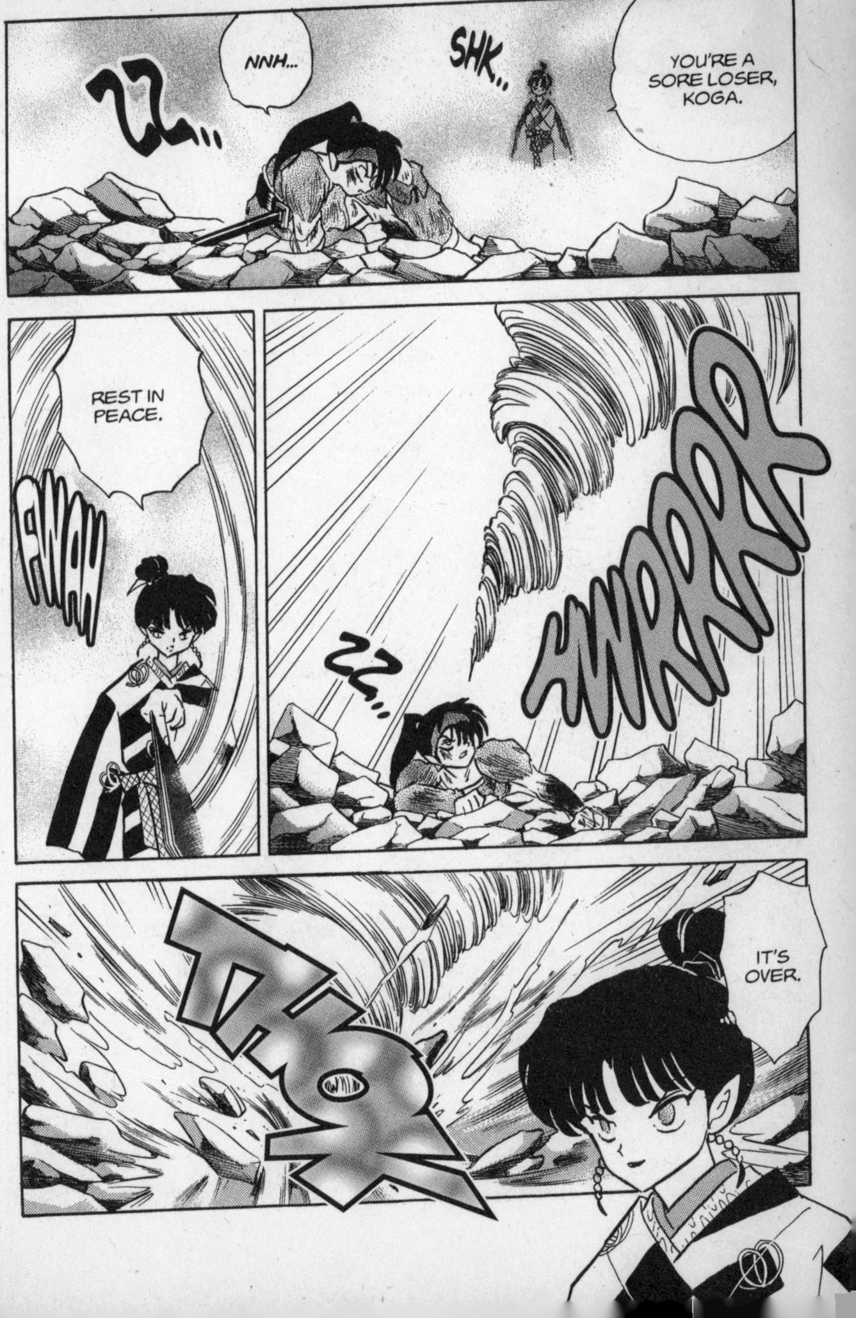
ZZ...
NNH...
SHK...
YOU'RE A SORE LOSER, KOGA.
REST IN PEACE.
FWAH
ZZ...
WHRRRR
THOK
IT'S OVER.

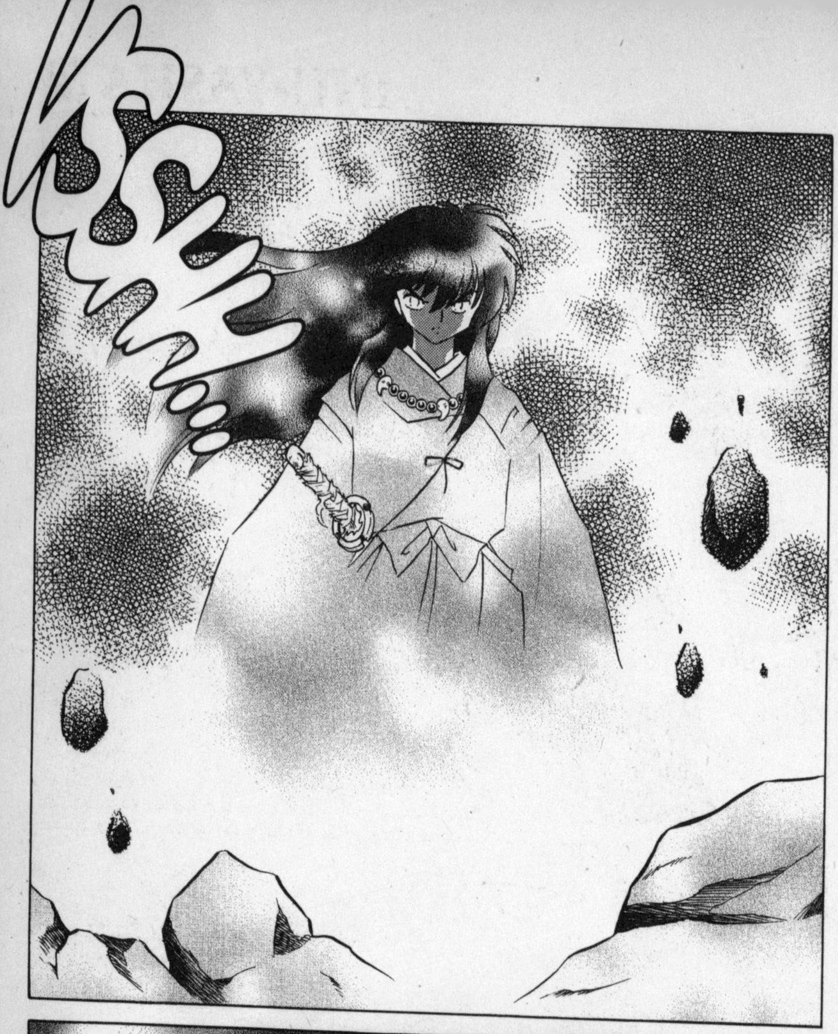
VSSHHOOO
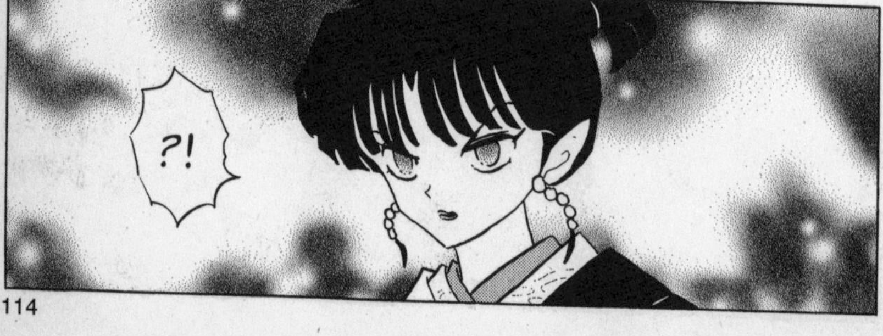
?!

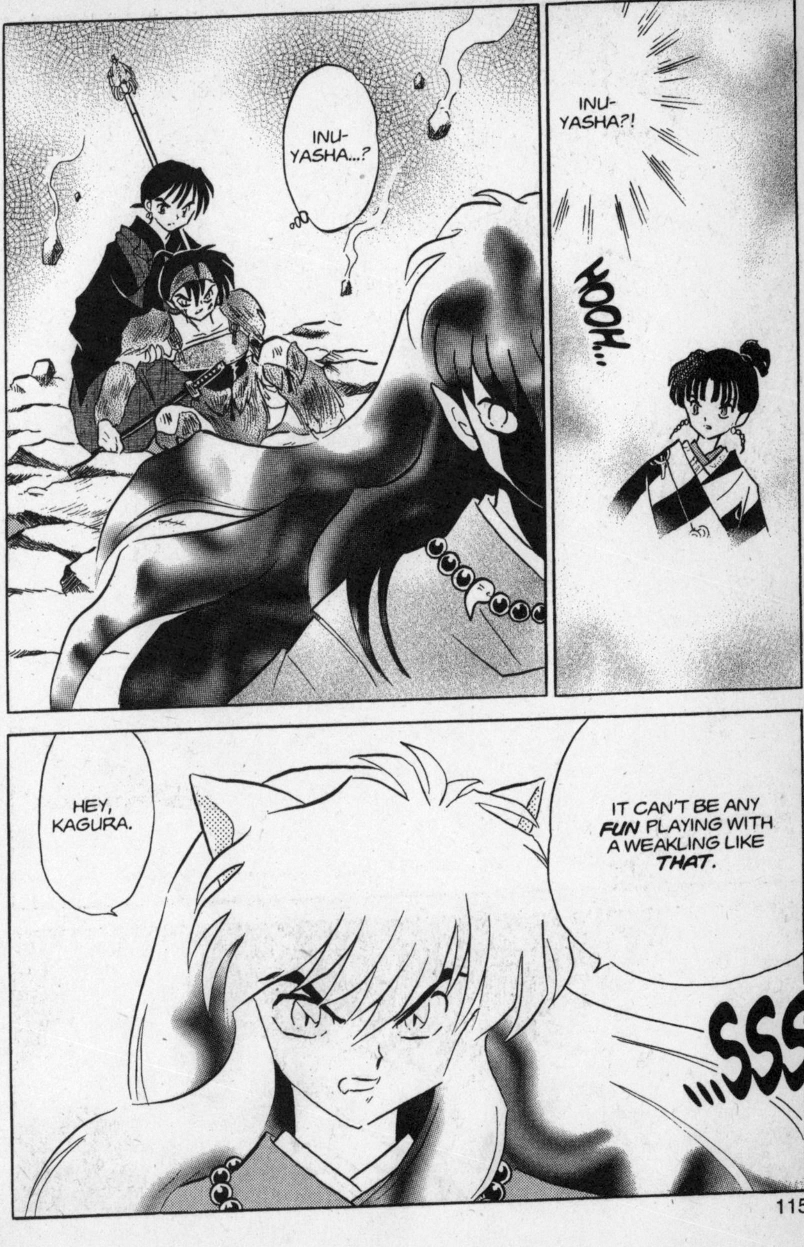
INU-YASHA...?
INU-YASHA?!
WOOH...
HEY, KAGURA.
IT CAN'T BE ANY **FUN** PLAYING WITH A WEAKLING LIKE **THAT**.
...SSS

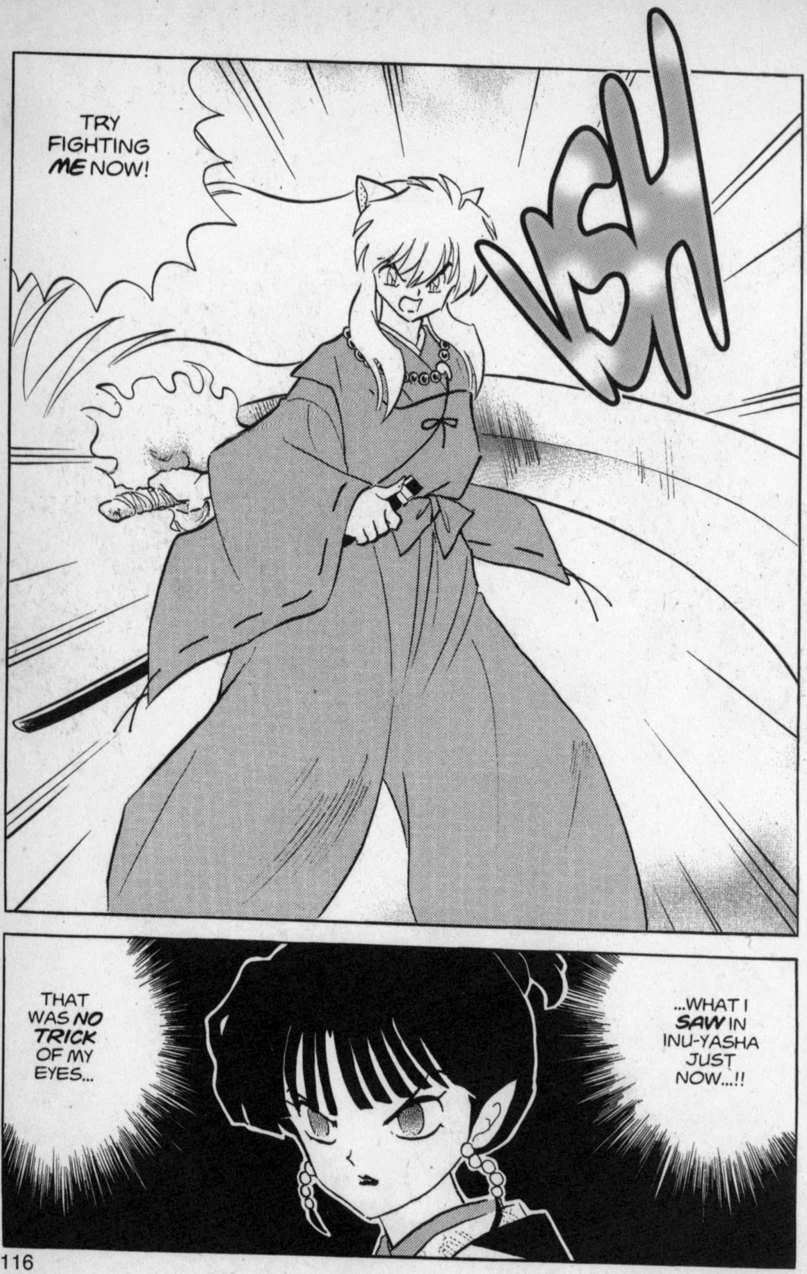
TRY FIGHTING ME NOW!
THAT WAS NO TRICK OF MY EYES...
...WHAT I SAW IN INU-YASHA JUST NOW...!!

SCROLL SEVEN

THE HALF-DEMON'S SECRET

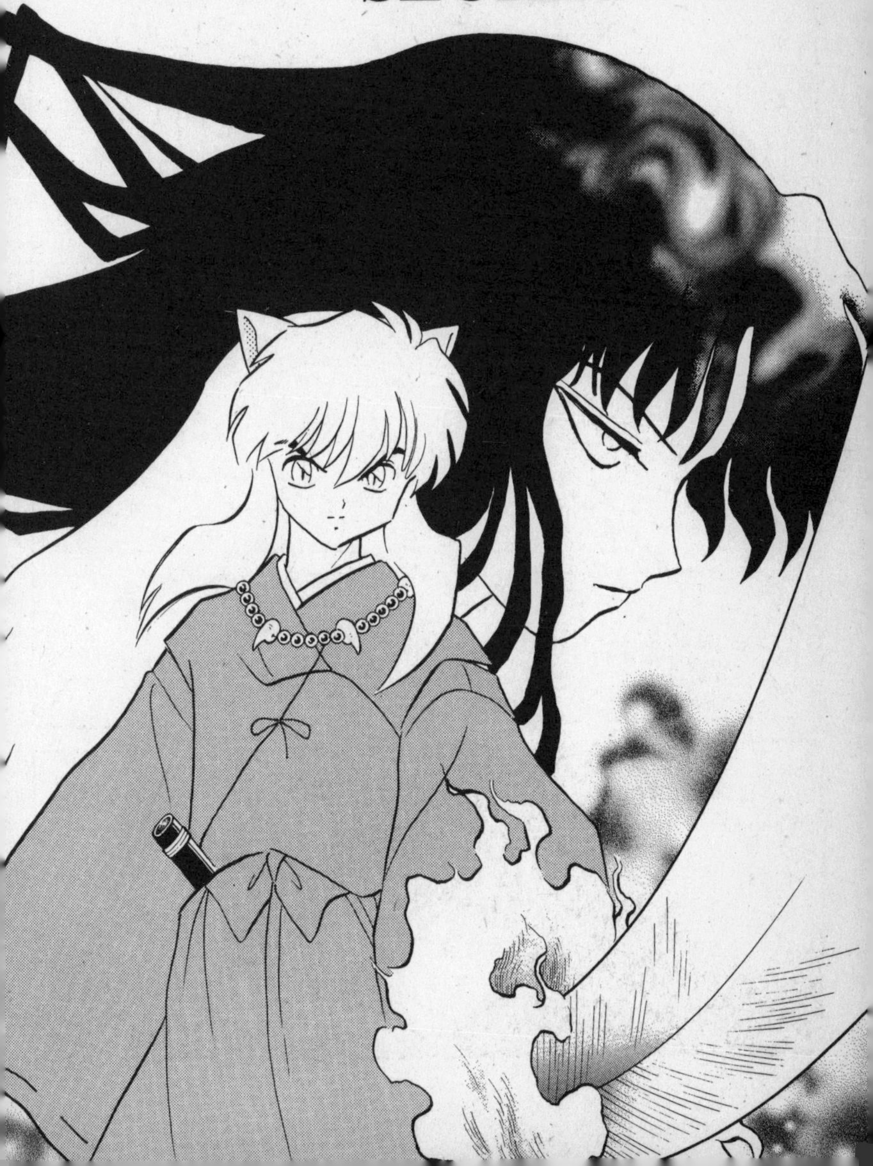

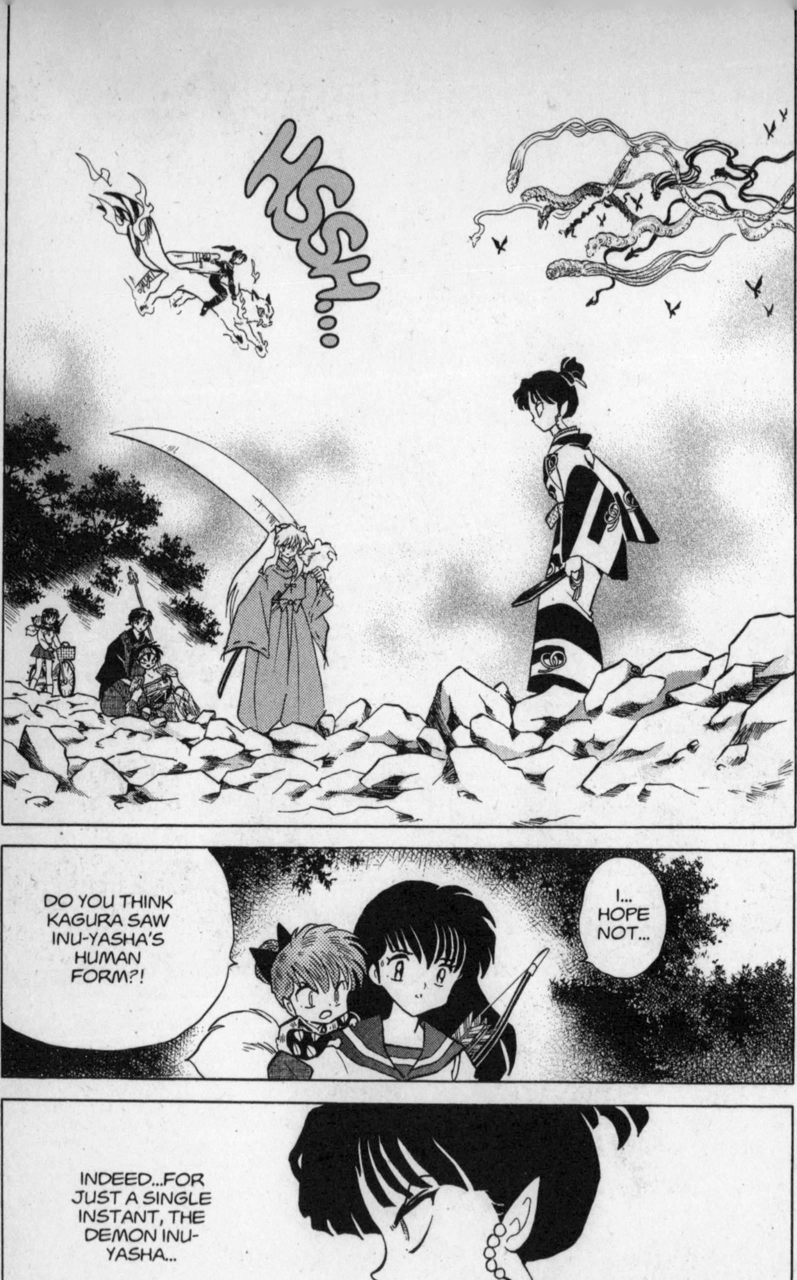
HSSH...
DO YOU THINK KAGURA SAW INU-YASHA'S HUMAN FORM?!
I... HOPE NOT...
INDEED...FOR JUST A SINGLE INSTANT, THE DEMON INU-YASHA...

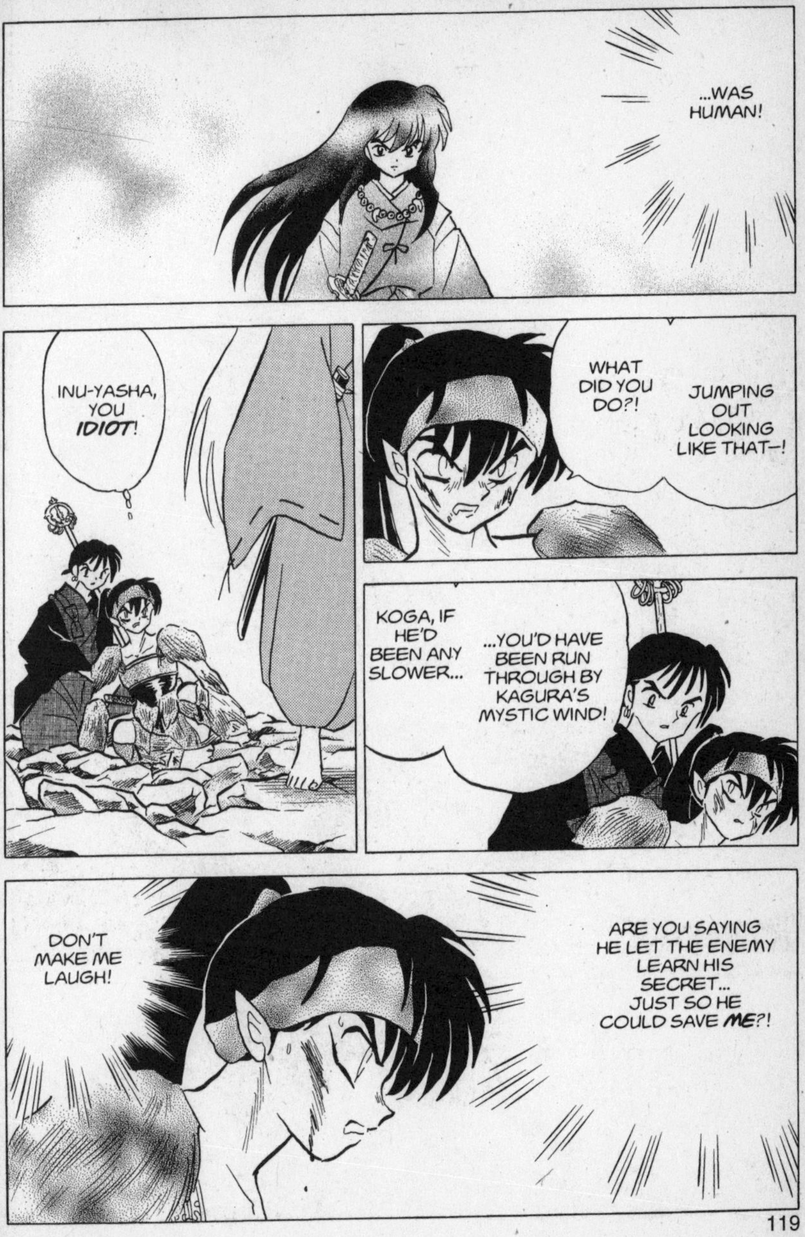
...WAS HUMAN!
INU-YASHA, YOU *IDIOT*!
WHAT DID YOU DO?!
JUMPING OUT LOOKING LIKE THAT–!
KOGA, IF HE'D BEEN ANY SLOWER...
...YOU'D HAVE BEEN RUN THROUGH BY KAGURA'S MYSTIC WIND!
DON'T MAKE ME LAUGH!
ARE YOU SAYING HE LET THE ENEMY LEARN HIS SECRET... JUST SO HE COULD SAVE *ME*?!

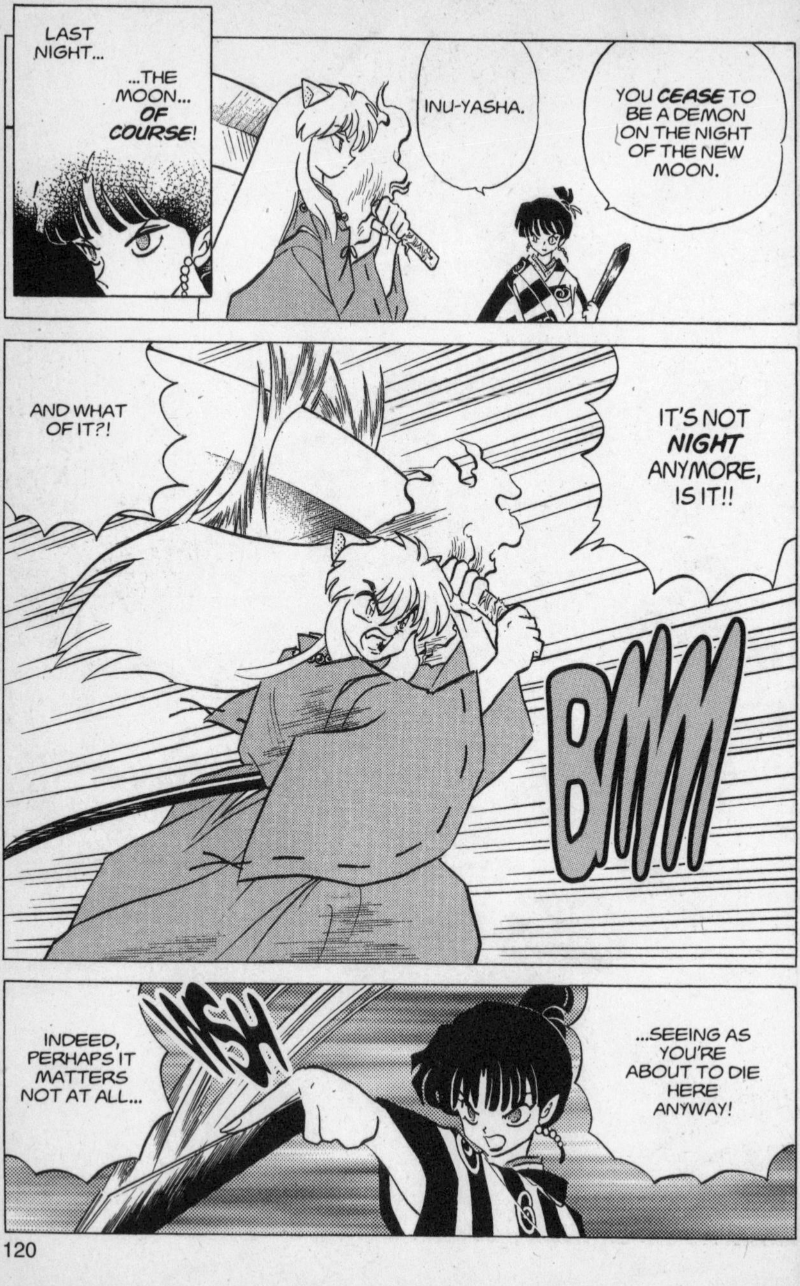
LAST NIGHT...
...THE MOON... OF COURSE!
INU-YASHA.
YOU CEASE TO BE A DEMON ON THE NIGHT OF THE NEW MOON.
AND WHAT OF IT?!
IT'S NOT NIGHT ANYMORE, IS IT!!
BMM
WSH
INDEED, PERHAPS IT MATTERS NOT AT ALL...
...SEEING AS YOU'RE ABOUT TO DIE HERE ANYWAY!

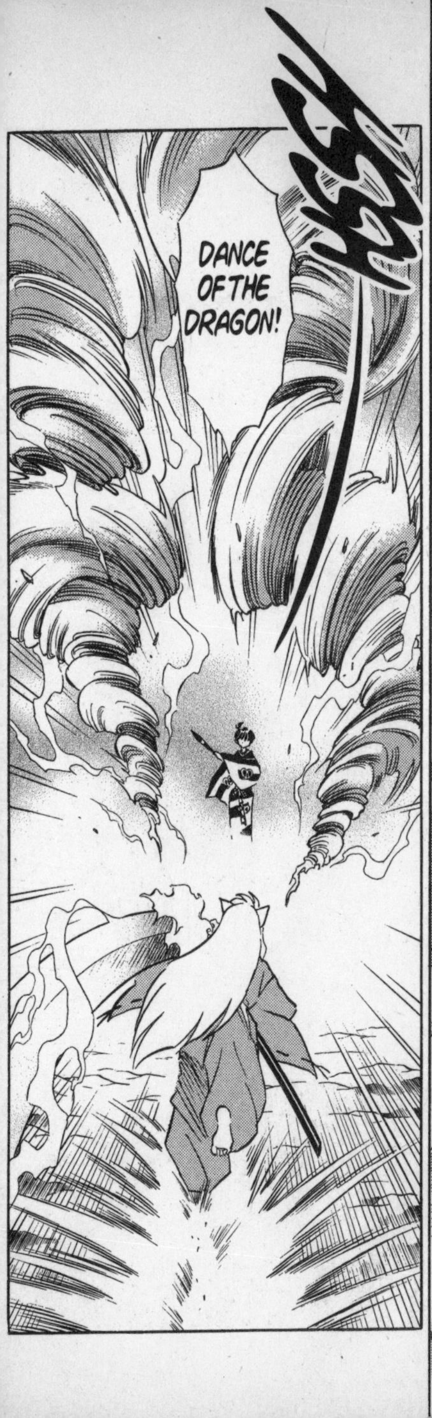
DANCE OF THE DRAGON!

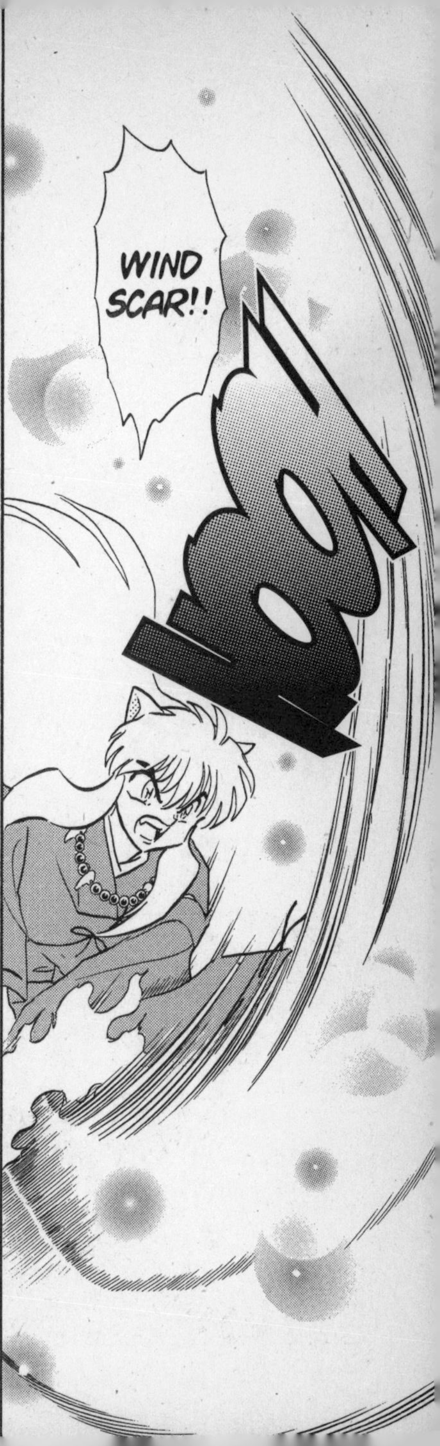
WIND SCAR!!
FOOM

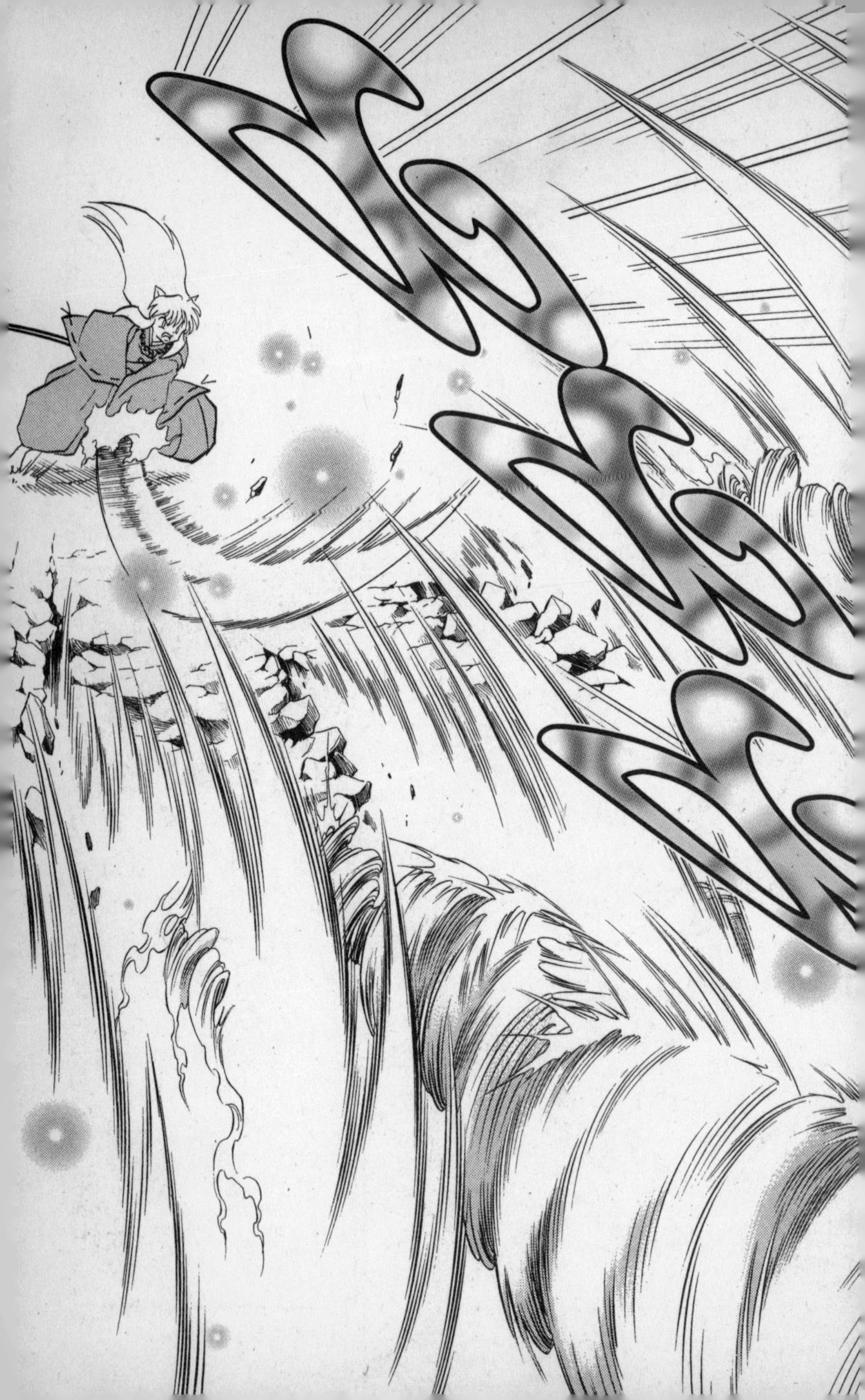

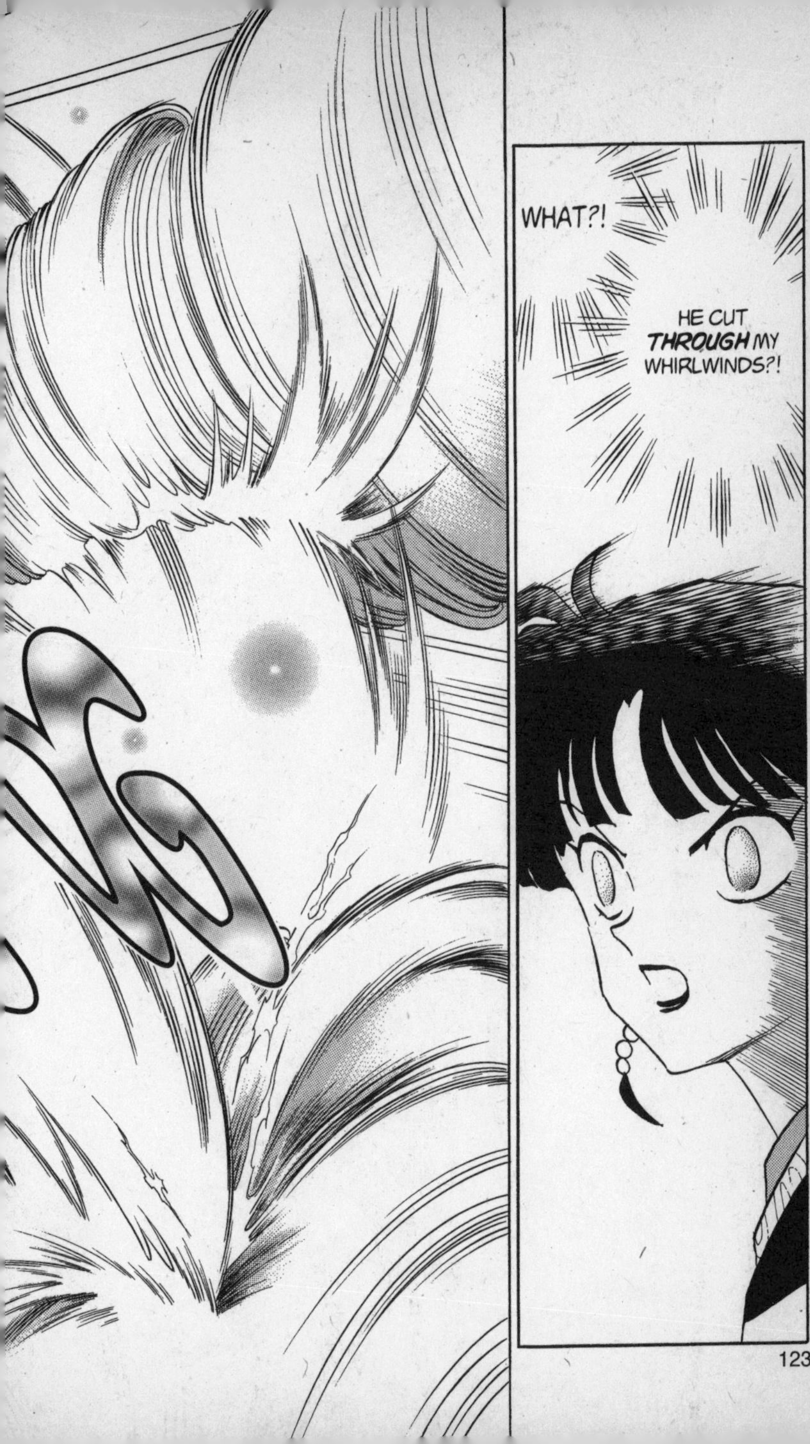
WHAT?!
HE CUT THROUGH MY WHIRLWINDS?!

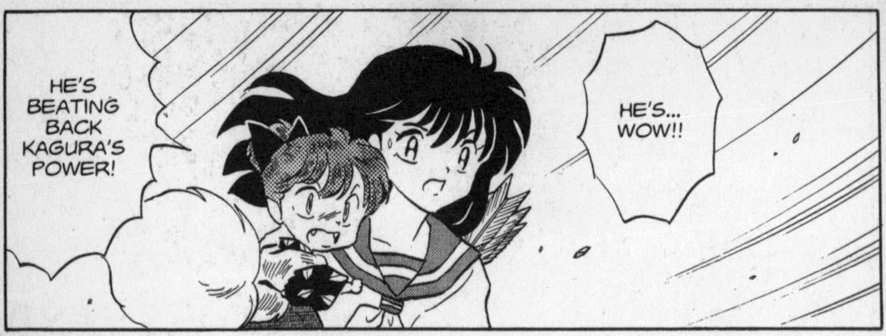
HE'S BEATING BACK KAGURA'S POWER!
HE'S... WOW!!

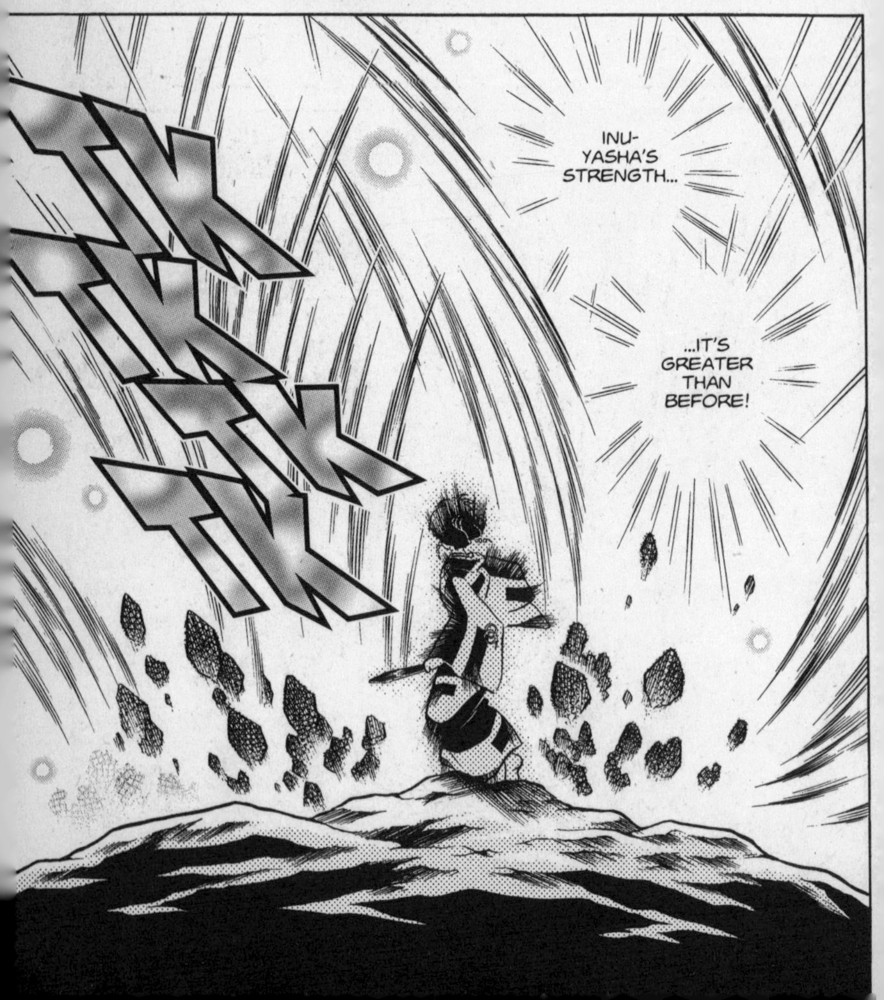
INU-YASHA'S STRENGTH...
...IT'S GREATER THAN BEFORE!

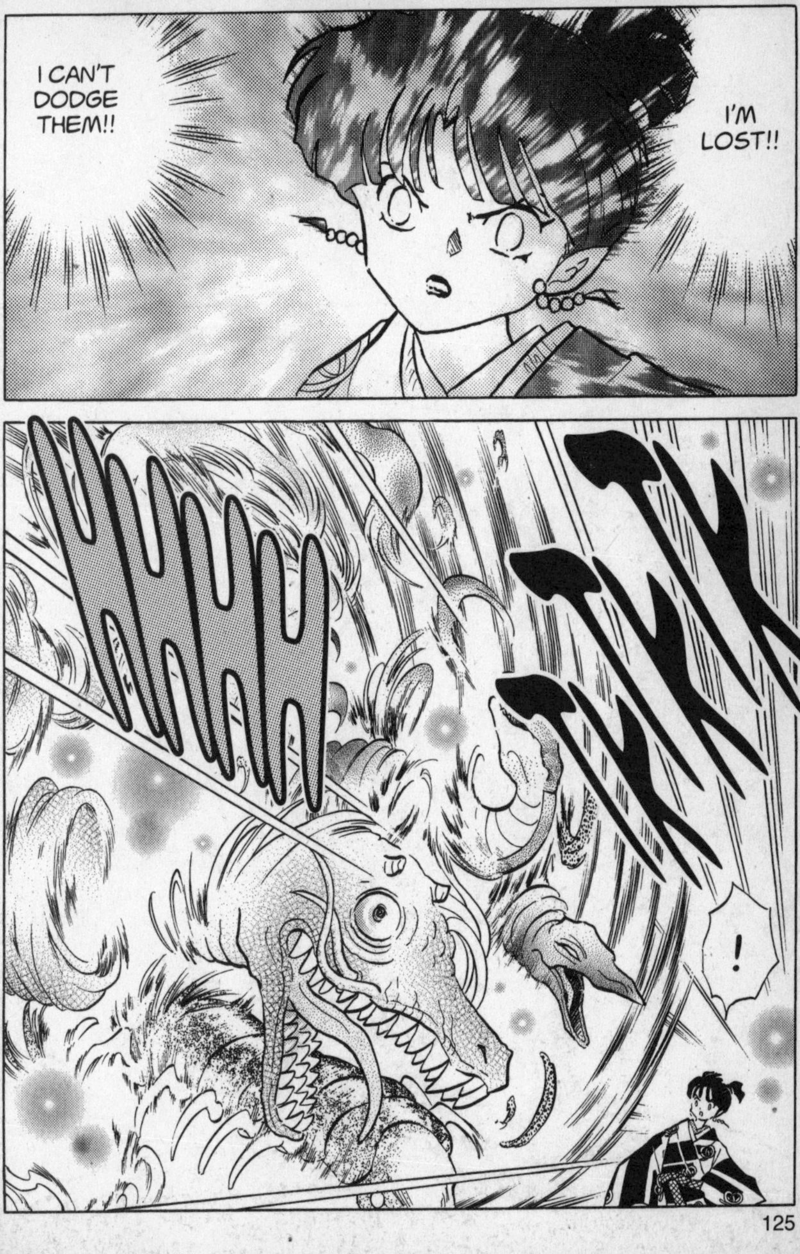
I CAN'T DODGE THEM!!
I'M LOST!!
!

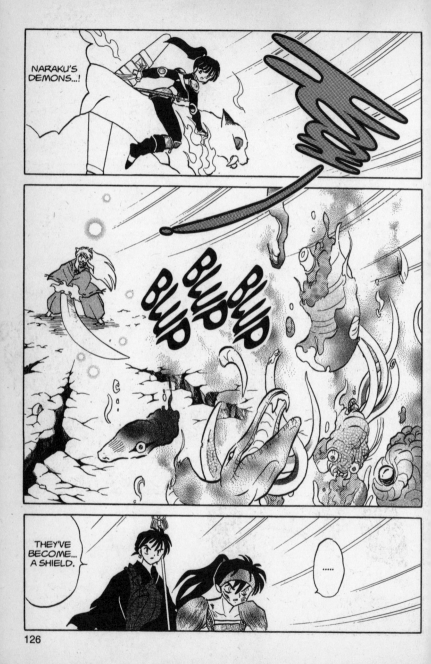

NARAKU'S DEMONS...!

BLUP
BLUP
BLUP
BLUP

THEY'VE BECOME... A SHIELD.

.....

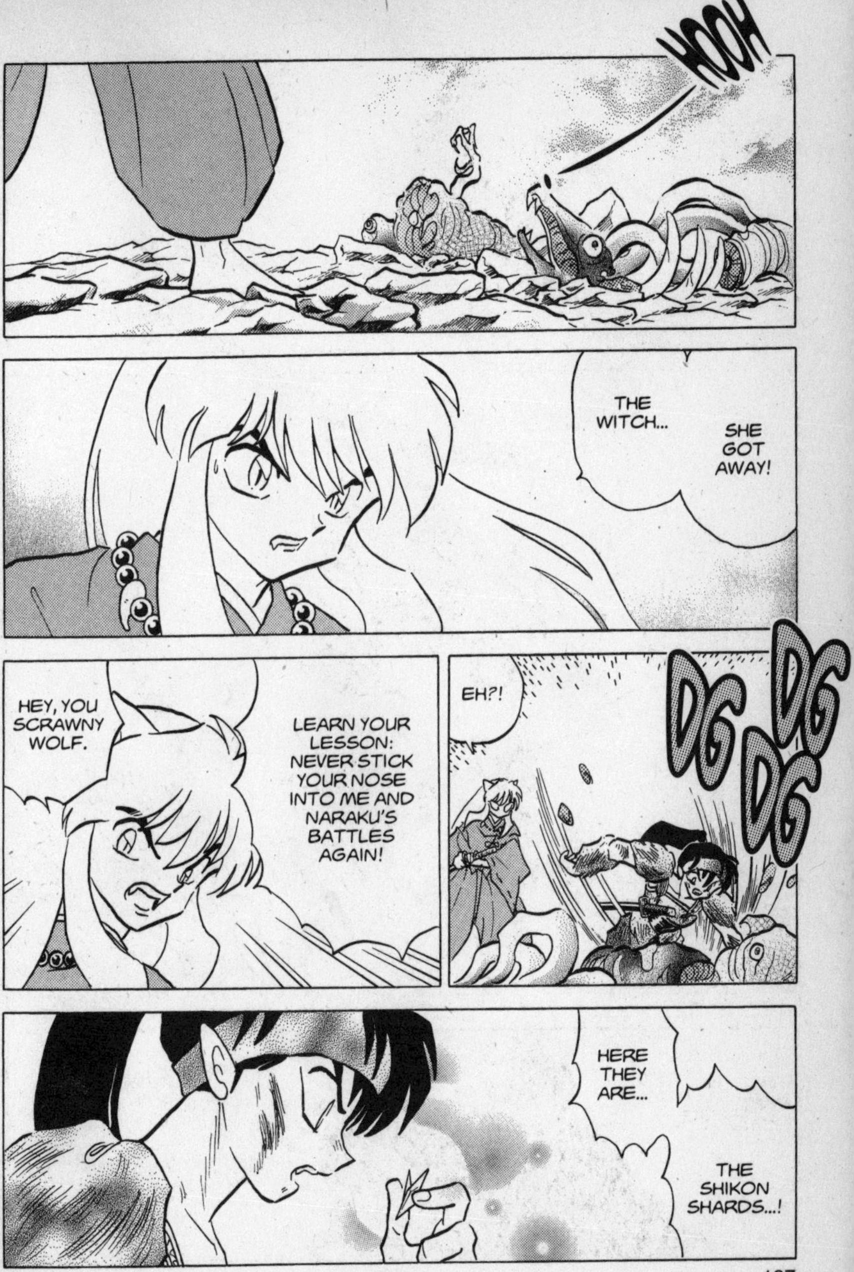

HOOH
THE WITCH...
SHE GOT AWAY!
HEY, YOU SCRAWNY WOLF.
LEARN YOUR LESSON: NEVER STICK YOUR NOSE INTO ME AND NARAKU'S BATTLES AGAIN!
EH?!
DG DG DG DG
HERE THEY ARE...
THE SHIKON SHARDS...!

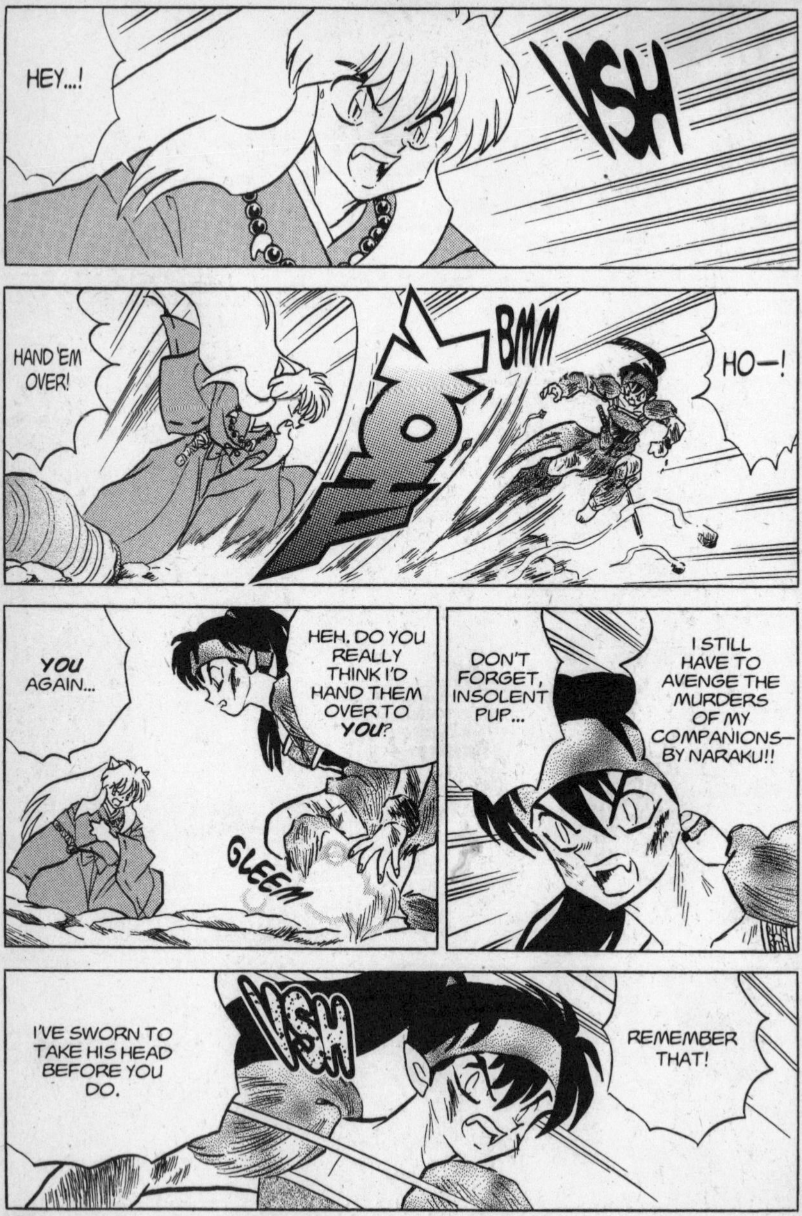
HEY...!
VSH
HAND 'EM OVER!
BMM
HO—!
YOU AGAIN...
HEH. DO YOU REALLY THINK I'D HAND THEM OVER TO YOU?
GLEEM
DON'T FORGET, INSOLENT PUP...
I STILL HAVE TO AVENGE THE MURDERS OF MY COMPANIONS—BY NARAKU!!
I'VE SWORN TO TAKE HIS HEAD BEFORE YOU DO.
VSH
REMEMBER THAT!

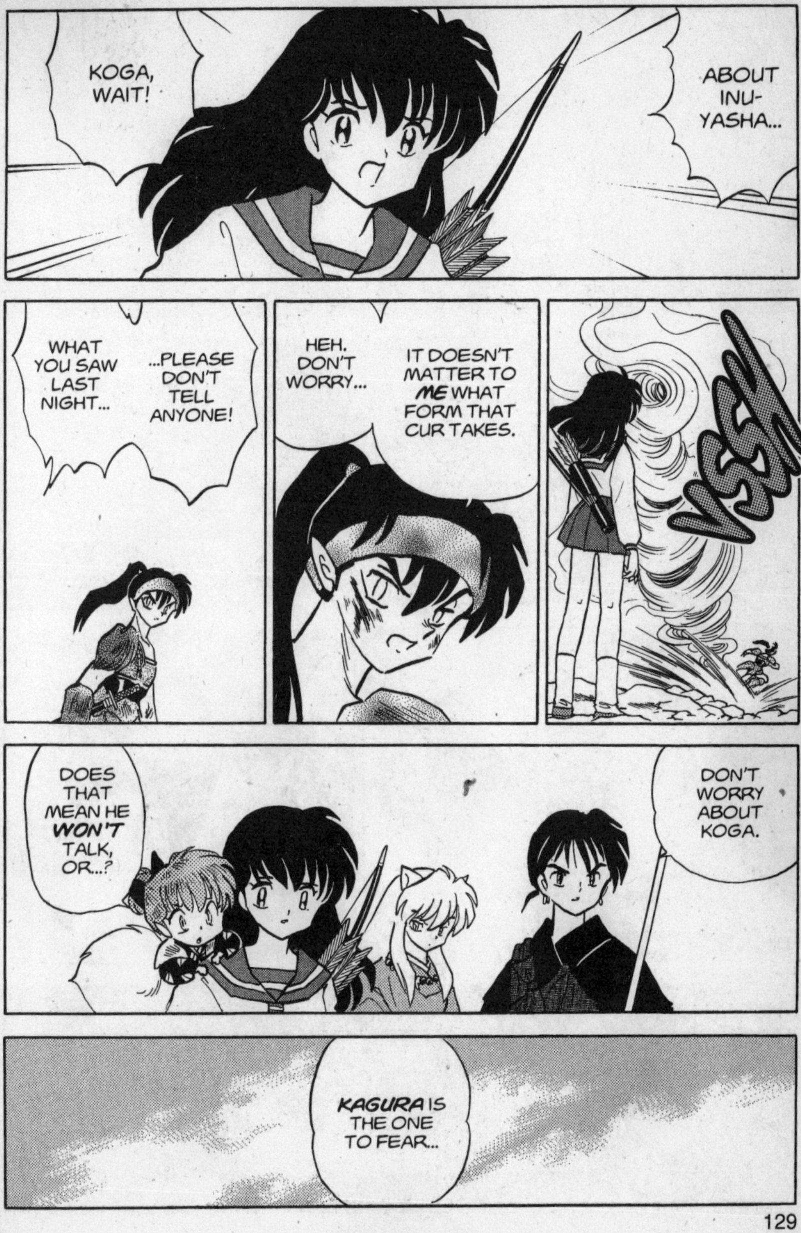
KOGA, WAIT!
ABOUT INU-YASHA...
WHAT YOU SAW LAST NIGHT...
...PLEASE DON'T TELL ANYONE!
HEH. DON'T WORRY...
IT DOESN'T MATTER TO *ME* WHAT FORM THAT CUR TAKES.
VSSSH
DOES THAT MEAN HE *WON'T* TALK, OR...?
DON'T WORRY ABOUT KOGA.
KAGURA IS THE ONE TO FEAR...

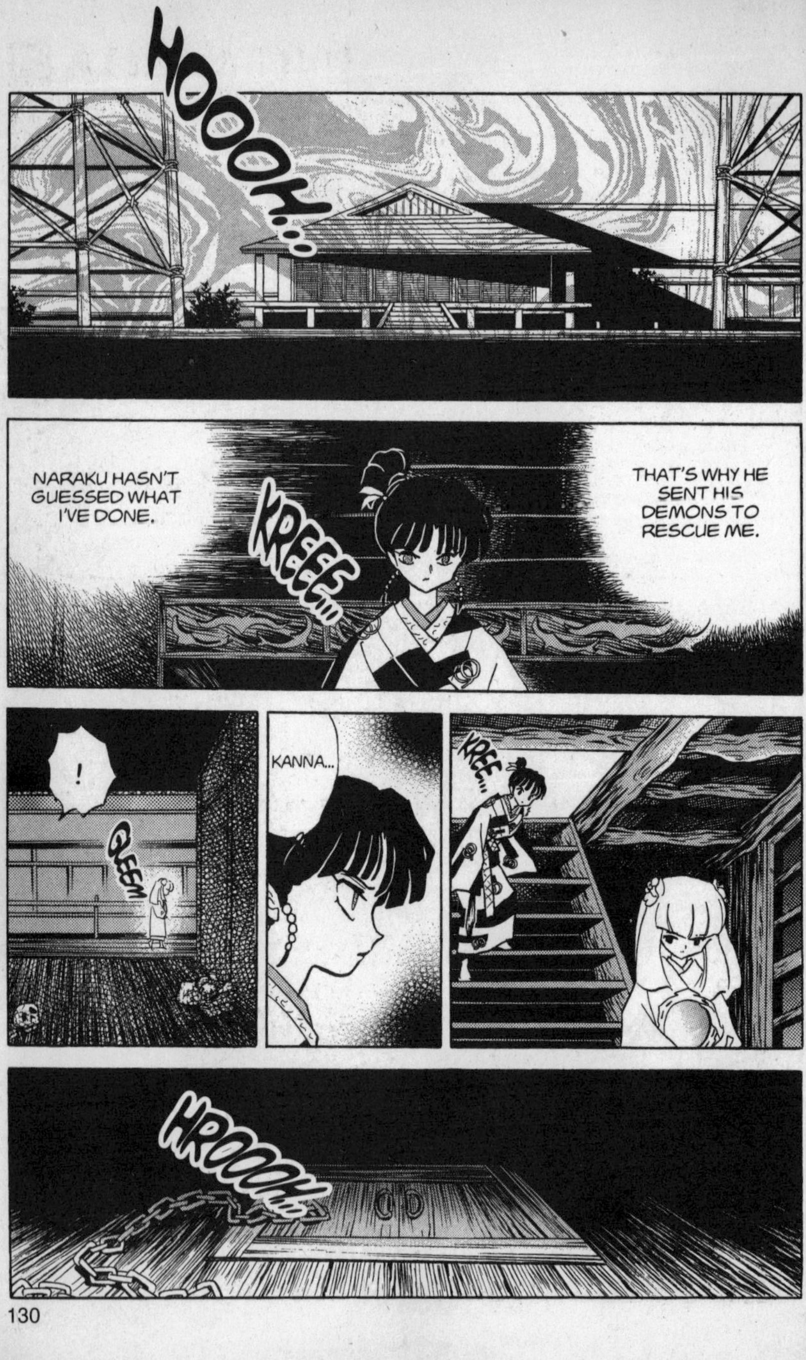
HOOOH...
NARAKU HASN'T GUESSED WHAT I'VE DONE.
KREEE...
THAT'S WHY HE SENT HIS DEMONS TO RESCUE ME.
!
GLEEM
KANNA...
KREE...
HROOOH...

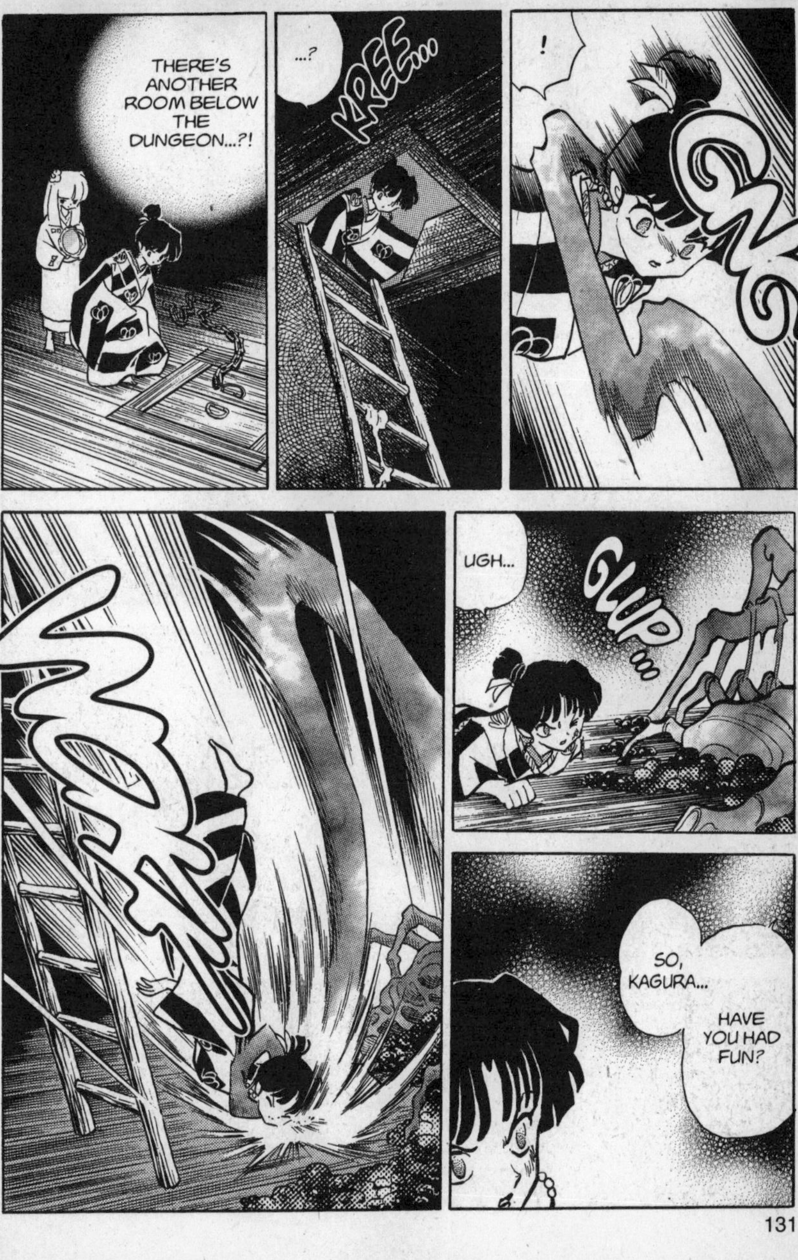
THERE'S ANOTHER ROOM BELOW THE DUNGEON...?!
...?
KREE...
!
UGH...
SO, KAGURA...
HAVE YOU HAD FUN?

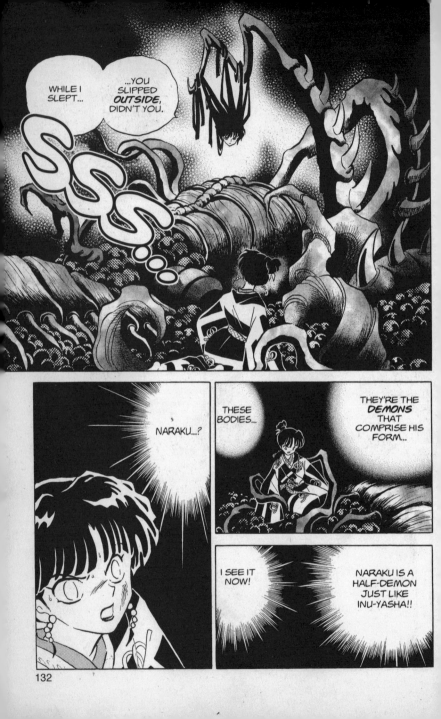

WHILE I SLEPT...

...YOU SLIPPED *OUTSIDE*, DIDN'T YOU.

SSS...

NARAKU...?

THESE BODIES...

THEY'RE THE *DEMONS* THAT COMPRISE HIS FORM...

I SEE IT NOW!

NARAKU IS A HALF-DEMON JUST LIKE INU-YASHA!!

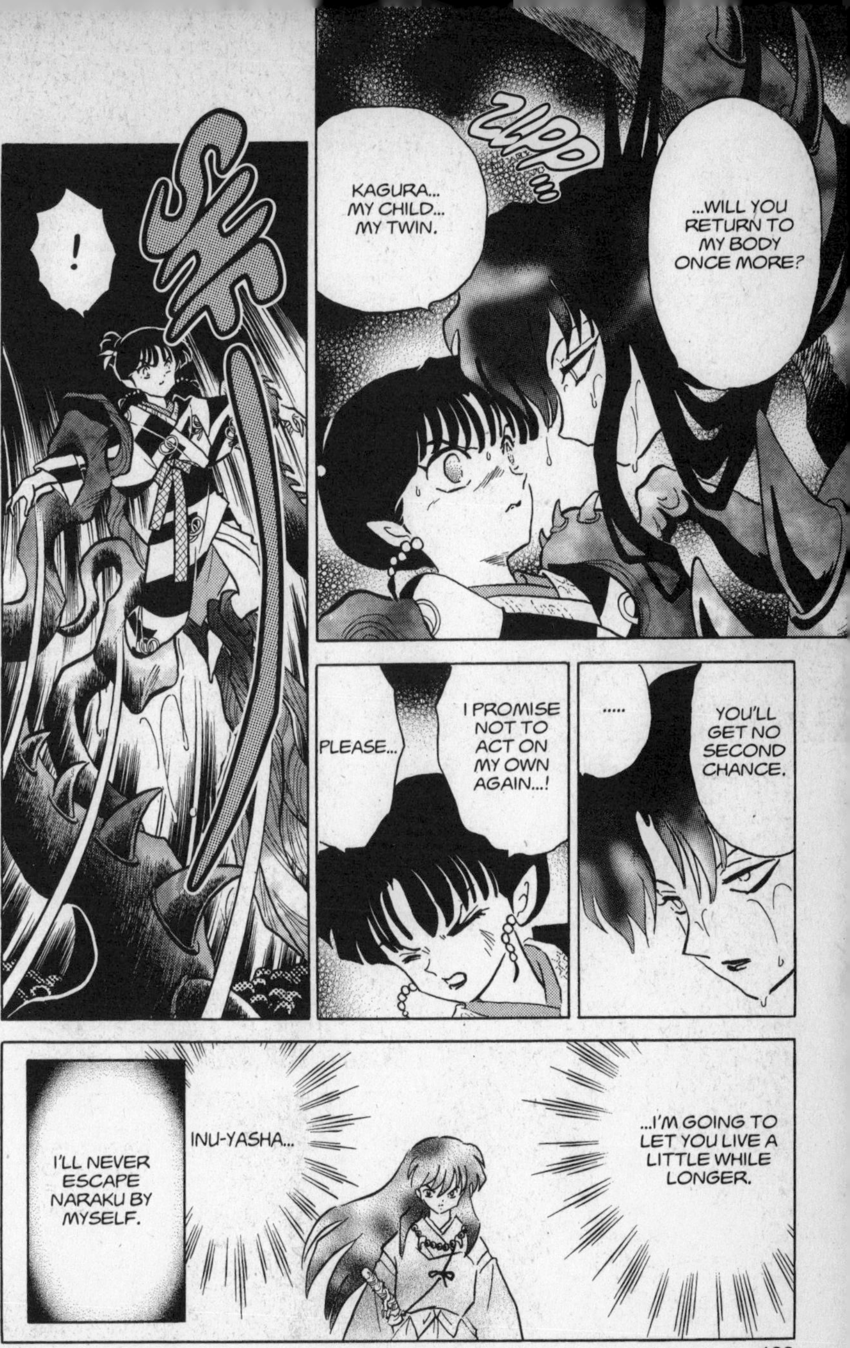
!
SHF
ZIPP...
KAGURA... MY CHILD... MY TWIN.
...WILL YOU RETURN TO MY BODY ONCE MORE?
PLEASE...
I PROMISE NOT TO ACT ON MY OWN AGAIN...!
.....
YOU'LL GET NO SECOND CHANCE.
I'LL NEVER ESCAPE NARAKU BY MYSELF.
INU-YASHA...
...I'M GOING TO LET YOU LIVE A LITTLE WHILE LONGER.

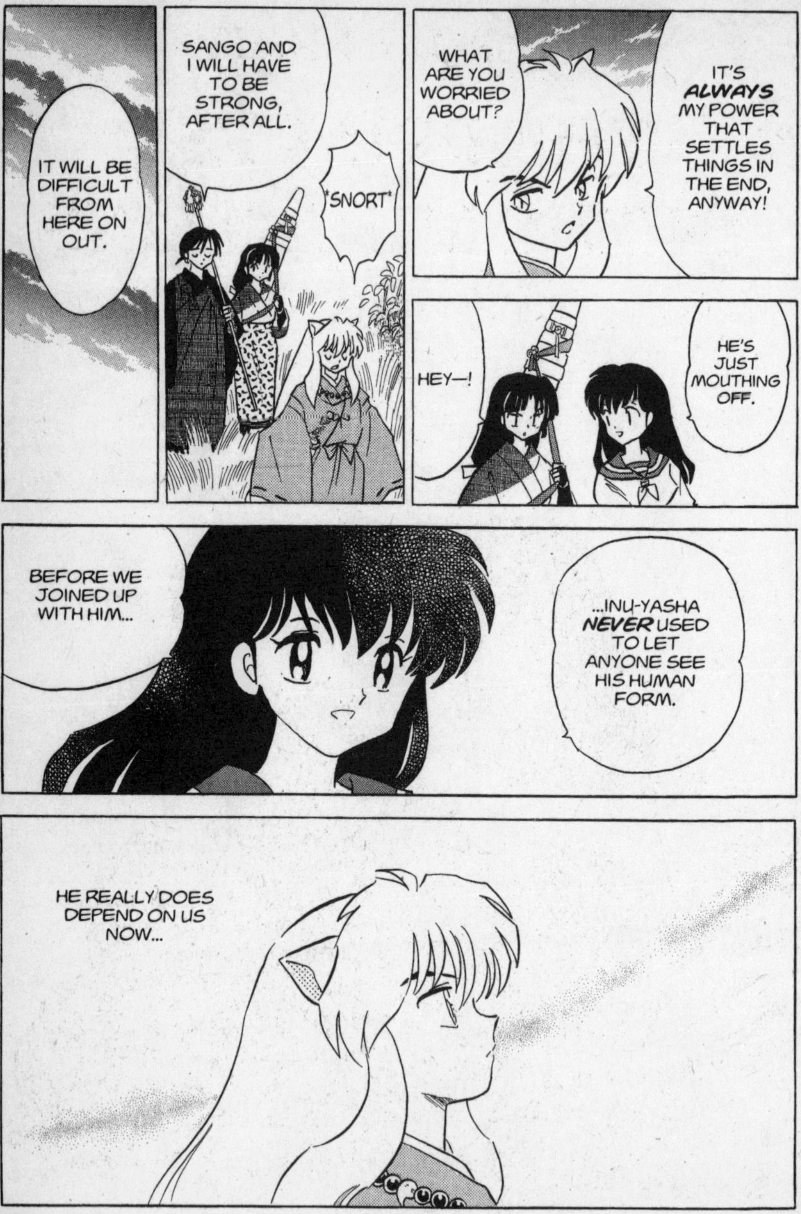
IT WILL BE DIFFICULT FROM HERE ON OUT.
SANGO AND I WILL HAVE TO BE STRONG, AFTER ALL.
SNORT
WHAT ARE YOU WORRIED ABOUT?
IT'S ALWAYS MY POWER THAT SETTLES THINGS IN THE END, ANYWAY!
HEY—!
HE'S JUST MOUTHING OFF.
BEFORE WE JOINED UP WITH HIM...
...INU-YASHA NEVER USED TO LET ANYONE SEE HIS HUMAN FORM.
HE REALLY DOES DEPEND ON US NOW...

SCROLL EIGHT
THE PRINCESS IN THE MOUNTAINS

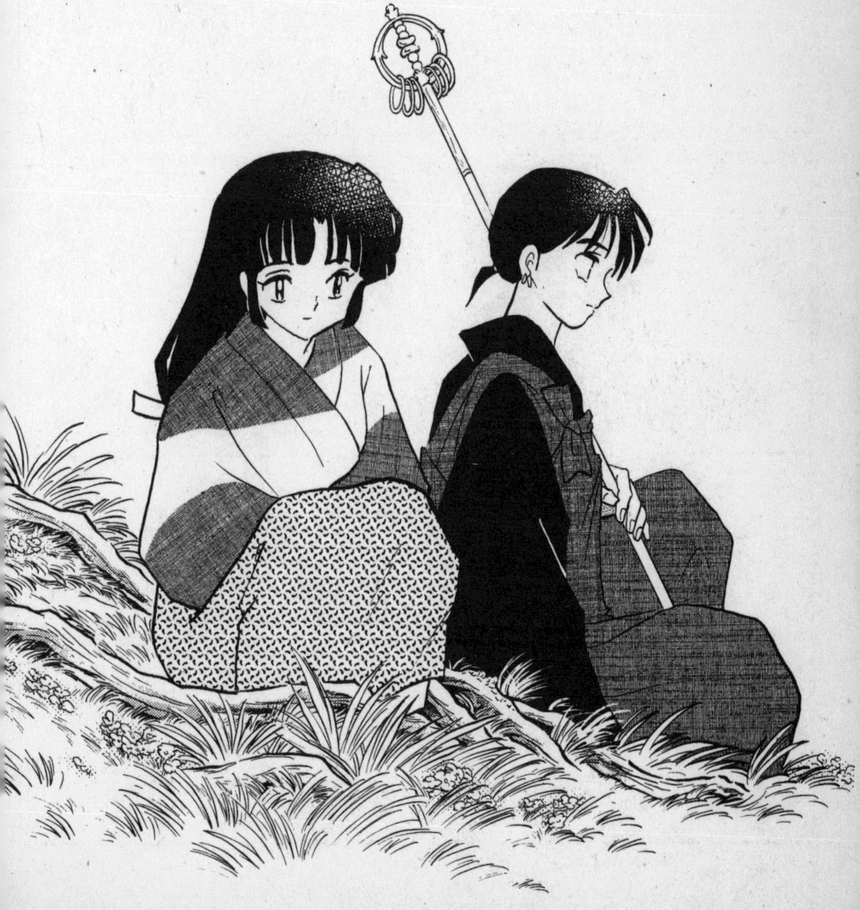

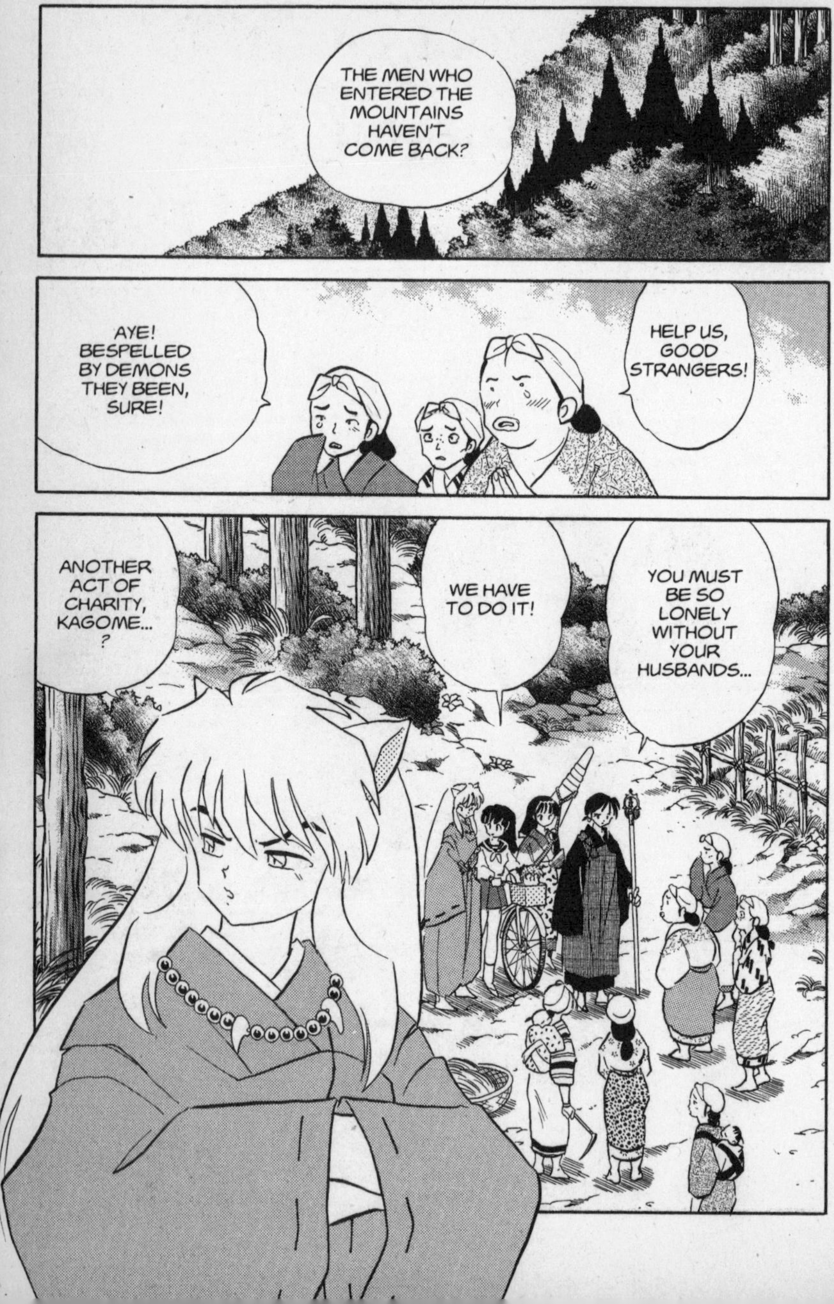
THE MEN WHO ENTERED THE MOUNTAINS HAVEN'T COME BACK?
AYE! BESPELLED BY DEMONS THEY BEEN, SURE!
HELP US, GOOD STRANGERS!
ANOTHER ACT OF CHARITY, KAGOME...?
WE HAVE TO DO IT!
YOU MUST BE SO LONELY WITHOUT YOUR HUSBANDS...

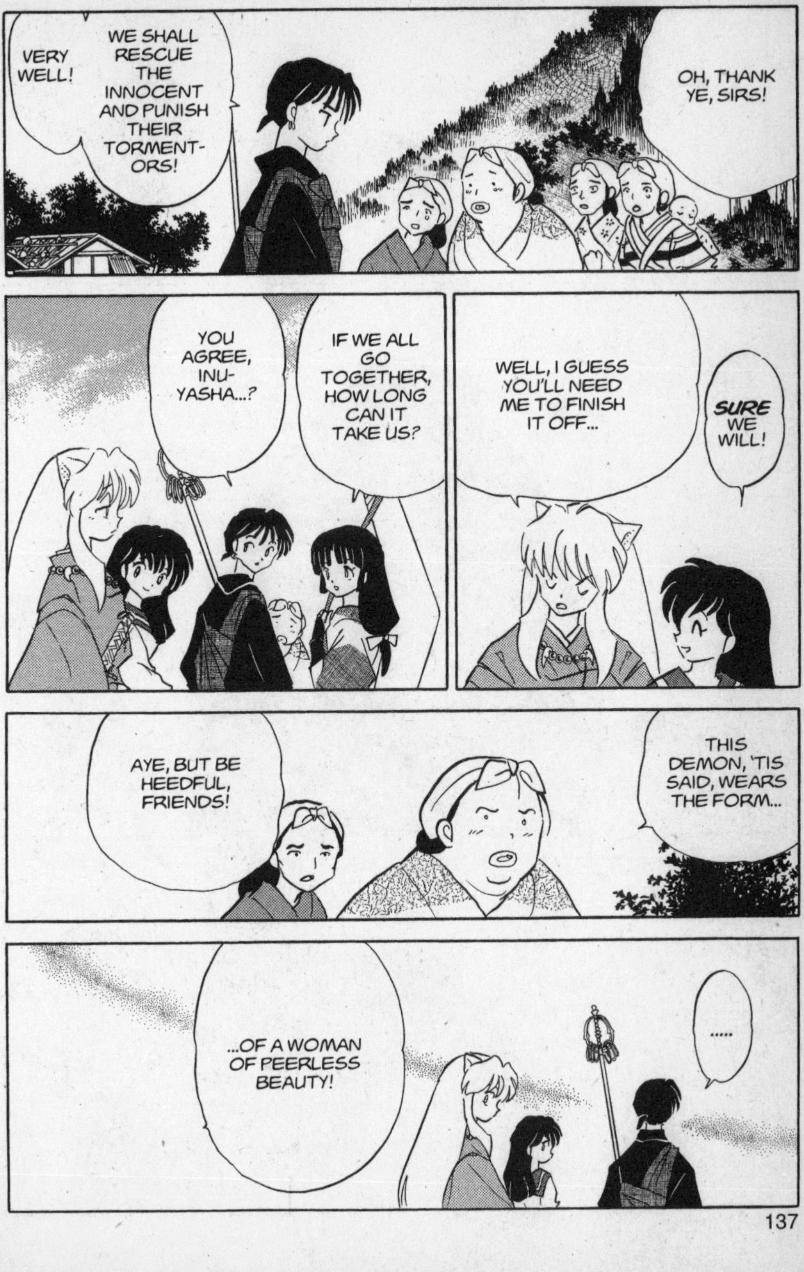
VERY WELL!
WE SHALL RESCUE THE INNOCENT AND PUNISH THEIR TORMENT-ORS!
OH, THANK YE, SIRS!
YOU AGREE, INU-YASHA...?
IF WE ALL GO TOGETHER, HOW LONG CAN IT TAKE US?
WELL, I GUESS YOU'LL NEED ME TO FINISH IT OFF...
SURE WE WILL!
AYE, BUT BE HEEDFUL, FRIENDS!
THIS DEMON, 'TIS SAID, WEARS THE FORM...
...OF A WOMAN OF PEERLESS BEAUTY!
.....

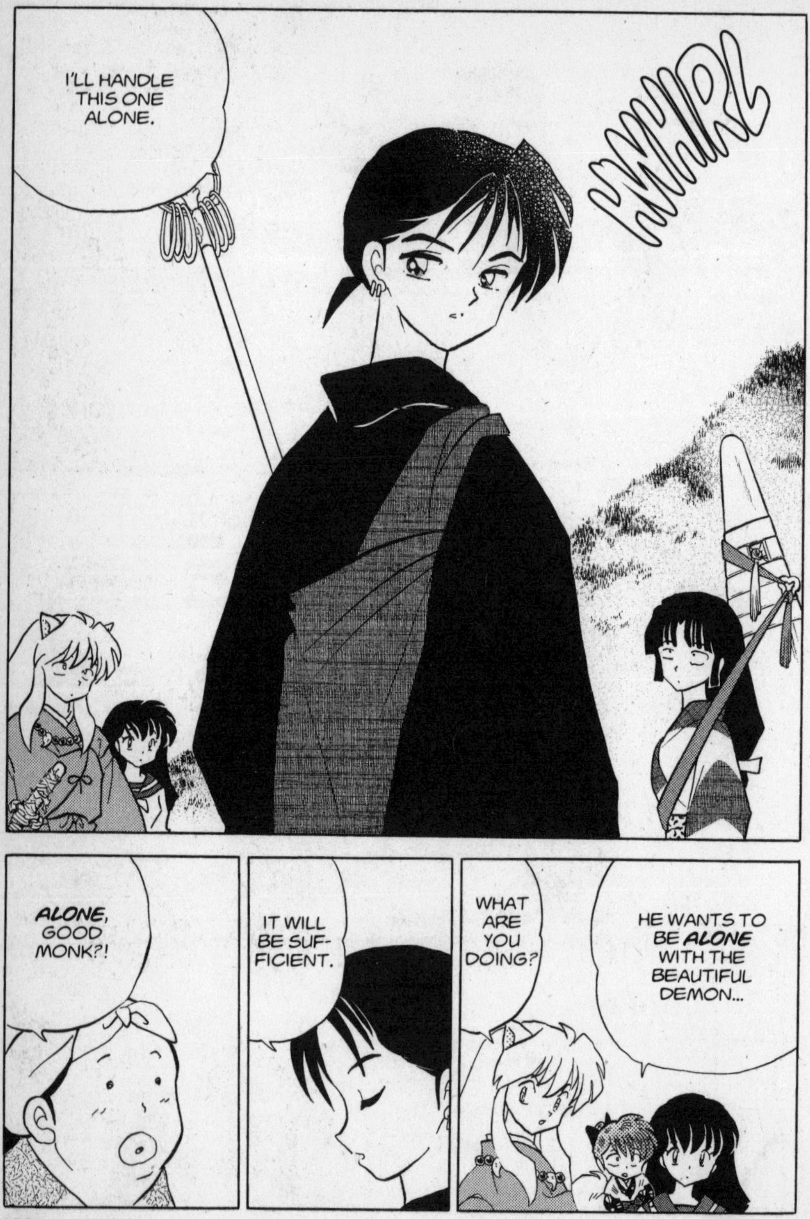
I'LL HANDLE THIS ONE ALONE.
WHIRL
ALONE, GOOD MONK?!
IT WILL BE SUF-FICIENT.
WHAT ARE YOU DOING?
HE WANTS TO BE ALONE WITH THE BEAUTIFUL DEMON...

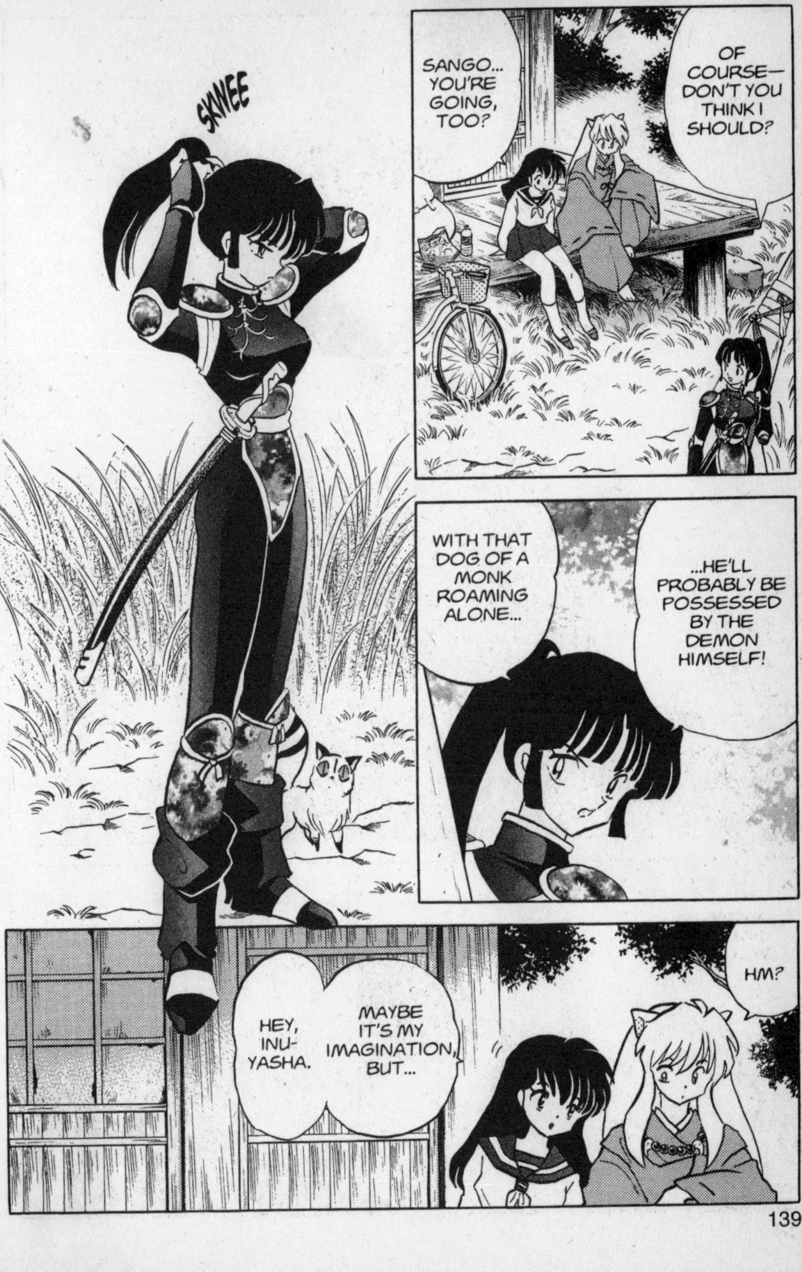
SKWEE
SANGO... YOU'RE GOING, TOO?
OF COURSE— DON'T YOU THINK I SHOULD?
WITH THAT DOG OF A MONK ROAMING ALONE...
...HE'LL PROBABLY BE POSSESSED BY THE DEMON HIMSELF!
HEY, INU-YASHA.
MAYBE IT'S MY IMAGINATION, BUT...
HM?

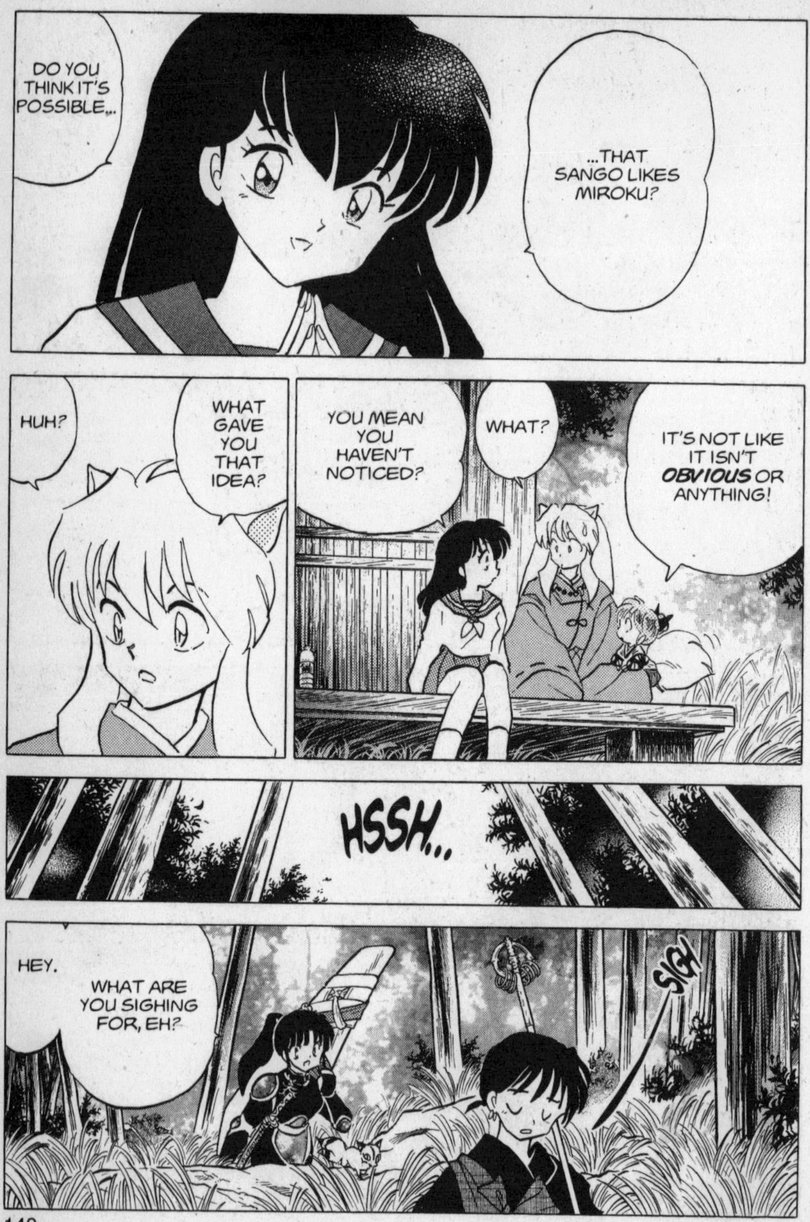
DO YOU THINK IT'S POSSIBLE...
...THAT SANGO LIKES MIROKU?
HUH?
WHAT GAVE YOU THAT IDEA?
YOU MEAN YOU HAVEN'T NOTICED?
WHAT?
IT'S NOT LIKE IT ISN'T **OBVIOUS** OR ANYTHING!
HSSH...
HEY.
WHAT ARE YOU SIGHING FOR, EH?
SIGH

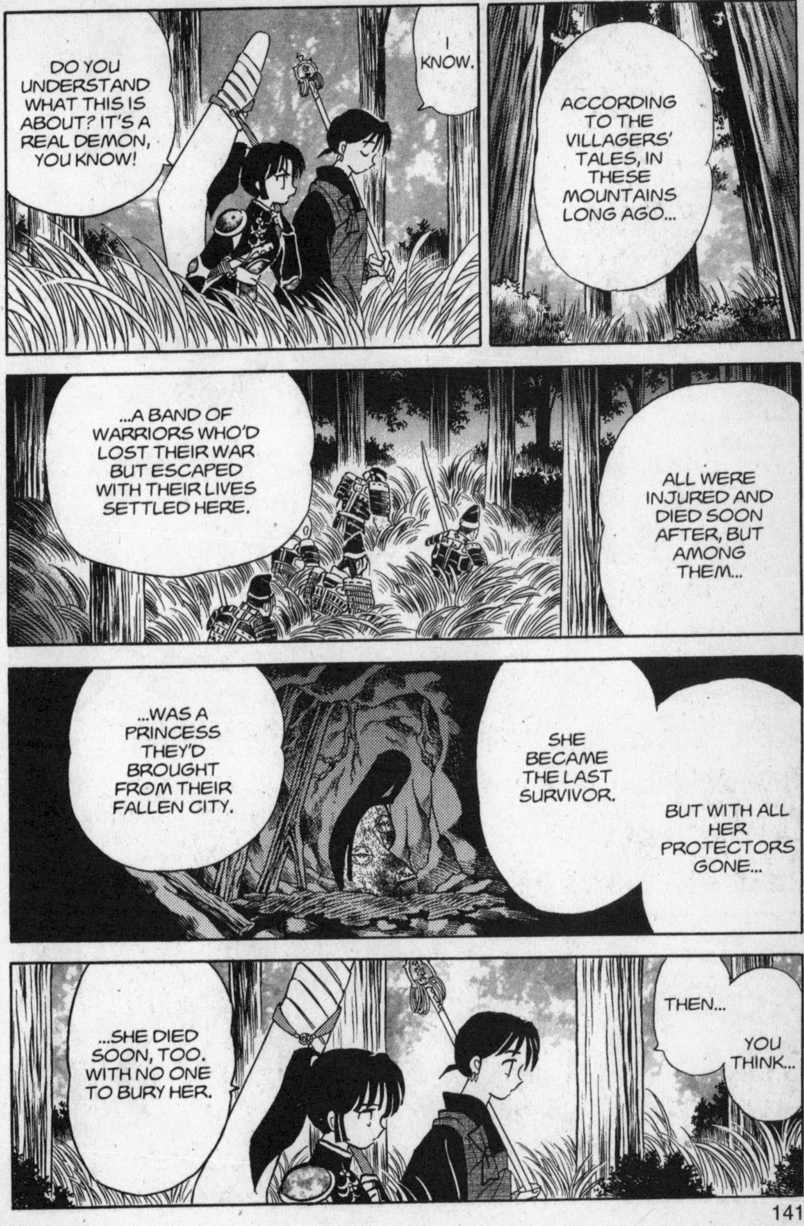
DO YOU UNDERSTAND WHAT THIS IS ABOUT? IT'S A REAL DEMON, YOU KNOW!
I KNOW.
ACCORDING TO THE VILLAGERS' TALES, IN THESE MOUNTAINS LONG AGO...
...A BAND OF WARRIORS WHO'D LOST THEIR WAR BUT ESCAPED WITH THEIR LIVES SETTLED HERE.
ALL WERE INJURED AND DIED SOON AFTER, BUT AMONG THEM...
...WAS A PRINCESS THEY'D BROUGHT FROM THEIR FALLEN CITY.
SHE BECAME THE LAST SURVIVOR.
BUT WITH ALL HER PROTECTORS GONE...
...SHE DIED SOON, TOO. WITH NO ONE TO BURY HER.
THEN...
YOU THINK...

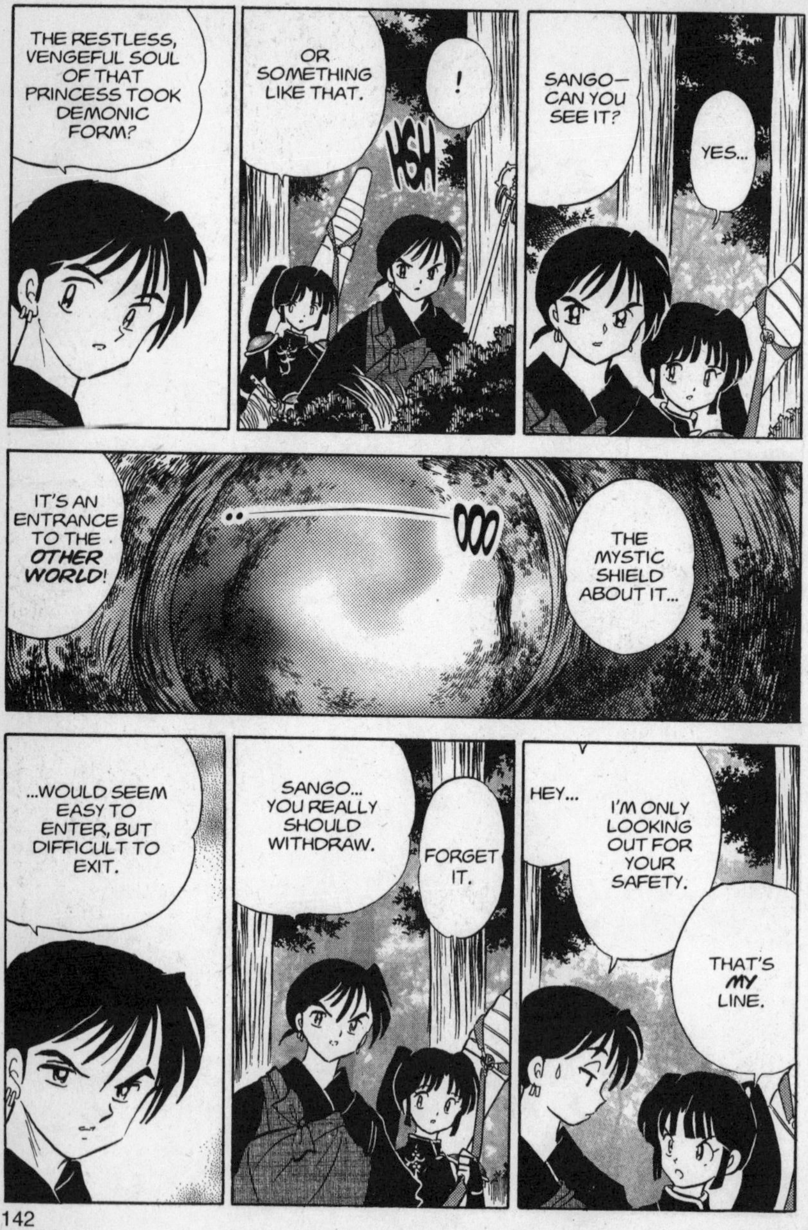
THE RESTLESS, VENGEFUL SOUL OF THAT PRINCESS TOOK DEMONIC FORM?
OR SOMETHING LIKE THAT.
!
HSH
SANGO— CAN YOU SEE IT?
YES...
IT'S AN ENTRANCE TO THE *OTHER WORLD*!
..
OOO
THE MYSTIC SHIELD ABOUT IT...
...WOULD SEEM EASY TO ENTER, BUT DIFFICULT TO EXIT.
SANGO... YOU REALLY SHOULD WITHDRAW.
FORGET IT.
HEY...
I'M ONLY LOOKING OUT FOR YOUR SAFETY.
THAT'S *MY* LINE.

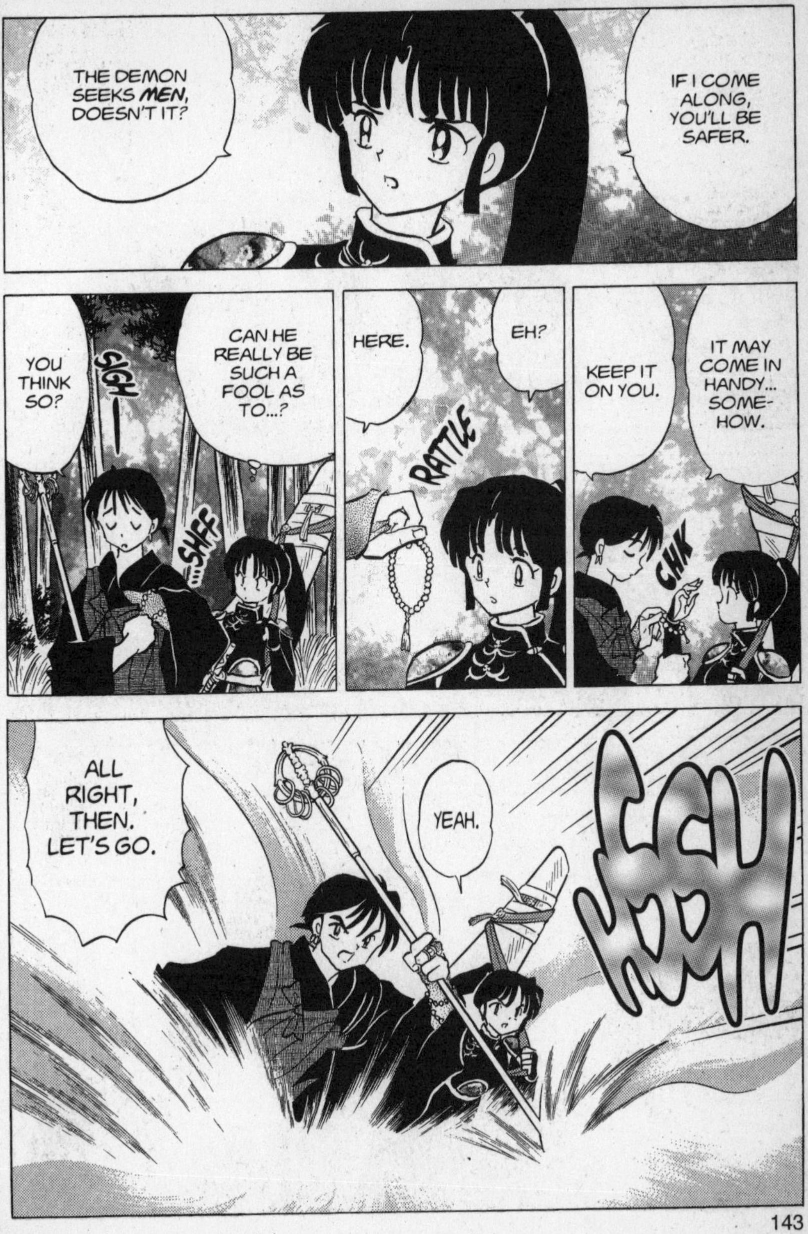
THE DEMON SEEKS *MEN*, DOESN'T IT?
IF I COME ALONG, YOU'LL BE SAFER.
YOU THINK SO?
SIGH
CAN HE REALLY BE SUCH A FOOL AS TO...?
...SHFF
HERE.
EH?
RATTLE
KEEP IT ON YOU.
IT MAY COME IN HANDY... SOME-HOW.
CHK
ALL RIGHT, THEN. LET'S GO.
YEAH.

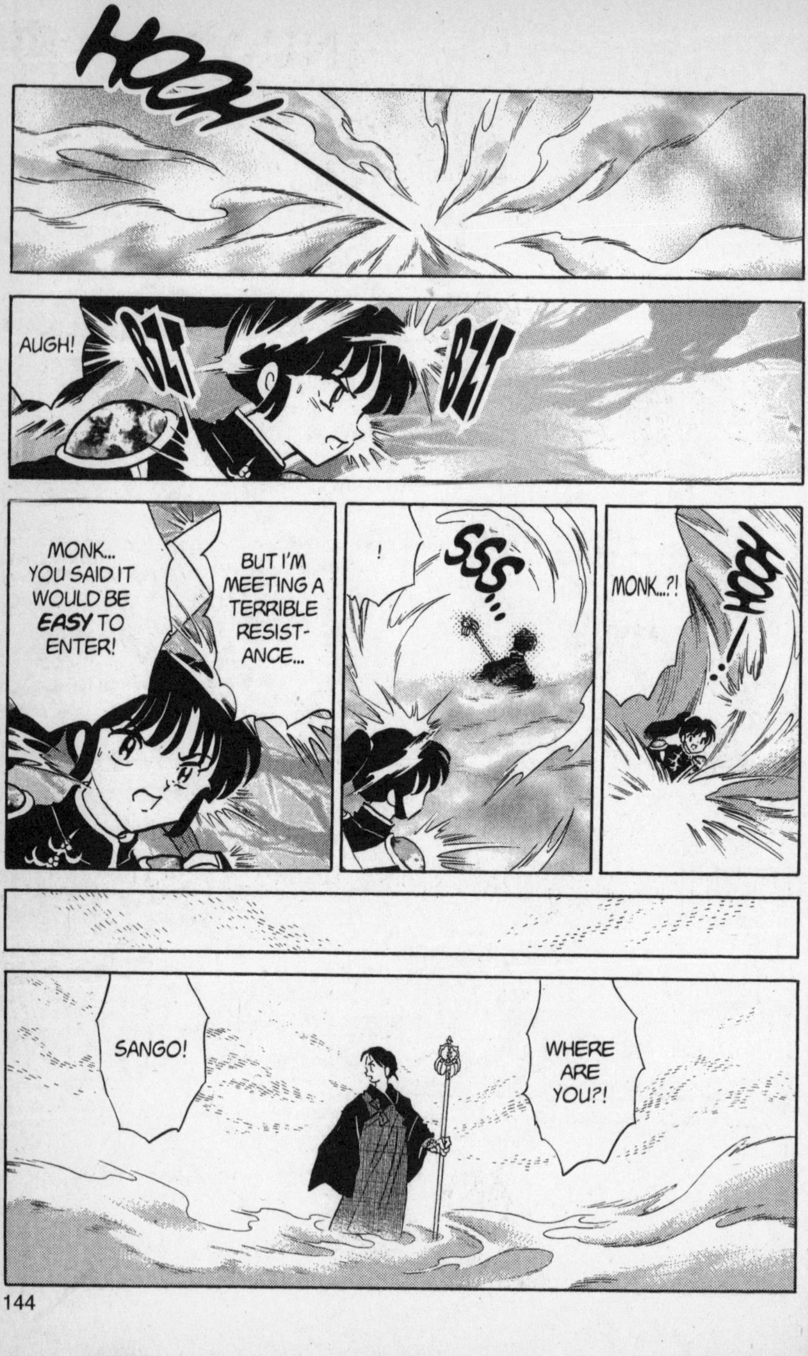
HOOH
AUGH!
BZT
BZT
MONK... YOU SAID IT WOULD BE EASY TO ENTER!
BUT I'M MEETING A TERRIBLE RESIST-ANCE...
!
SSS...
MONK...?!
HOOH
SANGO!
WHERE ARE YOU?!

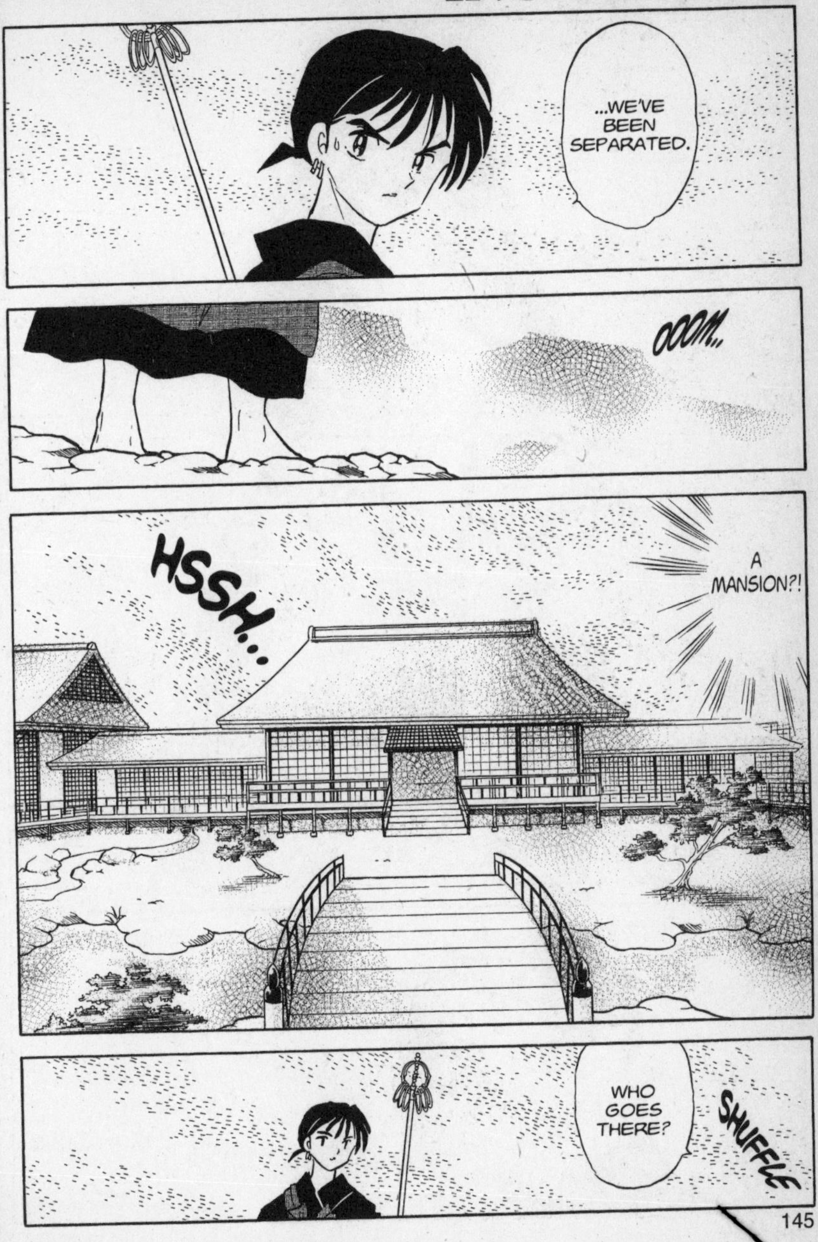
...WE'VE BEEN SEPARATED.
OOOM...
HSSH...
A MANSION?!
WHO GOES THERE?
SHUFFLE

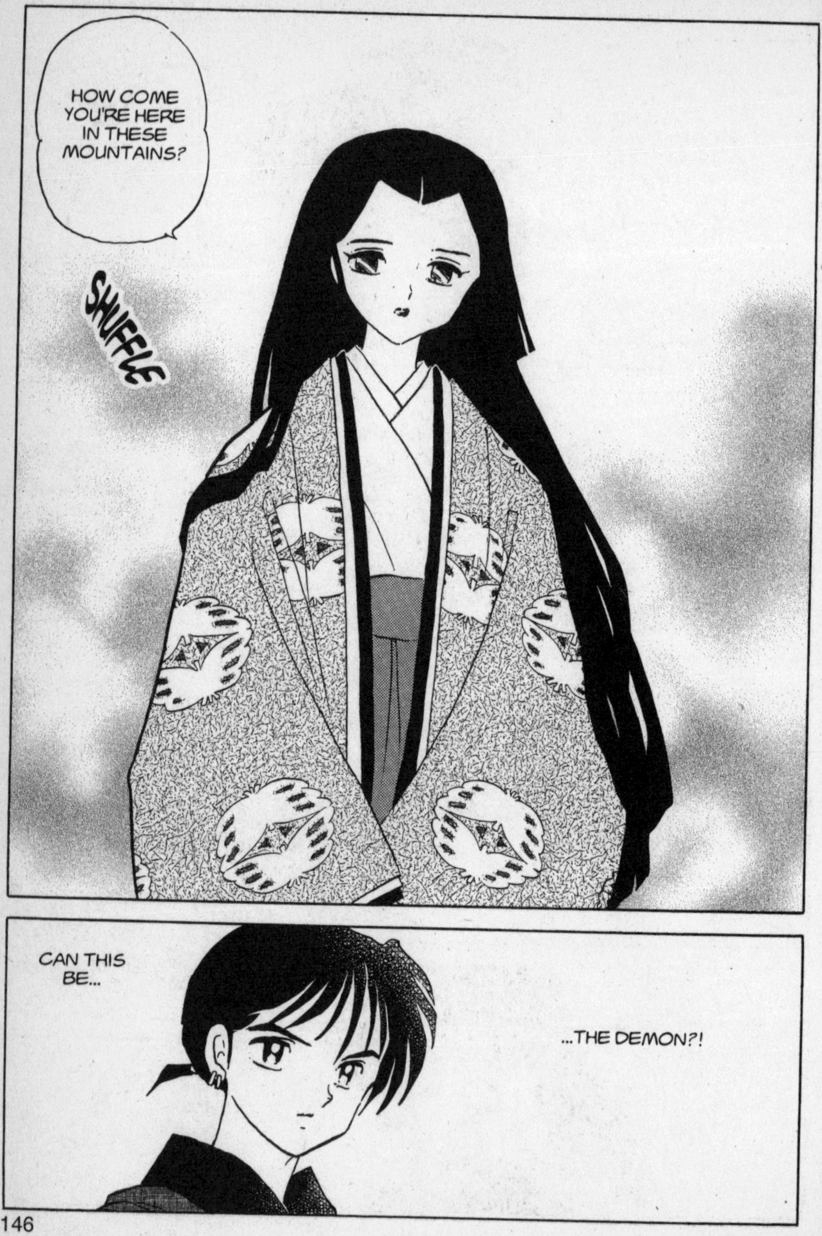
HOW COME YOU'RE HERE IN THESE MOUNTAINS?
SHUFFLE
CAN THIS BE...
...THE DEMON?!

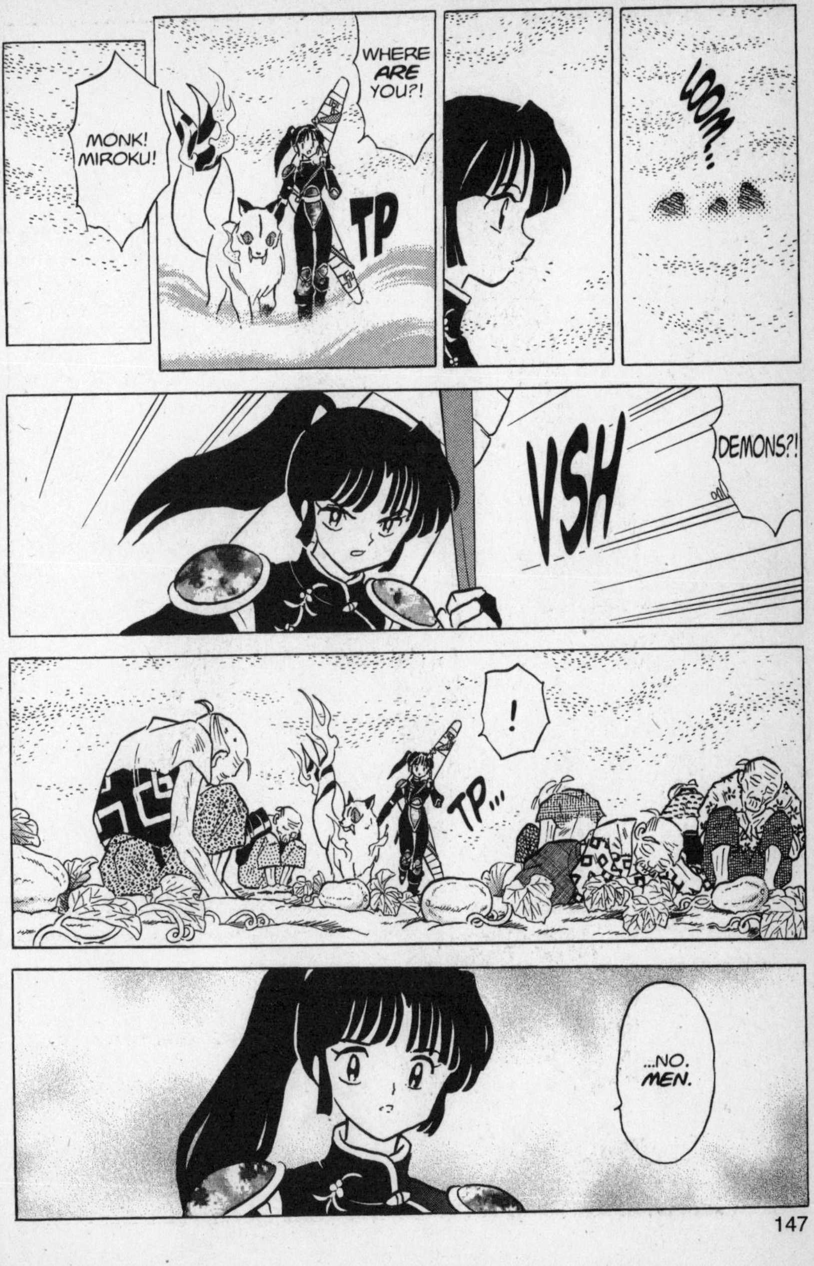
MONK! MIROKU!
WHERE ARE YOU?!
TP
LOOM...
VSH
DEMONS?!
!
TP...
...NO. MEN.

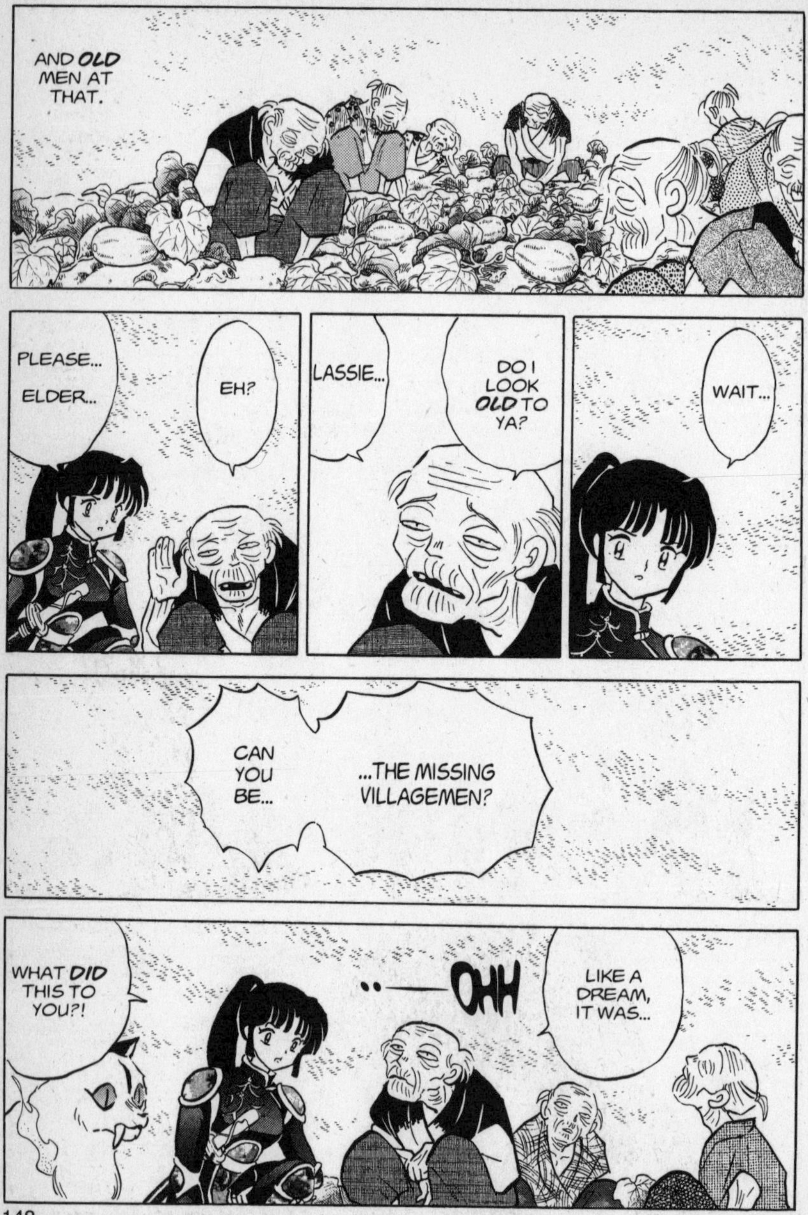
AND OLD MEN AT THAT.
PLEASE... ELDER...
EH?
LASSIE...
DO I LOOK OLD TO YA?
WAIT...
CAN YOU BE...
...THE MISSING VILLAGEMEN?
WHAT DID THIS TO YOU?!
..—OHH
LIKE A DREAM, IT WAS...

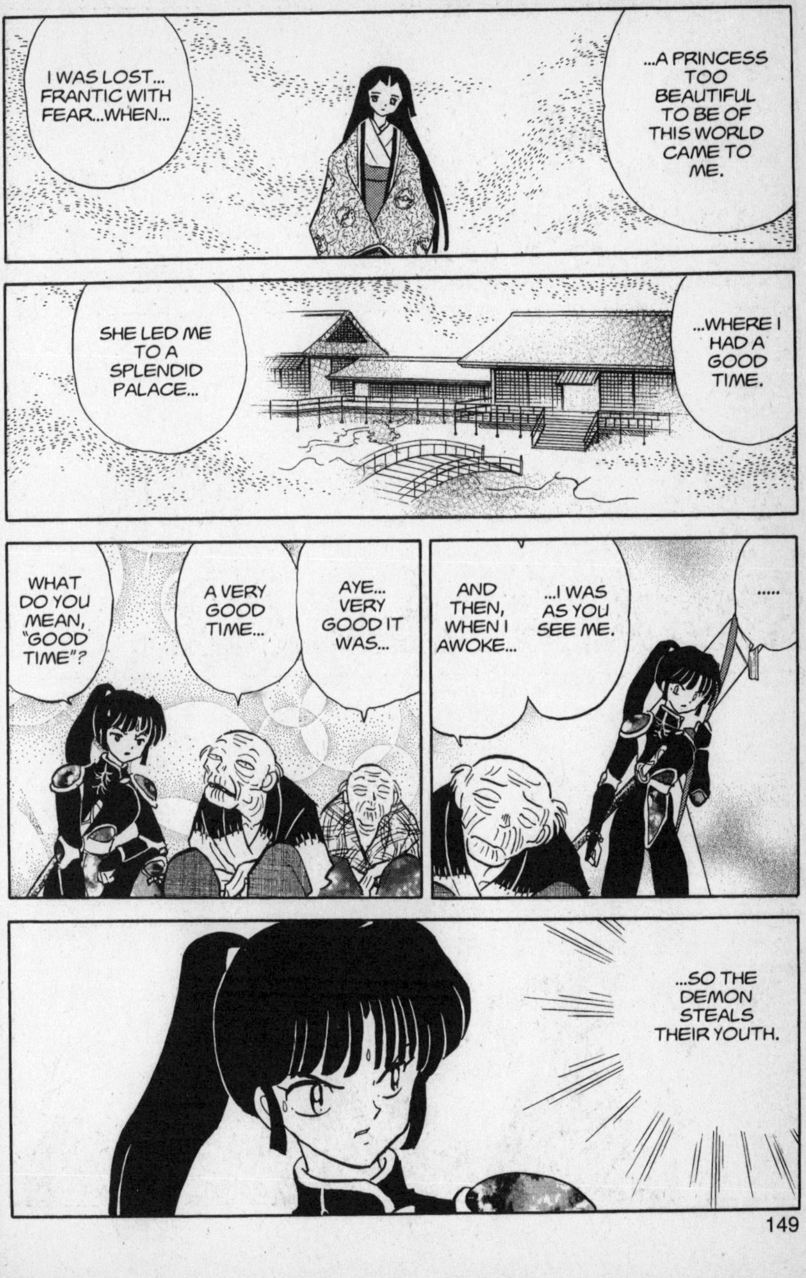
I WAS LOST... FRANTIC WITH FEAR...WHEN...
...A PRINCESS TOO BEAUTIFUL TO BE OF THIS WORLD CAME TO ME.
SHE LED ME TO A SPLENDID PALACE...
...WHERE I HAD A GOOD TIME.
WHAT DO YOU MEAN, "GOOD TIME"?
A VERY GOOD TIME...
AYE... VERY GOOD IT WAS...
AND THEN, WHEN I AWOKE...
...I WAS AS YOU SEE ME.
.....
...SO THE DEMON STEALS THEIR YOUTH.

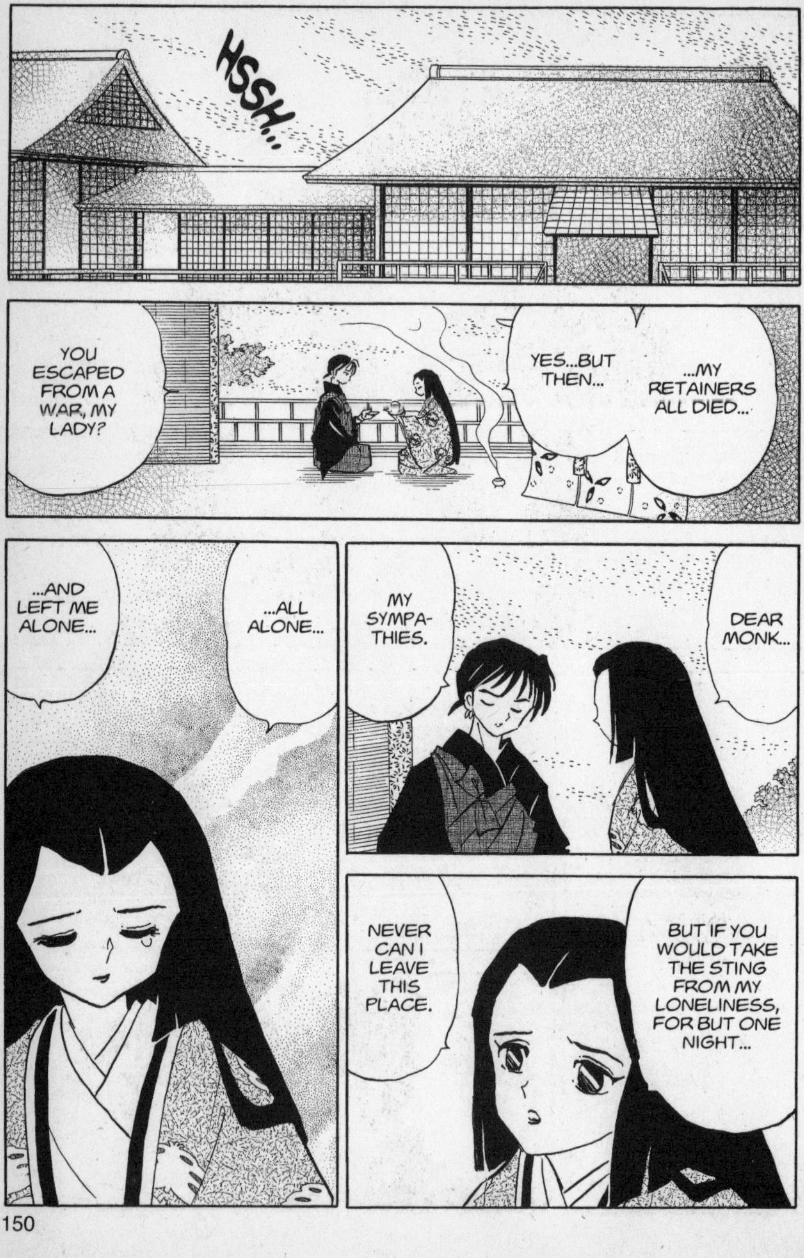
HSSH...
YOU ESCAPED FROM A WAR, MY LADY?
YES...BUT THEN...
...MY RETAINERS ALL DIED...
...AND LEFT ME ALONE...
...ALL ALONE...
MY SYMPATHIES.
DEAR MONK...
NEVER CAN I LEAVE THIS PLACE.
BUT IF YOU WOULD TAKE THE STING FROM MY LONELINESS, FOR BUT ONE NIGHT...

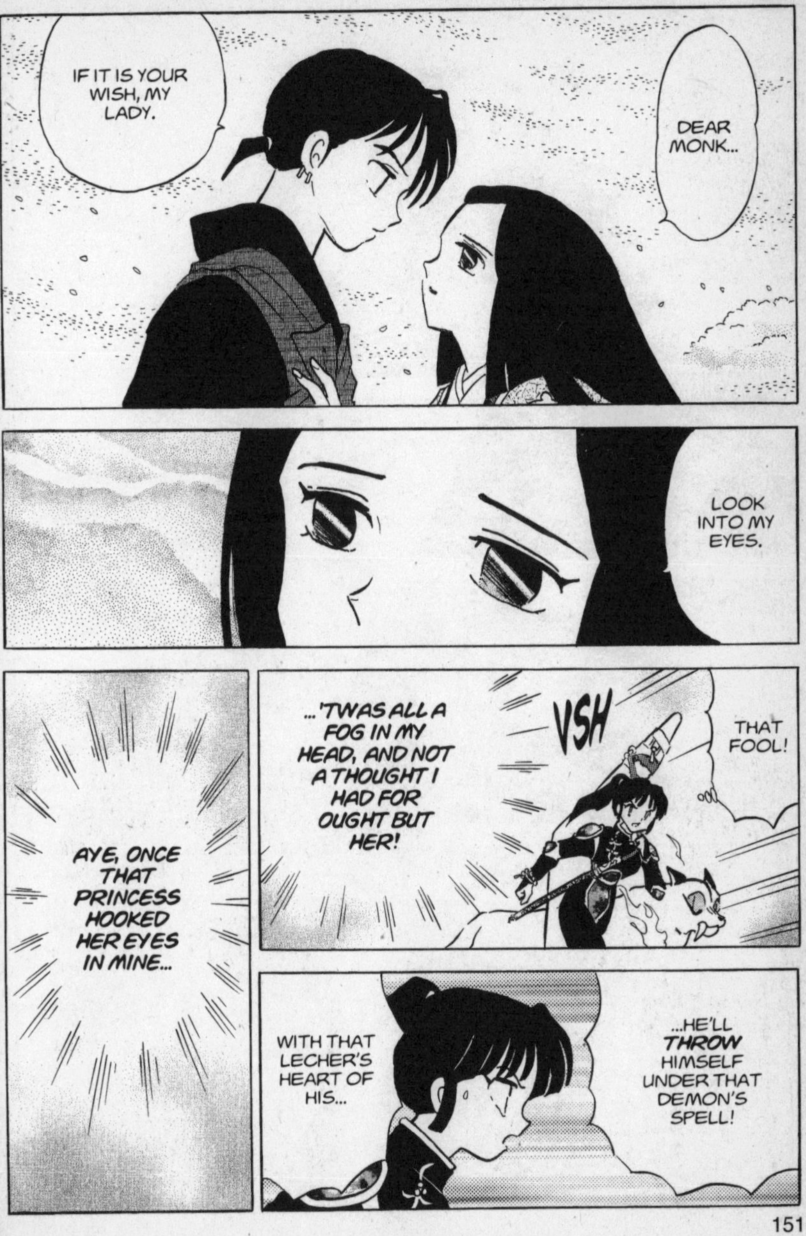
IF IT IS YOUR WISH, MY LADY.
DEAR MONK...
LOOK INTO MY EYES.
AYE, ONCE THAT PRINCESS HOOKED HER EYES IN MINE...
...'TWAS ALL A FOG IN MY HEAD, AND NOT A THOUGHT I HAD FOR OUGHT BUT HER!
VSH
THAT FOOL!
WITH THAT LECHER'S HEART OF HIS...
...HE'LL THROW HIMSELF UNDER THAT DEMON'S SPELL!

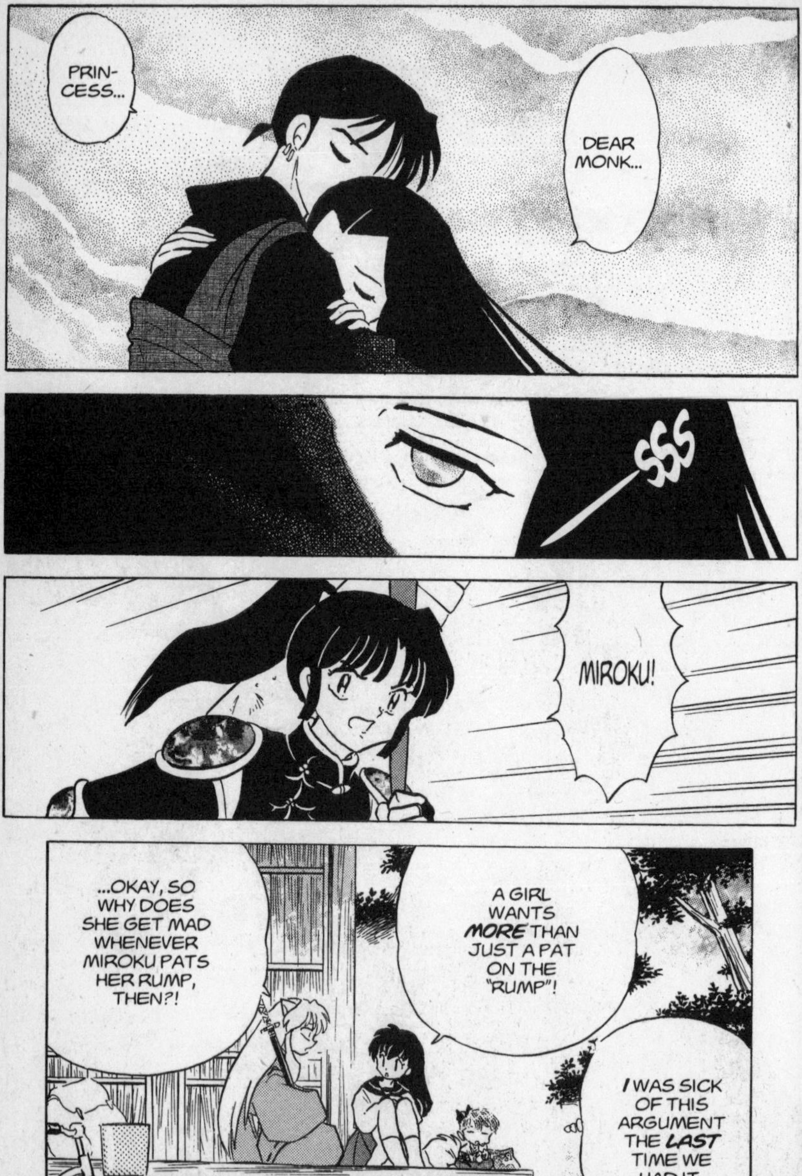
PRIN-CESS...
DEAR MONK...
SSS
MIROKU!
...OKAY, SO WHY DOES SHE GET MAD WHENEVER MIROKU PATS HER RUMP, THEN?!
A GIRL WANTS MORE THAN JUST A PAT ON THE "RUMP"!
I WAS SICK OF THIS ARGUMENT THE LAST TIME WE HAD IT.

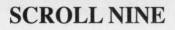

SCROLL NINE

A MAIDEN'S HEART

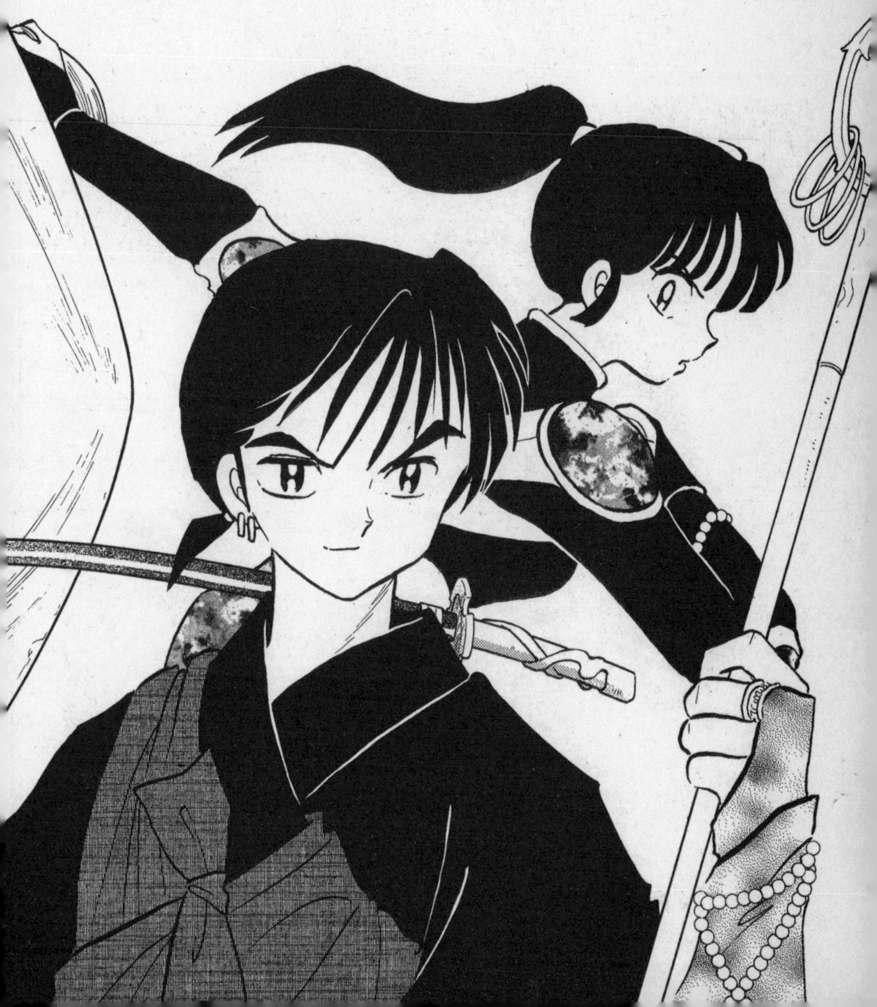

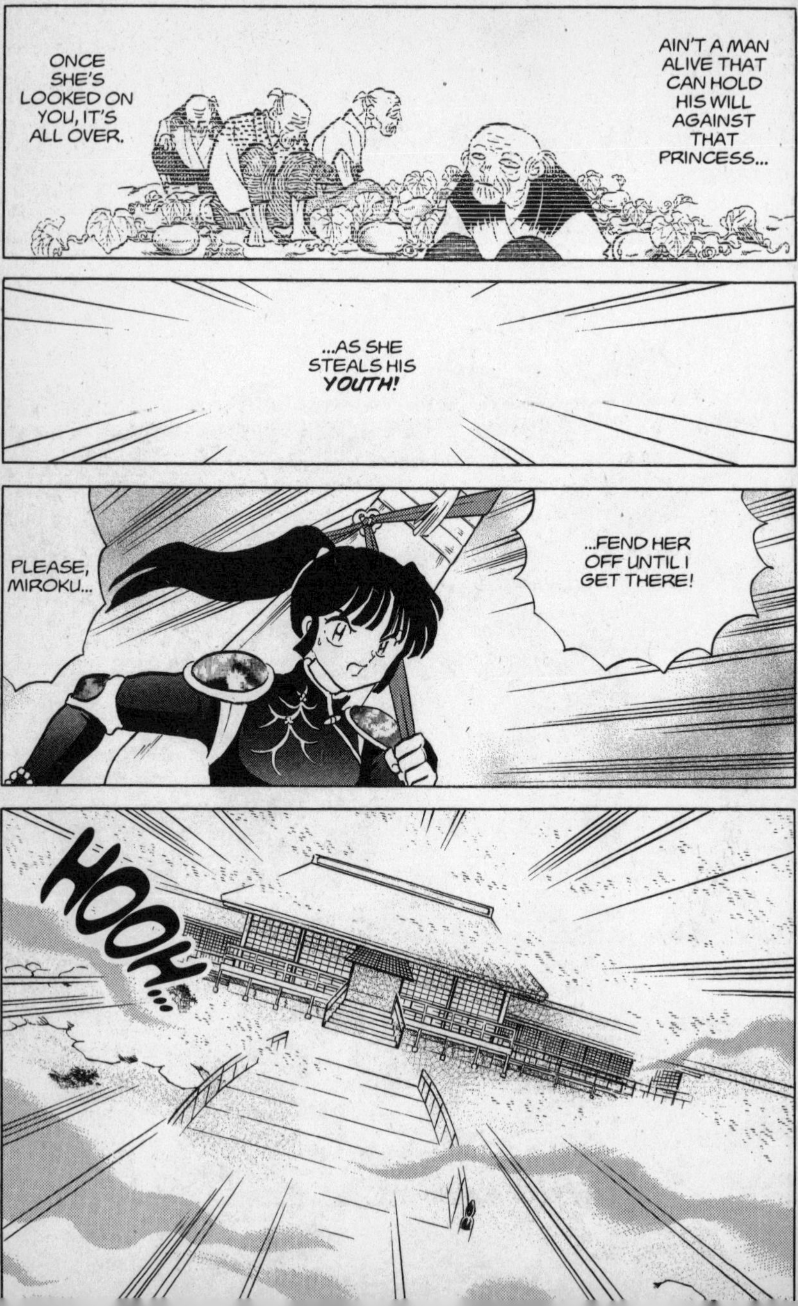
ONCE SHE'S LOOKED ON YOU, IT'S ALL OVER.
AIN'T A MAN ALIVE THAT CAN HOLD HIS WILL AGAINST THAT PRINCESS...
...AS SHE STEALS HIS *YOUTH!*
PLEASE, MIROKU...
...FEND HER OFF UNTIL I GET THERE!
HOOH...

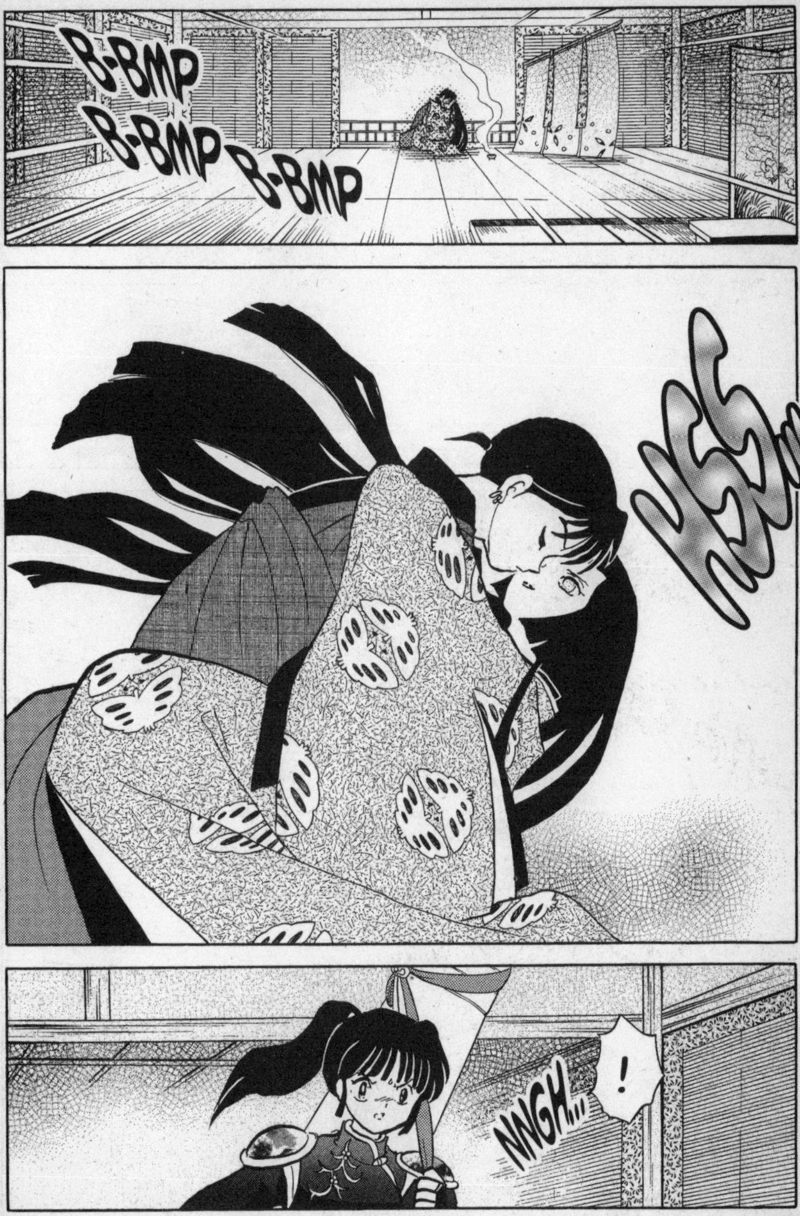
B-BMP
B-BMP
B-BMP
HSSS...
NNGH...
!

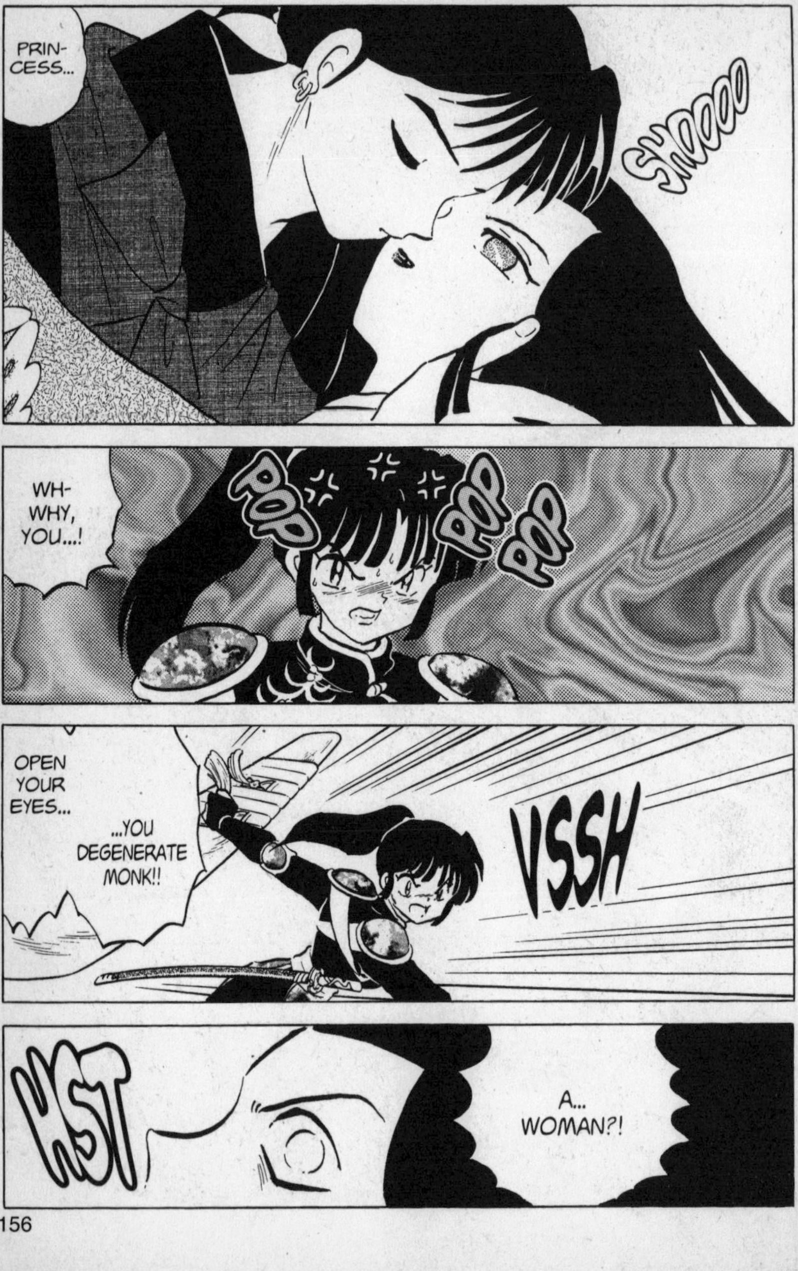
PRIN-
CESS...
SHOOOO
WH-
WHY,
YOU...!
POP
POP
POP
OPEN
YOUR
EYES...
...YOU
DEGENERATE
MONK!!
VSSH
HST
A...
WOMAN?!

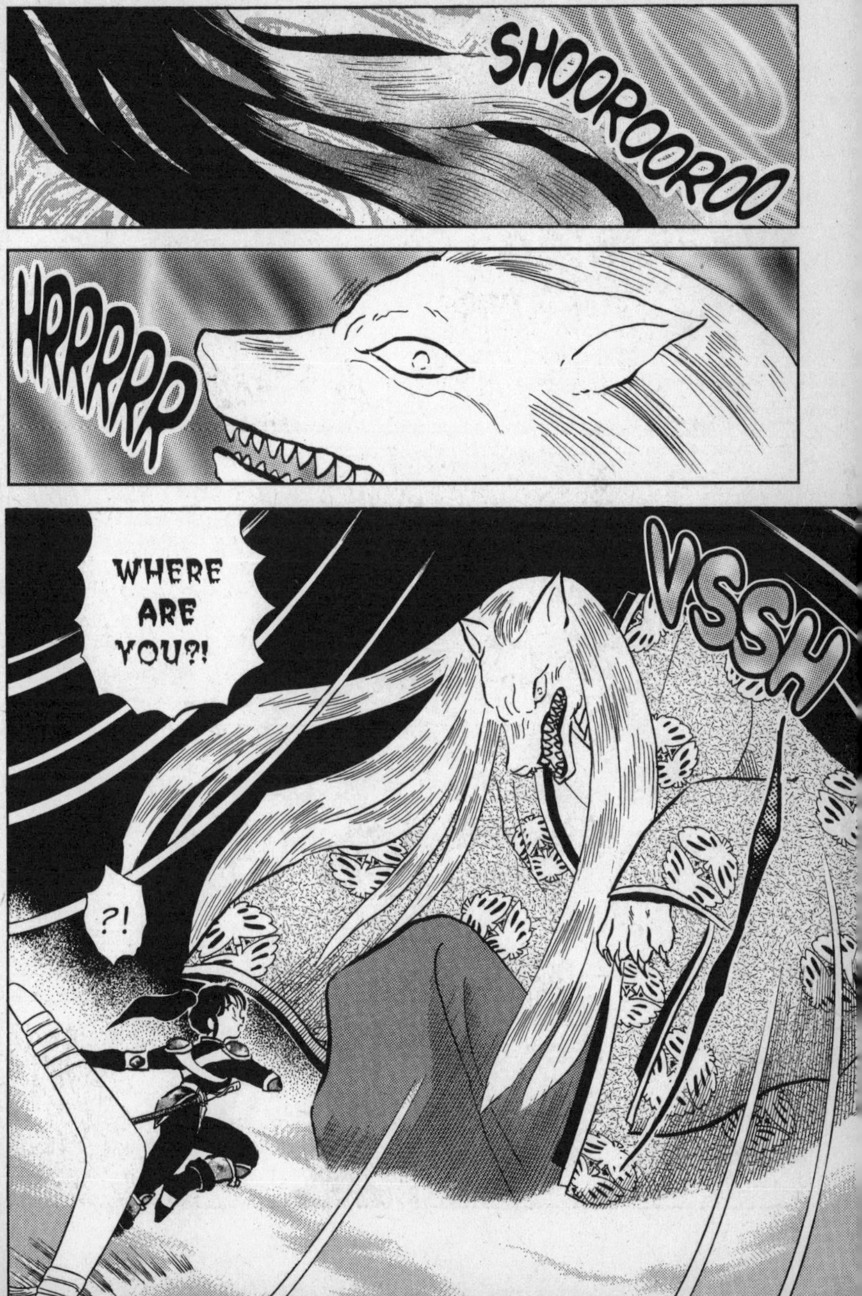
SHOOROOROO
HRRRRRR
WHERE ARE YOU?!
VSSH
?!

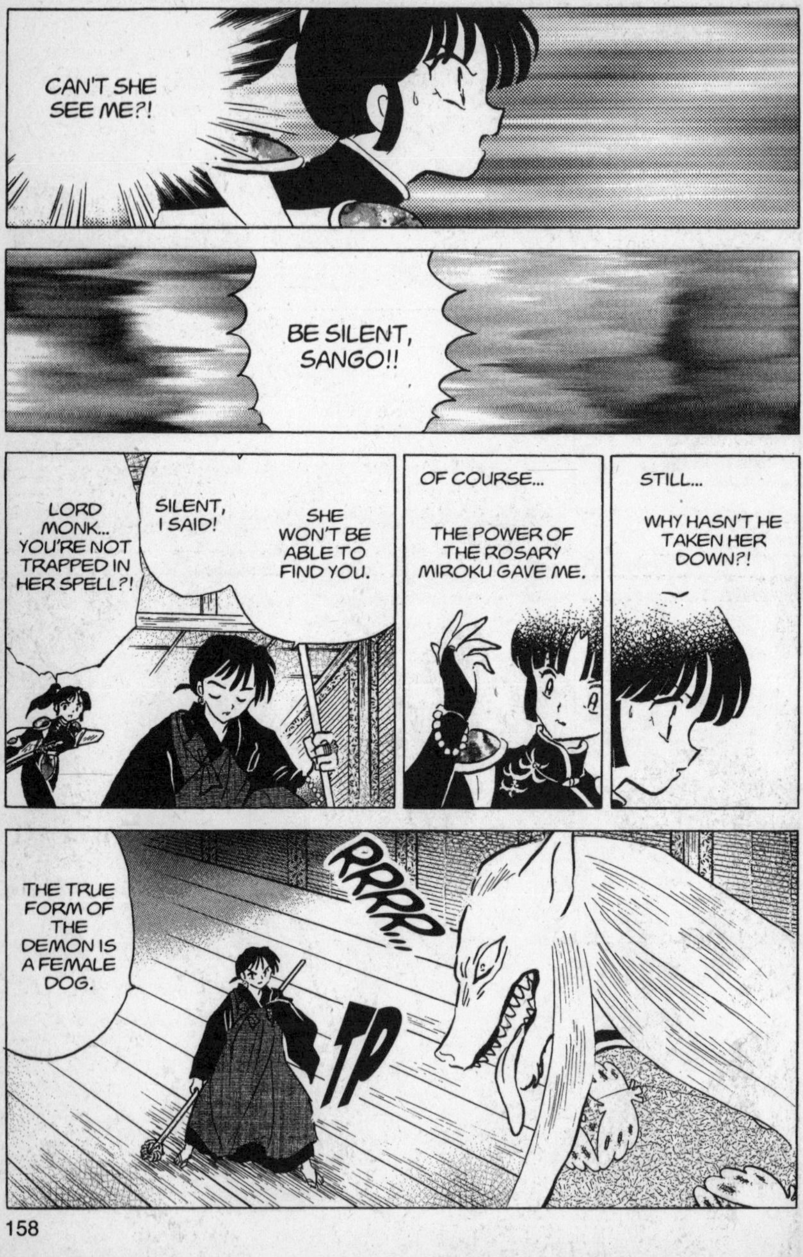
CAN'T SHE SEE ME?!
BE SILENT, SANGO!!
LORD MONK... YOU'RE NOT TRAPPED IN HER SPELL?!
SILENT, I SAID!
SHE WON'T BE ABLE TO FIND YOU.
OF COURSE...
THE POWER OF THE ROSARY MIROKU GAVE ME.
STILL...
WHY HASN'T HE TAKEN HER DOWN?!
THE TRUE FORM OF THE DEMON IS A FEMALE DOG.
RRRR...
TP

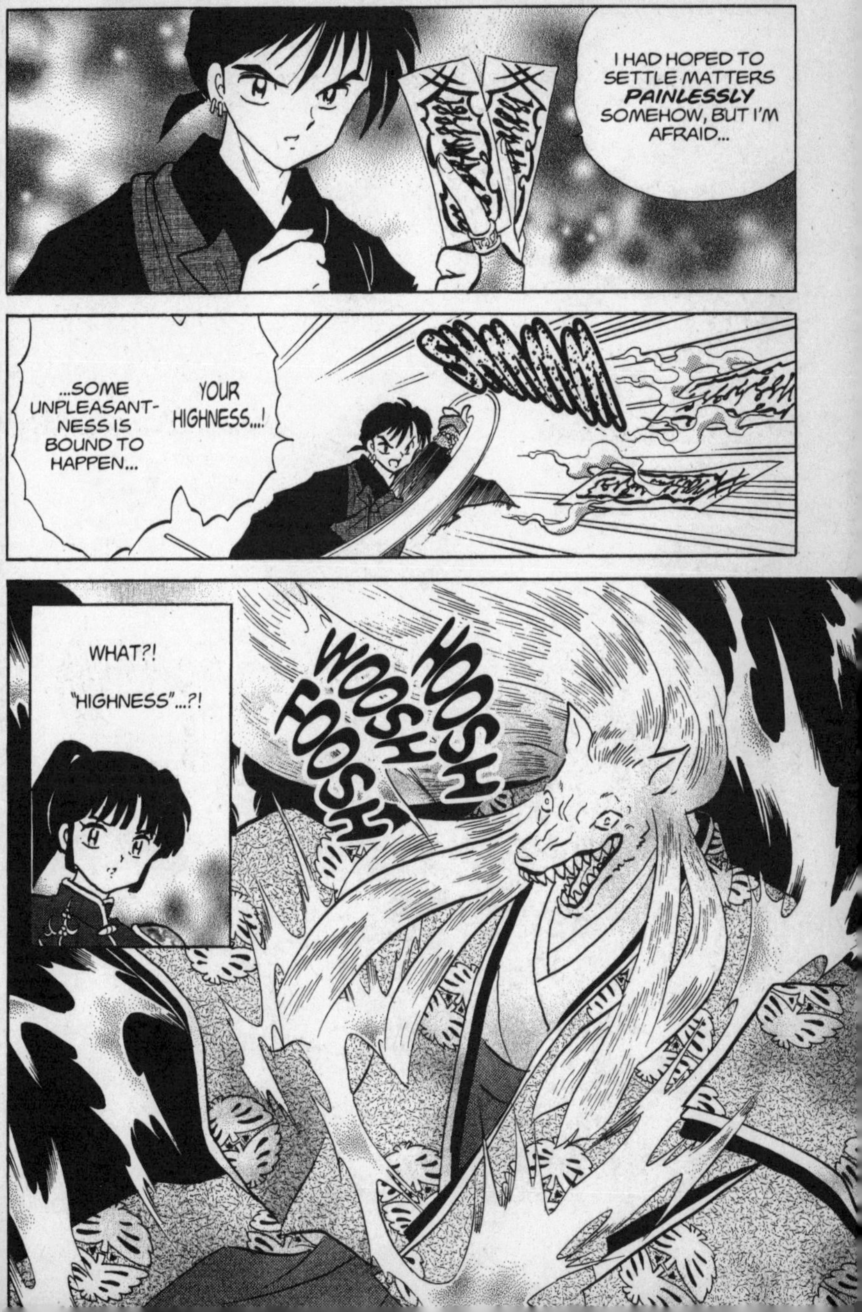
I HAD HOPED TO SETTLE MATTERS **PAINLESSLY** SOMEHOW, BUT I'M AFRAID...
...SOME UNPLEASANT-NESS IS BOUND TO HAPPEN...
YOUR HIGHNESS...!
WHAT?!
"HIGHNESS"...?!
HOOSH
WOOSH
FOOSH

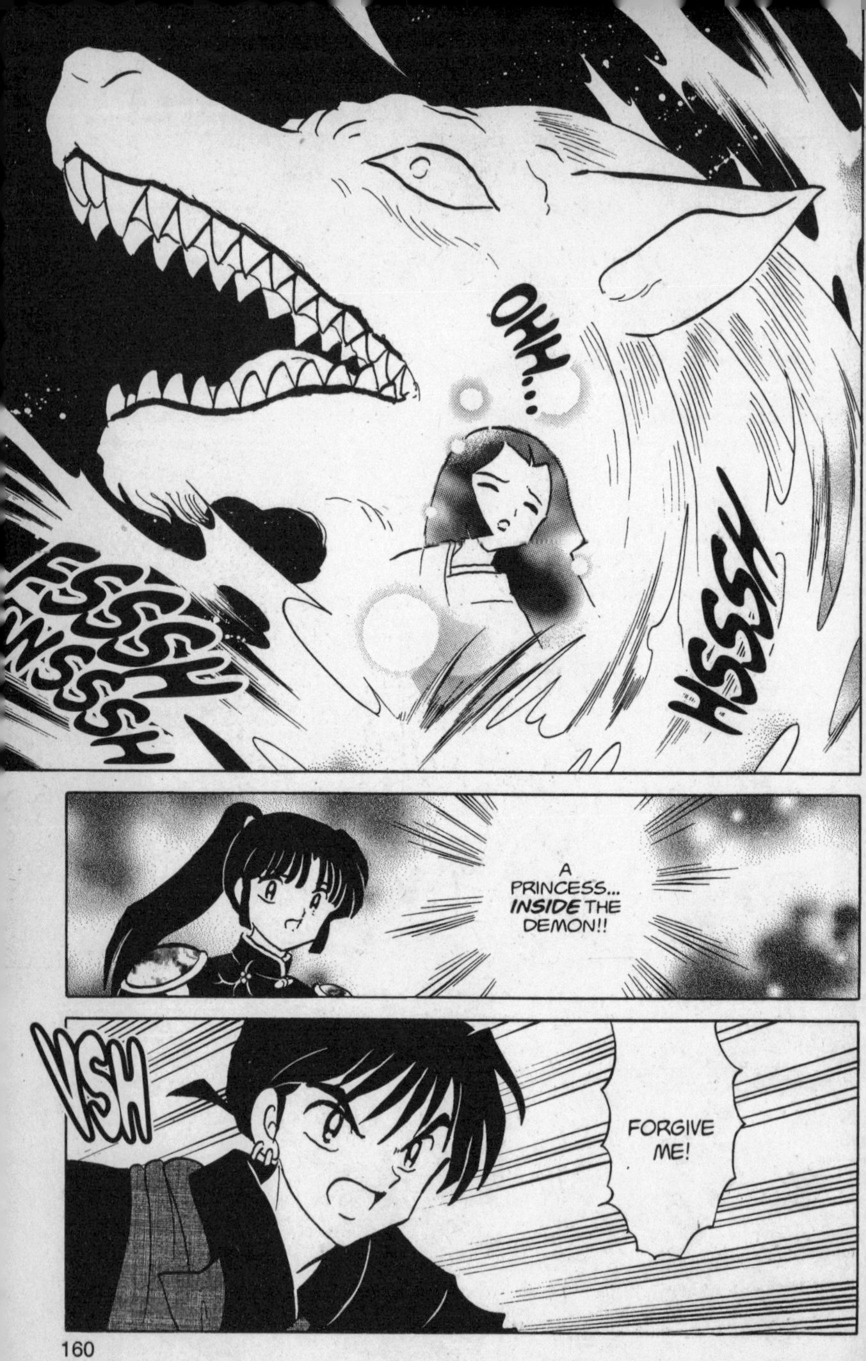
OHH...
FSSSH
WSSSH
HSSSH
A PRINCESS... ***INSIDE*** THE DEMON!!
VSH
FORGIVE ME!

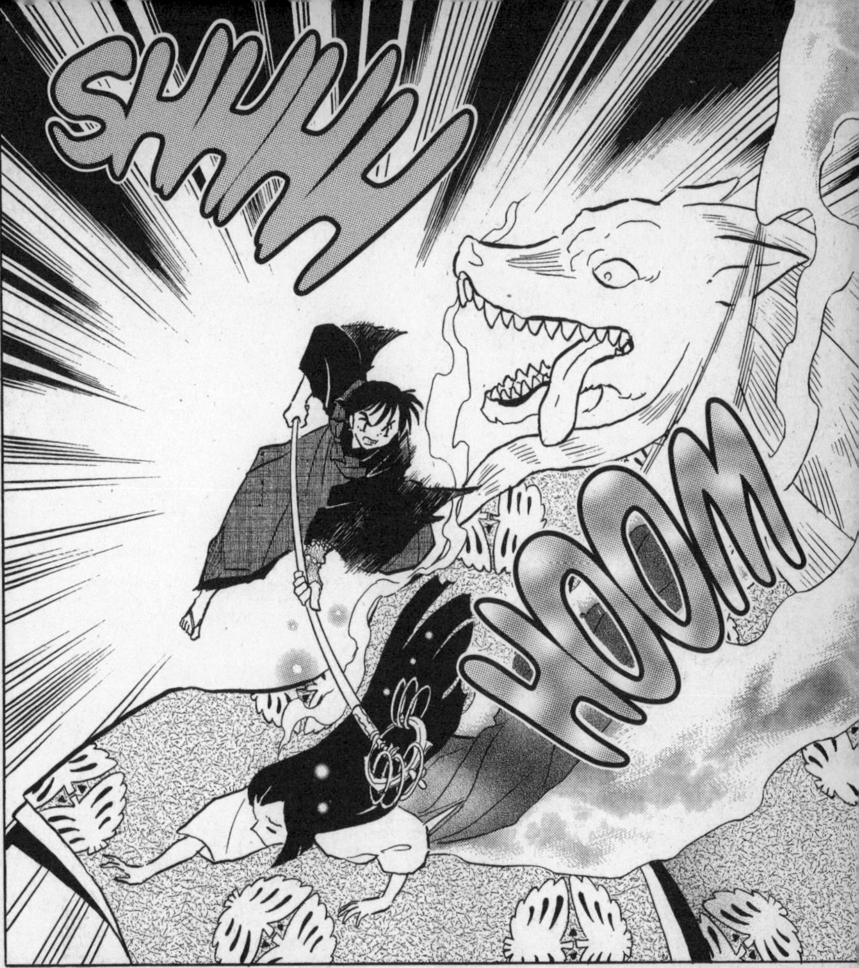
SHHH
VOOM
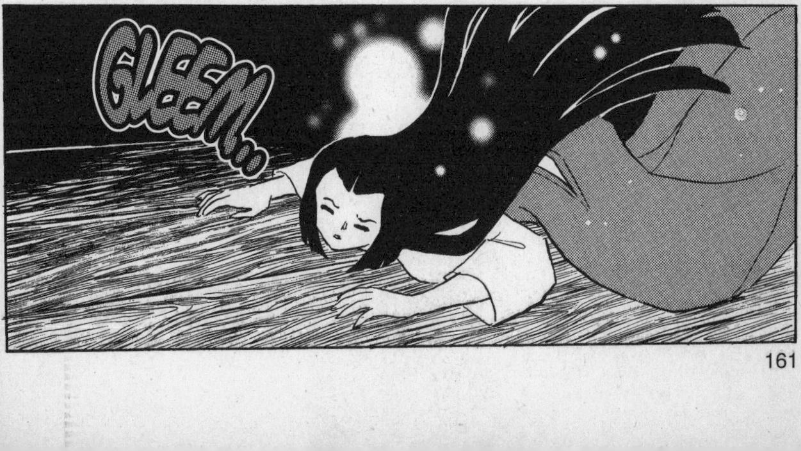
GLEEM...

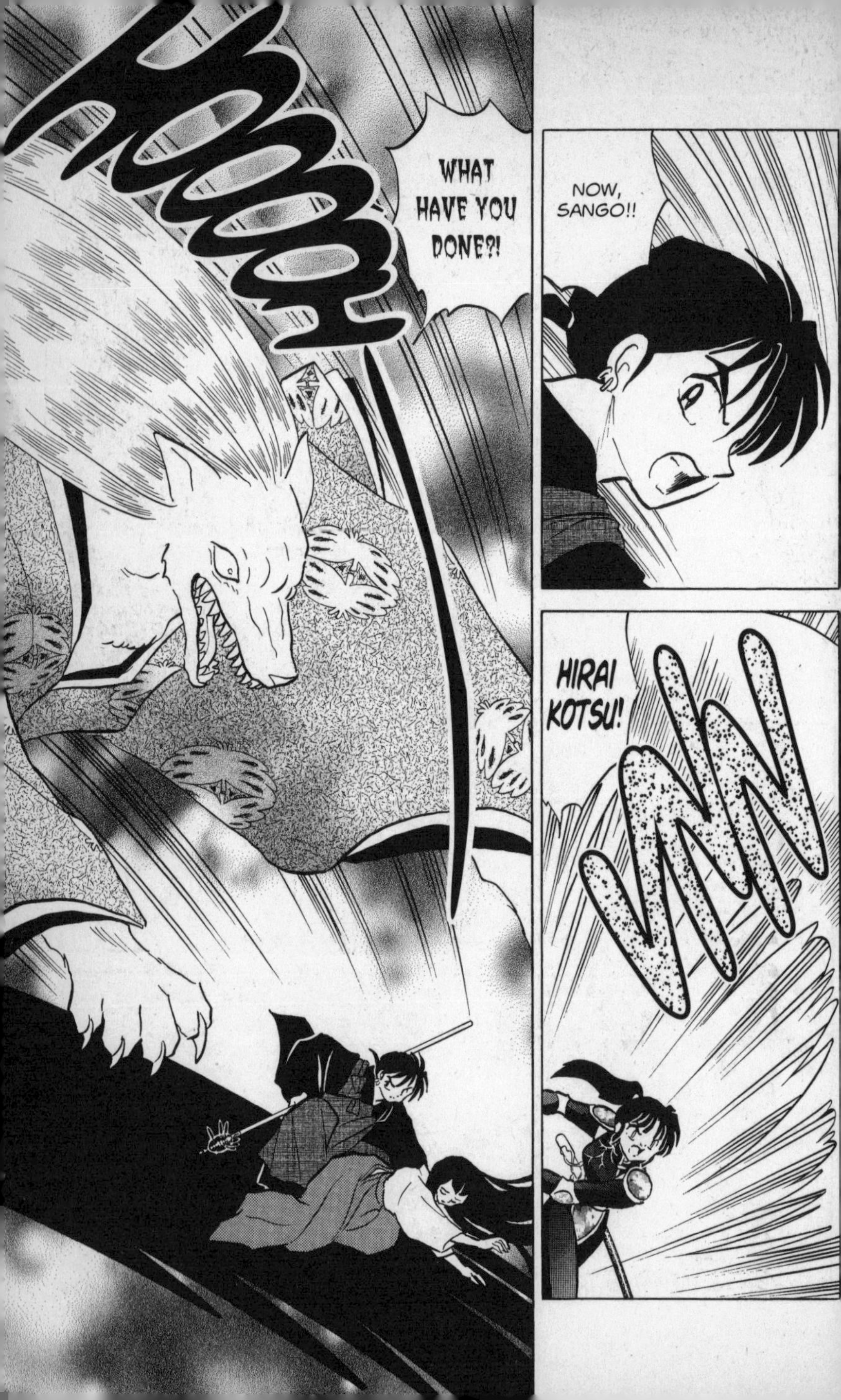
WHAT HAVE YOU DONE?!
NOW, SANGO!!
HIRAI KOTSU!

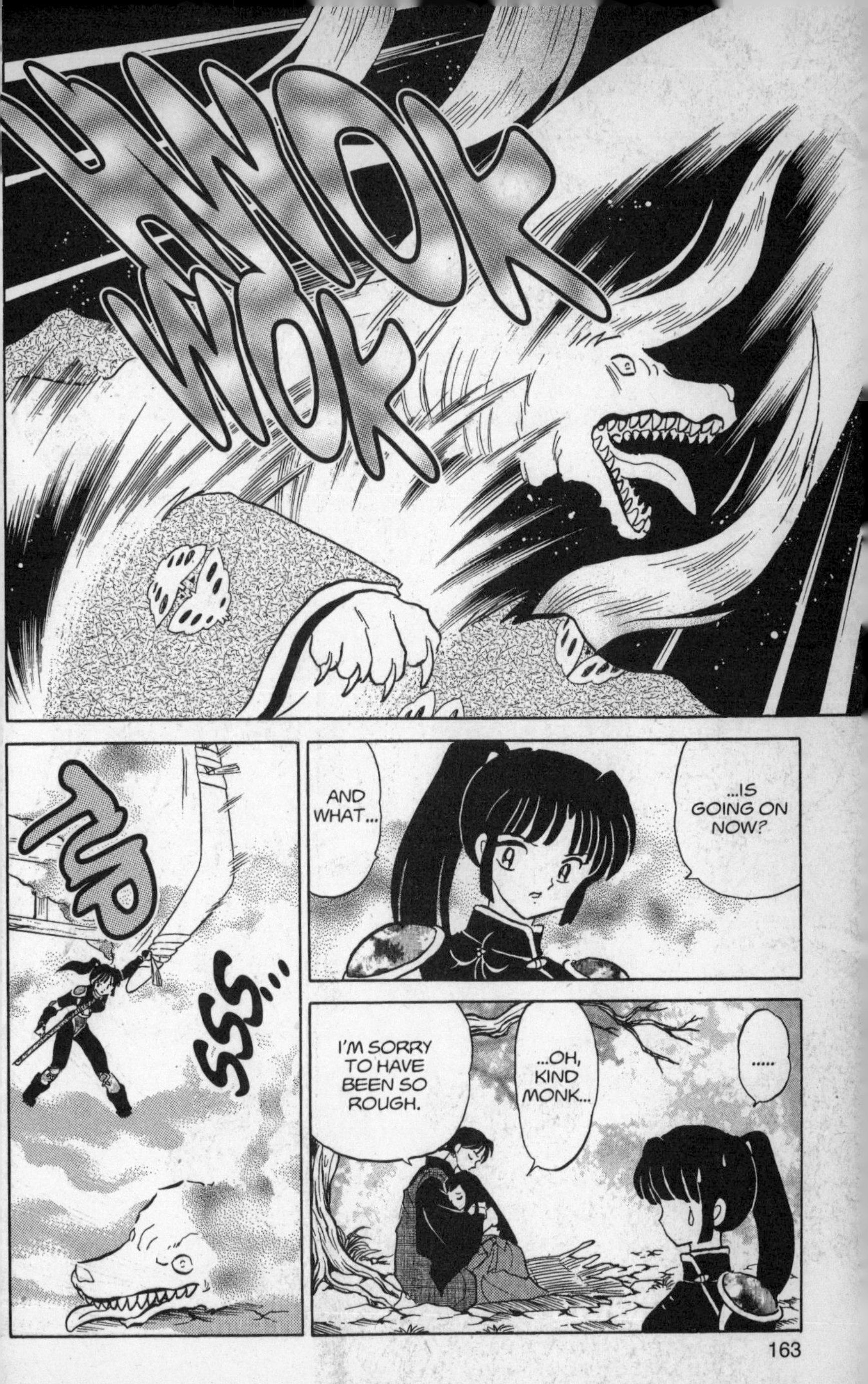
WOK
WOK
TUP
SSS...
AND WHAT...
...IS GOING ON NOW?
I'M SORRY TO HAVE BEEN SO ROUGH.
...OH, KIND MONK...
......

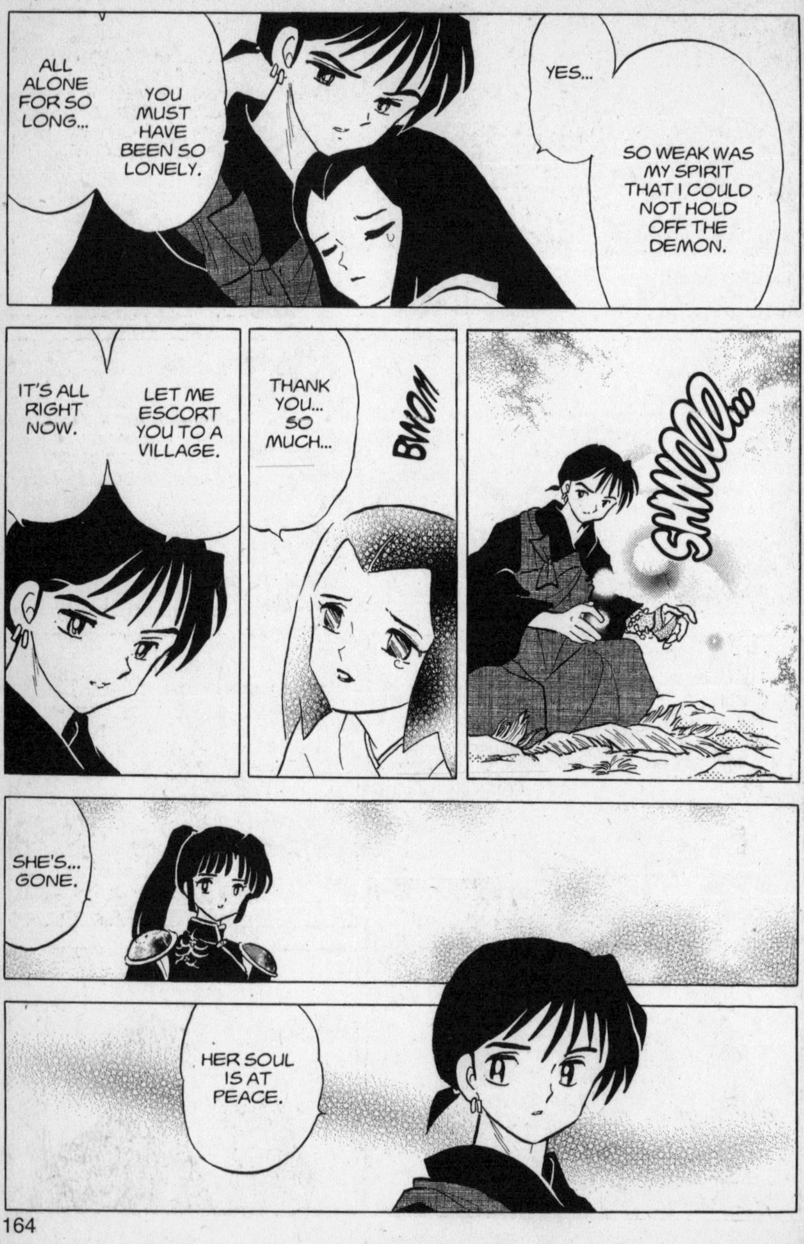
ALL ALONE FOR SO LONG...
YOU MUST HAVE BEEN SO LONELY.
YES...
SO WEAK WAS MY SPIRIT THAT I COULD NOT HOLD OFF THE DEMON.
IT'S ALL RIGHT NOW.
LET ME ESCORT YOU TO A VILLAGE.
THANK YOU... SO MUCH...
BWOM
SHWOOO...
SHE'S... GONE.
HER SOUL IS AT PEACE.

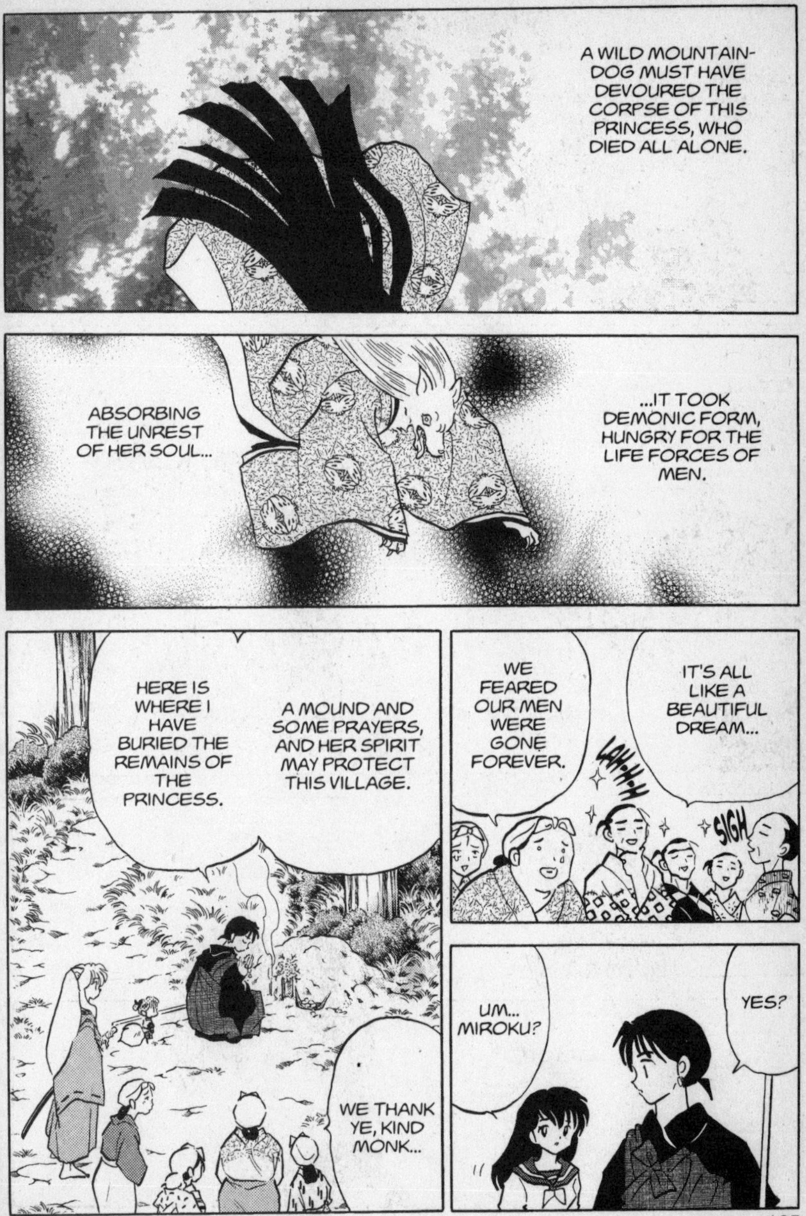
A WILD MOUNTAIN-DOG MUST HAVE DEVOURED THE CORPSE OF THIS PRINCESS, WHO DIED ALL ALONE.
ABSORBING THE UNREST OF HER SOUL...
...IT TOOK DEMONIC FORM, HUNGRY FOR THE LIFE FORCES OF MEN.
HERE IS WHERE I HAVE BURIED THE REMAINS OF THE PRINCESS.
A MOUND AND SOME PRAYERS, AND HER SPIRIT MAY PROTECT THIS VILLAGE.
WE THANK YE, KIND MONK...
WE FEARED OUR MEN WERE GONE FOREVER.
HAH-H-H
IT'S ALL LIKE A BEAUTIFUL DREAM...
SIGH
UM... MIROKU?
YES?

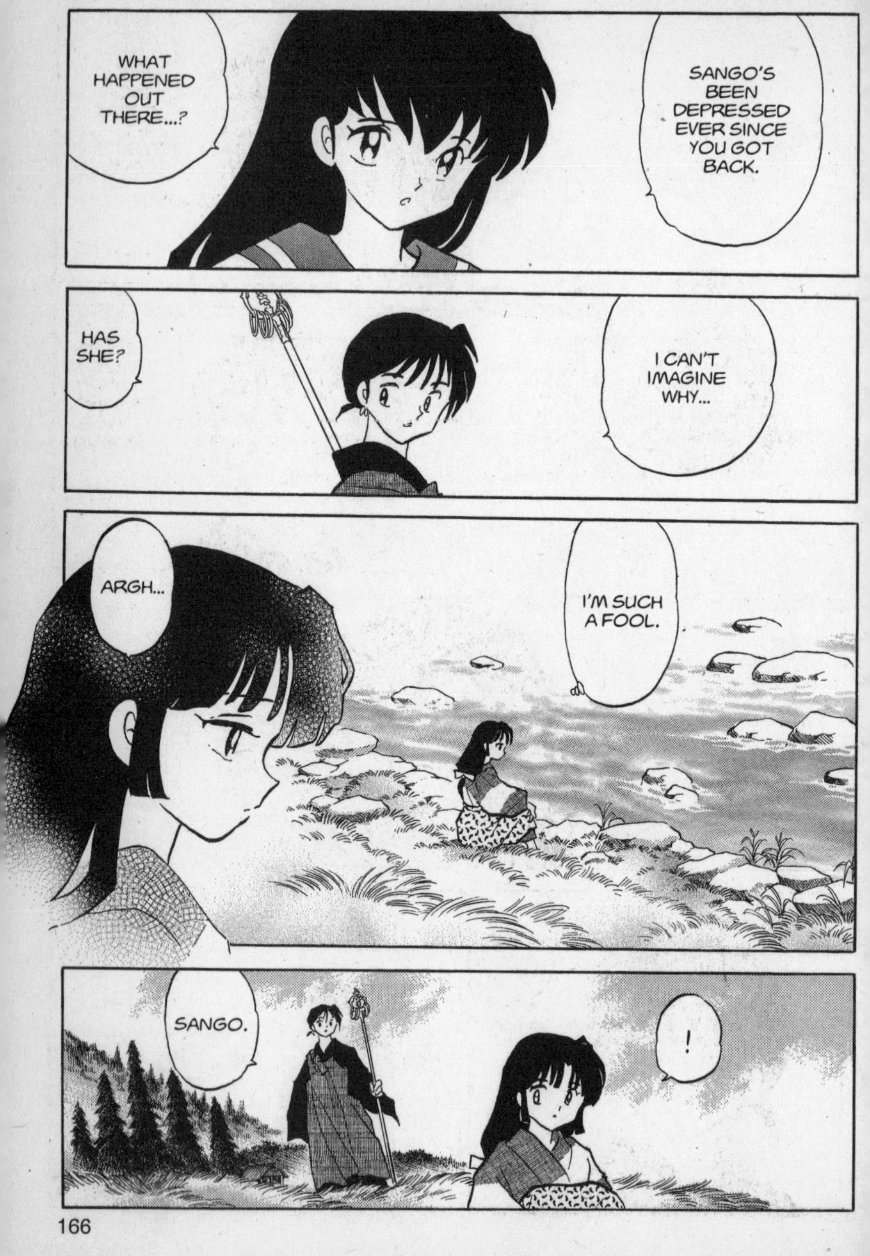
WHAT HAPPENED OUT THERE...?
SANGO'S BEEN DEPRESSED EVER SINCE YOU GOT BACK.
HAS SHE?
I CAN'T IMAGINE WHY...
ARGH...
I'M SUCH A FOOL.
SANGO.
!

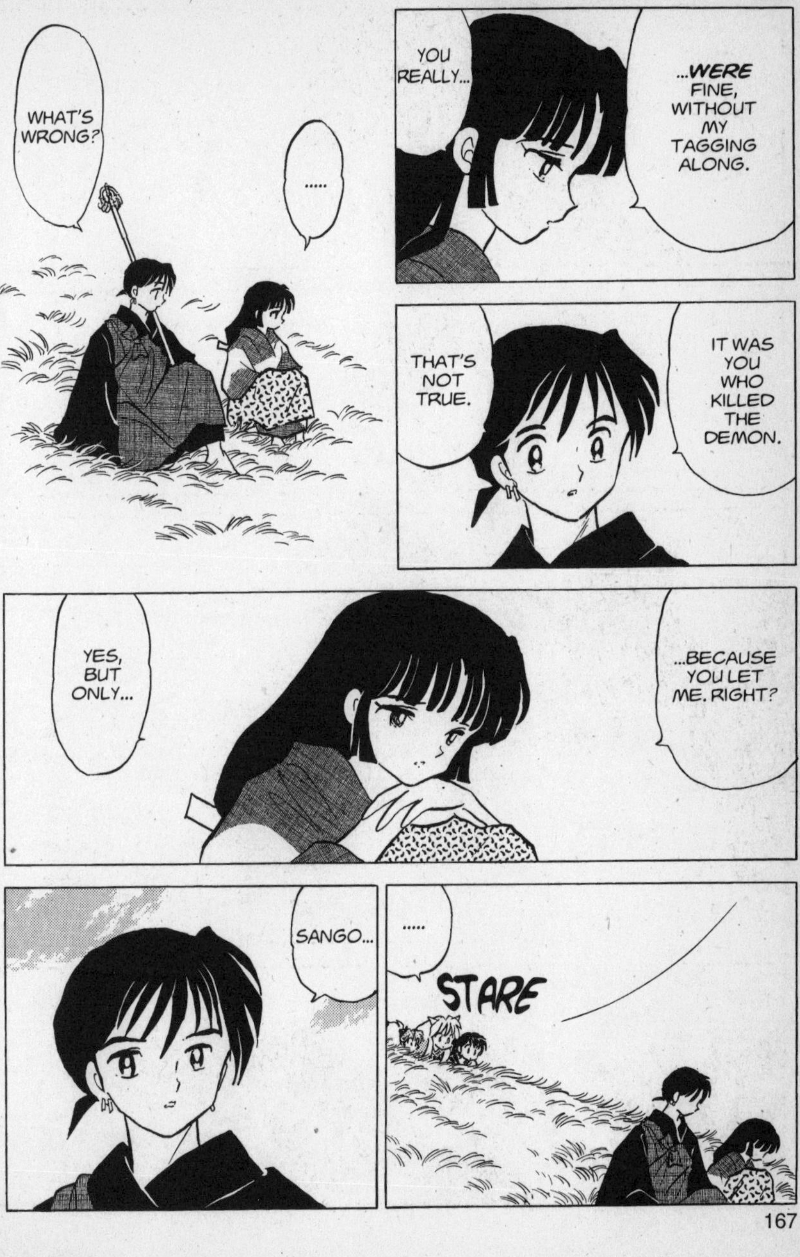
WHAT'S WRONG?
.....
YOU REALLY...
...WERE FINE, WITHOUT MY TAGGING ALONG.
THAT'S NOT TRUE.
IT WAS YOU WHO KILLED THE DEMON.
YES, BUT ONLY...
...BECAUSE YOU LET ME. RIGHT?
SANGO...
.....
STARE

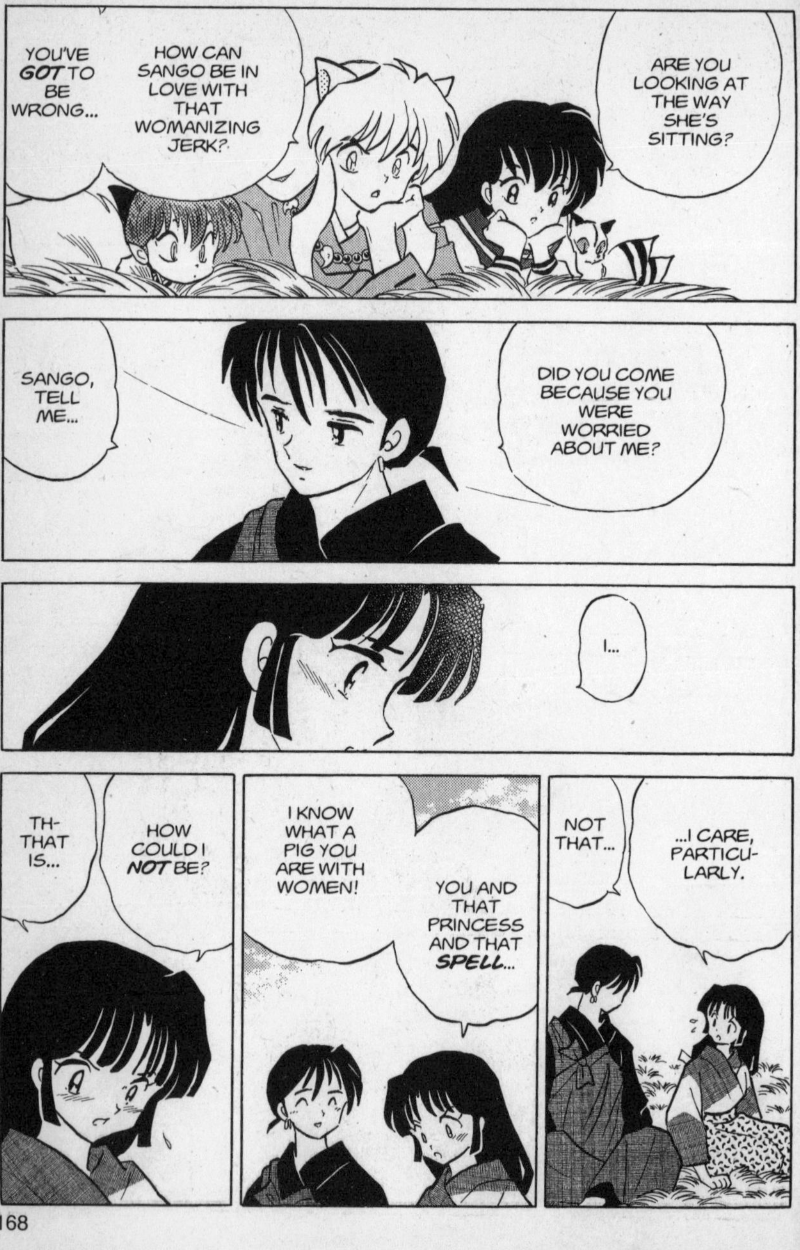
YOU'VE GOT TO BE WRONG...
HOW CAN SANGO BE IN LOVE WITH THAT WOMANIZING JERK?
ARE YOU LOOKING AT THE WAY SHE'S SITTING?
SANGO, TELL ME...
DID YOU COME BECAUSE YOU WERE WORRIED ABOUT ME?
I...
TH-THAT IS...
HOW COULD I NOT BE?
I KNOW WHAT A PIG YOU ARE WITH WOMEN!
YOU AND THAT PRINCESS AND THAT SPELL...
NOT THAT...
...I CARE, PARTICU-LARLY.

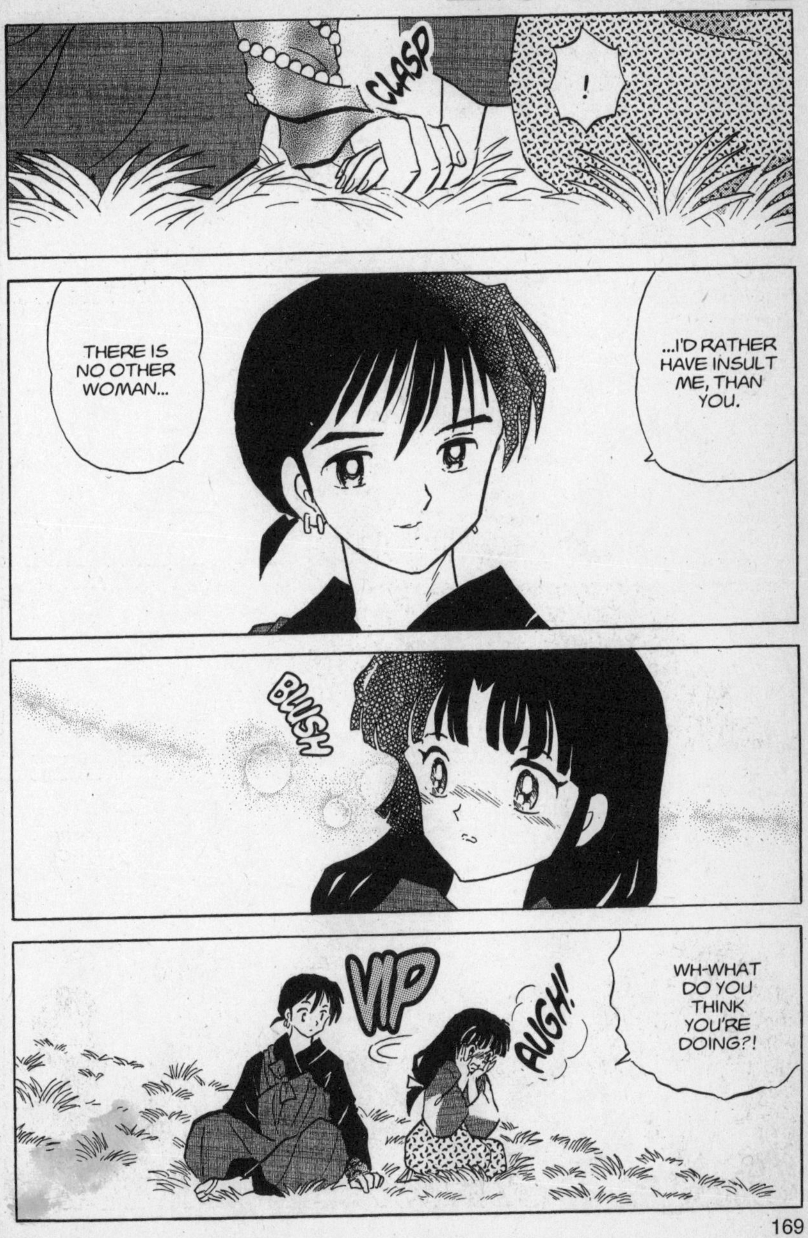
CLASP
!
THERE IS NO OTHER WOMAN...
...I'D RATHER HAVE INSULT ME, THAN YOU.
BLUSH
VIP
AUGH!
WH-WHAT DO YOU THINK YOU'RE DOING?!

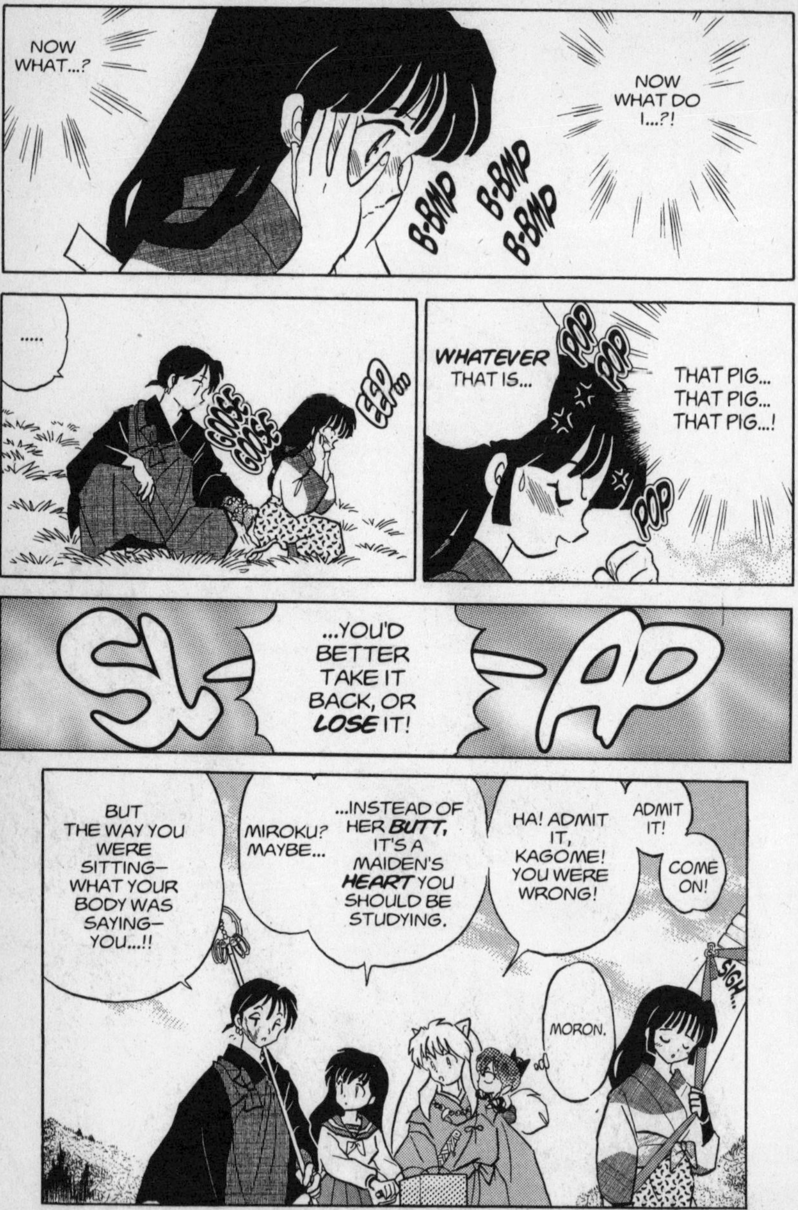
NOW WHAT...?
NOW WHAT DO I...?!
B-BMP
B-BMP
B-BMP
.....
WHATEVER THAT IS...
POP
POP
THAT PIG... THAT PIG... THAT PIG...!
POP
SL-AP
...YOU'D BETTER TAKE IT BACK, OR LOSE IT!
BUT THE WAY YOU WERE SITTING— WHAT YOUR BODY WAS SAYING— YOU...!!
MIROKU? MAYBE...
...INSTEAD OF HER BUTT, IT'S A MAIDEN'S HEART YOU SHOULD BE STUDYING.
HA! ADMIT IT, KAGOME! YOU WERE WRONG!
ADMIT IT!
COME ON!
MORON.
SIGH...

SCROLL TEN

THE MAN WITHOUT A FACE

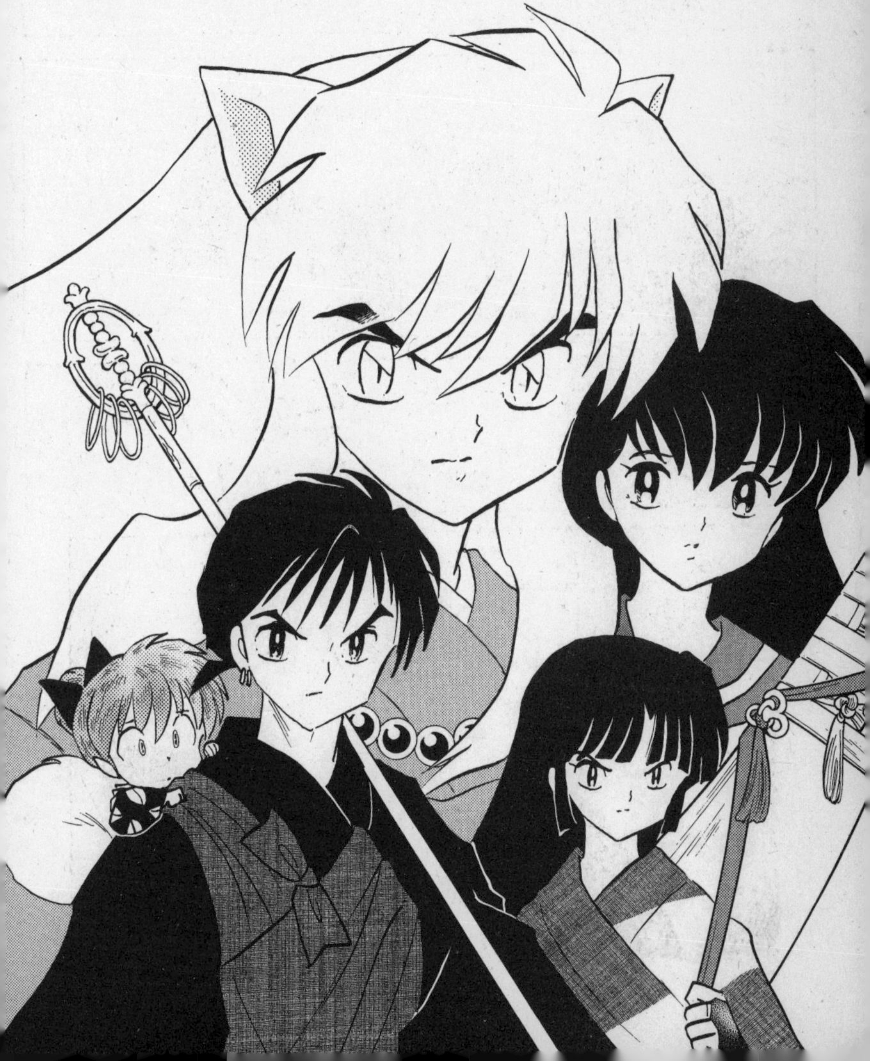

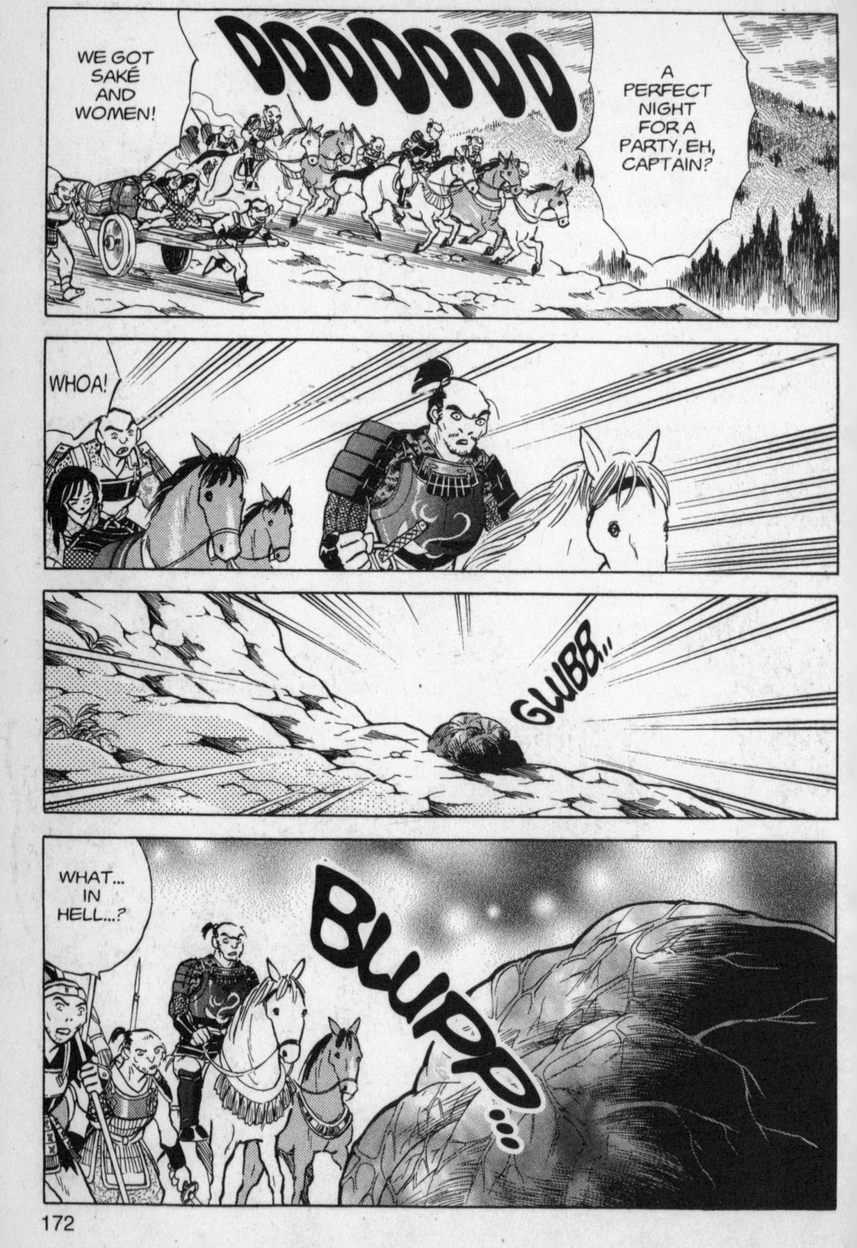
WE GOT SAKÉ AND WOMEN!
DDDDDDD
A PERFECT NIGHT FOR A PARTY, EH, CAPTAIN?
WHOA!
GLUBB...
WHAT... IN HELL...?
BLUPP...

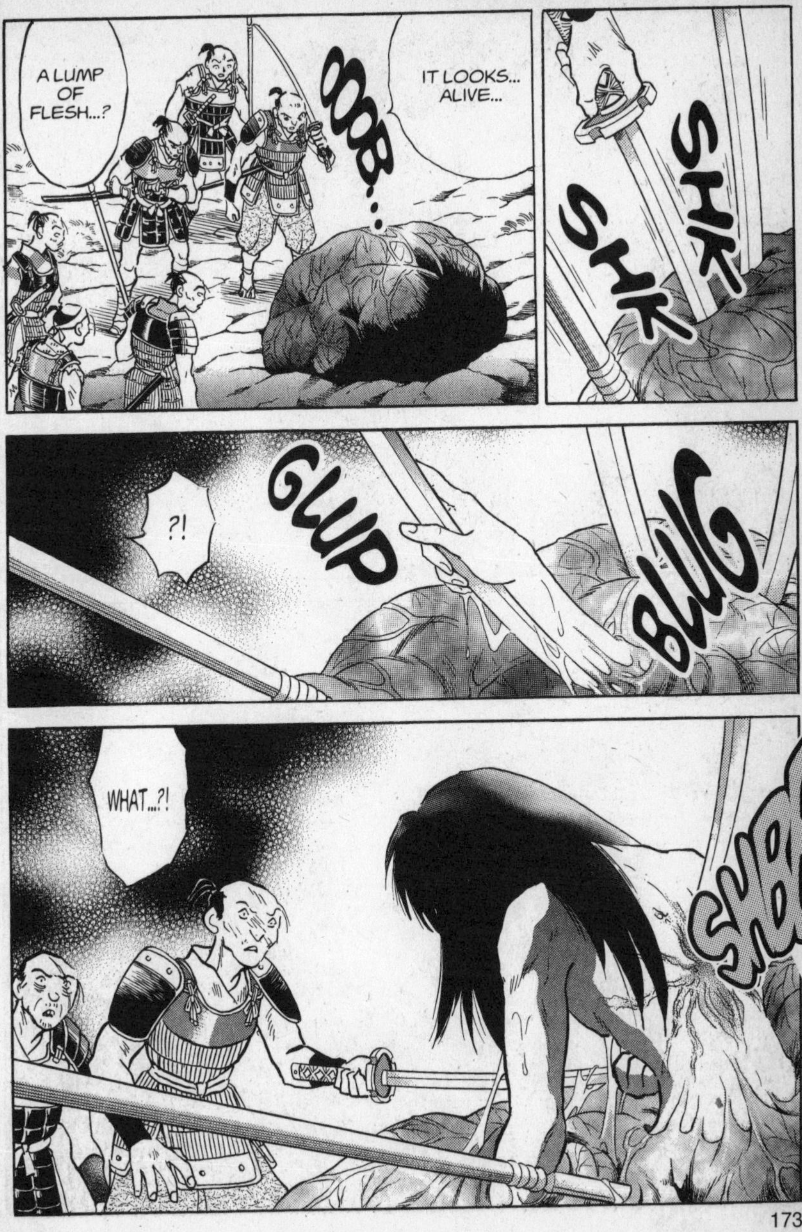
A LUMP OF FLESH...?
SOOOB...
IT LOOKS... ALIVE...
SHK
SHK
?!
GLUP
BLUG
WHAT...?!
SHBBB

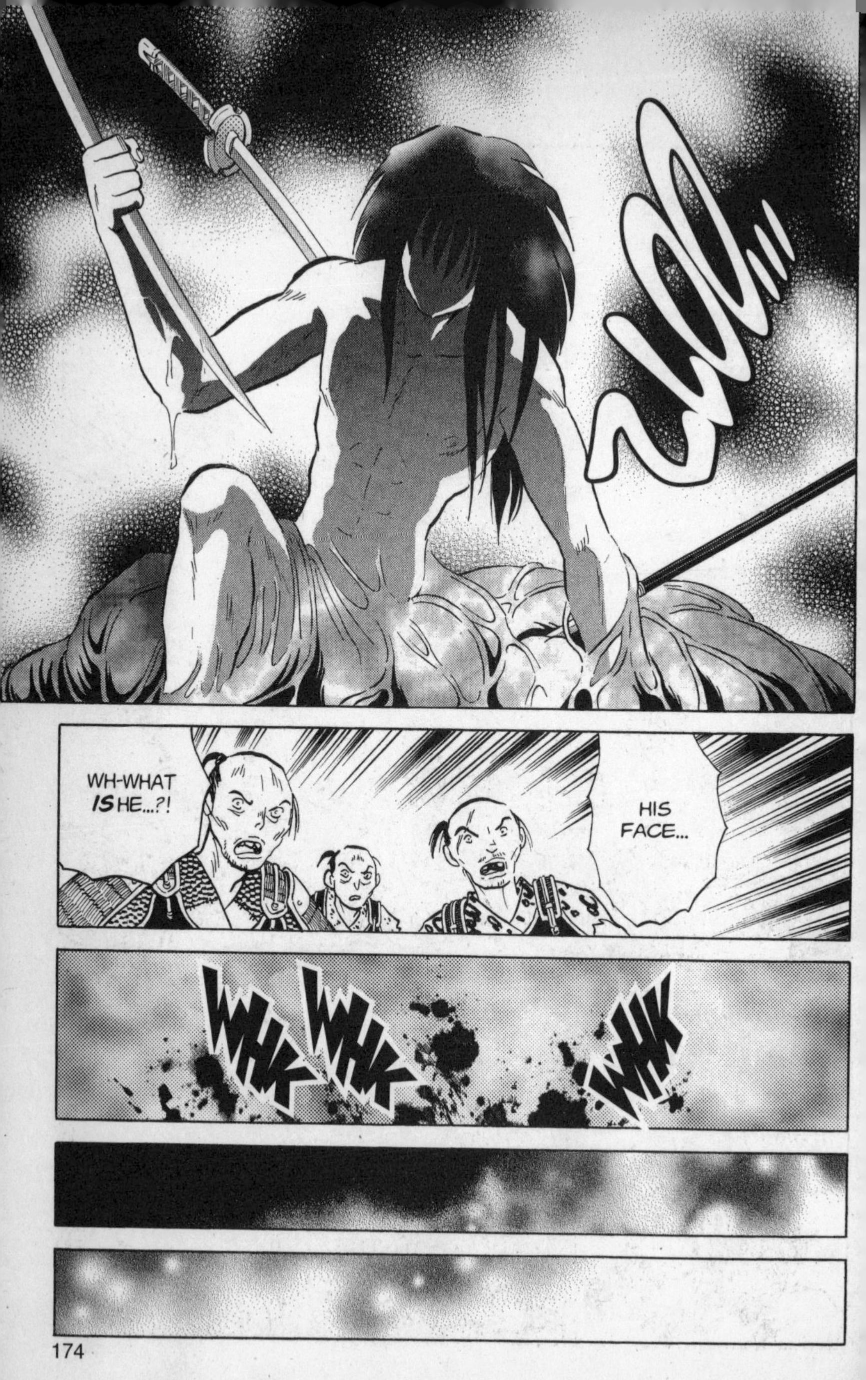
WH-WHAT *IS* HE...?!
HIS FACE...
WHK
WHK
WHK

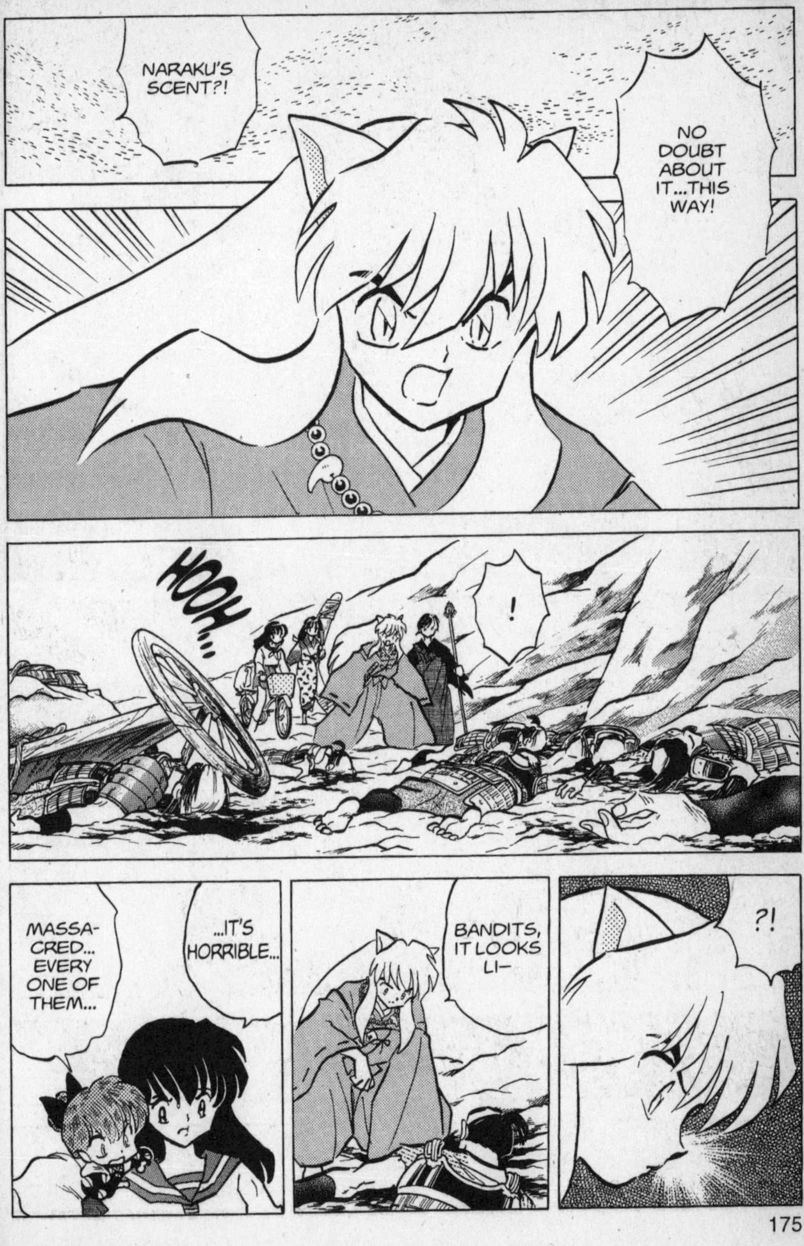
NARAKU'S SCENT?!
NO DOUBT ABOUT IT...THIS WAY!
HOOH...
!
MASSA-CRED... EVERY ONE OF THEM...
...IT'S HORRIBLE...
BANDITS, IT LOOKS LI—
?!

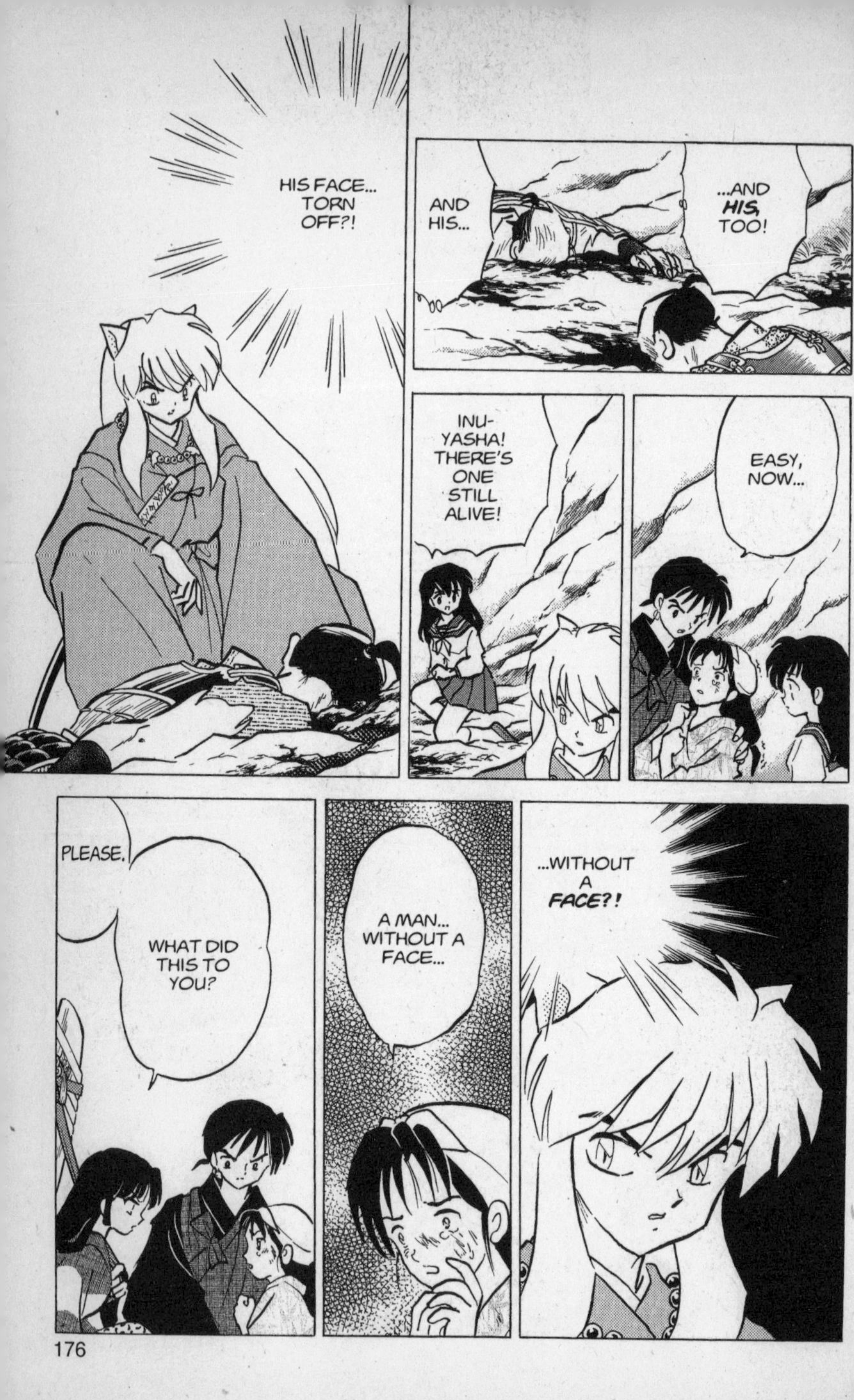

HIS FACE... TORN OFF?!
AND HIS...
...AND **HIS,** TOO!
INU-YASHA! THERE'S ONE STILL ALIVE!
EASY, NOW...
PLEASE.
WHAT DID THIS TO YOU?
A MAN... WITHOUT A FACE...
...WITHOUT A ***FACE?!***

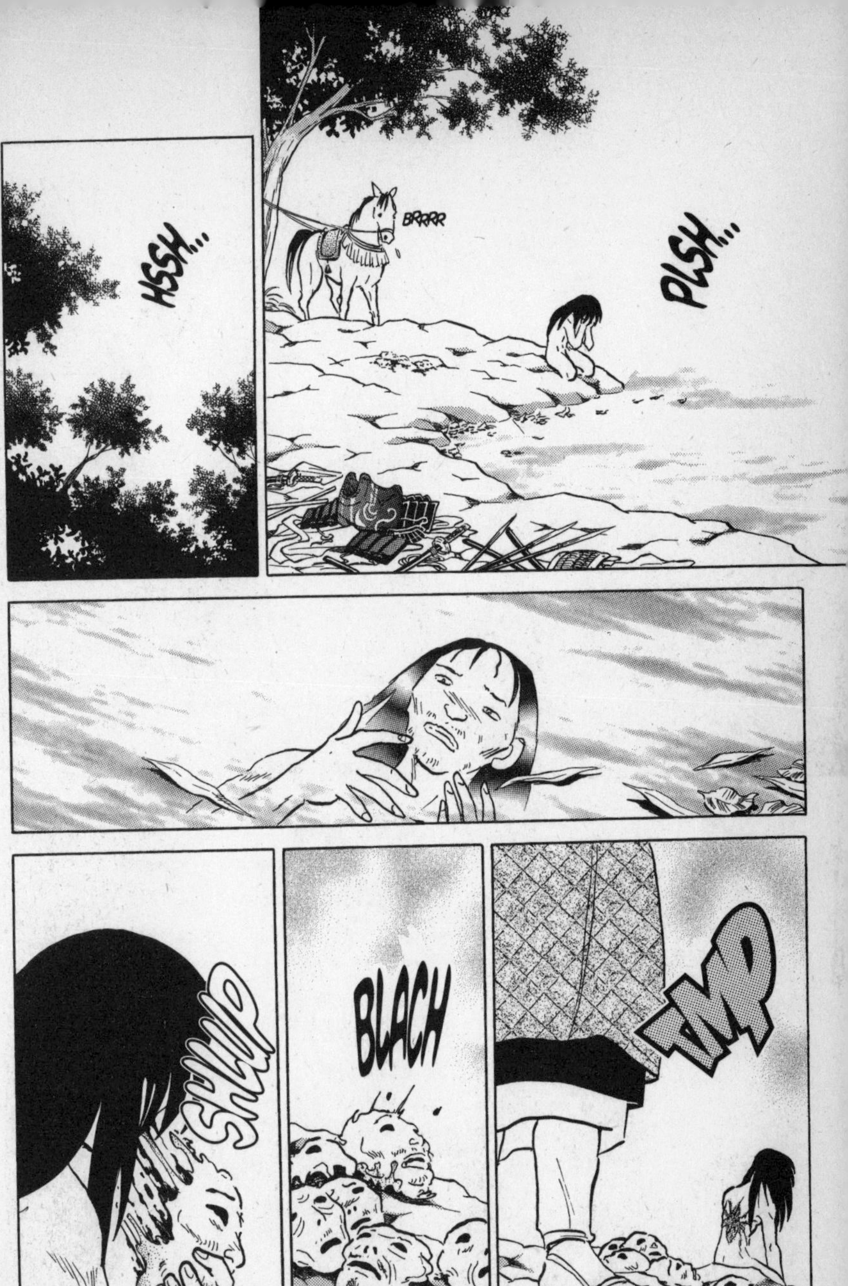
HSSH...
BRRRR
PLSH...
SHLUP
BLACH
TMP

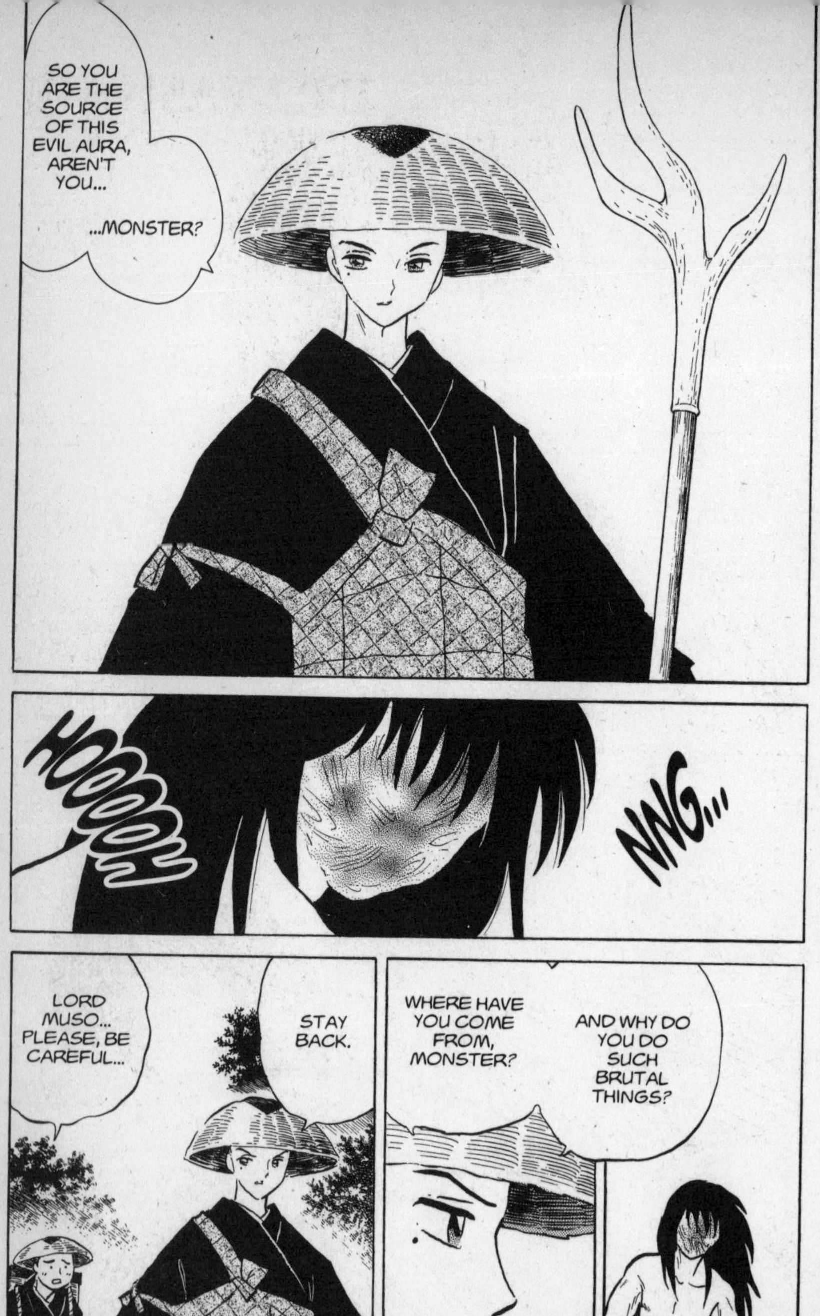
SO YOU ARE THE SOURCE OF THIS EVIL AURA, AREN'T YOU...
...MONSTER?
HOOOOOH
NNG...
LORD MUSO... PLEASE, BE CAREFUL...
STAY BACK.
WHERE HAVE YOU COME FROM, MONSTER?
AND WHY DO YOU DO SUCH BRUTAL THINGS?

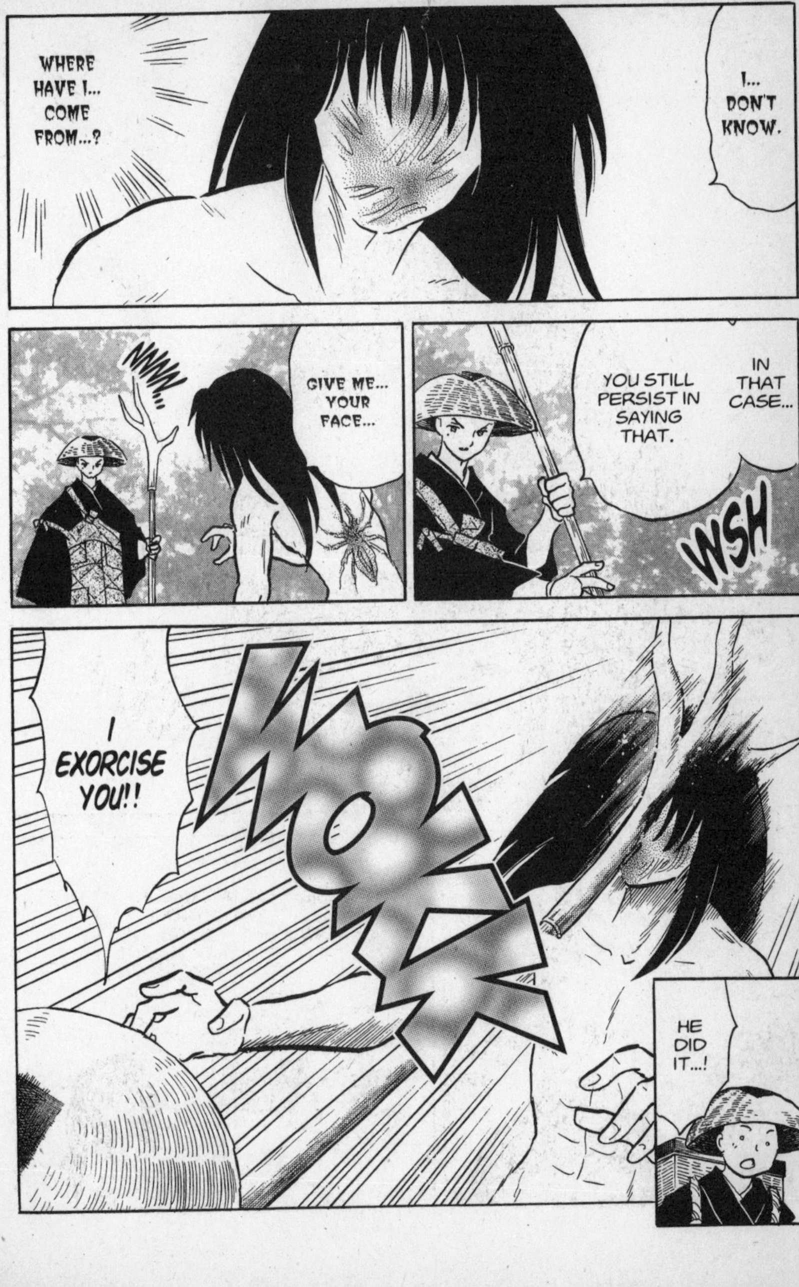
WHERE HAVE I... COME FROM...?
I... DON'T KNOW.
GIVE ME... YOUR FACE...
YOU STILL PERSIST IN SAYING THAT.
IN THAT CASE...
WSH
I EXORCISE YOU!!
HE DID IT...!

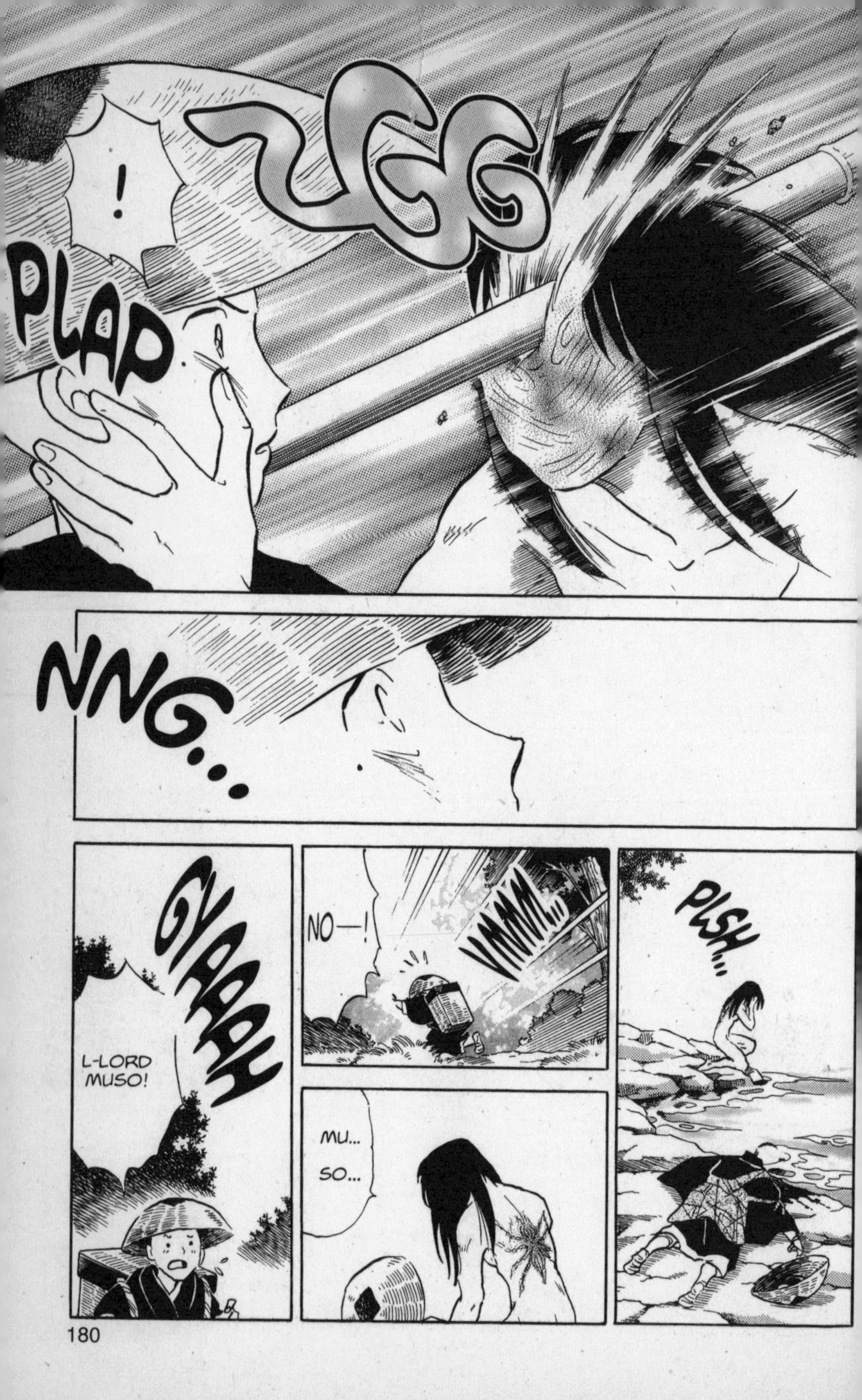
ZGG
!
PLAP
NNG...
GYAAAH
L-LORD MUSO!
NO—!
VMMM...
MU... SO...
PLSH...

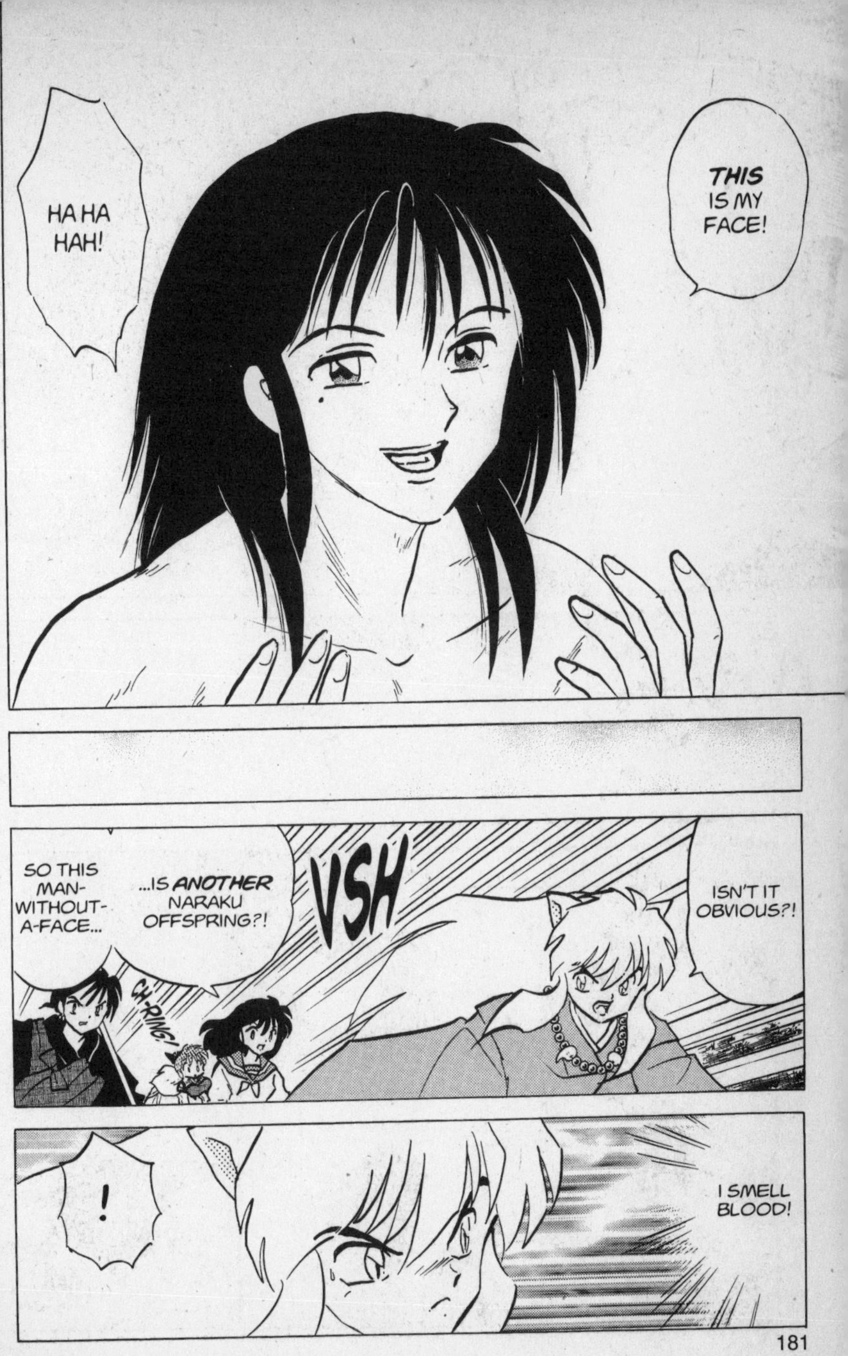
HA HA HAH!
THIS IS MY FACE!
SO THIS MAN-WITHOUT-A-FACE...
...IS **ANOTHER** NARAKU OFFSPRING?!
VSH
CH-RING!
ISN'T IT OBVIOUS?!
!
I SMELL BLOOD!

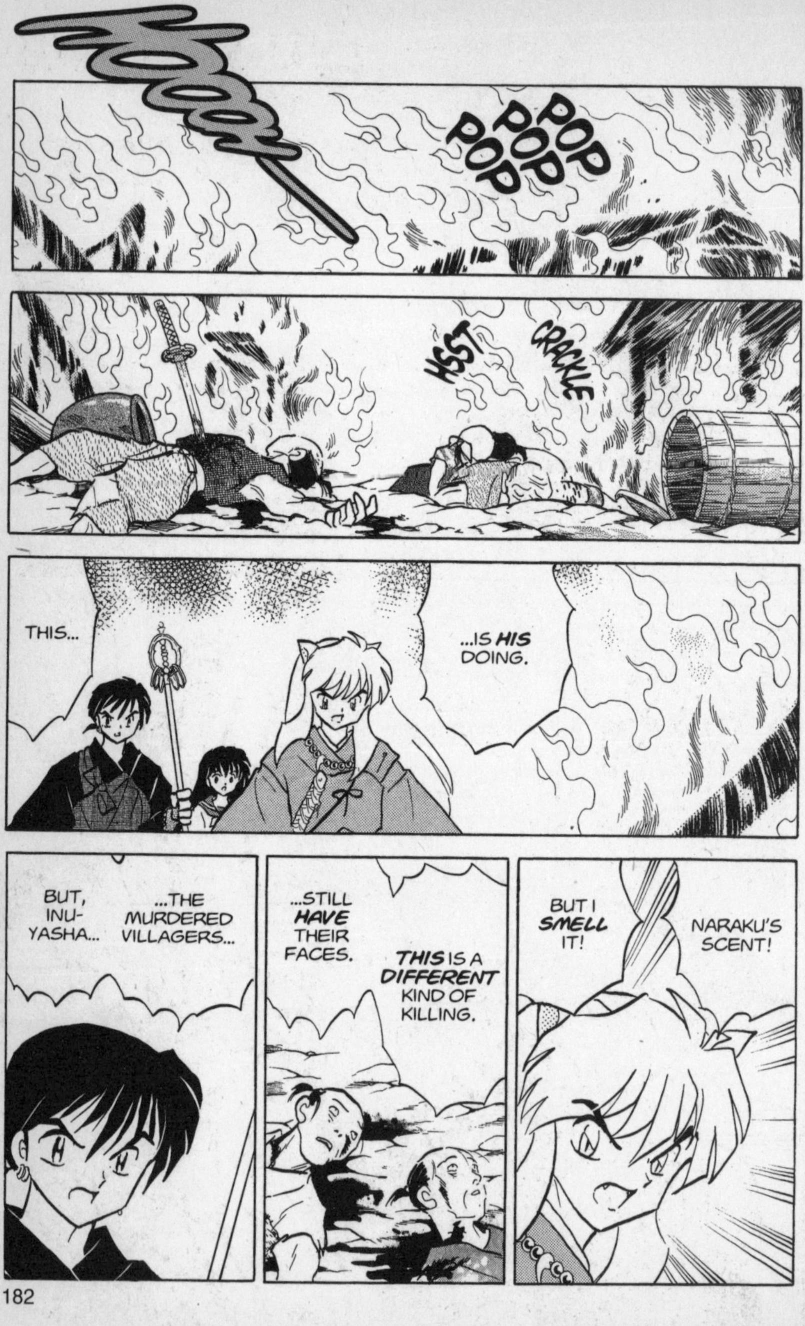
HOOOOH
POP
POP
POP
HSST
CRACKLE
THIS...
...IS HIS DOING.
BUT, INU-YASHA...
...THE MURDERED VILLAGERS...
...STILL HAVE THEIR FACES.
THIS IS A DIFFERENT KIND OF KILLING.
BUT I SMELL IT!
NARAKU'S SCENT!

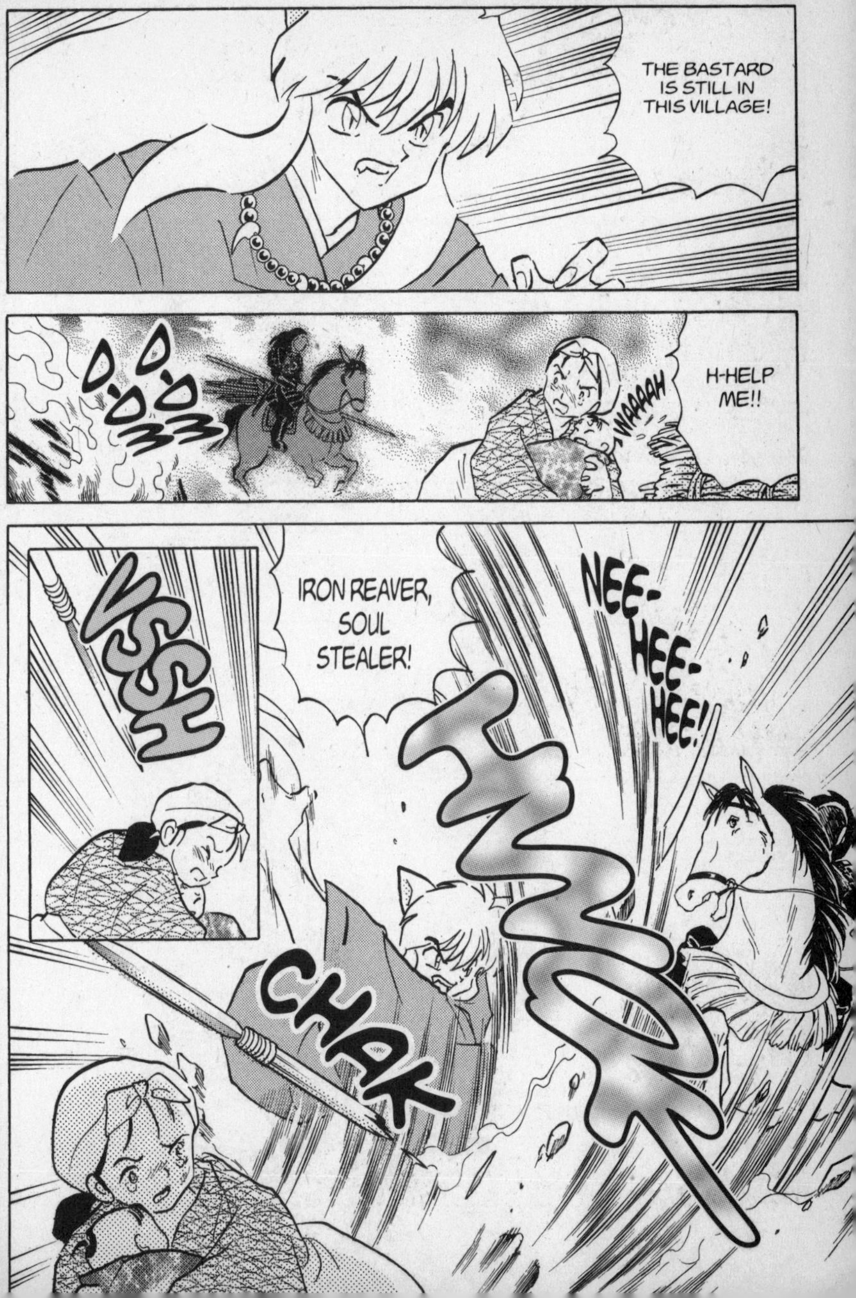
THE BASTARD IS STILL IN THIS VILLAGE!
WAAAAH
H-HELP ME!!
VSSH
IRON REAVER, SOUL STEALER!
NEE-HEE-HEE-HEE!
CHAK

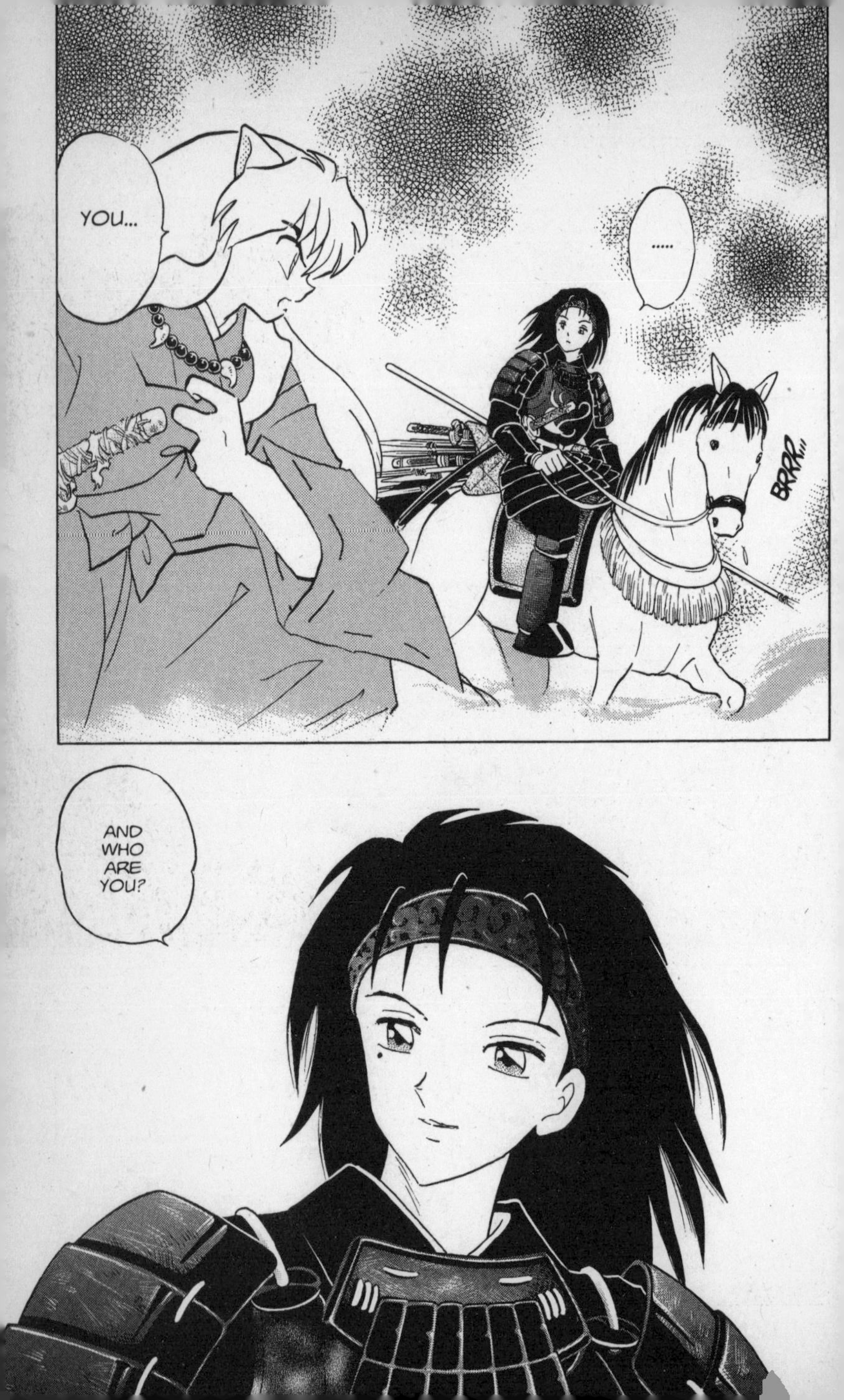
YOU...
.....
BRRR...
AND WHO ARE YOU?

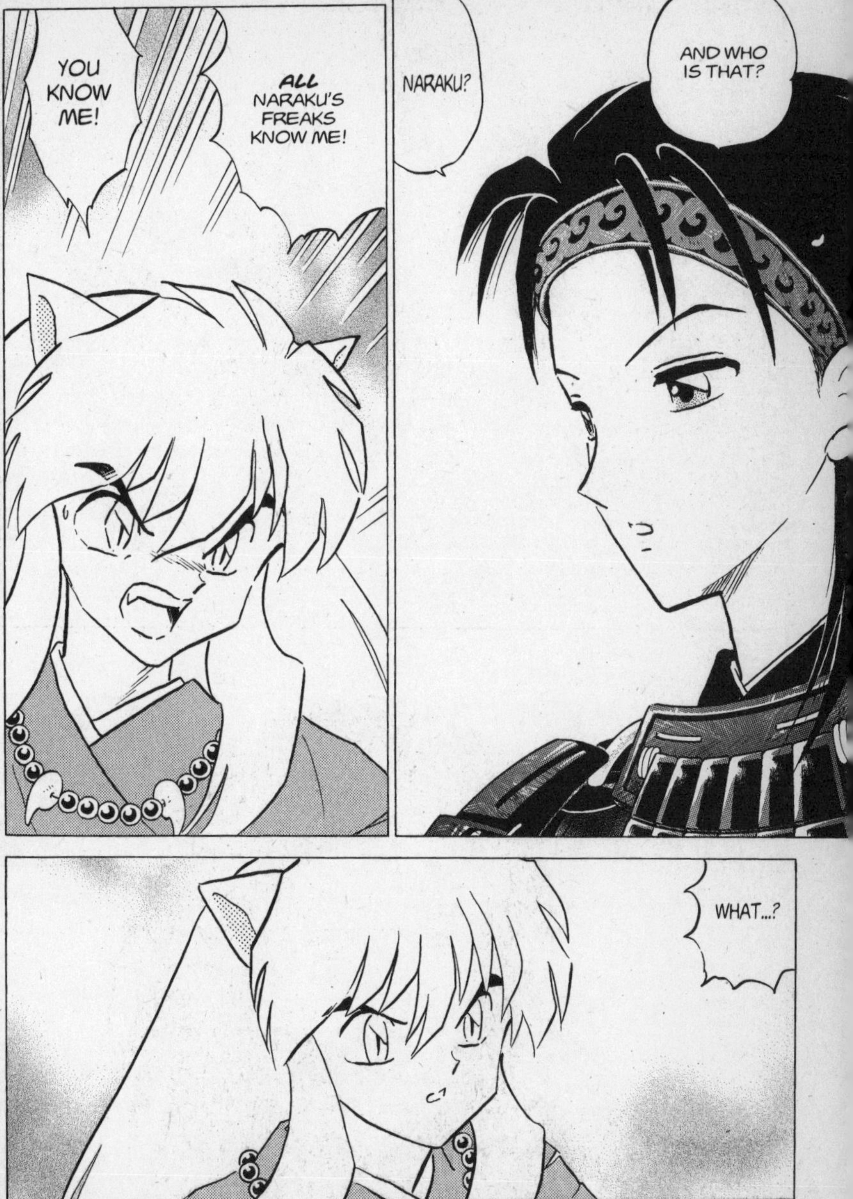
YOU KNOW ME!
ALL NARAKU'S FREAKS KNOW ME!
NARAKU?
AND WHO IS THAT?
WHAT...?

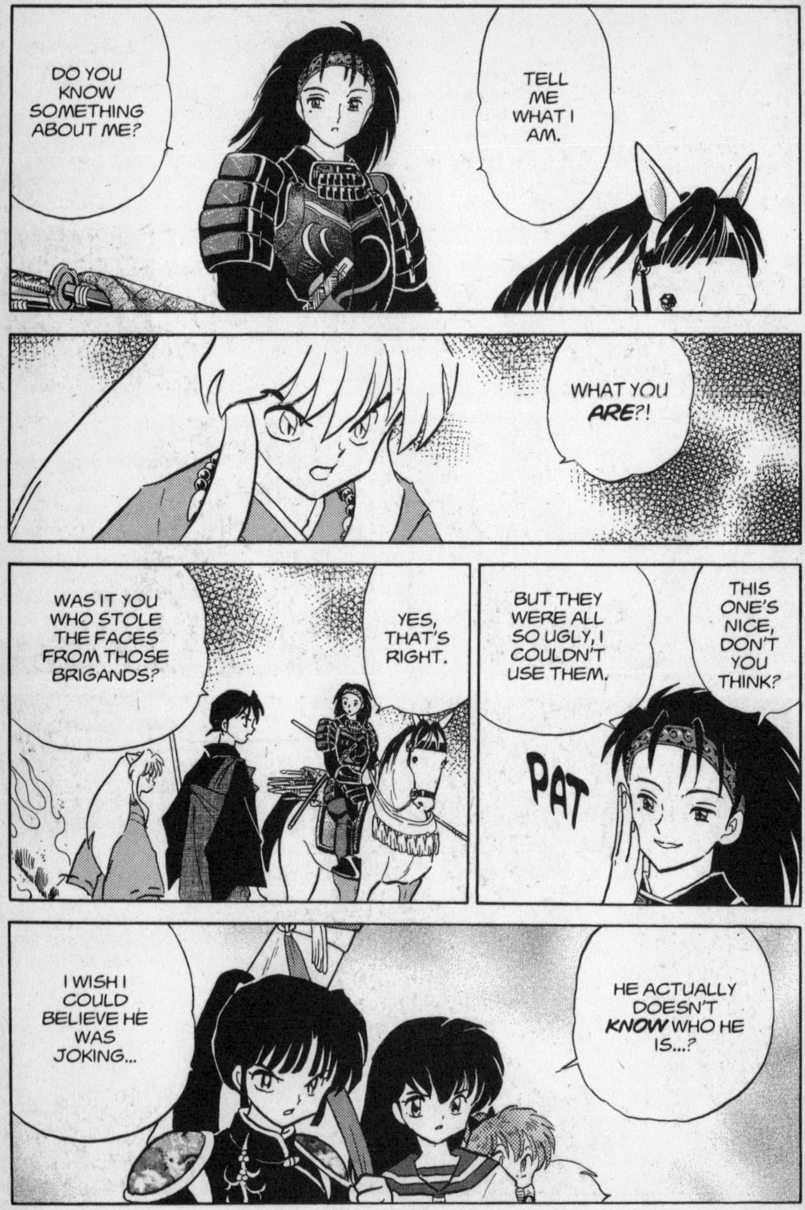
DO YOU KNOW SOMETHING ABOUT ME?
TELL ME WHAT I AM.
WHAT YOU ***ARE***?!
WAS IT YOU WHO STOLE THE FACES FROM THOSE BRIGANDS?
YES, THAT'S RIGHT.
BUT THEY WERE ALL SO UGLY, I COULDN'T USE THEM.
THIS ONE'S NICE, DON'T YOU THINK?
PAT
I WISH I COULD BELIEVE HE WAS JOKING...
HE ACTUALLY DOESN'T ***KNOW*** WHO HE IS...?

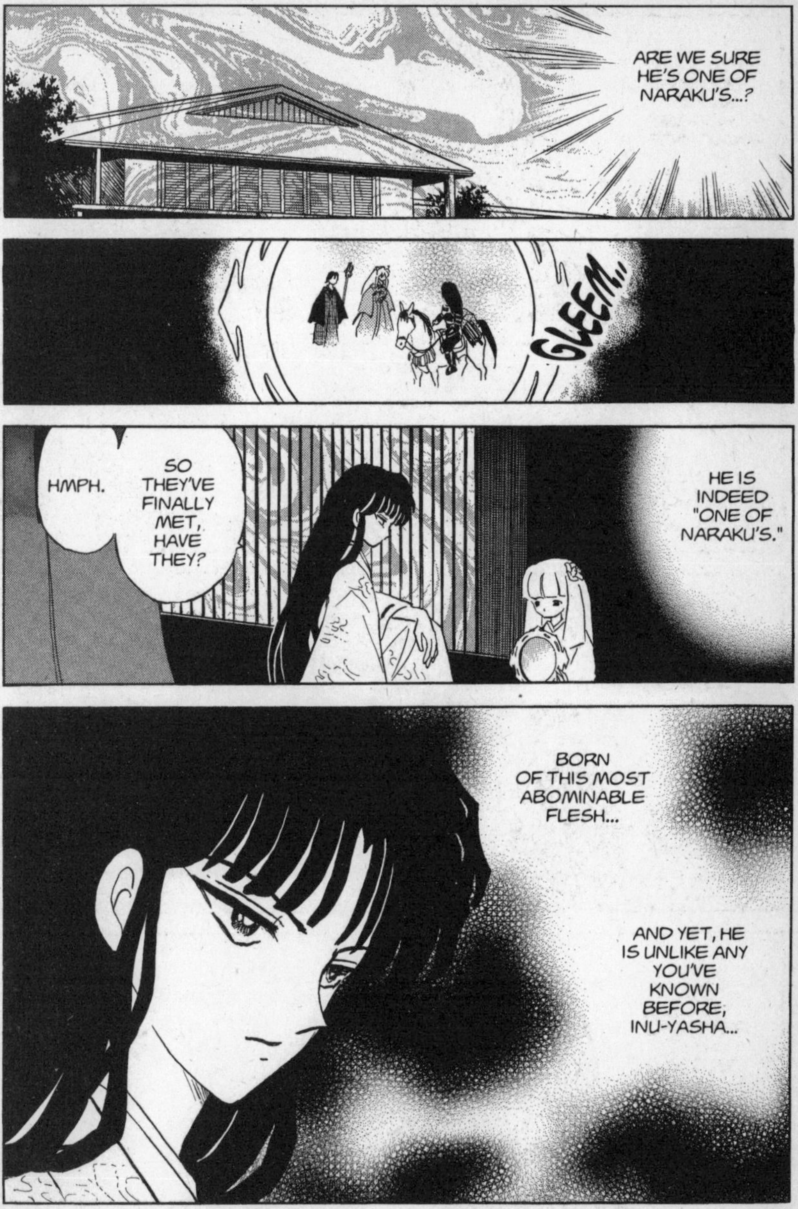
ARE WE SURE HE'S ONE OF NARAKU'S...?
GLEEM...
HMPH.
SO THEY'VE FINALLY MET, HAVE THEY?
HE IS INDEED "ONE OF NARAKU'S."
BORN OF THIS MOST ABOMINABLE FLESH...
AND YET, HE IS UNLIKE ANY YOU'VE KNOWN BEFORE, INU-YASHA...

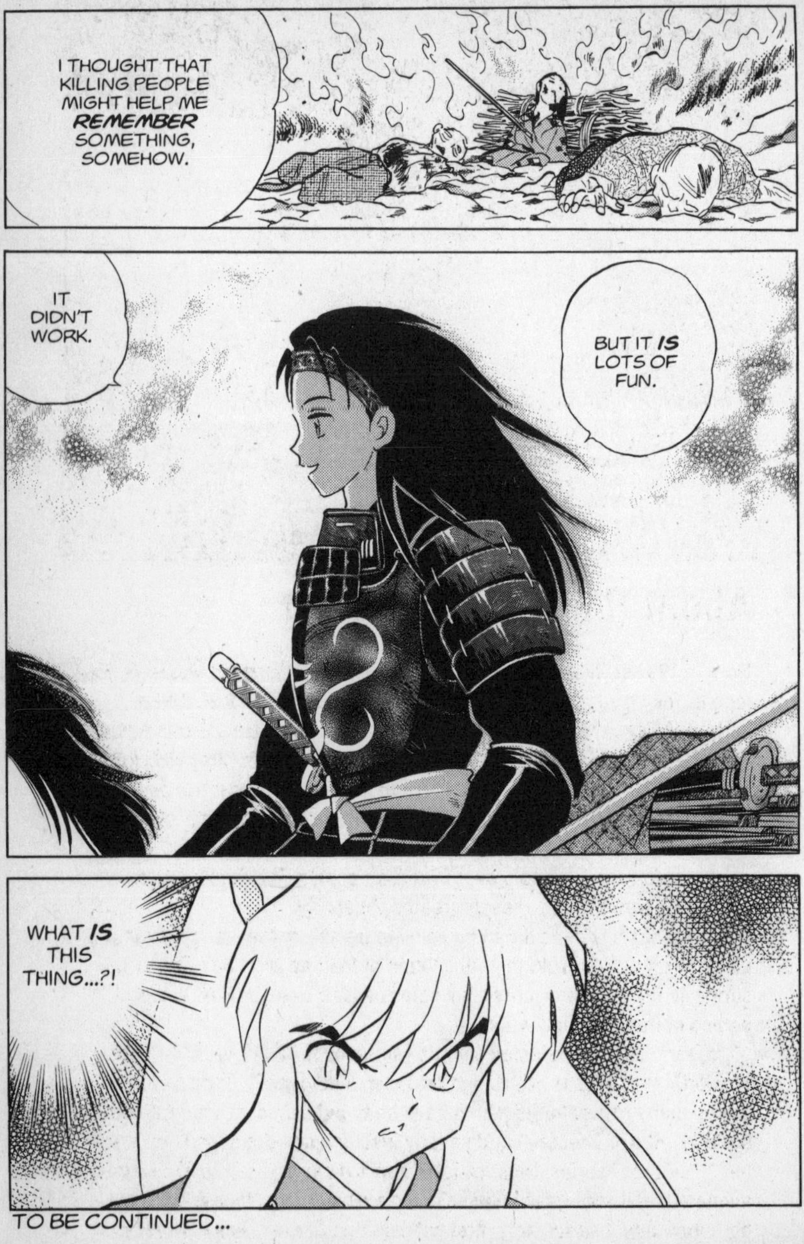
I THOUGHT THAT KILLING PEOPLE MIGHT HELP ME REMEMBER SOMETHING, SOMEHOW.
IT DIDN'T WORK.
BUT IT IS LOTS OF FUN.
WHAT IS THIS THING...?!

TO BE CONTINUED...

About Rumiko Takahashi

Born in 1957 in Niigata, Japan, Rumiko Takahashi attended women's college in Tokyo, where she began studying comics with Kazuo Koike, author of *CRYING FREEMAN*. She later became an assistant to horror-manga artist Kazuo Umezu (*OROCHI*). In 1978, she won a prize in Shogakukan's annual "New Comic Artist Contest," and in that same year her boy-meets-alien comedy series *URUSEI YATSURA* began appearing in the weekly manga magazine *SHŌNEN SUNDAY*. This phenomenally successful series ran for nine years and sold over 22 million copies. Takahashi's later *RANMA 1/2* series enjoyed even greater popularity.

Takahashi is considered by many to be one of the world's most popular manga artists. With the publication of Volume 34 of her *RANMA 1/2* series in Japan, Takahashi's total sales passed *one hundred million* copies of her compiled works.

Takahashi's serial titles include *URUSEI YATSURA, RANMA 1/2, ONE-POUND GOSPEL, MAISON IKKOKU* and *INUYASHA*. Additionally, Takahashi has drawn many short stories which have been published in America under the title "Rumic Theater," and several installments of a saga known as her "Mermaid" series. Most of Takahashi's major stories have also been animated, and are widely available in translation worldwide. *INUYASHA* is her most recent serial story, first published in *SHŌNEN SUNDAY* in 1996.